MICHAEL FREEMAN ON...

COMPOSITION

The Ultimate Photography Masterclass

An Hachette UK Company
www.hachette.co.uk

First published in the United Kingdom in 2022 by
Ilex, a division of Octopus Publishing Group Ltd
Carmelite House
50 Victoria Embankment
London, EC4Y 0DZ
www.octopusbooks.co.uk
www.octopusbooksusa.com

Distributed in the US by Hachette Book Group
1290 Avenue of the Americas, 4th & 5th Floors,
New York, NY 101014

Distributed in Canada by Canadian Manda Group
664 Annette Street, Toronto, Ontario,
Canada M6S 2C8

Publisher: Alison Starling
Commissioning Editor: Richard Collins
Managing Editor: Rachel Silverlight
Assistant Editor: Ellen Sandford O'Neill
Art Director: Ben Gardiner
Designer: Eoghan O'Brien
Picture Research: Giulia Hetherington
Production Controller: Serena Savini

ISBN 978-1-78157-836-0

A CIP catalogue record for this book is available from the British Library

Printed and bound in China

10 9 8 7 6 5 4 3 2 1

MICHAEL FREEMAN ON...

COMPOSITION

The Ultimate Photography Masterclass

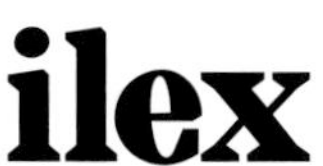

CONTENTS

46 CHAPTER 3: FRAMED

66 CHAPTER 4: SECRET GEOMETRY

134 CHAPTER 7: THE DIRECTOR'S CHAIR

146 CHAPTER 8: SWIMMING UPSTREAM

INTRODUCTION

It's now fifteen years since I wrote *The Photographer's Eye*, on composition in photography, and by good fortune it has stayed the course, in almost 30 languages around the world. The reason I am returning to composition with this book is that the world of photography has not stayed still, and neither have I. I've shot more, and thought more, and certainly have more than enough new ideas to fill this new book.

Composition, or design if you like, is the one ingredient of a photograph that you reliably have control over, and which you can use to influence how people will look at your work. You can point things out or delay their recognition. You can make images easy to look at or challenging. You can simplify or complicate. You can harmonize or shake things up. Perhaps more importantly, by doing such things intentionally and to your liking, you can put your stamp on your photography; give it your look, your style, your character. Photography is intensely personal. There is only one eye behind the camera, and it's yours, and composition is a powerful way of showing your individuality.

There's an approach to composition that has some traction in the art world. Writing for the catalogue of the 2003 Tate Modern exhibition *Cruel and Tender*, David Campany made the case against conscious composition: 'The straight photograph is often thought of as uncomposed and artless, a "degree zero" of composition, which in some senses it is.'[1] Here, the writer is using the term 'straight photography' not in the original sense, as used by Edward Weston, Ansel Adams and other West Coast photographers who

1 Campany, David, 'Almost the Same Thing: Some Thoughts on the Photographer as Collector' in *Cruel and Tender: The Real in the Twentieth-Century Photograph* [exhibition catalogue], London: Tate Publishing, 2003.

were arguing for precision and clarity in opposition to Pictorialism but as photography without direction. He continued, 'If we understand composition as an orchestration of the picture and an orchestration of its viewing, then the straight image refuses to lead the eye, refuses to lead the reading of the image. On the one hand this makes it a thoroughly generous, open and democratic kind of photograph, but it also makes it resistant and demanding.'[2]

Among participating photographers, the American Lewis Baltz wrote 'The ideal photographic document would appear to be without author or art,' and went further: 'I certainly wanted my work to look like anyone could do it...I was looking for the things that were most typical, the things that were the most quotidian, everyday, unremarkable, and trying to represent them in the way that was the most quotidian, everyday and unremarkable.'[3]

With the best will in the world, and looking at all the ways in which you could actually perform 'degree zero' composition, (short of throwing a camera in the air to let it capture a shot by chance), I think it's self-deceiving at best, fraudulent at worst. Composition-deniers use conceptual arguments but argue against skill, although even a glance at the work of Baltz and others shows that composition is indeed being employed. In Baltz's case, as also with Bernd and Hilla Becher, squared-up is the tactic mainly used (see page 42), and that's definitely not 'like anyone could do it'. Composition-deniers also face an intractable problem – the closer you get to 'degree zero', the more boring the picture. In the end, the strongest case for composition is that most people actually want to enjoy photographs.

2 Ibid.

3 Baltz, Lewis, 'Architecture as Photography: Document, Publicity, Commentary, Art' in *Constructing Worlds: Photography and Architecture in the Modern Age* [exhibition catalogue], Munich and London: Barbican Gallery/Prestel, 2014.

CHAPTER

1

DESIGN IS GOOD FOR YOU

Most good photographers work intuitively. Indeed, most photography demands speed, and in particular fast reactions, to cope with changing events, moving situations and shifting light. Only planned shooting, of the kind performed commercially to an art director's brief and most studio work, allows the luxury of time to consider and alter the design of the image. Even then, the time doesn't feel luxurious because decisions pile on top of each other in ever-increasing detail, and working to a sketch – even if it's only in your mind's eye – can create more difficulties than it solves. In fact, whether planned or unplanned, there can be a huge gap between wanting things to come together in the frame and actually making them fit. Intuition, then, figures strongly in most photography.

Like any creative activity, the compositional side of shooting a photograph calls for effort. There's hard graft involved, much of it in the form of training, because you're likely to have to perform quickly and at short notice. That means constantly imagining how scenes can be translated into framed images in interesting ways, and for committed photographers that tends to be always turned on in the background, with or without a camera in hand. It also means training your visual senses to be fully up and running as soon as you see a likely shot.

Anyone who works long enough with images, whether making them, selecting them or using them in layouts, 'sees' a kind of stylized, graphic version of them at the same time as the full photographic version. Images, particularly when they're strong and effective ones, have an internal construction that takes into account distinct elements, contrast, the distribution of light and colour, and shapes. Some people have used the word armature, others geometry. Throughout the book I've included what I privately call schematics to try and get this across. They are illustrations that attempt to show the underlying dynamics and graphic influences at work.

Finally, there's something quite new that I'm including in this book, and that's real-world testing of the compositional ideas that I'm suggesting. With the help of a human behavioural software company, iMotions, we've put photographs through the latest eye-tracking technology to see exactly how viewers look at them, and whether the photographer's ideas (mine, in this case) bore fruit. In other words, to find out whether design ideas actually work. Most of the time they did (phew), but some failures and bad ideas were ruthlessly exposed. At least there are lessons to be learned from those, which I'll share with you. Some people will oppose this kind of scrutiny, but frankly it's time we started proving what we think we know.

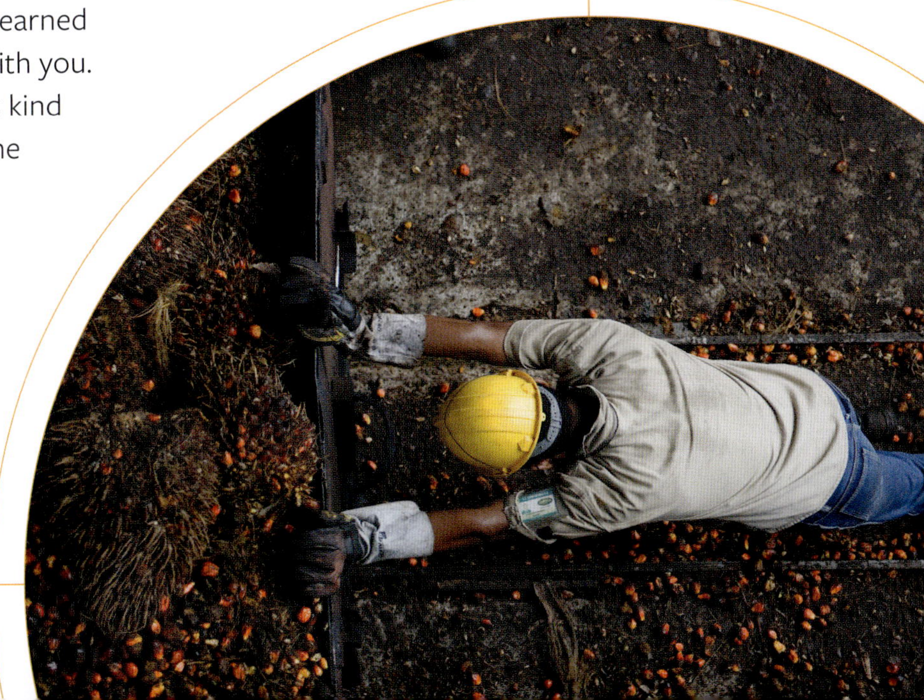

ORDER, DIRECT, INTEREST

Just to clear up any doubts about why you would or should take an active interest in the design of any photograph you're taking, there are three possible things it can do.

Three jobs, if you like. It can bring visual order to the random arrangement of a scene in front of the camera. It can help you nudge the way someone will look at your photograph. And it can make the image simply more interesting to look at. In a nutshell, you can create order, direct attention and add interest. Any photograph will be improved by having this effort and care put into it.

Different scenes have different needs, as of course so do we as individual photographers, and it's likely that one of these three – order, direction or interest – will dominate. At the same time, they often reinforce each other. Finding a structure that brings a sense of order, for example, may encourage the viewer's eye to move from one part of the picture to another, while using a line to direct attention, as in the case of the beach scene overleaf, can suggest a shape and therefore an order – in this example a suggestion of a pyramid or triangle. Making an image more interesting to look at often involves structure of some kind, and in both of the cases overleaf, there are suggestions of shapes being evoked or manipulated.

CREATING ORDER

For some, the word order suggests rigidity, compulsion, restriction and the very opposite of freedom and liberal ideas, so I'd like to start by saying this has nothing to do with what order can be in an image. A better starting point is the idea of 'order out of chaos', almost a cliché but on target for photography. The world in front of the camera is often (maybe usually) visually chaotic. It's disorganized, and as a photograph is something that we choose to take out of that real world, it's practically inevitable that we're going to put some structure into it. The Iranian photographer Abbas, who spent much of his career shooting events that involved violence and social upheaval, notably the Iranian Revolution, explained that the word for chaos in Farsi is *shulughi*, and in its benign, non-violent form has a place in the Iranian psyche, but continued, 'I can't seem to photograph *shulughi*. Even when it's in front of me I try to organise it.'[1] Indeed, it's a natural, unavoidable photographers' trait, the habit to organize and to connect all the picture elements, even if there are many. Most of the compositional techniques and strategies that follow are, to some degree, ways of bringing order to unruly visual situations, and they're many and varied.

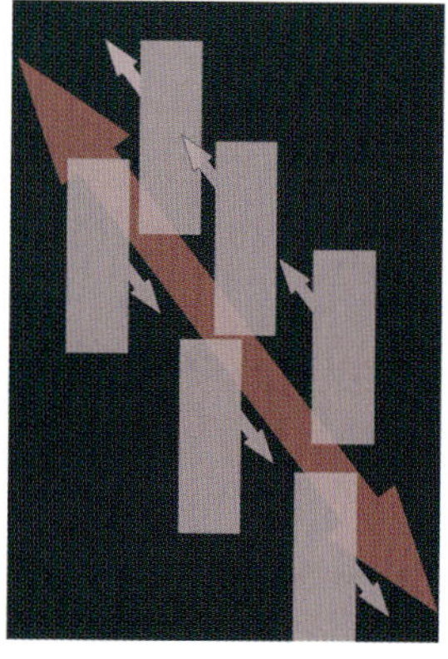

→ This was a fluid situation with a fixed viewpoint, looking down on planks from a Burmese riverboat as passengers embarked and disembarked. Two kinds of organization sprang to mind. One was the framing: tight to exclude anything but the planks and people, in a corner-to-corner diagonal. The other was timing the shot so as to separate the figures visually, and eventually, after some minutes, this arrangement happened, as the schematic above shows. An earlier, less organized moment is seen below.

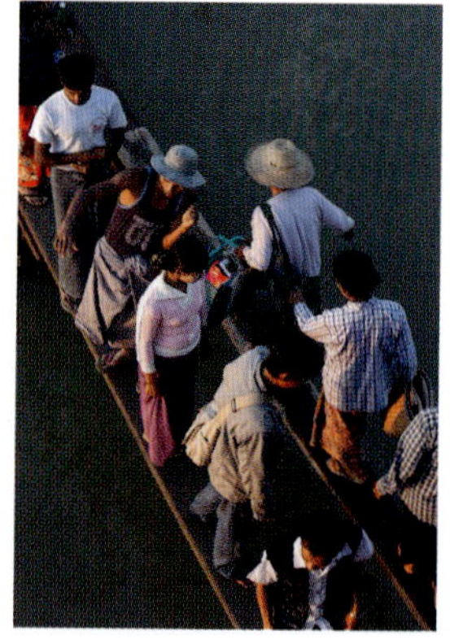

1 Pakdel, Kamy (director), *Abbas by Abbas*, 2019, 56 min.

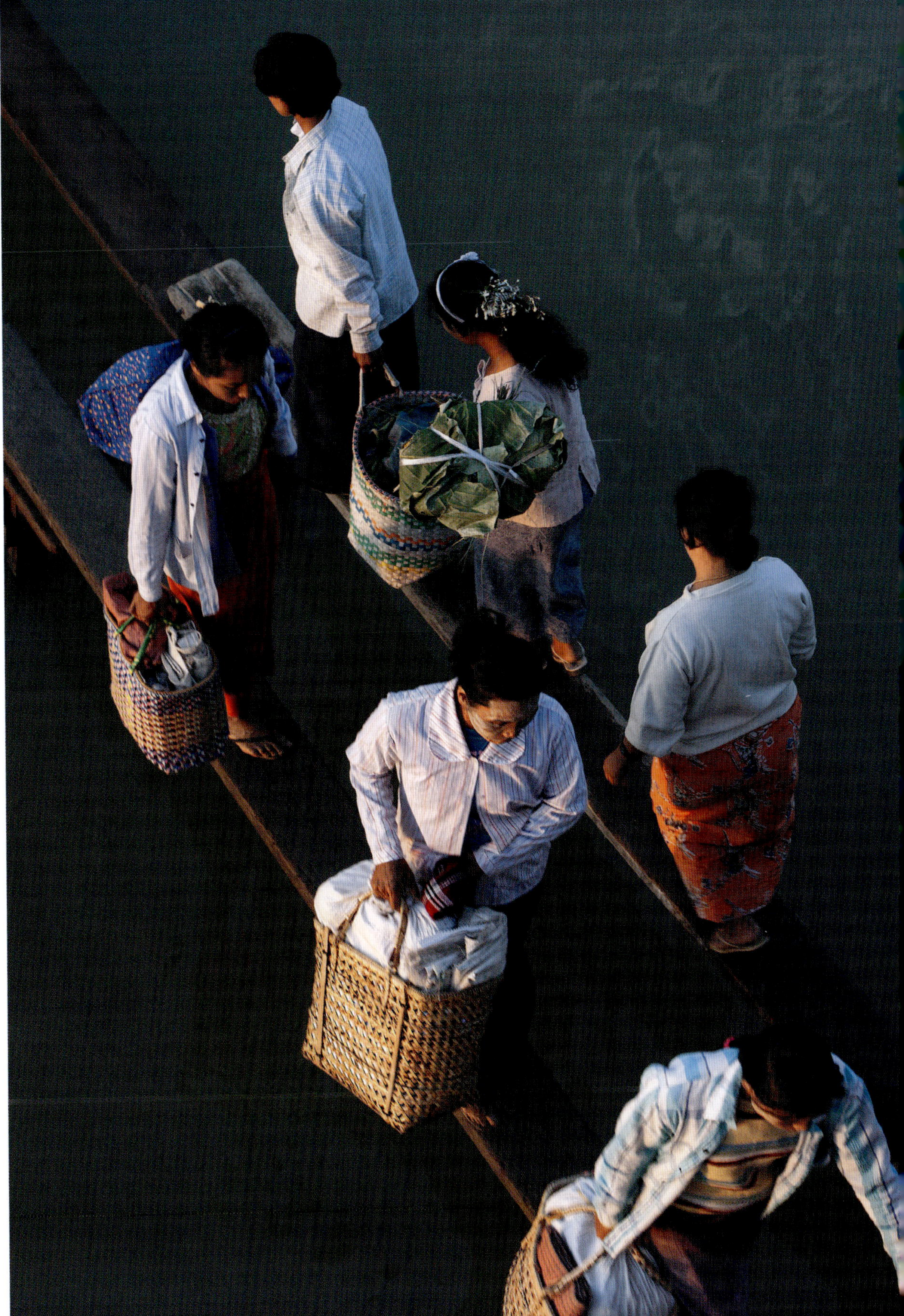

DIRECTING ATTENTION

The second job of composition relates particularly to the audience. It's a way of framing and arrangement to make some aspects of the image stand out and others fall back. Clearly, this is connected to bringing order, but it has a purpose that goes beyond creating a structure. It's a way of trying to persuade the viewer to see what you see, and in your way. You might think there's some hubris in thinking to control the way people look at your photographs, but it's often subtler than that, more to do with nudging and emphasis than with full-on 'orchestration', as Campany puts it (see page 7). For example, take the Enclosing strategy on page 122. Using an arrangement or a curve to suggest a frame within the picture frame is a way of inviting the viewer inside. In the example here on this page, I was concerned mainly with lowering the insistence of a lone figure, so that it wouldn't take over the picture but rather, with luck, be seen a fraction of a second later.

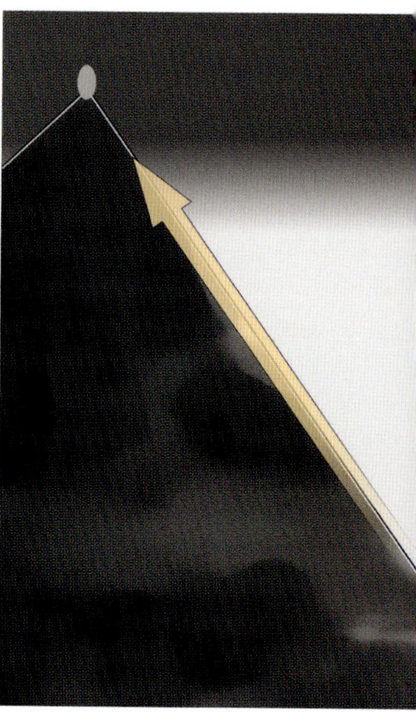

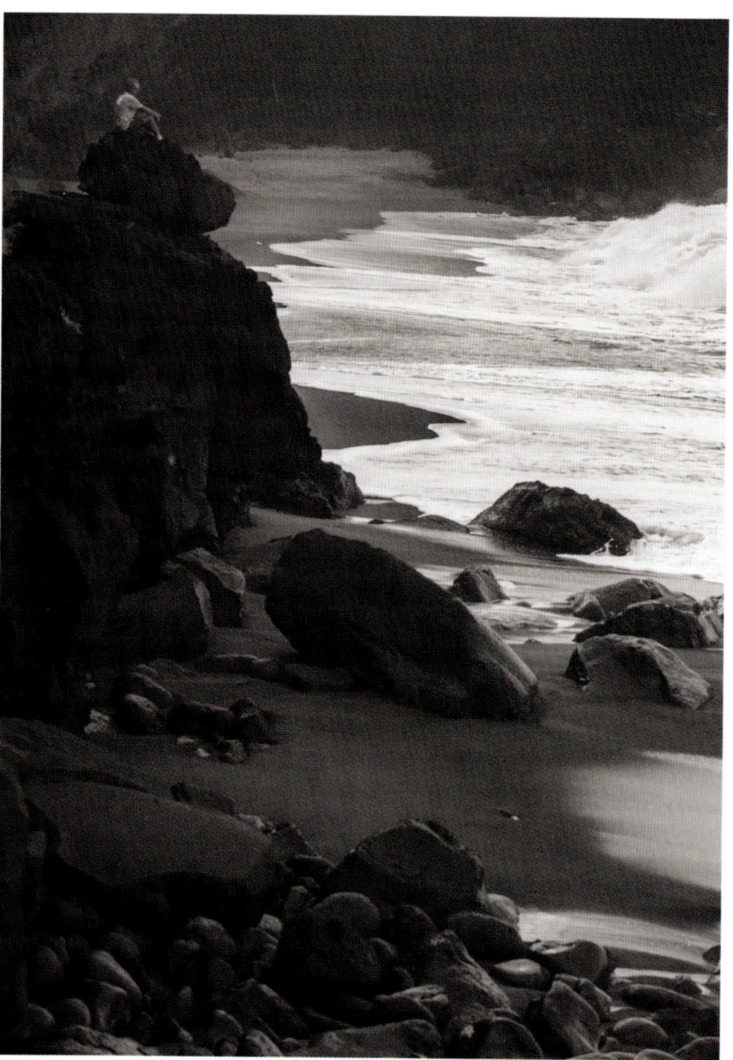

This shot was for a book on the French island of La Réunion in the Indian Ocean, and it needed to do two things: one was to show a very recent volcanic beach, because the island is an active shield volcano; the other was to show a fisherman studying the waves in preparation for his work the next day. They were both part of the story. The black lava was the main event, but I realized that by finding the right viewpoint, then framing with a medium telephoto (125mm), I could keep the fisherman high and left, almost right in the corner, and the diagonal would lead to him eventually (I didn't position him, he was just sitting there). Beyond the left edge was messy vegetation, but framed like this the fisherman seems at the apex of a rocky pyramid.

CREATING INTEREST

Third on the list of what effective composition can do – maybe should do – is simply to make the photograph more interesting to look at. That usually translates into attractive, but it could also be edgy or uncomfortable in some way. In either case, more striking than an under-designed version would be. This is an assignment I set in my online teaching, and it's the one I seem to have most difficulty explaining, because it does not have to do with how interesting or otherwise the subject is. It's about what composition can bring to the mix of subject, moment, lighting and possibly colour. Can it enhance? Can it add another layer of interest that will help the enjoyment of looking at the picture?

Basically, this is a candid shot of a Burmese man working on one of the public ferries that ply the Irrawaddy River. His strong, high-cheekboned face and intense gaze are the essential content, but it is the precise composition emphasizing simple geometric shapes – and the colour combination – that bring structural interest to the picture.

Pulling back on the framing allowed the use of rectangle, circle and line to bring an unexpected geometric design to this shot on a riverboat. For non-Burmese viewers, the distinctive script appears also as a pattern of rounded rectangles.

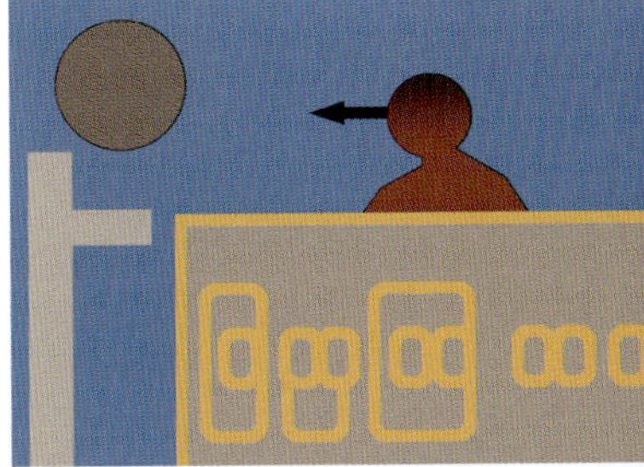

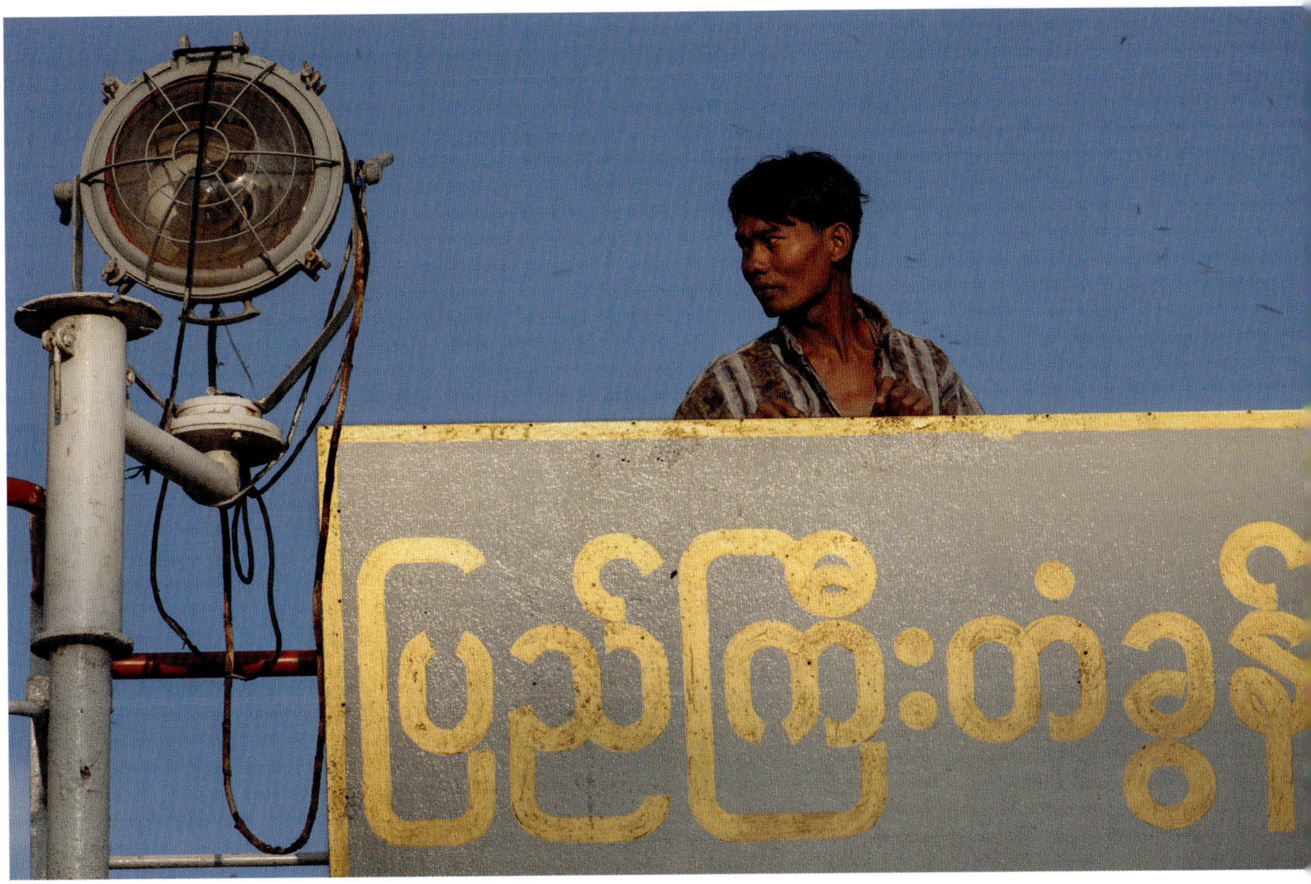

IMPROMPTU OR MANAGED

The process of composition flips completely between what most people photograph most of the time, which is the uncontrollable flow of events in front of the camera, and situations in which you dictate what happens in the scene.

In other words, from the real world to the studio – and I use that last word loosely to describe any staged space where you create scenes rather than just witness them. In the real world, we have to do the best we can with what's in front of us – Henri Cartier-Bresson called it taking pictures *à la sauvette*, which translates loosely as 'on the run' or 'on the fly' (it was his American publisher who changed that to *The Decisive Moment*, which doesn't mean the same thing). Typically, composing images 'out there' means trying to make them work in a race against time and movement. You may have quite a bit of time for a landscape or a building, or a second or so in

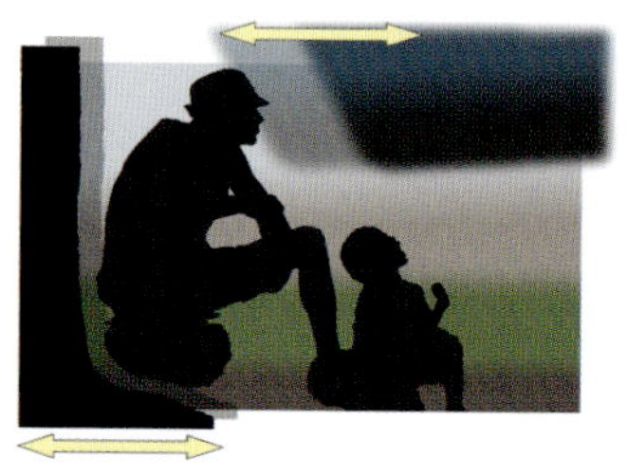

Apart from this being the best moment to shoot, with both heads in profile, the finer points of camera position were separating the man from the boat beyond and not having his back merge with the tree.

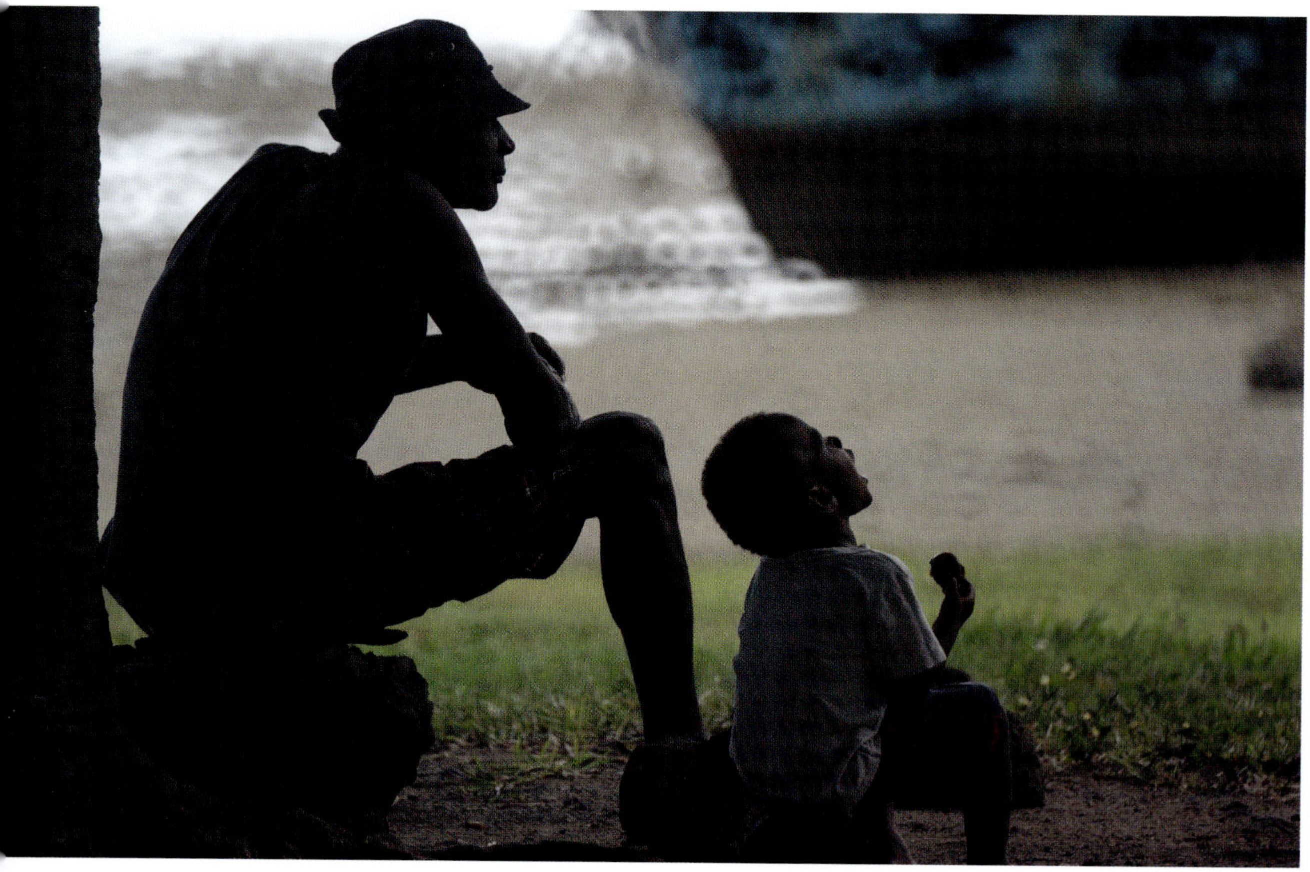

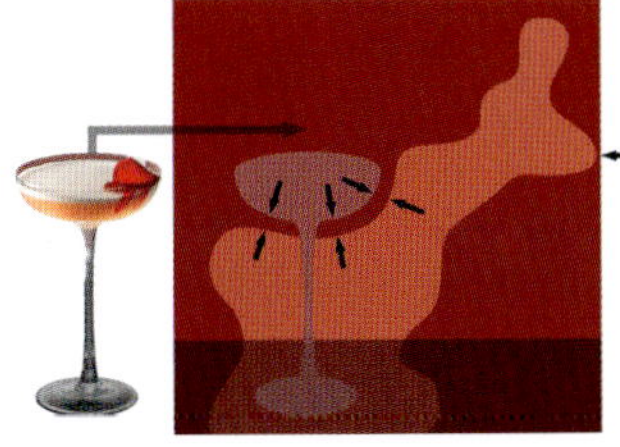

The main compositional issue here was fitting the cocktail glass to the design of the background wall, which was a given. The floral design itself had to fit neatly into the square format, which was also required. This precise position and camera elevation allowed the curved bowl of the glass to correspond with the arrangement of flowers.

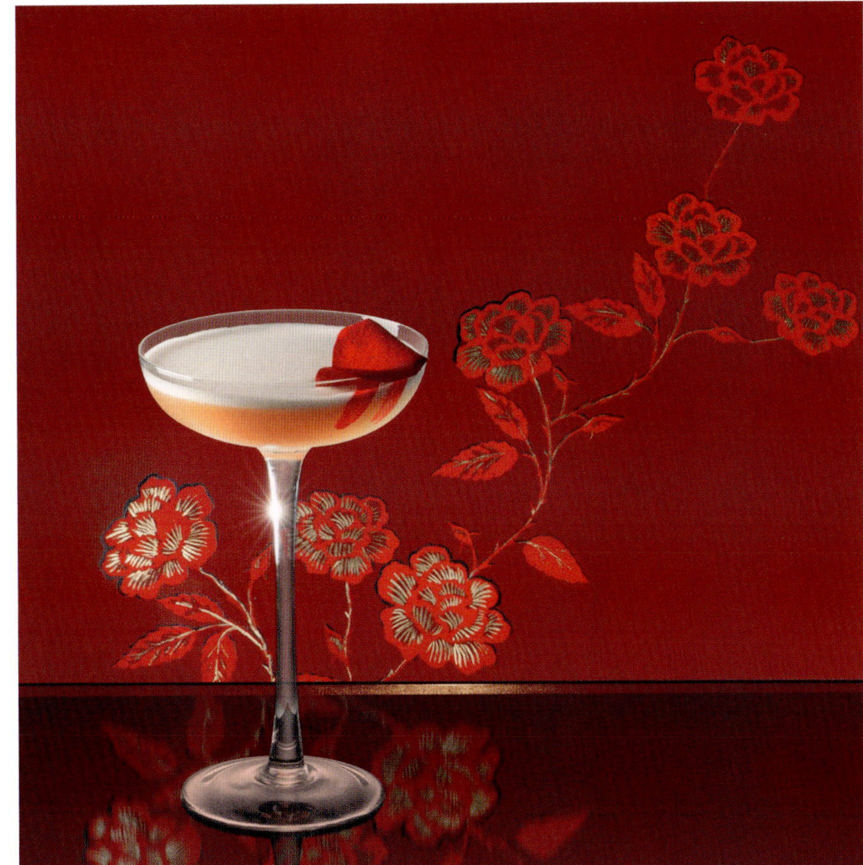

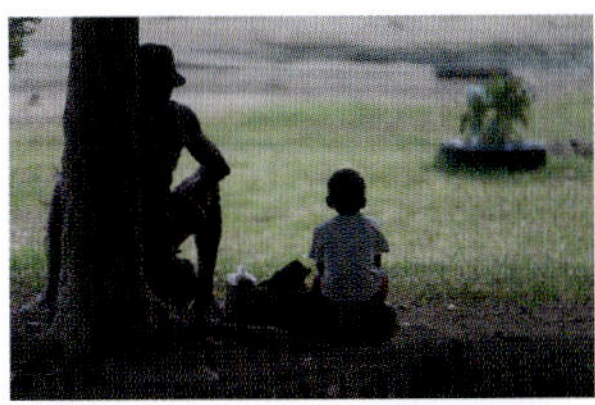

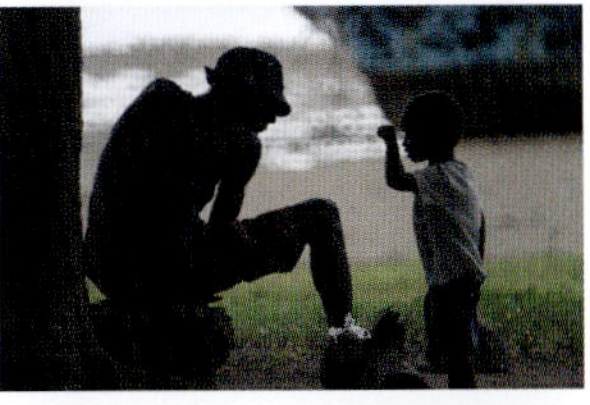

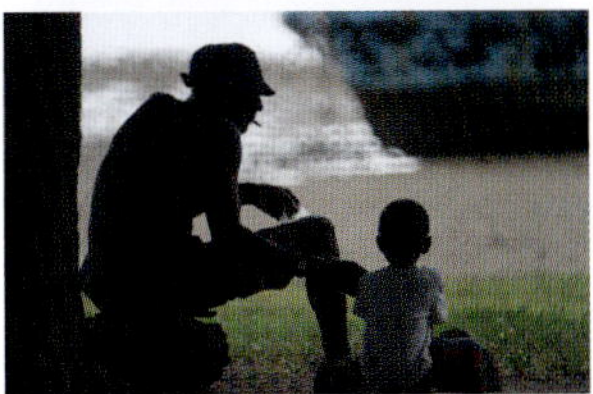

From first coming across the scene (not a useful shot), the sequence works toward finding a good moment and good separation between man and boy.

the case of street shooting, but either way you're applying the skills you've learned to situations that are often not as you'd like them to be. The advantage you gain is that every so often the real world, and your attempts to capture it, will throw up some unexpected and unpredictable prizes.

Move to the studio, however, and almost everything is reversed. You can do anything at all, exactly as you wish, but it comes with not one but two major disadvantages. First, if it looks predictable you don't score any brownie points. Second, how do you create surprises when it's all entirely at your command? Well, there are techniques for the first, as we'll see on pages 124, 128 and 158, some of them swiped from painting. And once you enter the self-absorbed flow of adjusting, moving, turning, adding and subtracting, some happy coincidences do occur that you hadn't planned in advance.

HOW WE LOOK AT PICTURES

I've just described the typical goals of composition, but do they actually work? As photographers, we think we know how our pictures will be looked at, and in all the compositional strategies that follow in this book we are, in effect, anticipating a reaction. But how do people look at photographs? It's an important question, and there have been equally important advances in recent years in studying the psychology of viewing.

The first issue is whether people are at all genuinely interested in your photographs to begin with. Are they going to flip through them casually or are they going to pay real attention? That's a matter of concern to the advertising industry, for instance, and to web designers, but for once most of us here have an advantage, as I assume we care only about the reaction from people interested in photography – our peers and professionals – and that's an audience already with the intention to look and judge.

The usual comfortable view of any image or screen for most people is at a viewing angle of approximately 30°. Typically, people will step back from a large image or move closer to a small image to approach this. The viewing angle sets how large it appears – how much of your field of view it occupies – and it matters because it affects how we see what's inside the frame. That in turn is heavily influenced by how our eyes are constructed. We see at different levels of detail, from very detailed to very coarse, and it's the coarse view that lets us take in the larger scene and sectors of it. We examine in detail only the central 5°, and that's called foveal or central vision, and while intuitively it seems reasonable to think that this is what's important, in fact it's the broader view, called peripheral, that controls how we understand the bigger picture.

Most people, if they think about peripheral, understand it as the very edges of vision – all the stuff going on indistinctly at the edges – but it has different levels, from just around the central, detailed view all the way to what's on either side of us. Here's not the place to go into the biology, but the different areas shown in the illustration opposite are backed up by the structure of the eye. This is why around a 30° viewing angle is the most comfortable for looking at a picture. Inside this there are different sizes of the view that give us different information. Some of this is disputed, but generally there's a broad area of taking in the view around about 18°, a narrower and a little more detailed at 8°, and the ultimately detailed inside 5°.

Viewers look at images in two phases. The first is called the pre-attentive phase – taking in the entire picture before deciding what to look at more carefully. In popular terms, this is the 'first glance'. It involves what's called parallel processing, meaning that different kinds of visual information, such as colour, shape and contrast, are handled at the same time. It works at the near peripheral level that

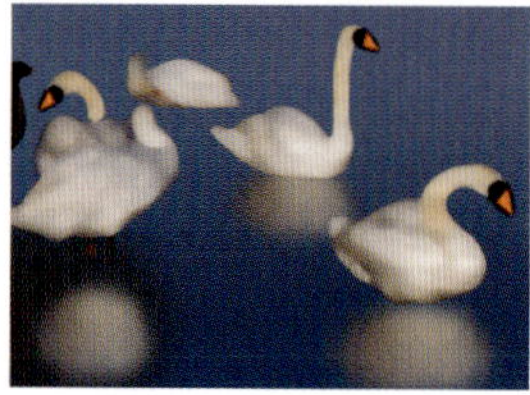

A glance (pre-attentive) takes everything in but without detail. It's understood immediately that these are swans on the water, and that the main colour components are white on blue with orange and black spots.

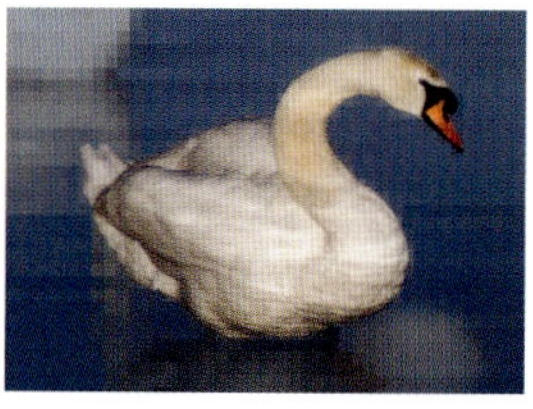

The attention moves in to macular level to look at an individual swan, for example (depending on the viewer), which fills the attention.

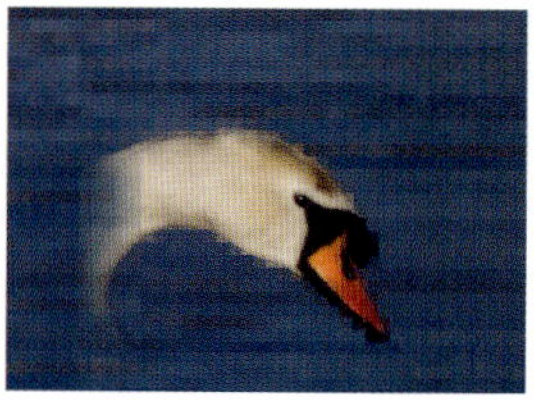

The viewer might then focus in closer on the head because of its strongly contrasting colours, and this detail view fills the attention to the exclusion of other parts of the scene.

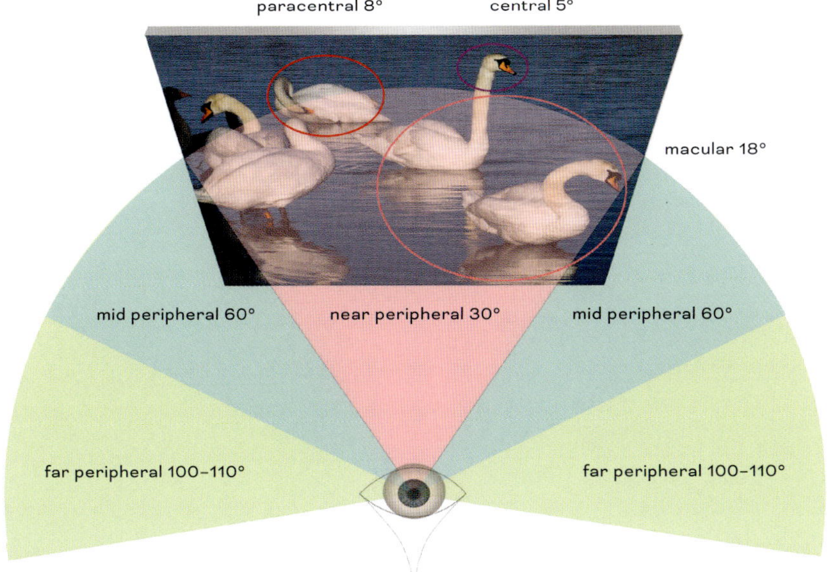

Our field of view is not fixed and not sharply defined, but these are the generally recognized fields, changing from very coarse at the widest angles to detailed in the centre. Looking at a photograph rather than the real world changes the way we look because it has edges, and most people position themselves so that it comfortably fills their near peripheral vision.

Looking at a picture is not the same as looking at the real world. A picture is self-contained and we're primed to search inside the frame for anything interesting.

takes in an entire image, and typically lasts for up to half a second. In all the eye-tracking tests that you'll see in this book, every viewer started by looking at the exact centre of the image – essentially taking in the entire view broadly. Then the viewer dives in, looks in detail at what's most interesting, and builds up a more definite and complete view, all of this happening quickly. How quickly depends on things like how interested the viewer is in the picture. If they're bored with the picture, they'll give up and move on.

People bring their own individual interests and priorities to the action of looking at pictures, and we can expect variety. Not everyone will notice what you want them to, and some viewers will find things within your photographs that you didn't expect. Others will ignore or not be impressed by things that you thought were important or skillful. If you choose to make pictures that are generally pleasing, they'll be more predictably popular than if you try to be different and challenging, but they won't stand out among all the similar pictures that other people take.

EYE-TRACKING

It's now straightforward to measure how someone looks at an individual picture, millisecond by millisecond, although interpreting the result is anything but. Since I wrote *The Photographer's Eye*, eye-tracking technology has become almost mainstream. Exactly where and for how long the viewer looks at an image is tracked, and the results, as shown here, are overlaid on the image.

In the picture below, the lines are called gaze paths as the eye moves from the start (number 1 in the centre) from one point of interest to the next. These points where the eye halts are called fixations, and the time spent varies, generally according to how interesting that part of the picture is to the viewer. They're numbered in sequence, and for this picture and this viewer it was looked at for a timed 30 seconds, during which time the eyes went to 71 points, or fixations. The amount of time spent at each fixation (called dwell time) is colour-coded from short (green) to long (red).

Starting at the centre of the picture (this is the pre-attentive, taking-it-all-in phase), this viewer's eye rapidly scanned all points of interest and contrast (including the stripes on the T-shirt) but kept returning to and fixating on the central face, and also to the chess pieces. Each fixation lasted on average less than half a second, but longer for the face.

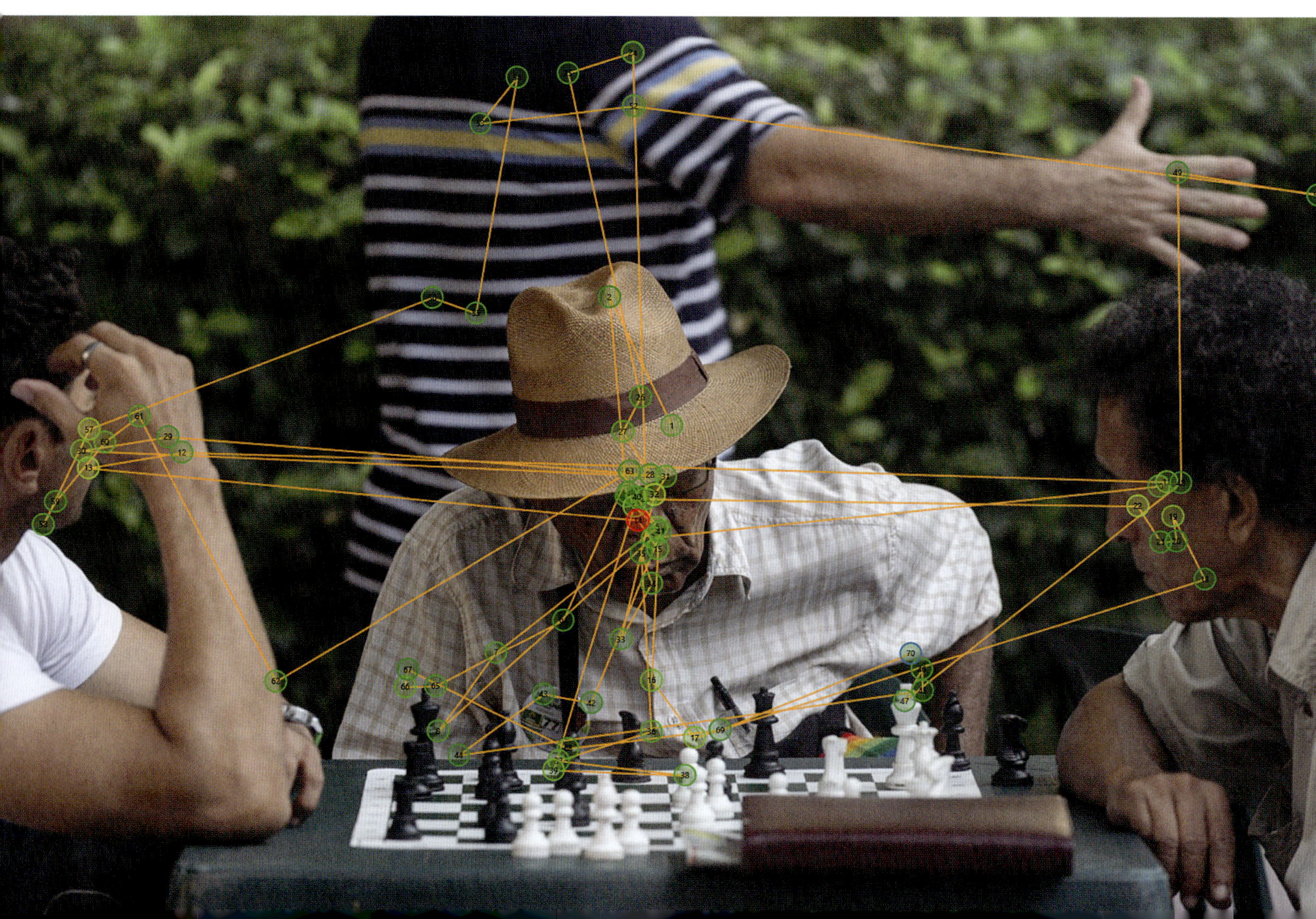

THE IDEA OF THE SHOT

This becomes interesting if you first know what the photographer was thinking about and trying to do – and then comparing that with how a viewer looked at it. In this case, naturally I can say exactly what I was trying to do. This is the city of Cartagena, Colombia, which I know well and visit frequently. I already knew this chess-playing location in a park, so would drop by every so often. For me it was an opportunity to photograph people candidly, absorbed in an activity and often in deep concentration – the actual chess boards were not so interesting to me. On this occasion, I was drawn by the face of the old man in the hat; it was full of character. And it was a good shooting position – a clear view from in front, and he was neatly flanked by two other men. That made me go for a tight and centred – symmetrical – composition. The hat itself was interesting and made up for the fact that I couldn't see his eyes clearly. I would have been quite satisfied with just this scene, although it wouldn't have made my list of favourites, until a man walked by behind and thrust out his hand firmly to greet someone else out of frame. People here are very demonstrative, and for me it was a valuable bonus to capture the open hand at just that moment and in a clear space.

At the time of shooting, the first two priorities were the interest of the central man's face and hat, and the symmetry around that, with two turned faces on either side. The chessboard was seen as just part of the setting, and the trigger for the moment was the asymmetrical action of the outstretched hand.

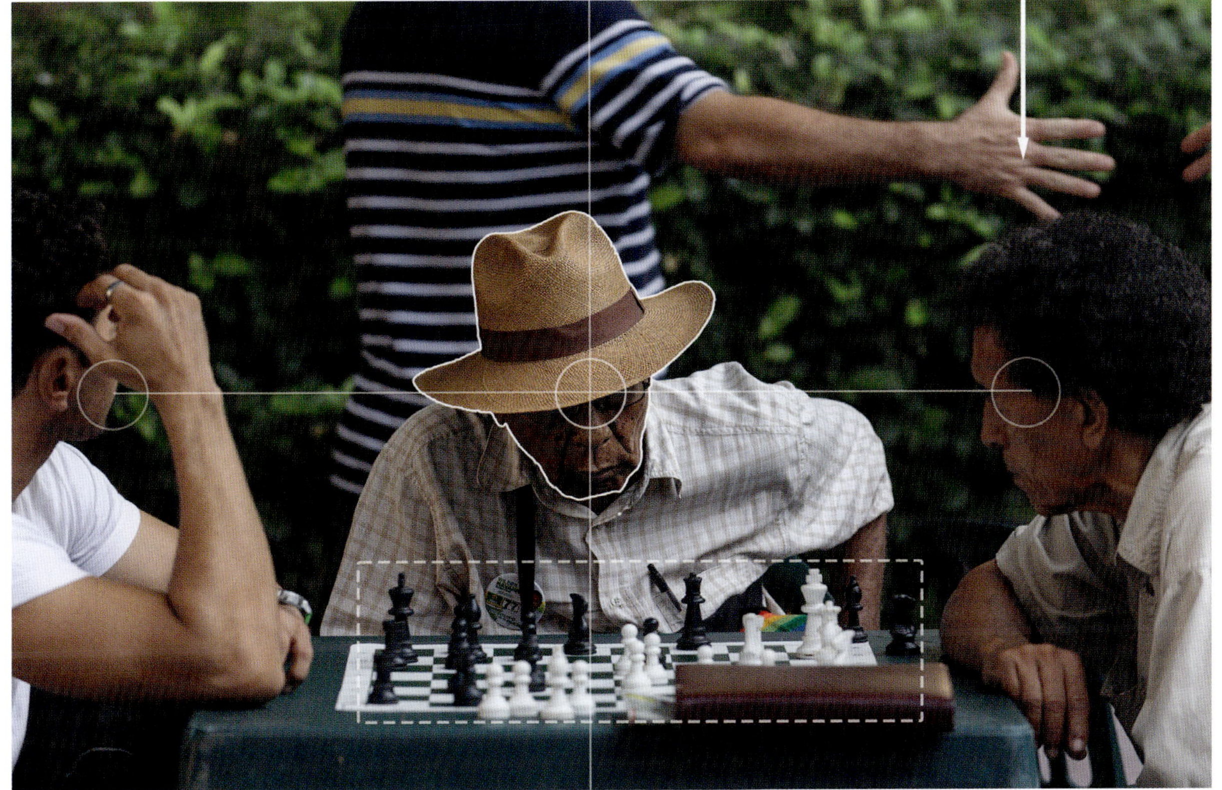

HOW IT WAS SEEN

I then gave this photograph, and others, to the human behavioural software company iMotions, who showed it to a number of test subjects in a controlled viewing situation. I was interested to see if these viewers would look at the picture in the same way that I had looked at the scene and moment, and if they would have the same priorities. Each person looked at the picture in a somewhat different way and different order, but the basic response was similar: starting with the older man's face and hat, then dropping to the chessboard, taking in some of the other two men's faces (not much, because they are turned away), and at some point later registering the outstretched hand.

So far so good, but what was I not expecting? Two things. One was the sheer amount of attention paid to the chess pieces, though actually this is logical. I wasn't interested much in these because I took them as a given and was concentrating on the people, but if I'm objective, they are indeed what most people would call the main subject of the picture. My second 'failure' was the relative lack of interest in the hand. One test viewer glanced there only once in the entire 30 seconds.

A 'heat map' is an easy-to-comprehend view of the amount of time spent by all subjects in the test on parts of the picture – in other words, an aggregate of fixations. It clearly shows the power of the human face to attract attention, but also the interest shown in the chess pieces and the lack of interest in the outstretched hand.

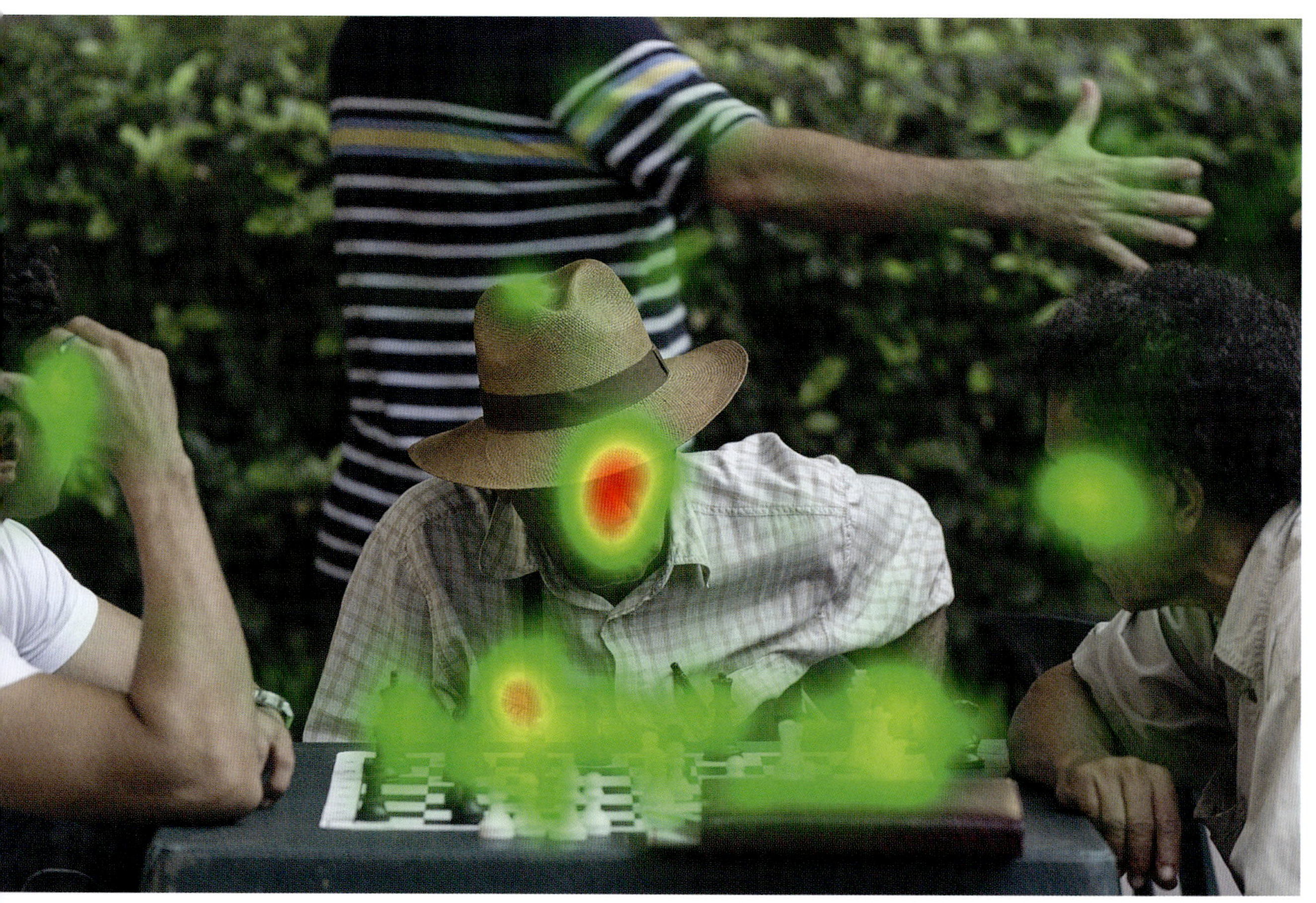

SUBJECT 1

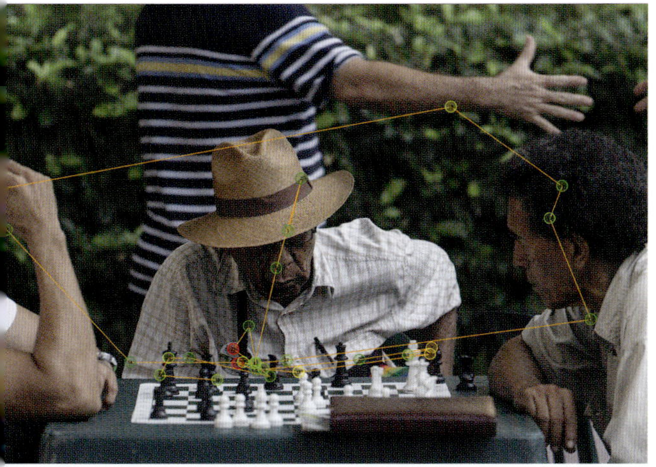

SUBJECT 2

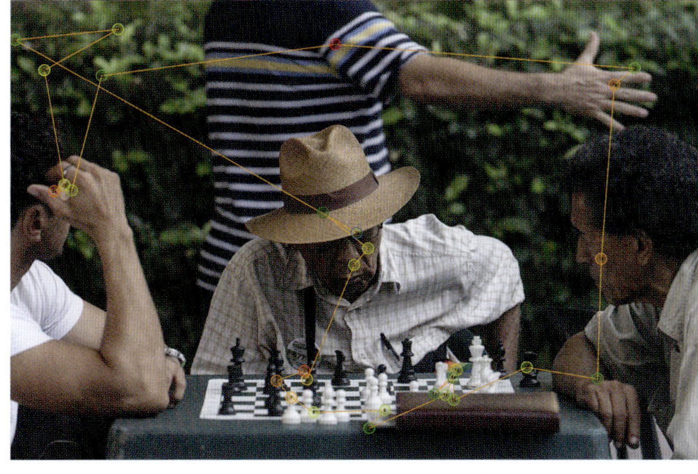

SUBJECT 3

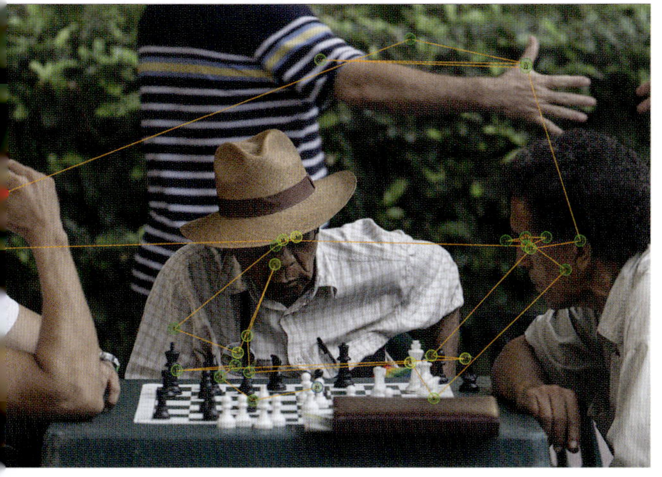

SUBJECT 4

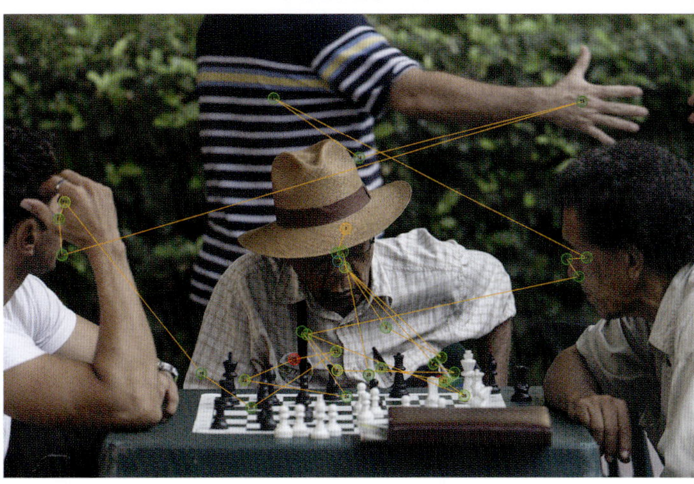

What counted as a nice bonus gesture for me was much less appealing to the viewers, as the aggregated heat map drives home. There are different ways of displaying this information, and the 'heat map' is probably the most useful for a quick grasp, as it combines all the tests and then colour-codes the time spent looking at different parts of the photograph. The intensity of attention paid by viewers increases from green, through yellow to red.

LESSONS LEARNED

Without a doubt, most viewers were far less interested in the outstretched hand than I was, and the sheer salience (see page 94) of a human face dominates, but another valuable lesson is the variation from one viewer to another. This really shows up when viewers have less time to look, so we took just the first ten seconds. It heightens just how different the viewers were.

↑ By taking just the first ten seconds of viewing, you can see the marked differences in how different test subjects looked at the image. While the heat map opposite evens out the responses, these individual gaze paths underline how viewers vary.

DESIGN TOOLS

You need surprisingly little to compose, and certainly no extra equipment, but it's worth thinking about what you have in your hand – camera and lens – and which parts are useful for how you put the picture together.

The first set of tools is the way in which the camera presents the view, and there's a choice. In fact, the displays have been changing since photography began. In the heyday of the film camera, just before digital took over, there were several. The purest and most awkward was the ground-glass screen located exactly where you would later put the film, on which you could see the exact image, upside down and dim, and I've included a shot of how this looked on a 4 × 5-inch view camera. This was a slow and traditional way of composing, but it was completely accurate.

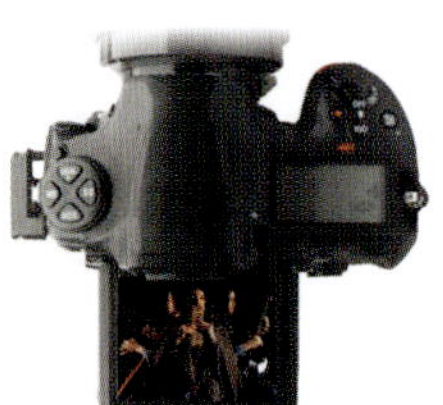

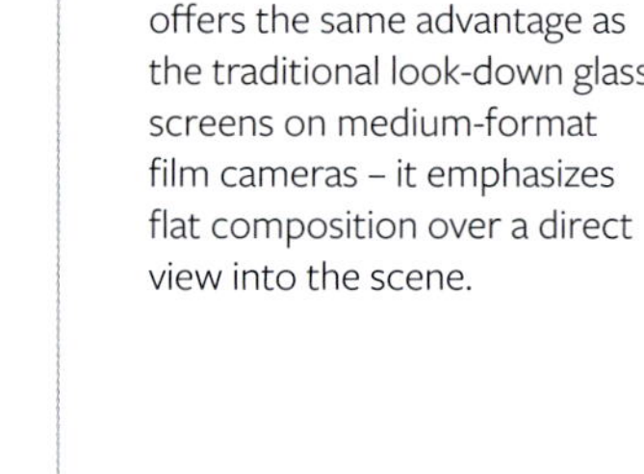

A hinged screen, standard on most good digital cameras, offers the same advantage as the traditional look-down glass screens on medium-format film cameras – it emphasizes flat composition over a direct view into the scene.

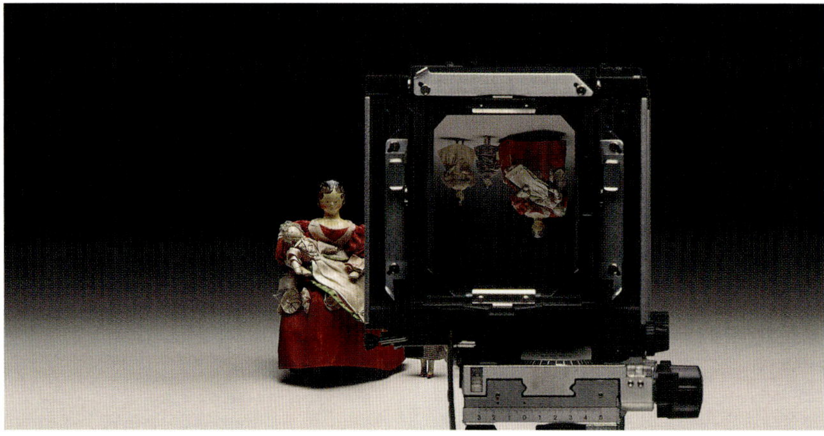

Traditional sheet-film photography, still practised by some photographers, offered great precision in framing and composing before the actual film was inserted. The inverted view, which is how the lens projects the image onto the glass screen and the film, actually helps to compose by concentrating on the arrangement rather than the meaning of the subject.

Other cameras had a viewfinder with its own lens that used a rangefinder for focusing, like the Leica, or a full duplicate lens in the case of a twin-lens reflex like the Rolleiflex, which called for looking down onto a screen inside a hood. Then there was the single-lens reflex (SLR), a groundbreaking invention that gave the actual view through the lens, bright and right way up, using a hinged reflex mirror and a roof pentaprism. For a combination of accuracy and speed, the SLR has hardly been beaten, and made it through the transition to digital as the DSLR.

This direct view through an eye-level viewfinder has a special influence on how we frame and compose. Physically, it makes the camera an extension of the eye, while giving a bright, sealed-in-black view. It accentuates the frame edges – makes them harder and more exact – and isolates the scene from the reality of the situation. This helps to focus on the composition, but its drawback is that it hides what might be coming into frame. For this reason, many professionals shoot with both eyes open.

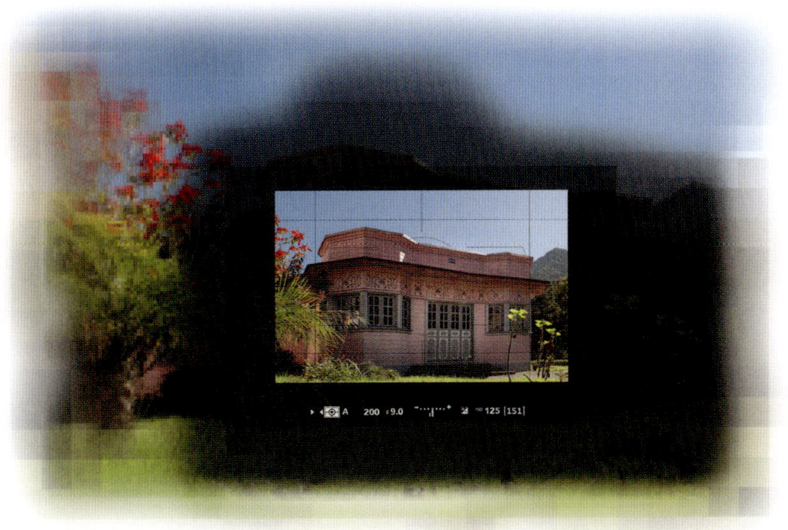

An approximation of how the view looks through an eye-level reflex or mirrorless viewfinder with both eyes open. Many professionals shoot this way in order to stay aware of what's happening just outside the frame. Priority is on the framed view, but there is still an awareness of the surroundings.

The alternative to the viewfinder on most cameras is the screen. It's a different way of framing a shot, maybe not quite as fast and a little disconnected, but it has the advantage that you're already looking at a flat picture, and that can help many people translate a three-dimensional real-world scene into a photograph. If you're using a phone camera, then the screen is automatically what you use. With some phones you can choose the frame shape, and with some the manufacturer uses the extra spaces on the longer side to show what's just outside the frame, and that can help in fine-tuning a composition.

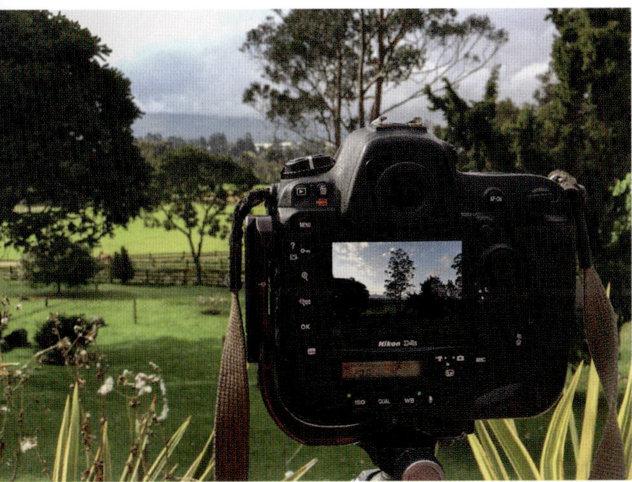

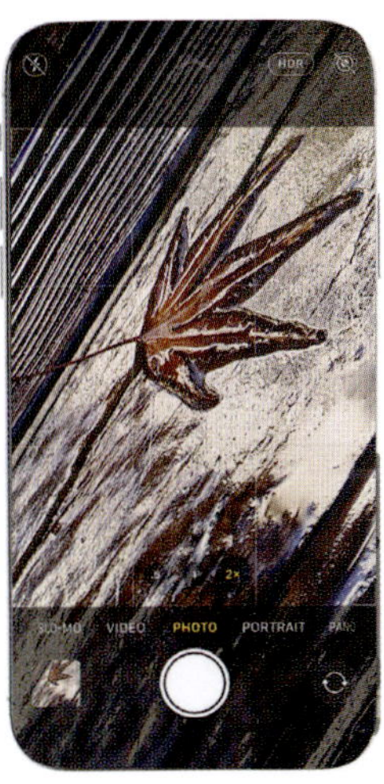

The live screen on a DSLR offers a two-dimensional view that contrasts with the more three-dimensional version through a viewfinder. Phone cameras may offer extra features, such as a greyed-out view of what is just outside the frame, to aid precise composition.

VIEWPOINT

The next 'tool', if I can call it that, is the means to change your viewpoint. In other words, the camera position. Actually, your two most useful pieces of equipment are your feet.

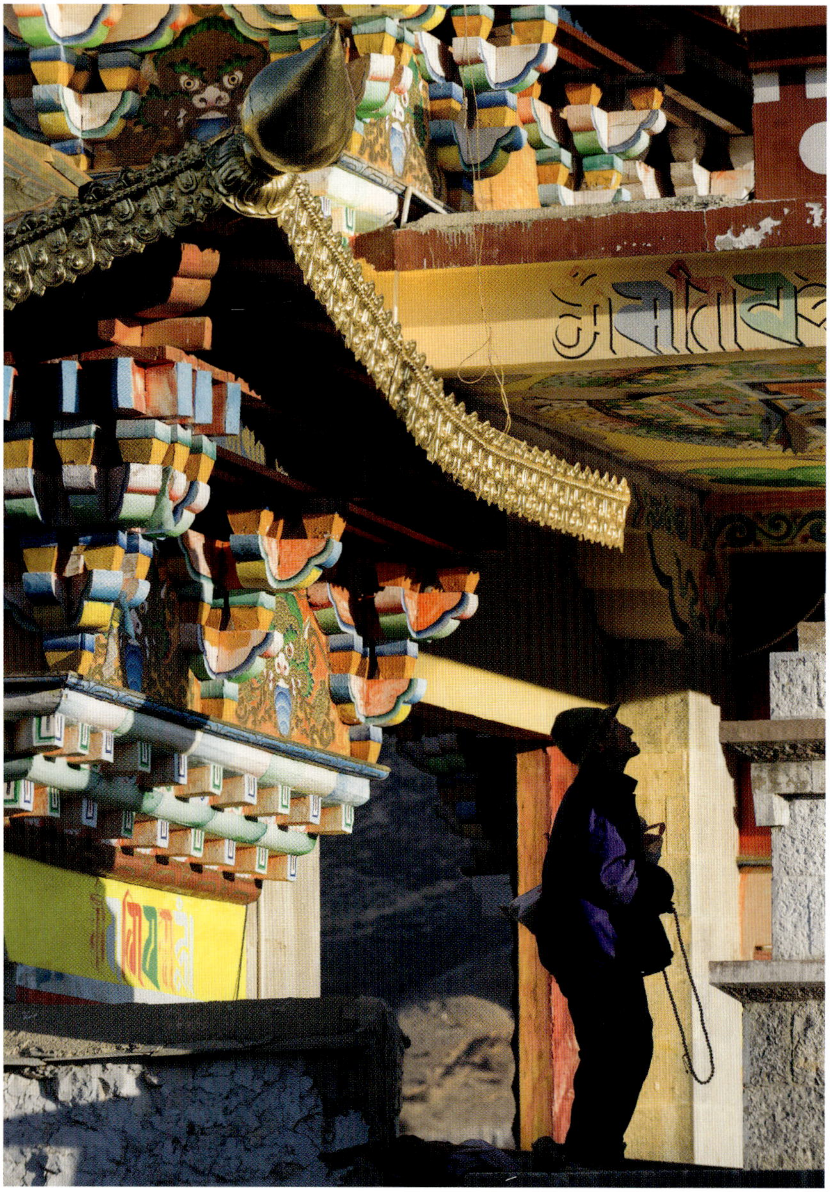

Moving with the camera forwards, backwards and sideways alters the relationships between elements in the scene, sometimes significantly. The elements in question here, in a Buddhist monastery in Yunnan, China, were the semi-silhouette of the man, the large ornate carved pillar on the left, the low foreground wall and the brightly lit doorframe. Compare the successful version on the left with the smaller photograph in which the man is hopelessly confused with the shadows.

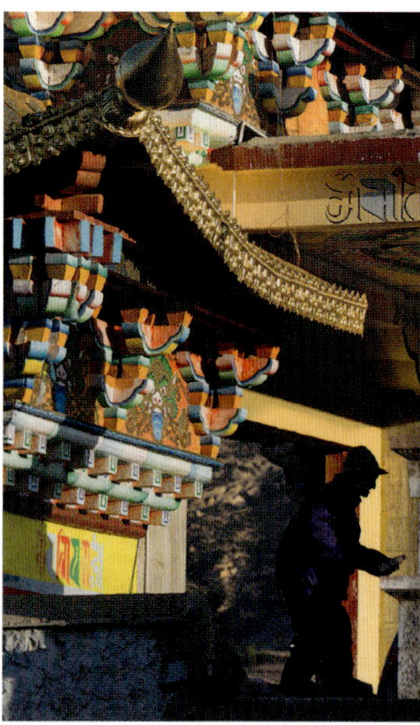

It surprises me sometimes how few people move around, even a little, for a better viewpoint and are just satisfied with the first view they get. Very small movements to one side, higher or lower, especially if you use a wider-angle lens, can make a considerable difference to the final picture.

In the picture of the brightly coloured monastery gate, the sheer exuberance and complexity of the decoration was the point of the shot, but there was also a man entering for prayer, and this would turn an architectural picture into a more human one. To make it work compositionally, as he was in silhouette, I needed to place him with a clear outline against a bright but uncomplicated area. The earlier shot of him bending down showed what wouldn't work. I needed a moment at which he stood up straight, because the sunlit patch of wall that was the only background possible was small and narrow. In that time, I had to move slightly forward and slightly to the left. The movements were small, but they were the difference between success and failure, with no halfway point.

That was an example of the fine-tuning use of viewpoint. Another use is for drastic change, and this typically means looking for an unusual or unexpected view that will add some graphic edge to the shot. This nearly always has to be opportunistic – taking advantage of whatever the situation has to offer. Overhead shots are probably the most typical, and while they can become formulaic, they are often able to lift a too-ordinary picture situation to the level of being worth shooting. This was the case with an oil palm processing plant, where workers moved hoppers full of the palm fruit along rails. This was a commercial assignment and so the shot could not be avoided, and there was indeed an overhead gantry. Complete changes of view like this depend at the very least on the subject making sense from the new viewpoint, and that is not always the case. Here, however, the stretched position that the man got himself into while pushing looked good from above, with the added bonus of a simpler and cleaner image.

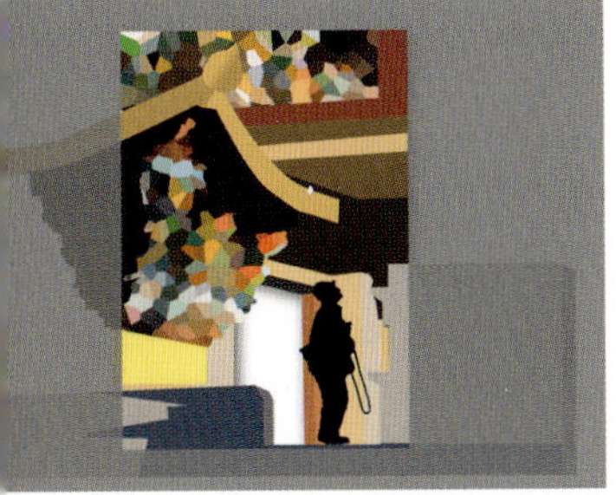

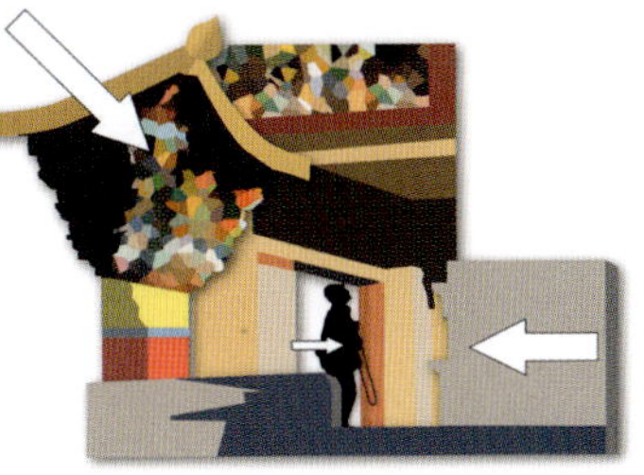

A radical change of viewpoint to directly overhead changed an ordinary and untidy industrial scene in a Colombian oil plant into a graphically ordered and simplified image, squared-up vertically downward (see also pages 42 and 78).

→

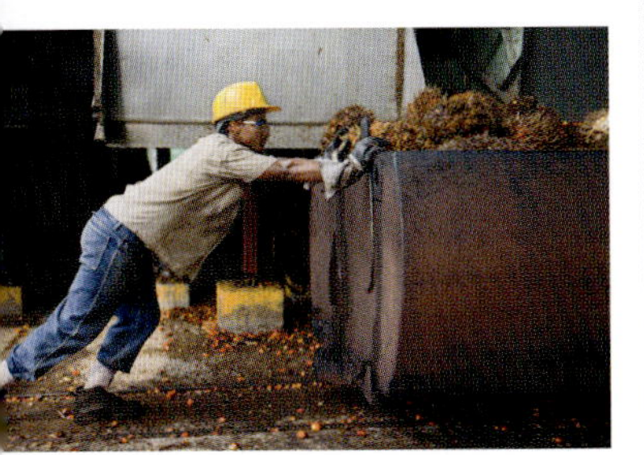

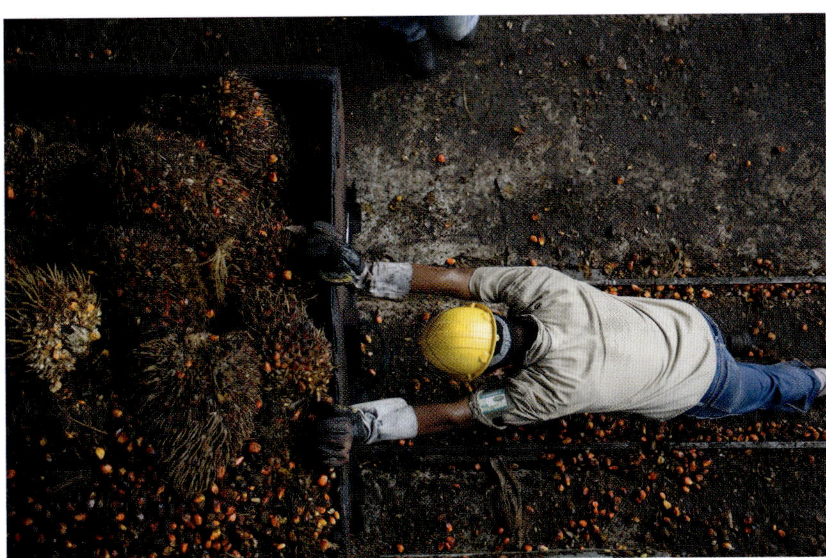

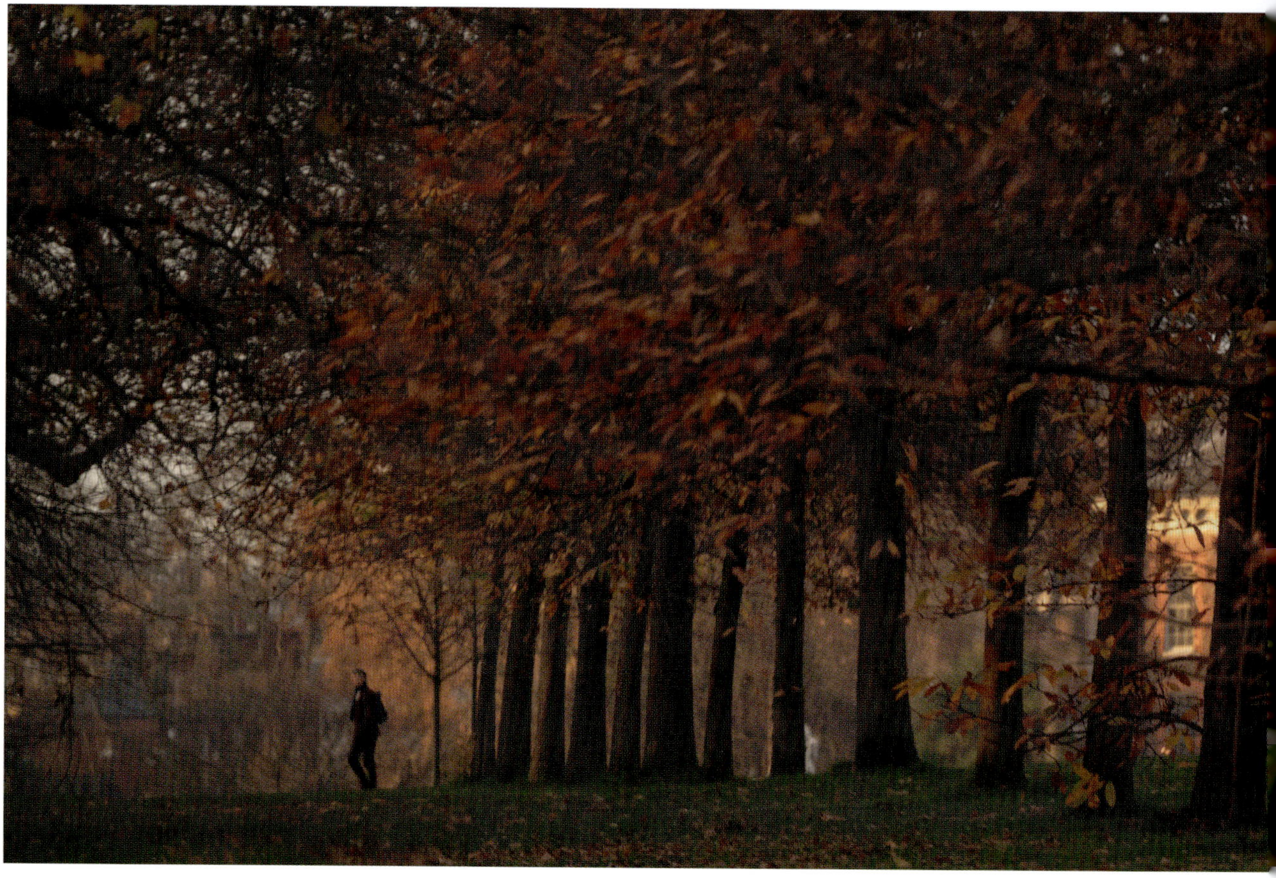

OPTICS

We're all used to the practical benefits of different lenses, and the difference is usually the focal length, which sets the angle of view and the magnification. Whether in the form of a zoom range in a single lens, or several lenses each with different focal lengths, this is what allows us to manage the space in front of the camera.

Wider takes in more of the scene, obviously useful in an interior space or to capture the vastness of a big landscape. Longer is a way of getting visually closer to a subject, useful if it's distant. Practicalities aside, however, the qualities of a lens also make it a design tool, every bit as important as the viewing system and the camera position.

There's a visually 'neutral' focal length that doesn't impose any special feeling on the image, and most people refer to it as 'standard' – it gives much the same view

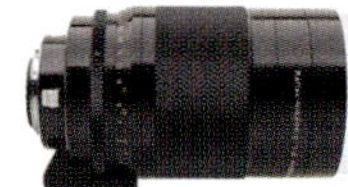

One of two extremes in focal length is a parkland scene shot with a very long 500mm lens (a compact mirror lens rather than the more usual telephoto). The angle of view is an extremely narrow 4° horizontally, just ten percent of what a standard lens gives, and the result is an unfamiliar framing, a much smaller section of the total view than we're accustomed to, equivalent to 'central' vision as seen on pages 16–17.

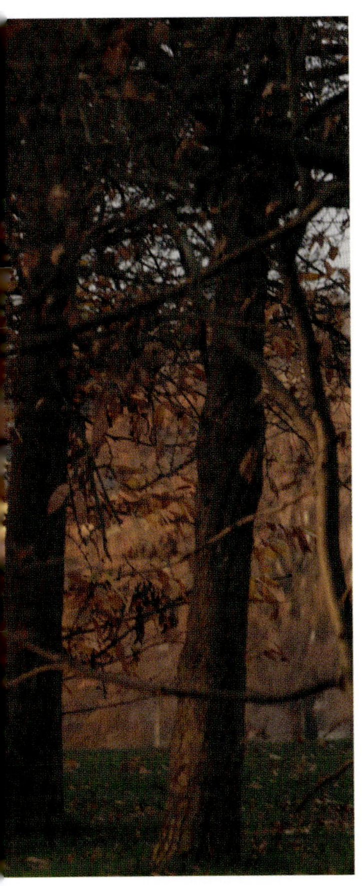

as we see with our eyes alone. That sounds logical but in fact is tricky to define, because of the quite different way in which we see the real world from how a lens images it onto a rectangular frame. Go back to the eye's different visual angles on page 17, and 'near peripheral' at 30° is probably the best candidate. With a full-frame DSLR or mirrorless camera that would be a 50mm lens, and indeed, since the earliest days of 35mm cameras, 50mm has traditionally been the standard. In reality, as we saw earlier, it can't be precise, but somewhere between about 40mm and 60mm looks standard to most people.

Going wide brings in angular distortion, which can be a useful design tool graphically, depending on your taste. I'm showing extreme examples here just to make the point. The shot of a covered bridge in China takes up an eye-straining 100° – a 12mm focal length – and this effect dominates the picture, for better or worse. For the record, Henri Cartier-Bresson, who hated talking much about equipment, thought 35mm way too wide: 'very often it is used by people who want to shout. Because you have a distortion, you have somebody in the foreground and it gives an effect. But I don't like effects.'[1]

Going in the opposite direction, long focal lengths narrow the viewing angle and create compression effects, as we'll see on page 36. Again, the example here is a deliberately extreme one, a 500mm lens with its 4° angle of view. From a design point of view, what dominate here are the feeling of the frame being well-filled, and the row of tree trunks acting as a single unit.

1 Henri Cartier-Bresson interviewed by Sheila Turner-Seed, 1971; quoted in 'Henri Cartier-Bresson: "There Are No Maybes"', *New York Times*, 21 June, 2013.

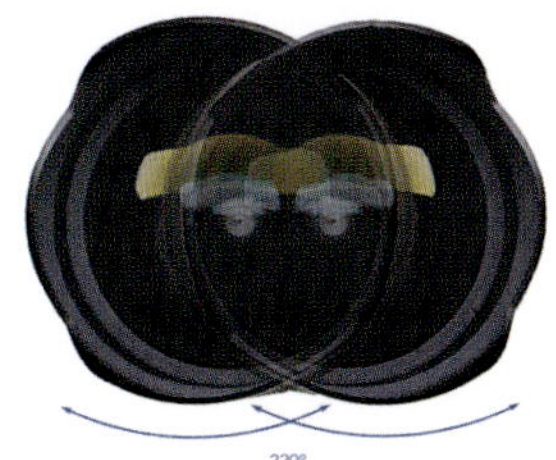

By panning and stitching two side-by-side frames shot with a 14mm lens, this view of a covered bridge and overhanging old tree in Zhejiang province, China, covers an extreme 220°. This is also outside our experience as a fully detailed image, and it is one justification for using extreme optics.

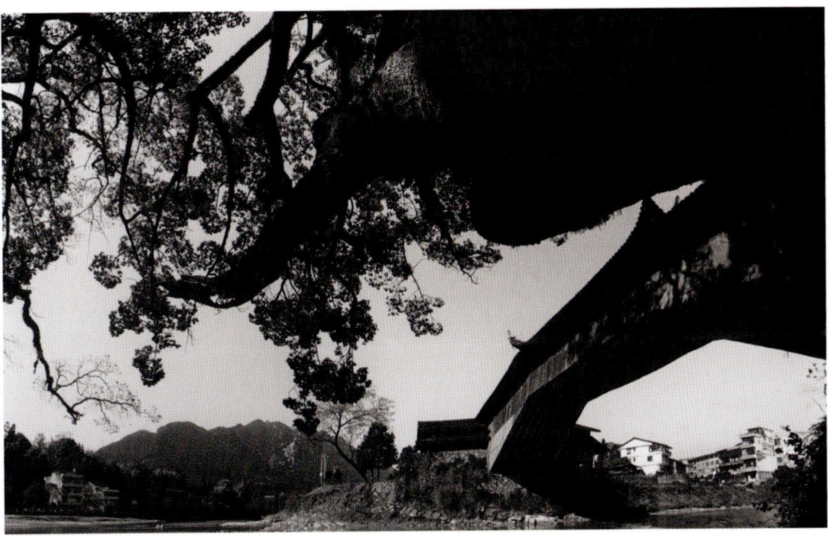

CHAPTER

2

DEEP OR FLAT

One of the most basic issues in photography – basic but often overlooked – is how to get the real-world, three-dimensional scene in front of you into a flat rectangle that's two-dimensional, while having it all make sense and look good. There are two opposite styles of doing this translation. In one, you're trying to preserve the illusion that there's depth in the scene you've captured. In other words, you're favouring the real scene and you're trying to stay faithful to what it feels like to be there. In the other, you care less about that sensation of foreground, middle ground and background, and more about the natural flatness of a picture and its graphic possibilities.

Both of these styles are worth striving for, but you can't do both at the same time. It's either, 'Do I want to project myself and the viewer into the scene?' or 'Do I want to create a more abstracted version, stepped back from the real thing?' However, there's no reason why you can't switch from one to the other between pictures.

In the real world, things move. We move, and this immediately shows us almost all we need to know about the depth of the scene we're in. Shift your head to one side even slightly, and parallax kicks in. This is the displacement of things in our line of sight, and close objects seem to shift more as we change our viewpoint than distant objects do. Even without that shift, we have stereopsis because we have two eyes side by side, which give us binocular vision. Neither parallax nor stereopsis are available in a still photograph, and this makes it possible to play with how you arrange close things against distant ones, as in the picture of the ancient Thai monument on page 41, by moving slightly to one side, especially with a wide-angle lens.

However, these techniques have to work on an audience that knows that there must be depth in the scene, and also, because they're looking at a photograph, trying to locate this picture in the real world. In other words, however hard you try to abstract and remove the sense of three dimensions from an image, the viewer will still be looking for the clues that make it an actual scene taken from life. If you use techniques to flatten a scene, this inevitably means disorienting the viewer, which may get you more attention. So there's rather more to this issue than first meets the eye.

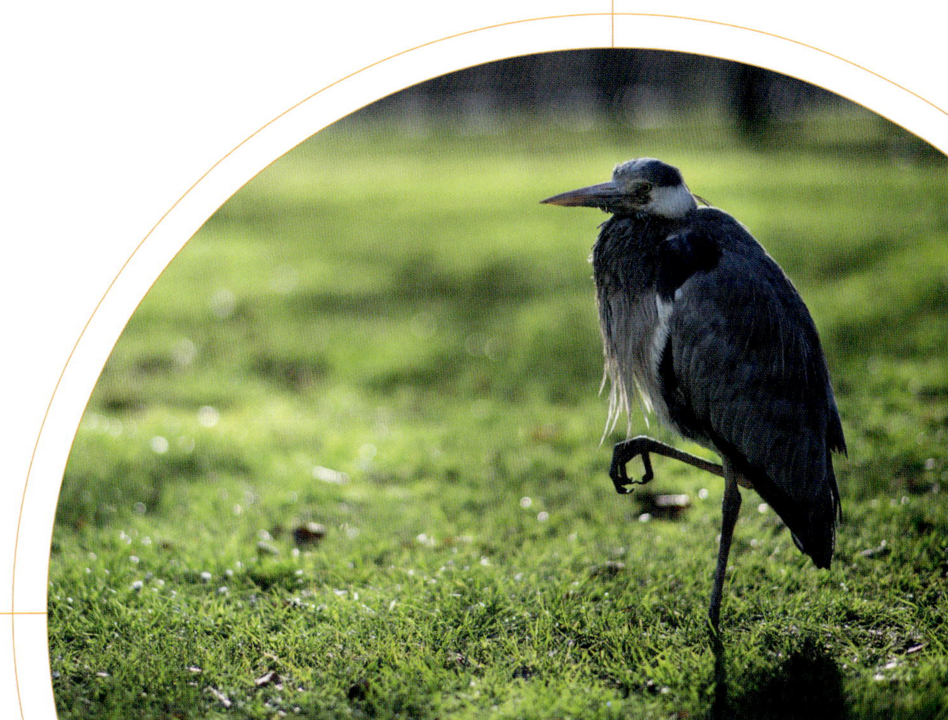

PERSPECTIVE: DIMINISHING

In all kinds of imagery, perspective defines the way in which the scene appears to have depth, just as in real life. It's a set of clues that show what parts are closer, which are farther away, and how they relate to each other.

In the history of painting and drawing, it was a major headache to deal with, but of course photography delivers it automatically because of the way lenses work. Even so, there are things you can do to enhance it, and this is where composition comes in, with viewpoint playing a major role. There are three main kinds of perspective effect in photography, and probably the most obvious is when similar things appear smaller at a distance. This is what's happening in the picture here, where the camera is deliberately close to the foreground figure, while several metres separate him from the couple having lunch on the patio of their house.

Gutting and selling locally caught fish in the barrio of Rafael Nuñes, Cartagena, Colombia, where the street is the focus of activity, from vendors to house porches. Reportage shots depend on information rather than expression, and so often call for full depth of field. That in turn needs an experienced balance between aperture and how close the camera can be to the foreground. Closer means stronger perspective and sense of depth.

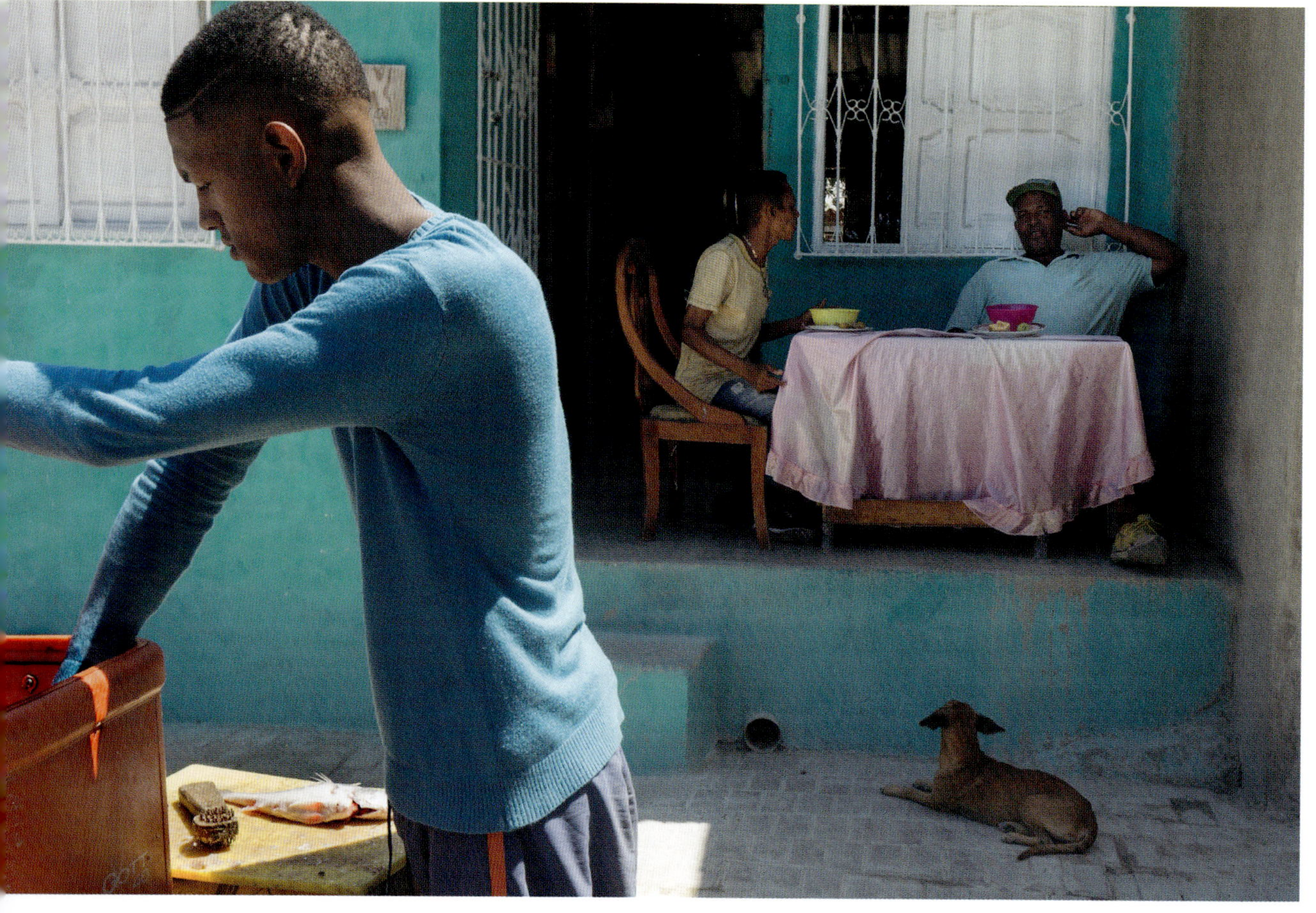

Yes, there's more going on in the shot than just perspective – the repetition of the aqua colour, the rectilinear division of the frame and the neat placement of the relevant subjects – but tangible depth is very much a part of the picture. The focal length is standard (48mm), because while a wide angle would exaggerate the difference in size between the people, having the foreground figure on one side of the frame would distort his shape unreasonably. Depth of field is strong (*f*/14) to cover the entire scene, because we want to see all the details and expressions. More on what depth of field does to the sense of depth shortly, on page 40.

Diminishing perspective may not seem so remarkable because we're so accustomed to it, but it involves our brain overriding the evidence of our eyes, a process called size constancy. We know that most people are more or less the same height, as are telegraph poles and automobiles, so we automatically interpret any size difference as perspective. Lens focal length plays a strong role because of the angle of view. At its widest with a wide-angle lens, this amplifies the difference in size between foreground and distance, as you see with this shot of hay bales. A telephoto reduces the difference in size, as we'll see soon, and that definitely has a flattening effect.

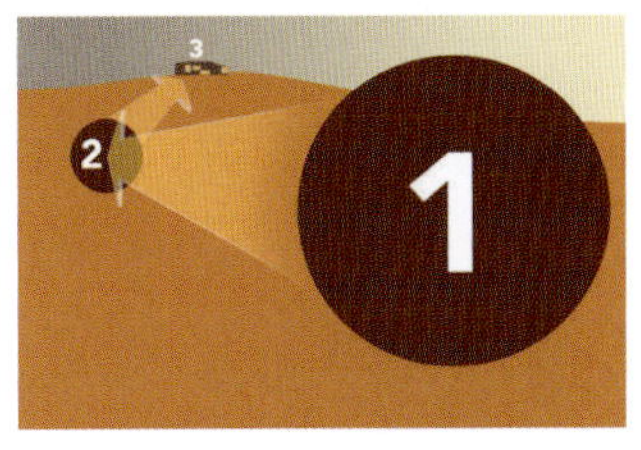

A simple three-point composition of wheat fields in Tuscany at harvest time, with a 20mm wide-angle lens. Hay bales are so obviously consistent in size that this framing strongly conveys perspective and distance, and leads the viewer's eye through the scene in a short sequence.

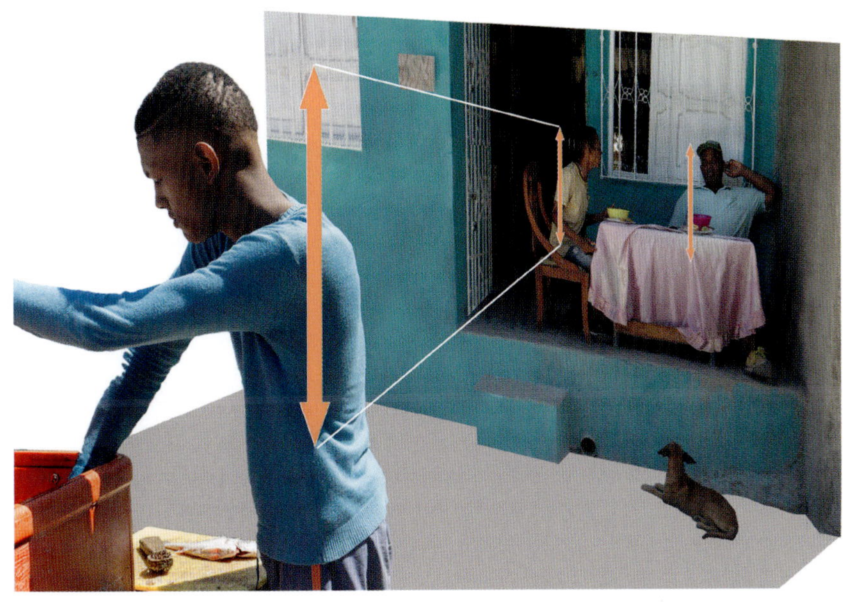

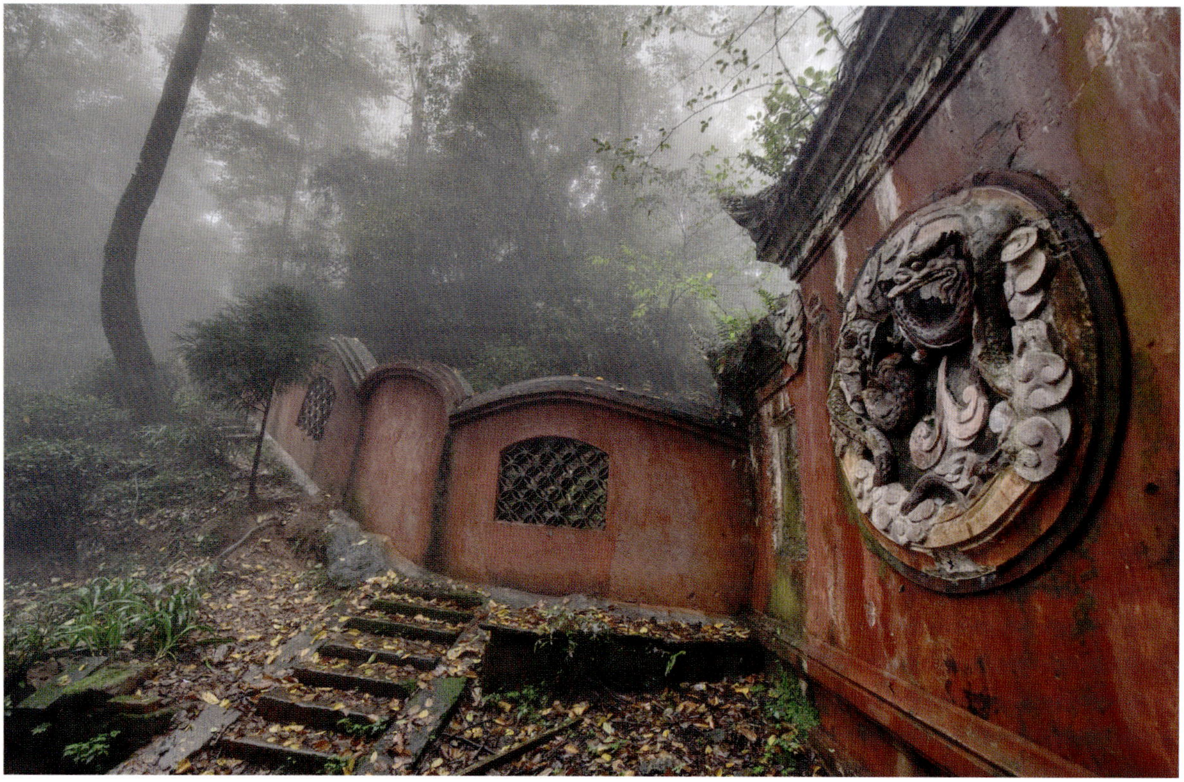

PERSPECTIVE: LINEAR

The second kind of perspective is linear, and it is all about converging lines. As with size constancy for diminishing perspective, it's what we naturally know about the scene that makes linear perspective work.

We know, or at least assume, that in the picture of a red Chinese wall the top and bottom of the wall are level and parallel, and that all the steps are the same width. That's our experience in play, and so we translate this view as receding sharply. I've chosen this picture for the purpose, rather than the usual example of a straight road converging to a point in the distance, to show that different kinds of perspective can combine. Here, it's a slightly foggy day, and that brings with it aerial perspective, which is next on our list on the following pages. Nevertheless, linear perspective is the main actor here, beginning with the very strong convergence on the right of the frame. That's the main clue to depth in the scene, and it's enhanced by two things: viewpoint and lens focal length. Moving close to the wall on the right and shooting at a very acute angle maximizes the convergence of the lines, and this

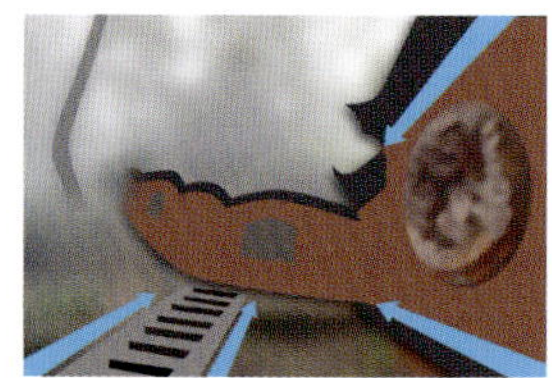

↑ The main depth dynamic here on this ancient Chinese tea mountain is the strong convergence of lines, which we can assume are parallel in real life. This comes from using an ultra-wide-angle lens, 14mm, positioned close to the wall, looking along it at a sharp angle and framed for maximum distortion on the right side.

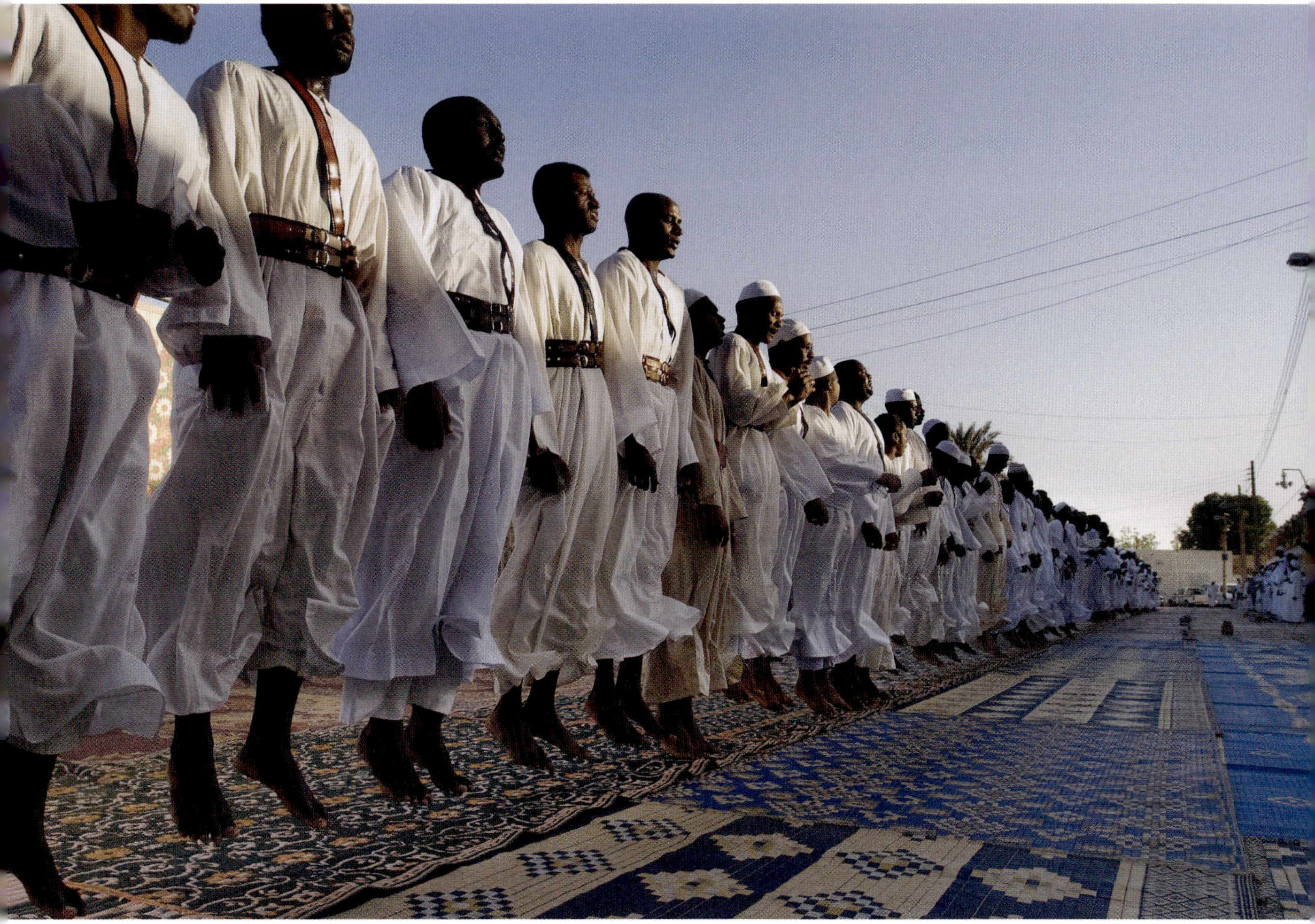

is exaggerated even more by using a lens with an extremely wide angle, 14mm. Note that the most active part of this perspective is right at the beginning, closest to the camera, so to make the most of the effect, position this decisively in the frame.

Similarly, in the picture of a Sudanese Sufi congregation leaping in unison during Friday prayers, the angle of view, dramatized by crouching, and a wide-angle focal length of 25mm, have all the lines in the picture – from the carpet to the men to the telephone wires – converging strongly to a point near the right edge. Just as the Chinese wall picture has an added aerial perspective, this one has diminishing perspective on top of linear – there are more than 60 men.

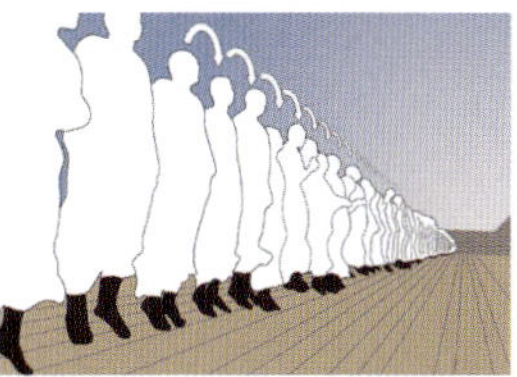

A similar lens/angle technique was used here for even greater linear perspective effect. A 25mm lens was used from an angle that makes the most of the number of Sufi men in Omdurman, Sudan – close enough to the men on the left to enhance the linear perspective, while far enough in front of the line to show all of them right to the end.

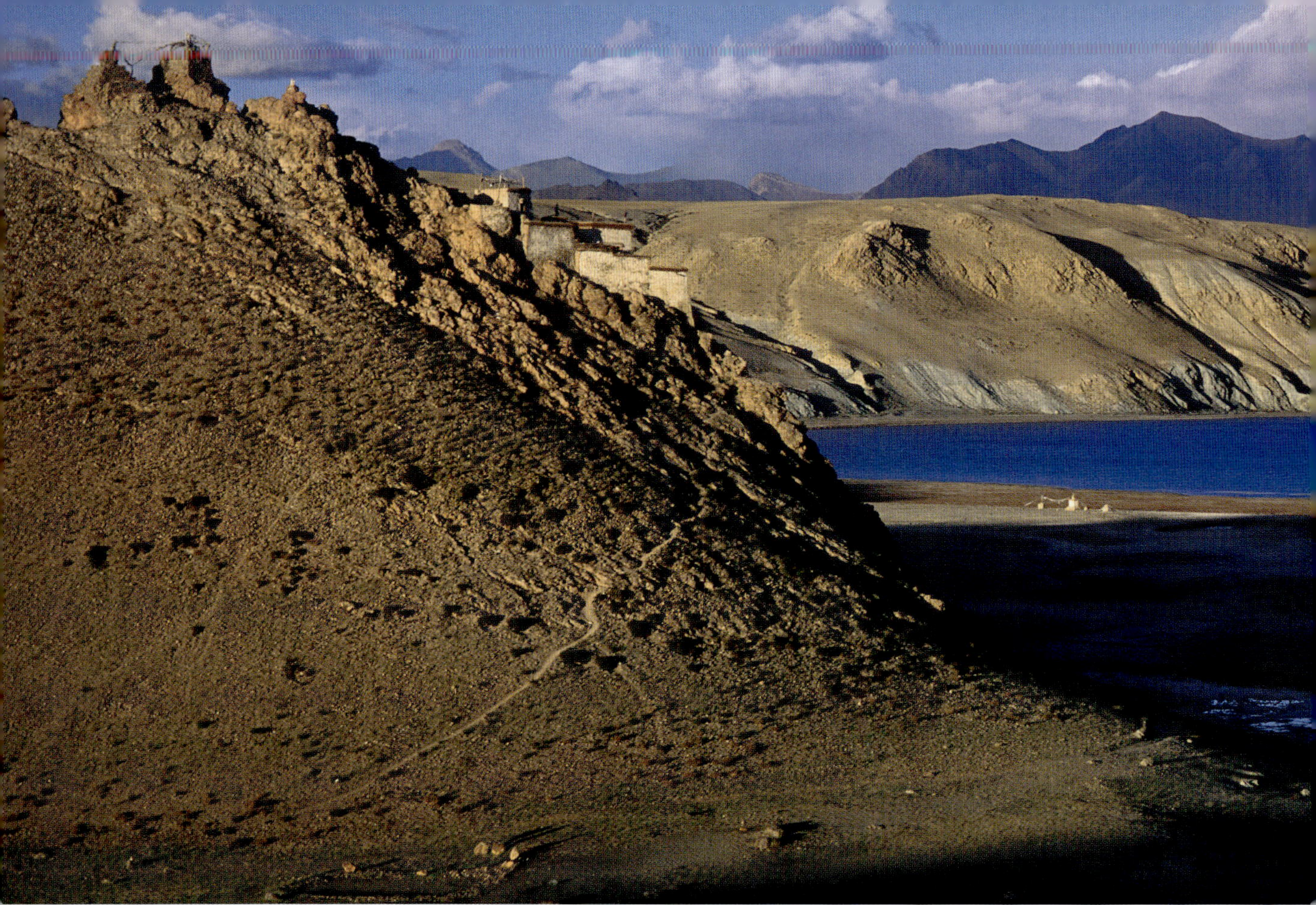

PERSPECTIVE: AERIAL

The third main kind of perspective depends on atmosphere. Minute particles suspended in the air are to all intents invisible across a short distance, but over longer distances give a misty or hazy effect.

Features look lighter, there's less contrast and we see less detail. The more particles in the air, the stronger the effect, and it's a very convincing clue to depth in a landscape. That has a lot to do with weather and pollution, because the particles are either tiny water droplets forming mist or fog, or else dry particles from dust and smoke. For mist, one typical situation is early morning after sunrise, especially in cold, clear weather when there's dew or frost on the ground that the sun begins to warm, and mist develops as the water evaporates. Lighting can also exaggerate aerial perspective, in particular backlighting, when you're shooting toward a low sun. A side effect is that beams of light become visible because of scattering by the particles.

↑ At one extreme of aerial perspective are high mountain landscapes in clear weather, as in this image of Lake Manasarovar, especially when the sun is low and behind the camera, which gives more even lighting across distance.

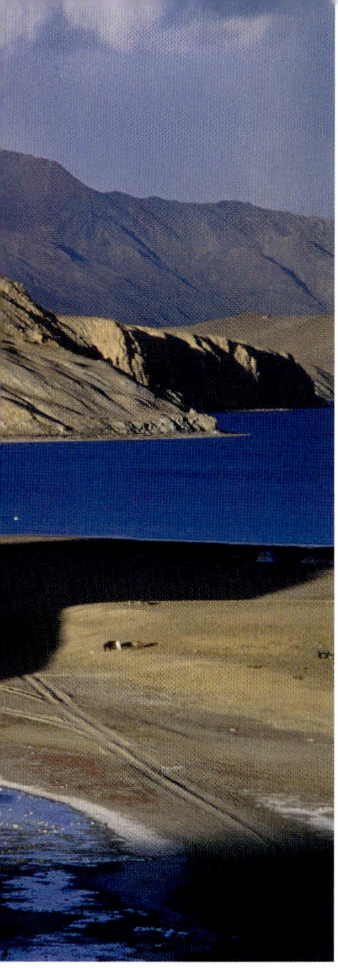

Using a wide-angle lens helps, as long as you include a foreground, simply because it covers a greater depth of atmosphere, as in the case of the Balinese landscape here. If you use a telephoto lens, you're basically cropping in on the distant part of the view without seeing the clearer foreground.

For the opposite effect, simply reverse the ingredients, as you can see in the landscape shown at left. This is at about 16,000ft (5,000m), where the air density is almost half of that at sea level. On top of that, this is a medium telephoto lens, and the sun is behind the camera, and the combination creates a vivid landscape with startling clarity. The hills across the lake are about 2 miles (3 km) away at their closest, and the mountains beyond, 12 miles (20 km). The shadow edges are another clue – they stay sharp across distance, and the total effect is striking because most of us don't experience this kind of light. UV and polarizing filters tend to cut down haze, and there are also de-hazing software filters.

By contrast to the lake scene, this wide-angle (20mm) shot of rice fields looking toward Mount Gunung Agung in Bali, more than 25 miles (40km) away, has exaggerated depth mainly because of the difference in clarity between the close foreground and the distant top of the volcano.

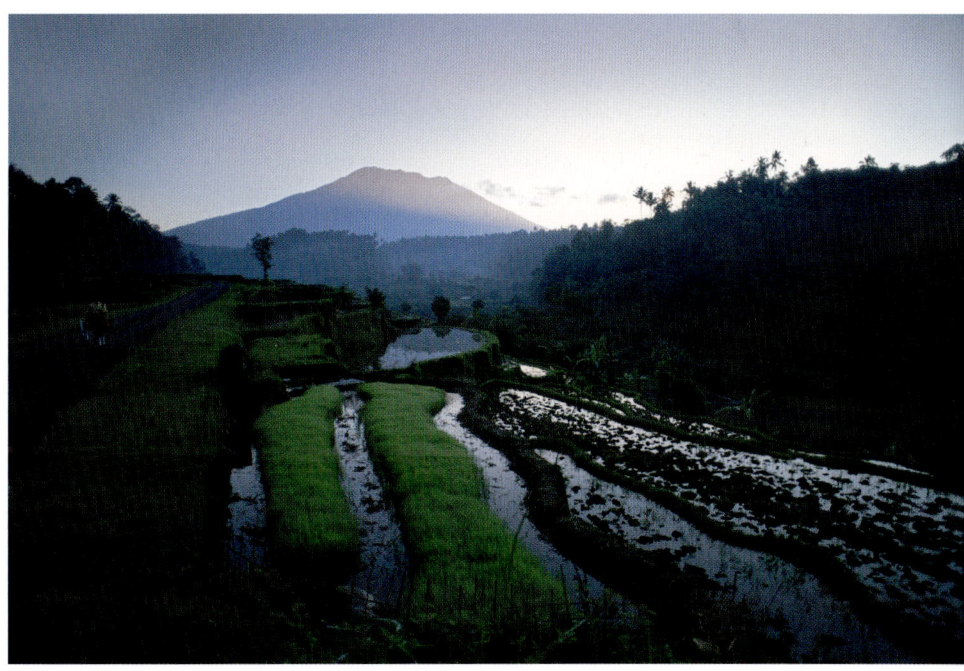

FLATTENING & COMPRESSION

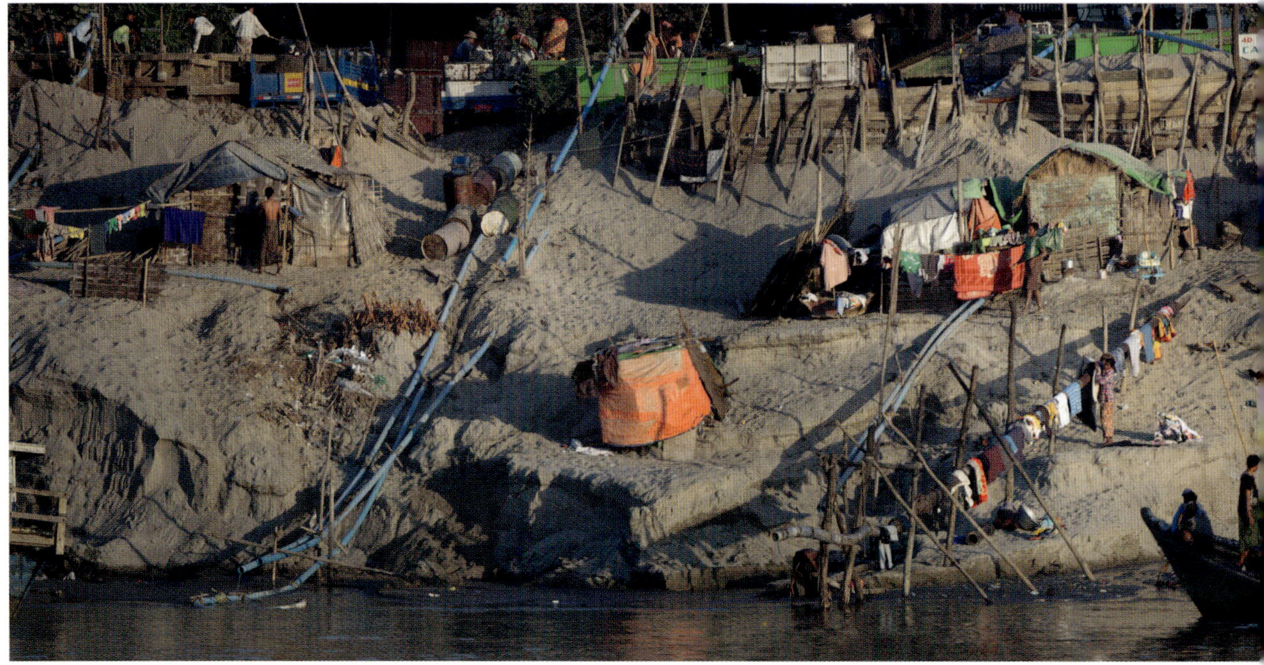

The Tibetan high plateau scene on the previous page showed how a longer focal length can work toward flattening a scene, and it does this in two ways. One is by cutting out foreground and middle ground. The other is by giving what looks to the viewer like a compressing effect.

Both of these are in proportion to the focal length, so that super-telephotos are very distinctive in this way. Both also depend on how you use the lens and the viewpoint you choose. Let's start with what I call the 'telephoto distanced' style. It works when the view is across an open space, so that you immediately lose the foreground and middle ground, and you project the viewer straight to the distance. This does two things: first, it gives the impression of having stepped back and of observing without getting involved. In terms of sensation and the viewer's relationship with what's in the frame, it has a remoteness and objectivity that is the complete opposite of the immersive style that we'll see next. This is one of the reasons why telephoto shooting is embraced by some photographers and rejected by others. Those who dislike it feel that photography is at its best when it's involved with its subjects. The second effect is that usually – certainly in the example here of a riverbank in Mandalay, Myanmar, shot from a boat on the River Irrawaddy – what's in view seems to be all at the same distance, simply because there are no nearer reference points. Graphically, it's flattened and coolly detached.

↑ Using a 500mm lens similar to that on page 26 – with an angle of view of only 4° horizontally, across about 300m of empty space – has the effect of compressing everything, from the riverboat to the huts on the bank, into what looks like the same plane.

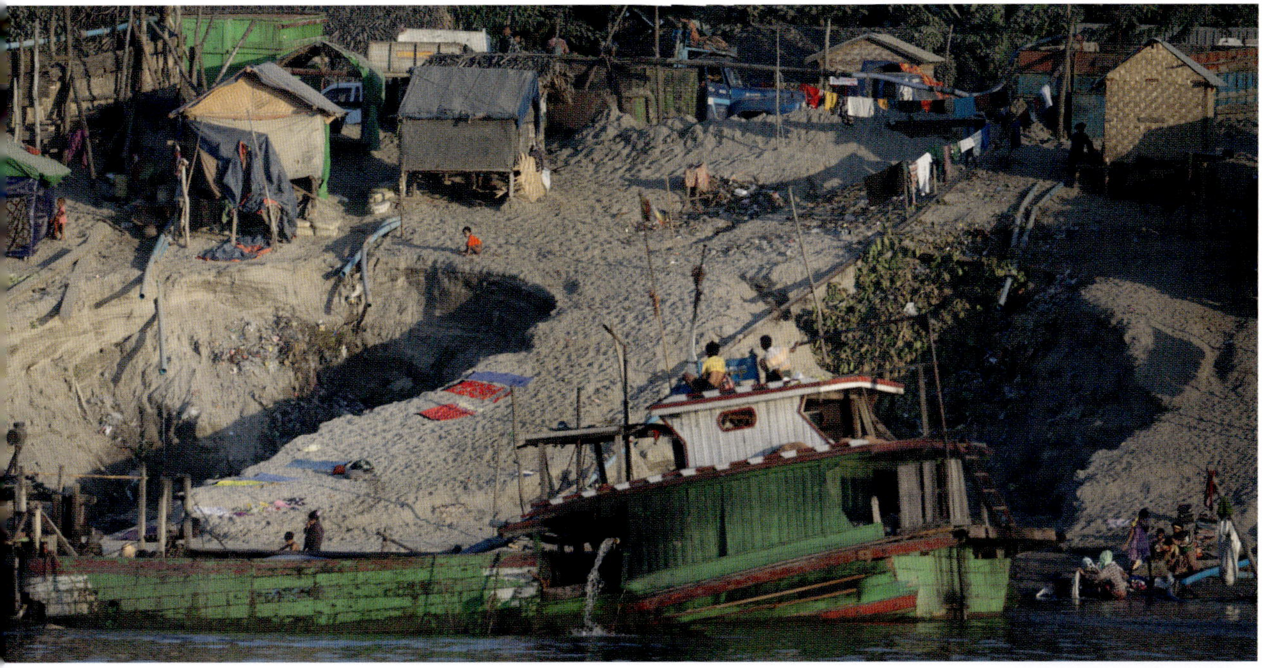

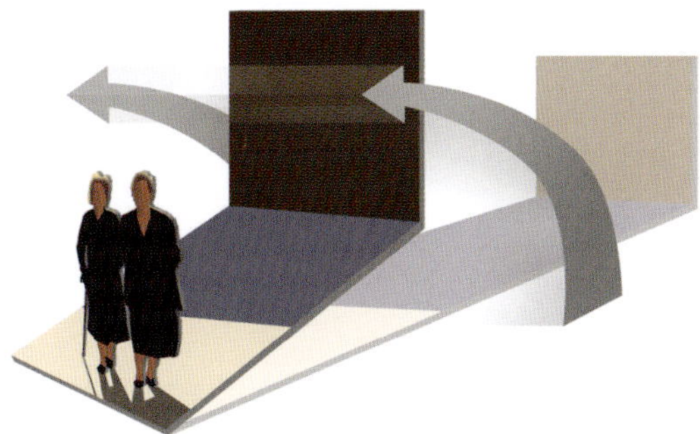

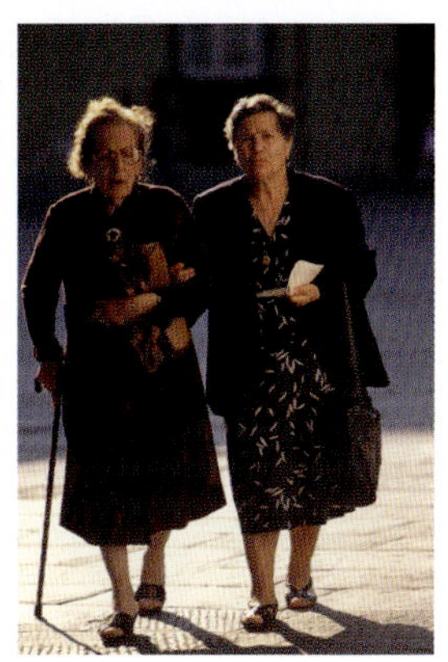

The other way in which a telephoto takes away the sense of depth in a scene is by a kind of compression. This is entirely perceptual, but even with a modest telephoto (180mm in the case of the two Italian women walking toward the camera) the effect is as if the background has been somehow tilted forward.

IMMERSION

Using a wide-angle lens in a particular way gives quite the opposite sensation to the distanced style of telephoto shooting we just looked at, and it can be one of the strongest ways of taking the viewer with you into a realistic impression of a scene.

It's subjective and immersive, as the examples here show, but to be effective and give the greatest sensation of depth, you need to maximize the range from near to far. That means, ideally, including something close to within several centimetres (a few inches), while looking through to a substantial distance, and a wide-angle lens manages this the most easily. That in turn means framing so that the distance is close to the centre of the frame, while the foreground is on one or both sides. If the close foreground elements break the frame at the sides, there's a wrap-around effect. We'll look next at how focus contributes to depth or flatness, but this immersive style favours good depth of field because it's natural to want to see detail in things that are very close to the camera. Again, this is easiest with a wide-angle lens.

An extreme corner distortion using a 14mm lens in a Sudanese Sufi religious school, or *khalwa* (left), but then corrected by applying spherical distortion in post-production (right). This correction creates barrel distortion, just noticeable on the edge of the tablet in the foreground.

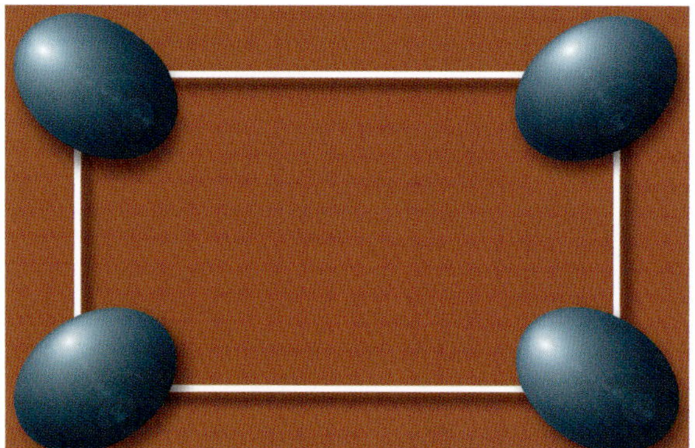

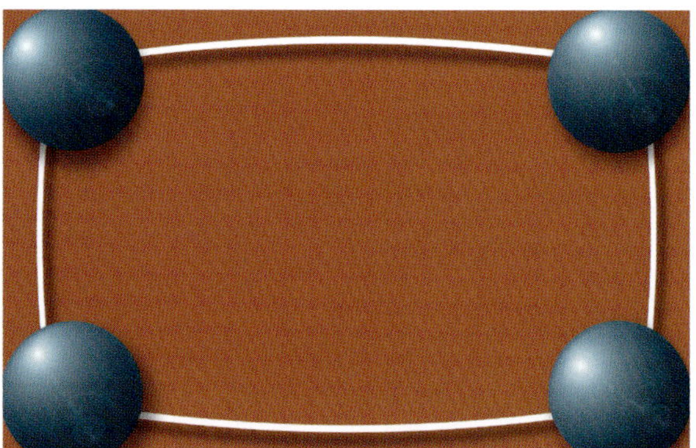

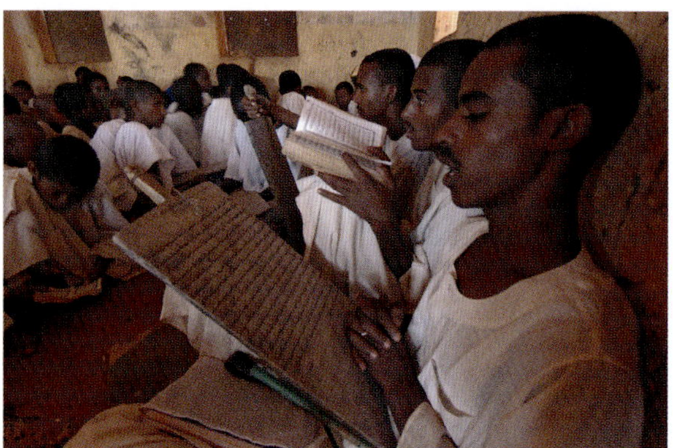

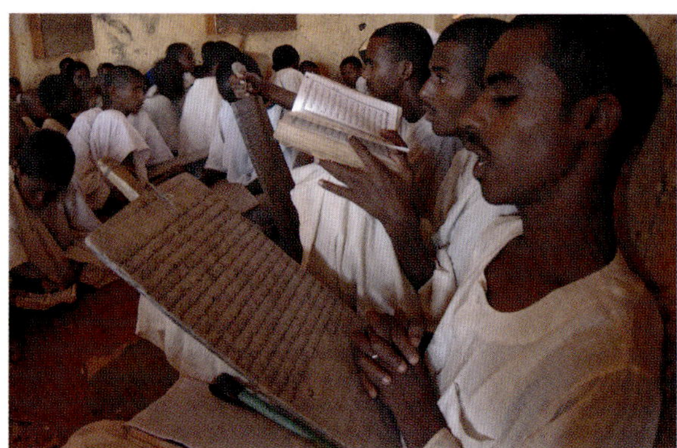

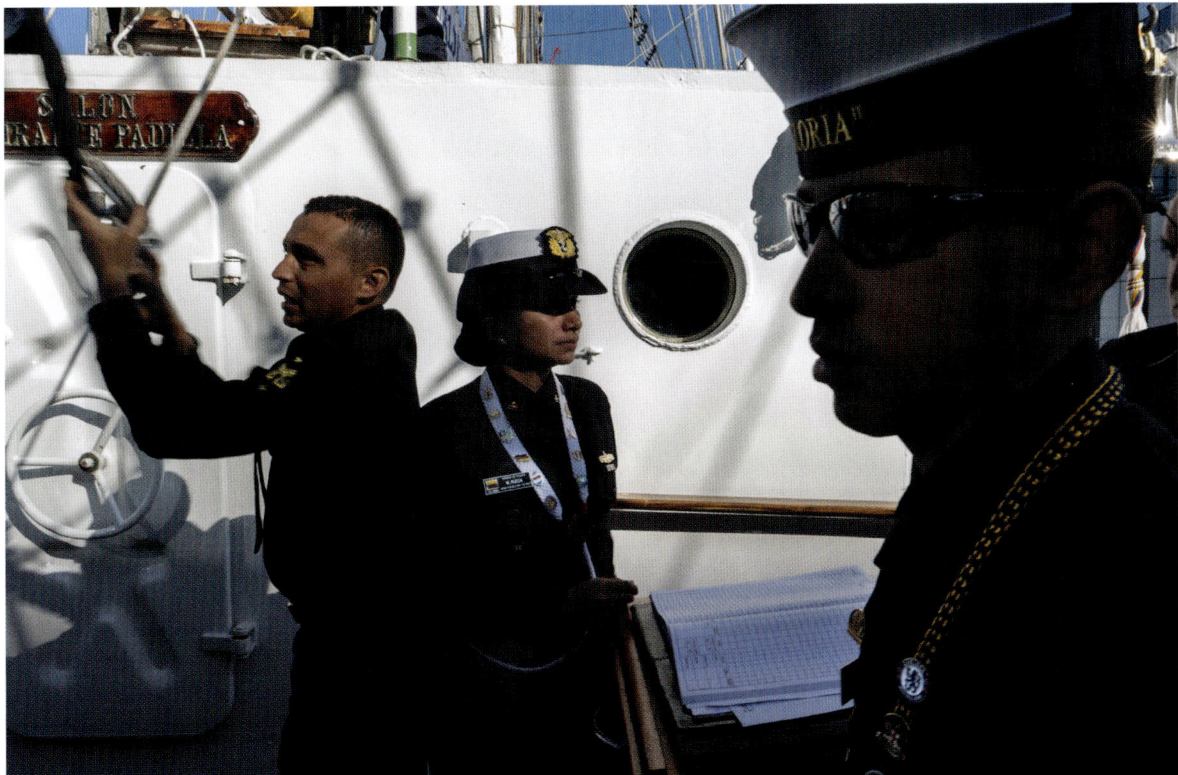

However, this strategy brings with it a special difficulty, which is that very wide-angle lenses not only have radial distortion, but even less acceptably, when there are people close to the camera, volume deformation. This is perceptual but no less important, and the typical scenario is that faces and heads become elongated on an outward axis. The sailor's head and cap show some of this in the picture here, while the head of the Sudanese man reading the Qur'an even more so. This is all to do with expectations and familiarity. There is a digital solution, by applying spherical distortion, but while it reduces volume deformation it increases the radial distortion. You can't solve both. Ideally, avoid obvious and long vertical and horizontal lines, especially close to the corners.

↑ A drill on a Colombian naval flagship, shot with a 31-mm focal length lens, which from close deforms the sailor at right, but this was judged just about acceptable. Balancing distortion with composition is a constant issue with immersive wide-angle shooting.

FOCUS DEPTH

As focus is all about distance, it's clearly a candidate for manipulating the sense of depth, but it's not straightforward. It involves two actions: the point where you focus, and the choice of aperture that will set how much of the scene will be sharply focused front-to-back.

Full depth of field from a 20mm-equivalent lens (actually 47mm on a 5x4-in camera) stopped down to its minimum, and a viewpoint stressing the depth of the scene from the small foreground stone pillar to the distant large tower.

The complication is that a shallow, selectively focused shot (as below) is certainly three-dimensional and makes the focused subject stand out, but it also makes the background less readable. This rather misses the point if you want to show the depth, because while the sense of depth is there, the viewer can't make most of it out. Full depth of field from a small aperture as in the archaeological scene opposite (this is more effective with a wide-angle lens than a telephoto) might seem to reduce depth impression, but as we've already seen, other things such as perspective can simply do a better job – and the sharpness throughout helps us appreciate that.

Quite often we're faced with a choice of how much sharpness for a scene, and it could go either way, toward full depth of field or toward shallow, selective focus. When you have subjects at well-separated distances, do you want them all in focus or just one of them? If the scene is deep, and we've already looked at a number of ways of dealing with this, either stressing it or reducing it, the depth of field can work independently of the other techniques. Most photographers I know tend to go strongly in one direction or the other – either everything sharply focused or else just one point in focus that leaves the rest blurred (which we'll come to in

An 85mm lens at a wide aperture (*f*/1.4) was used in a classic selective-focus style, with two elements on the same plane (the Buddha carving and wavy architectural feature) in sharp focus, and sufficient distance behind to throw the background into a soft blur.

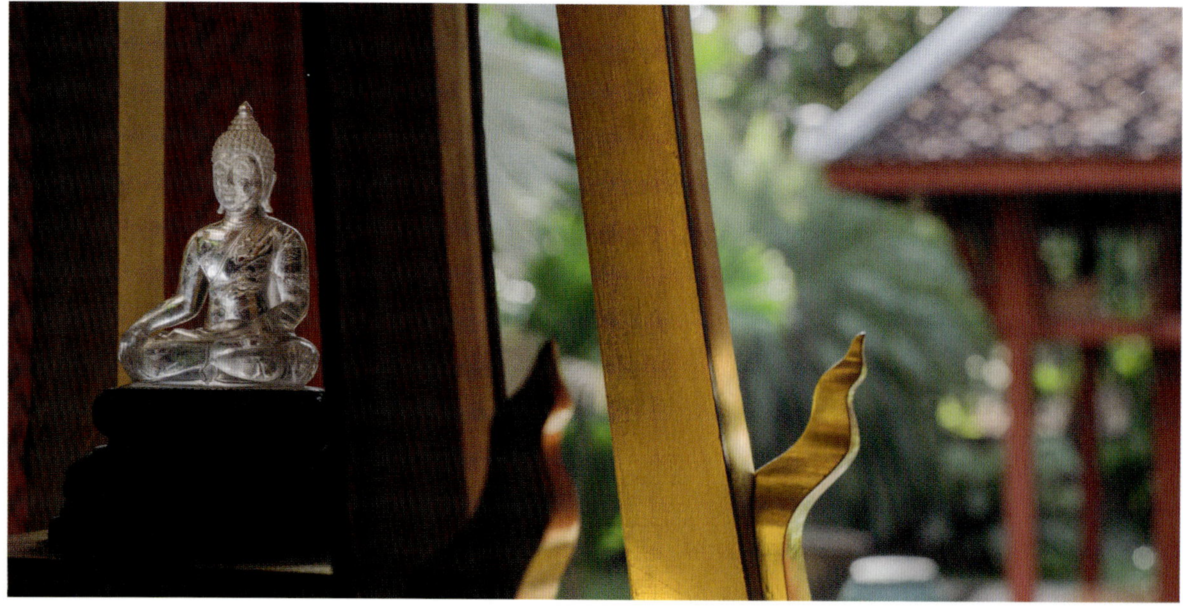

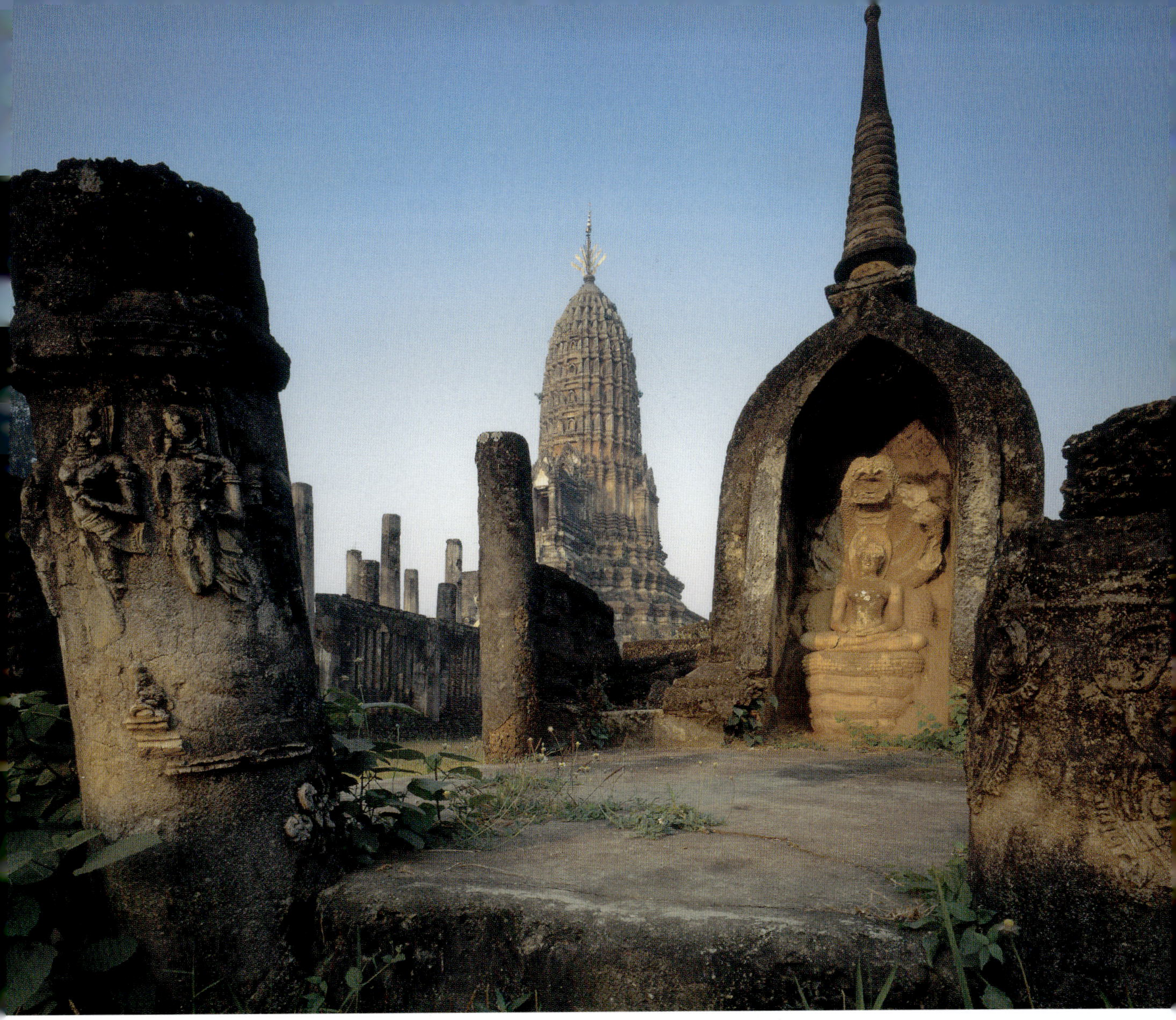

Focus Pull, page 144). There's a reason for preferring one extreme or the other, which is that in-between versions – mostly or partly sharp – often look weak, as if the photographer couldn't decide or couldn't make it work. The problem with having parts of a picture that are almost-but-not-quite sharp is that this makes us actually want to see the detail, yet we're denied that. These two pictures show the two extreme versions, both conveying depth successfully, but in different ways.

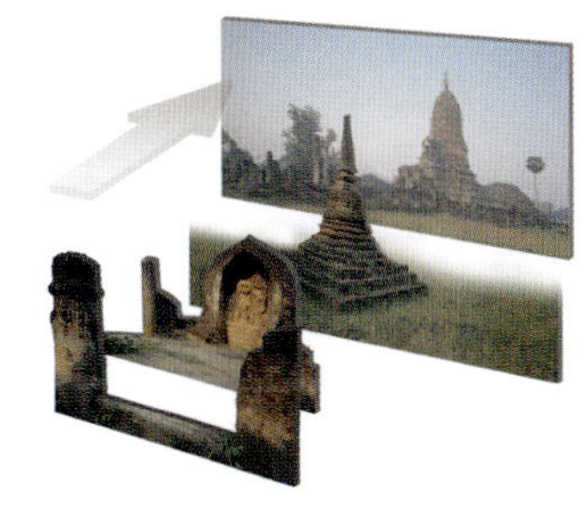

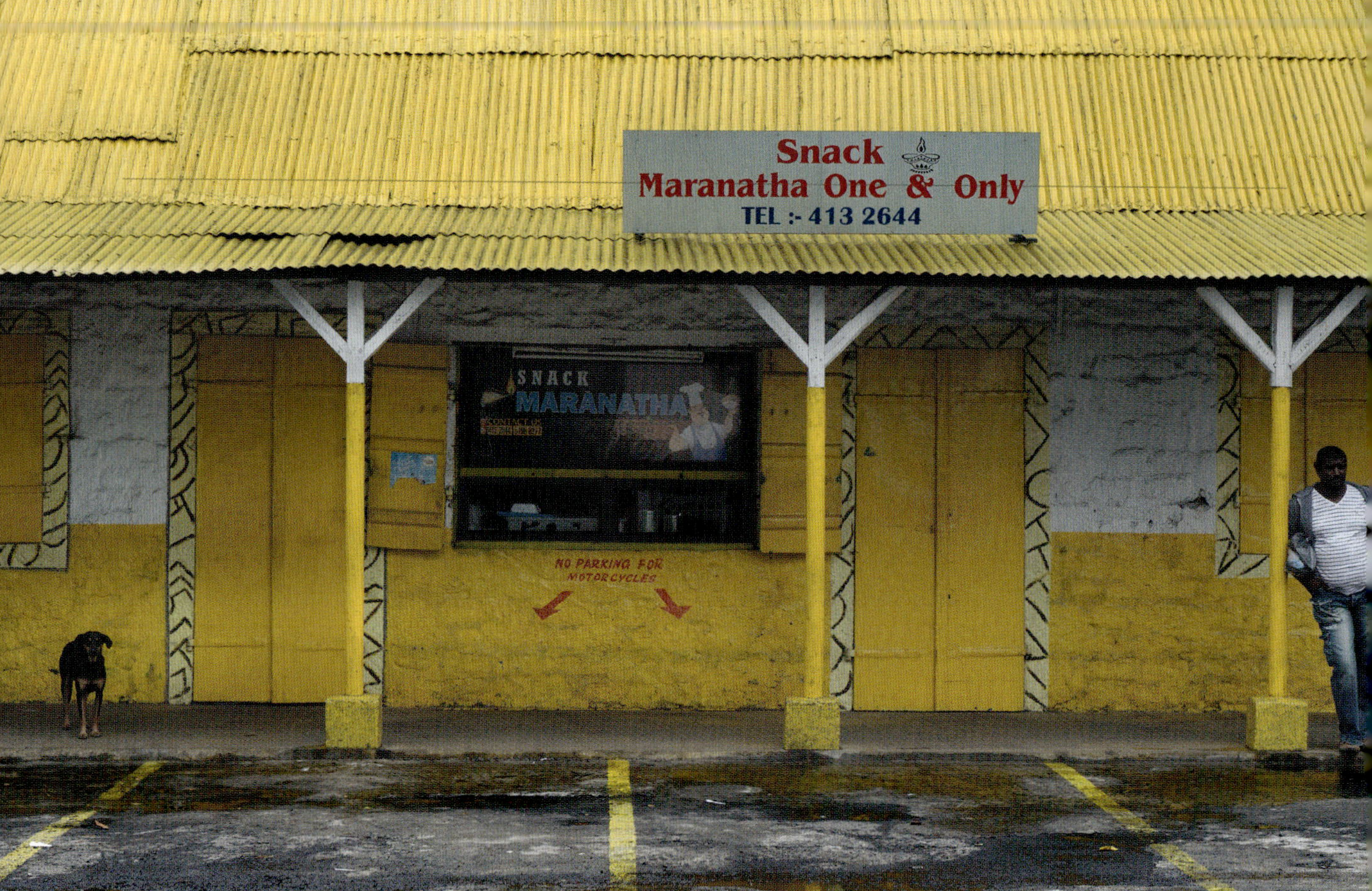

SQUARING UP

Beloved of art directors and no-frills documentary photographers (for entirely different reasons), squaring up to the scene and shooting it full frontal is one way of removing depth and replacing that with two dimensions.

The rationale is straightforward: most man-made structures feature verticals and horizontals, and if the camera view is exactly at right angles, you eliminate convergence. There's a little more to it than that, because this works best when the subject itself has little depth, like the façade of a building. If it has the kind of depth that you can see in the picture of the Thai building (opposite above), with wings appearing on either side, then it will unavoidably look deep, because of horizontal convergence. For this reason, squared-up shots are easier to pull off with a standard or long focal length, as is the case with the yellow building, shot at 62mm; and closing in or even cropping in often helps.

↑ Even though the yellow parking bay lines converge and give depth clues, the overall impression of this Mauritian café is two-dimensional due to the precision of the viewpoint and framing, and the flat lighting on a rainy day.

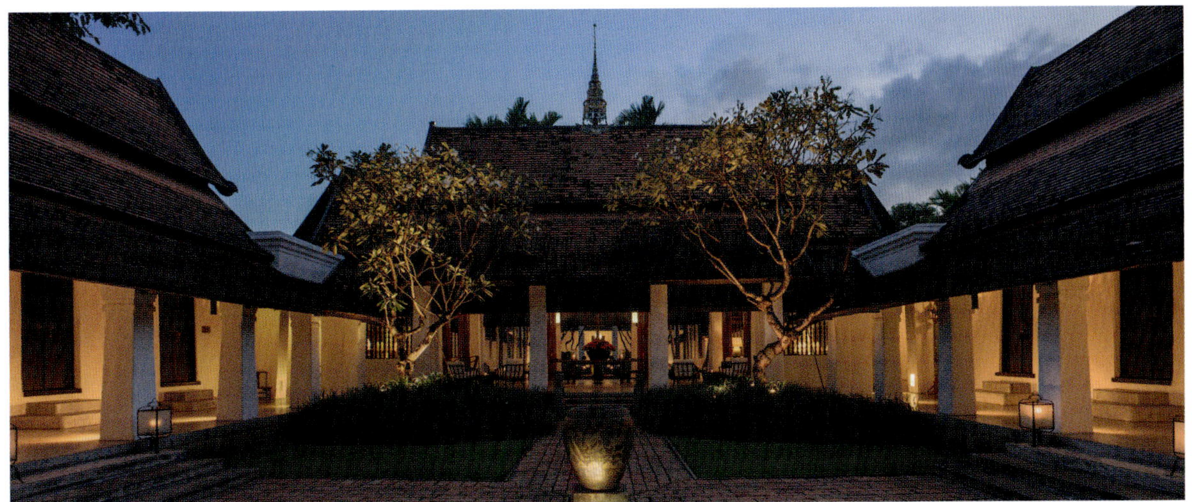

They are popular with designers working on graphic publications, including books, websites and magazines, for the simple reason that the neat verticals and horizontals take typography easily, and this qualifies them especially for cover shots. The picture of a miniature Tokyo house (below) illustrates this well – it was a natural choice for the cover of a book on small living spaces. In fact, neatness and the ability to fit seamlessly into page layouts explains much of their popularity. They are made, in other words, for flat usage, and the alignment of their lines with frame edges only strengthens this sensation.

Although precisely squared-up, this Thai building loses any sense of flatness because of the wide-angle lens used (18mm), which stretches the two wings on either side.

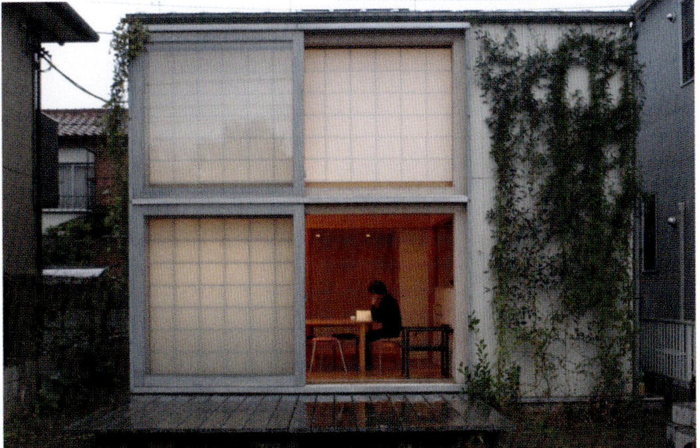

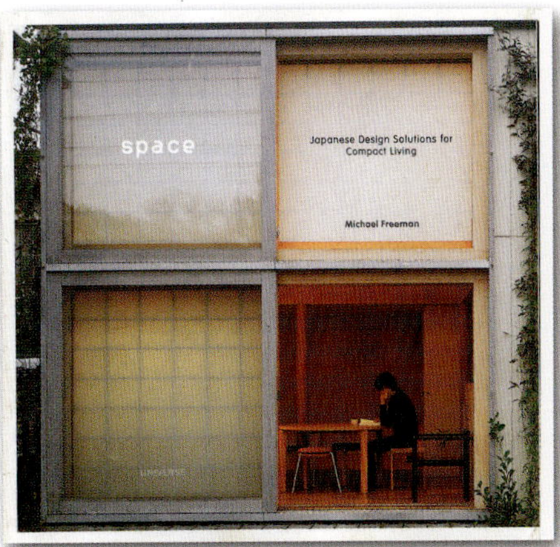

Squared-up images are, however, prone to repetitiveness, and are far from exciting. This inherent lack of drama and energy is what appeals to the kind of documentary photographer who is concerned mainly with objective recording, and you'll see them used plentifully in typologies – the kind of series of pictures, usually architectural, made popular by the photography couple Bernd and Hilla Becher and the so-called Düsseldorf School that they inspired.

Shooting this extremely small contemporary Japanese dwelling (called the 9-tsubo House) squared-up echoed the square-divided design theme of the architecture, and was appropriate for the cover of the square book.

FLAT LIGHTING

Finally, lighting can play a major part in flattening or deepening a scene. This is a huge topic in its own right, one that I'll be dealing with in the next book in this series, *On Light and Shadow*. Here, I'll concentrate on using light to reduce the sensation of depth, contrary to its normal job of contributing to the three-dimensionality of a scene in most shooting situations.

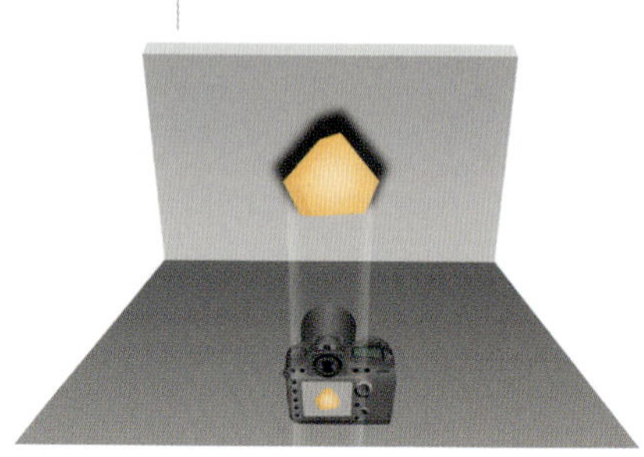

Both sidelighting and backlighting – and all the intermediate directions – create an interplay of light and shade that give us clues about volume and depth. Sidelighting of any kind helps to reveal and accentuate the volume of an object by contrasting the lit side with the shadowed side, while backlighting typically stresses aerial perspective (see page 34) by heightening atmosphere.

The morning sun low and behind the camera casts only thin shadows on a gilded Thai temple, creating a flattening effect on its tiered roofs, enhanced by a medium telephoto lens.

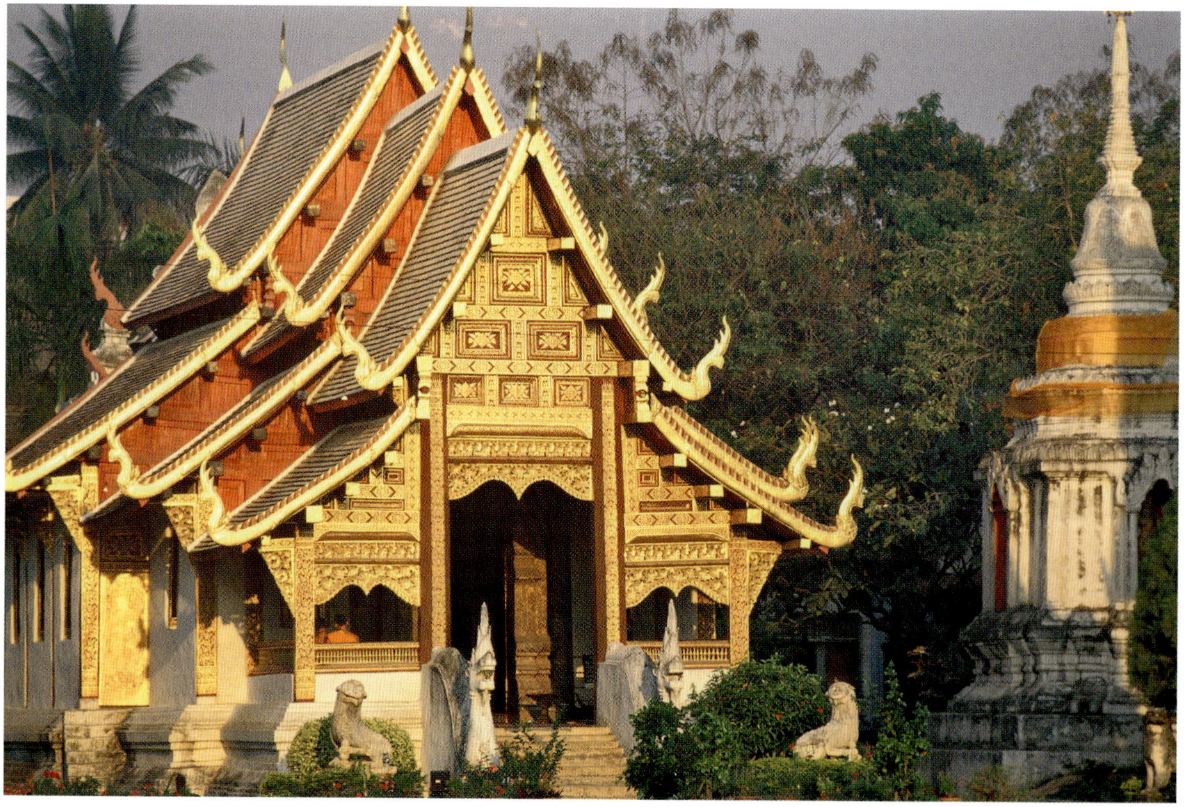

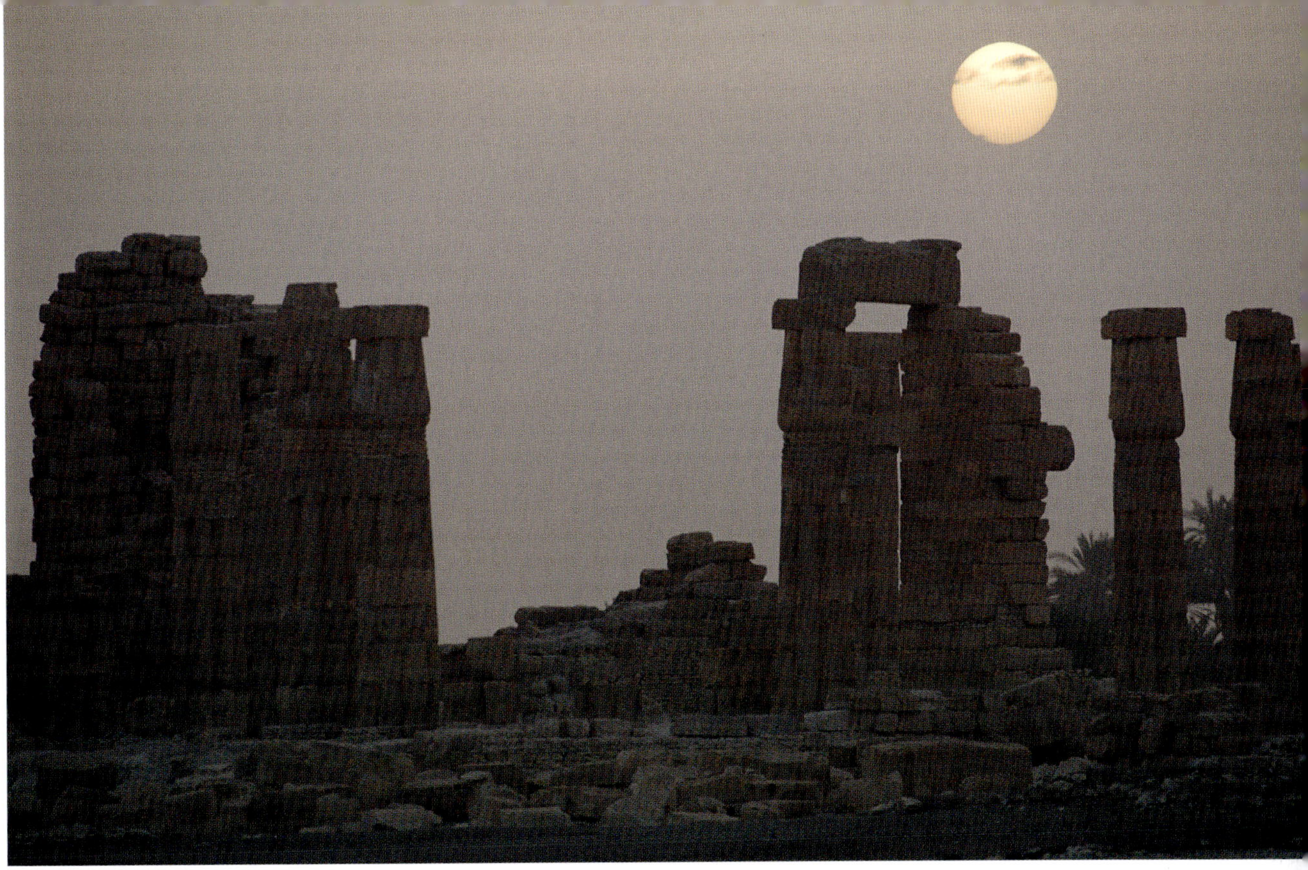

However, two other kinds of lighting work against the sense of depth. The first is axial lighting, so-called because the light source is on the same axis as the camera view, which is flattening because the shadows it casts are invisible from the camera. At most, there's a thin dark edge. This is the same when the sun is behind the camera as it is with an on-camera flash, or even more so with the more specialized ringflash that surrounds the front of the lens. The sunlight conditions are actually quite limited, because if you're shooting level, the sun has to be very low, as in the example here of the gilded Thai temple.

A second flat-light condition is when the lighting is so diffuse that there are no shadows anywhere. This happens with overcast skies (see the stone barns set in fields), haze (as in the picture of an ancient Nile temple here) and twilight. Haze, however, also brings with it atmospheric perspective, which restores a sense of depth, unless the viewpoint and a long lens keep attention fixed on a middle-distance section, as in the example above.

↑ Finely suspended dust particles after a sandstorm in northern Sudan flatten the light and also reduce depth information.

↘ Dull, even daylight is consistent across this detail of a Yorkshire landscape, suppressing the sense of depth.

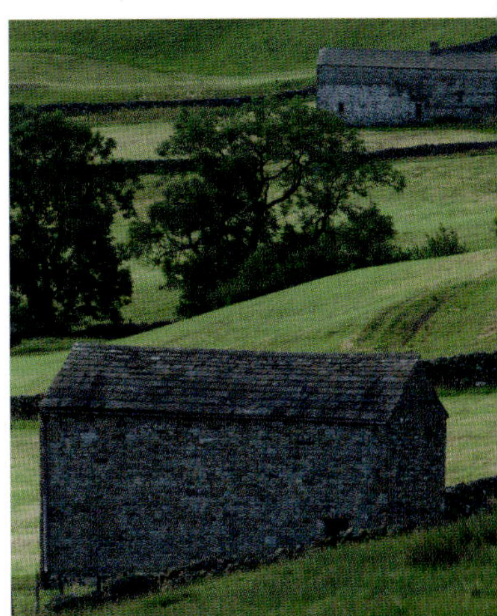

CHAPTER

3

FRAMED

Most conversations about composition are about what goes on inside the frame – how to fit things, line things up, connect or disconnect and so on – but for that to happen you first have to choose the limits of your view. The one unavoidable feature of every photograph, or any picture for that matter, is that it has a frame. You could fool around with its shape, and we'll see more of that soon, but it still has edges. Shooting first involves choosing how much of the scene in front of the camera gets to be inside the frame – and why. What stays inside has its counterpart in what you choose to leave out, and there are always reasons why each of us make these decisions, even if we do it intuitively.

While framing may be the first and most fundamental decision in making a photograph, it is not and cannot be a separate operation from the rest of composition. If you start with a clear idea of a subject, you'd typically look for a way to frame it, and then maybe adjust the position, which might then suggest a slightly different framing, and so on, in a rapid series of tweaking. Nevertheless, what I want to do in this chapter is to disentangle it a little, and look at different types of framing and the reasons for choosing them. We start with making clear what exactly the subject is and how it can fit in the frame, then move on to different frame shapes (known as aspect ratios) and conclude with how, and when, the frame can be divided into segments – a foretaste of the geometry of images that the following chapter covers.

One thing about framing that has always intrigued me is the idea of matching the frame to the subject. This seems a natural thing to do when you have the time, and it is made all the more possible not only by large zoom ranges, but by pan-and-stitch allowing us to extend the frame in any direction and choose the frame without losing image size by just cropping. The choice is huge, but I wonder if this is a totally good thing. Sometimes, there may just be too much choice. Interestingly, you can approach the whole framing operation from the other direction, finding ways to fit a scene or subject into a fixed frame. That's what happens when you use a single prime lens and stick to the frame the camera gives you. It turns out that you can always make it work to a degree and, much of the time without regrets for the restriction of choice.

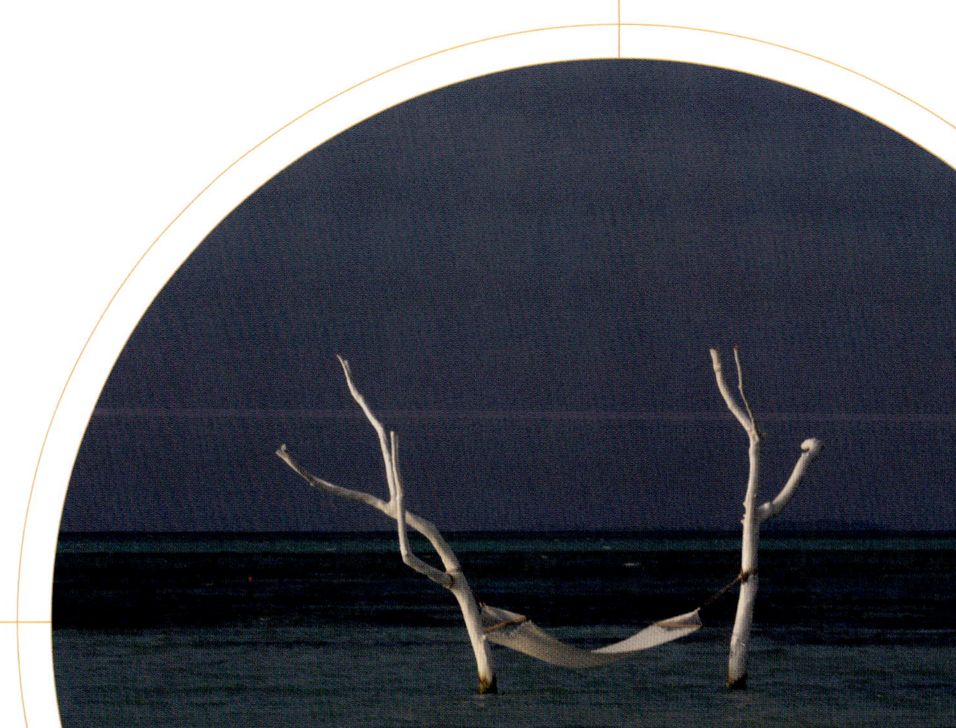

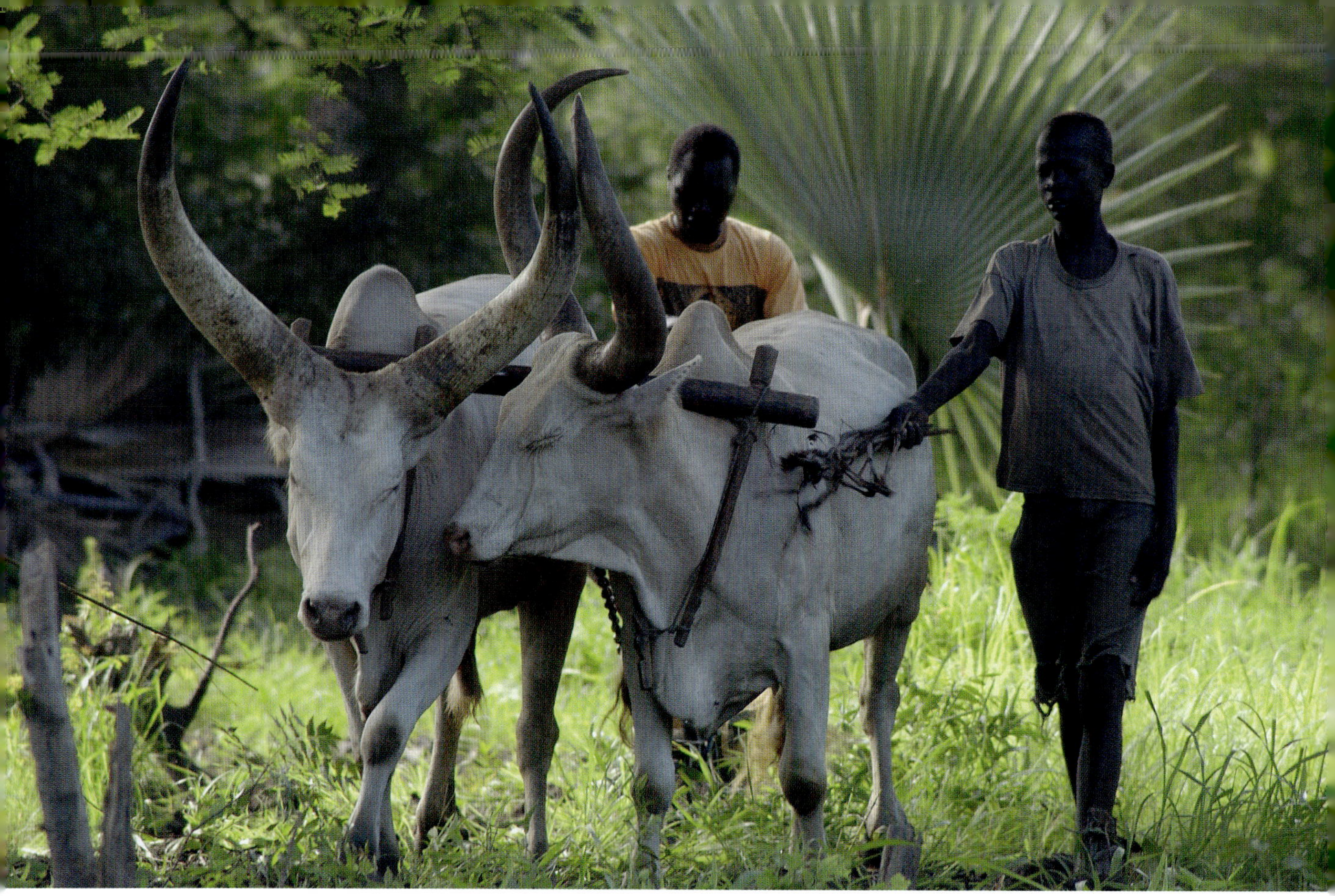

SUBJECT & FRAME

In a sense, composition begins with the idea of the subject and how to fit the frame around it, and if it's small, where to place it in the frame. That all sounds reasonable but it assumes a very particular kind of photograph – one that may not be as common as many would think.

Certainly, if you're setting out to make a portrait, or shoot a house, or a flower, or a bird, then you have a clear target. But many situations offer more complex subjects, or subjects that exist in a different way, or even no obvious subject at all. What's in question is the meaning of 'subject', and it's fundamental.

For image-making of any kind, there are three kinds of subject. First, there are concrete subjects; the tangible, discrete kind, like those just mentioned. The two long-horned cattle with their owners are a concrete subject. Though there are two animals and two men, they form an obvious unit that anyone would see as a small group. Then there are visual subjects, which may or may not coincide with the first kind.

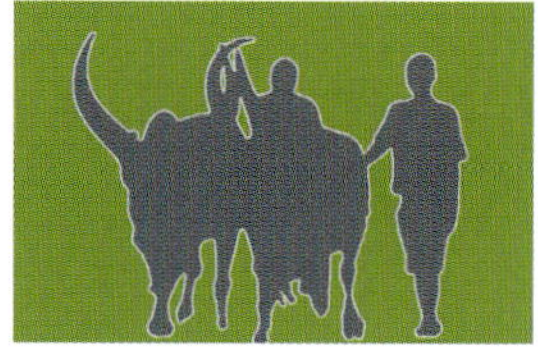

↑ Even though some tones on the left are similar to the background, the two cattle and two men are easily recognized semantically as a unit and as the subject.

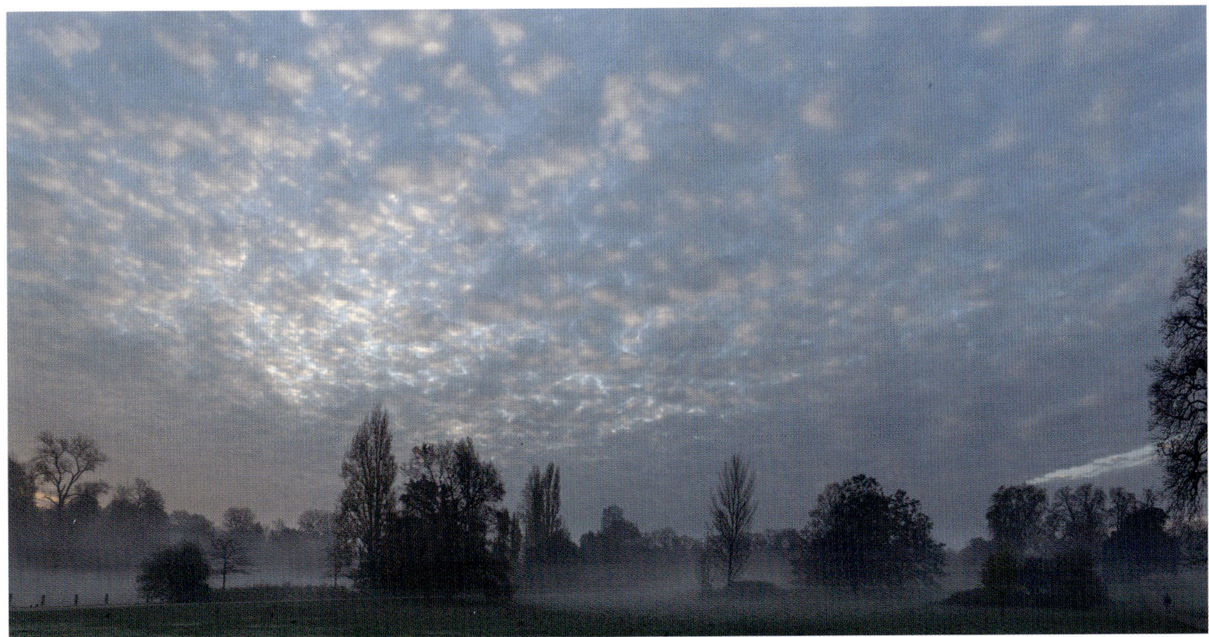

In composition, what often matters more is a unit, a shape that stands out from a background because it contrasts with the scene, which might be because of light and shade, or contrasting colour. A visual subject doesn't call for any recognition; it just needs to be distinctly different from the rest of the picture. The cattle and men qualify, just, because the setting is greenery, although there might be a little doubt about the upper left corner, and it's a little out of focus. But in the picture of the Indian man applying religious markings to his face, the subject that matters for composition is the band of light. This is the visual subject here, rather than the entire figure of the man, which is unclear around the edges.

Third, there are conceptual subjects, and those depend entirely on the photographer. Again, as with visual subjects, it can coincide with the concrete subject. If you say that a head-and-shoulders shot is a portrait, then it is. But if you shoot a landscape that has no single, clear, stand-out feature, then what? As in the dawn view here, the subject is the entire landscape that fills the frame and goes beyond. Compositionally, there's no subject to place. And what about a picture halfway between portrait and landscape, where you have a small figure in a setting? The figure could be the subject, but only if you decide so. Is the really tiny figure in the lower-right corner of the view here a potential subject? Probably not. But you see the uncertainty that's possible.

↑ Many landscapes are themselves the entire subject of a photograph, with the individual elements like trees simply contributing rather than standing apart.

↘ Although in a semantic sense the subject is a man, visually the subject is the central bright bar of light.

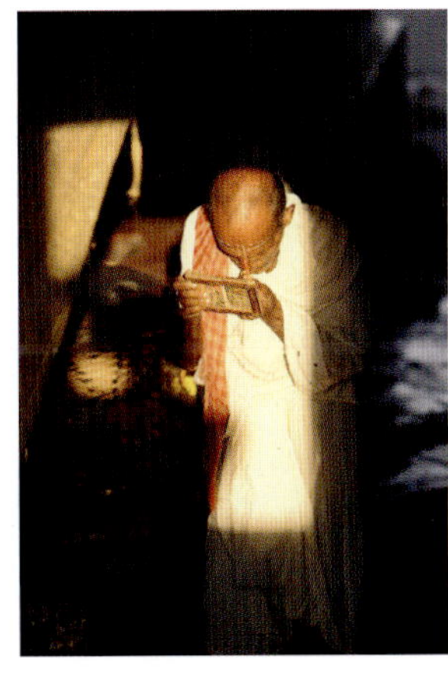

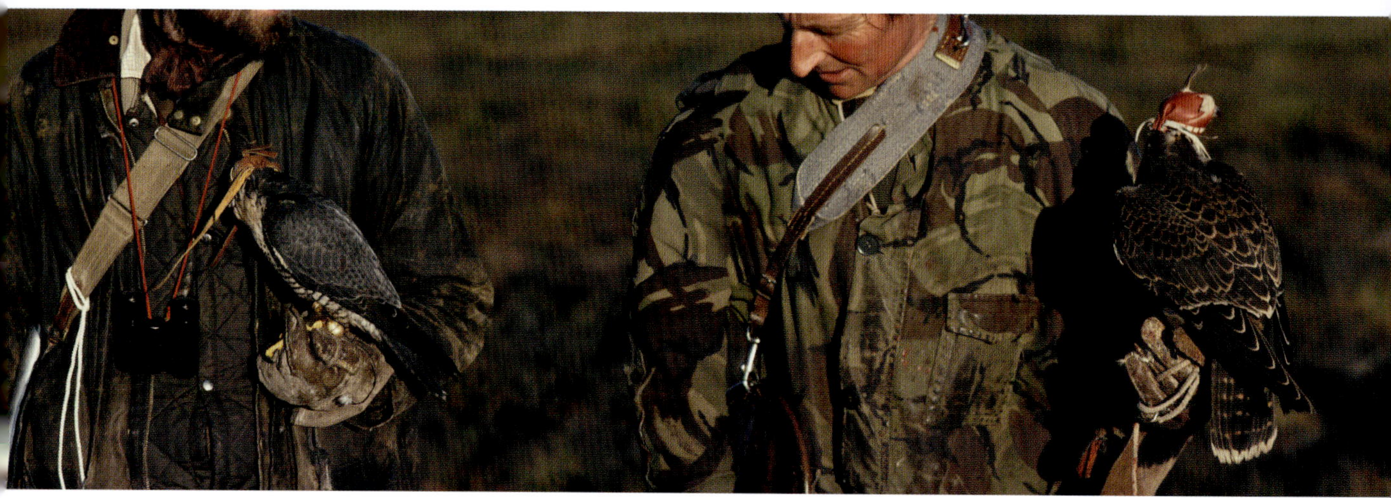

TIGHT

There's a difference of opinion among photographers around how tightly or loosely to frame a subject.

↑ An unusually tight crop with a purpose, of two falconers out hunting with their birds. This was part of a story, and it accompanied several other pictures that showed faces. The reason for cropping out the faces here was to keep attention firmly on the birds in the gloved hands.

The argument for closing in, either by moving forward or zooming, is that it concentrates attention and improves the 'fit' of the subject. The counter-argument for opening up or stepping back is that you give the subject room to breathe and allow the viewer's eye more choice in looking at and around the picture. The actual type of subject has a strong influence, inevitably, and the more concrete and compact it is, the more obvious the sense of tightness or looseness. Going back for a moment to the previous pages, the landscape shot is so amorphous and wide-ranging that it hardly lends itself to tightening the framing.

Here, I'm arguing the case for tightening the framing, at least identifying the kind of shooting situation where it can help to strengthen the picture. Whenever you do it, you're exercising more control over the composition than usual, so it's definitely more forceful and generally wouldn't suit photographers who prefer to let viewers

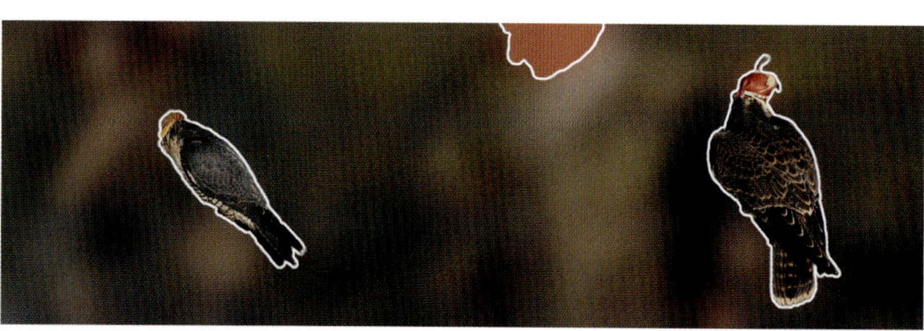

find their own way around a picture. Both the examples here very much dictate what the audience should look at. While they both appear to be frontally shot portraits, they are in fact quite different. In one, the focus is single-mindedly on the eyes of the subject and the direct, almost confrontational relationship with the camera and viewer, while the other tries to take attention away from the men and shift it to the two falcons.

The portrait of a South Sudanese man has to balance two photographic qualities. One is the expression – part of the moment, if you like – and the other is the compelling colour combination of very dark skin and yellow. There were two ways to go. One was to follow the lines of the man's arm, elbow and hand, which could have a graphic relationship with the frame, and which helped to enclose his face and torso. The only problem with that was the distracting scene behind him, including patches of red and blue. Shooting for black and white would have lost those, but, given the power of the yellow, this was not an option. The more radical choice was to step forward slightly and lower the framing to cut into his forehead. This simplifies the elements, while the eyes with their direct gaze are powerful enough as an attractant to still hold the attention.

Both shots have their strengths. The slightly looser one below has a good angular structure from the arm, elbow and hand, while the tight version on the left has simplicity and a more extreme arrangement of face and hand top and bottom, similar to the 'end-to-end' style on page 150.

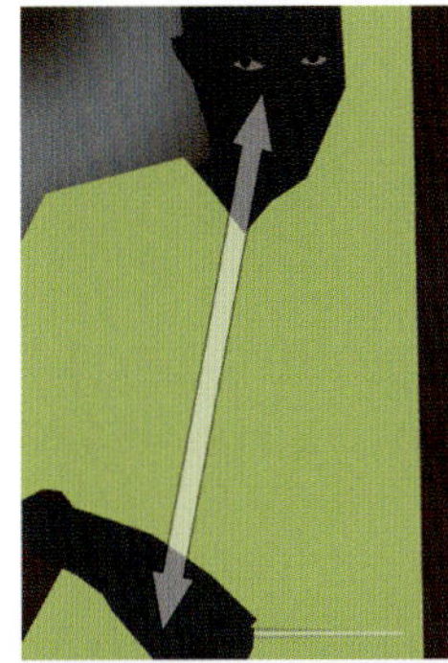

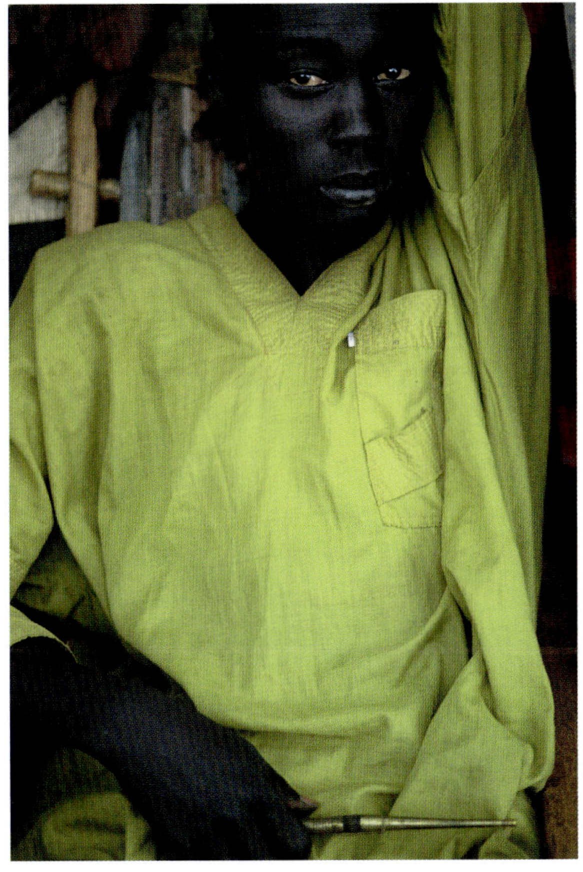

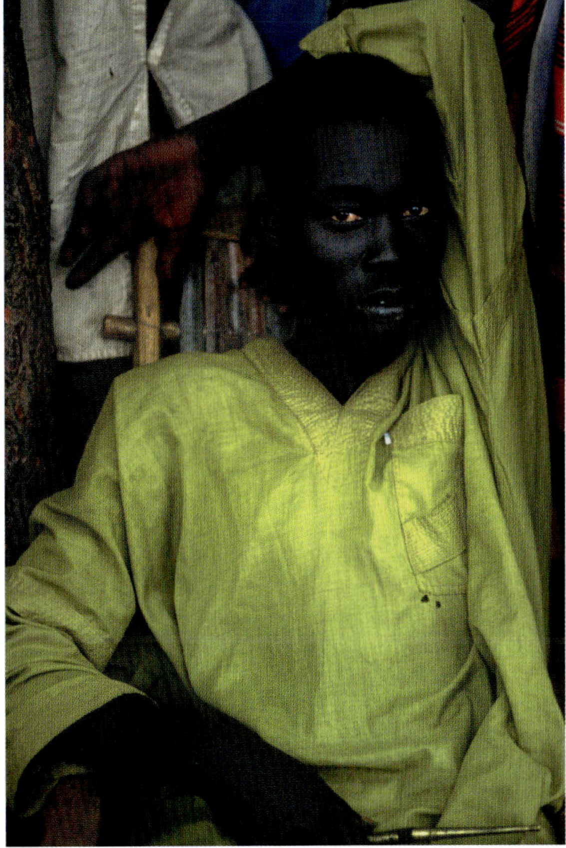

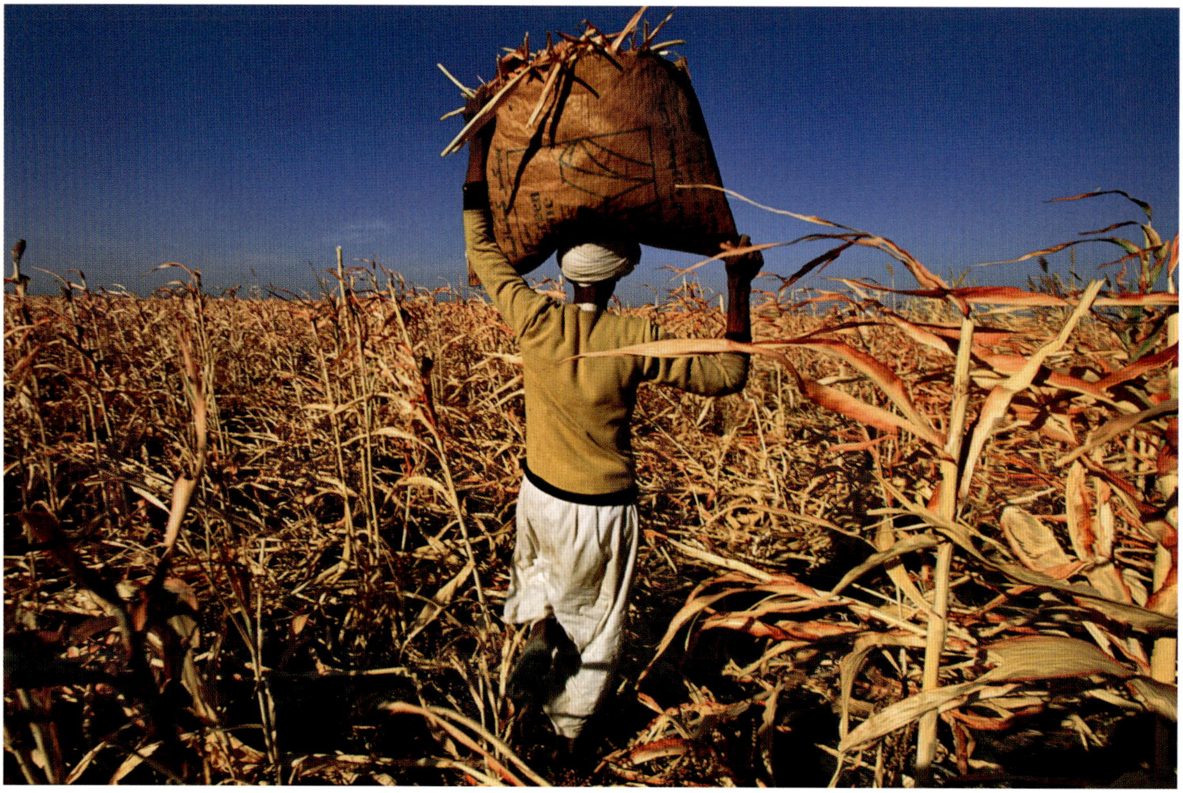

PLACEMENT ZONES

Only when a clear subject is small enough to move around in the frame does the question of where exactly to put it arise. That size may be your choice if you have time and some control, or it may be outside your control and something you have to react to and do your best with, as happens in street photography, for example. In either case, it needs to be thought about, even if you have only a tiny fraction of a second. The subject needs a reason to be where it's placed. Is it to feel comfortable, or unexpected, or to relate in some way to the rest of the picture?

↑ For a full-height vertical subject in a horizontal frame, there are basically five choices and three types of position. The inherent symmetry of this figure, and that he is moving directly away, made the centre of the frame a reasonable choice.

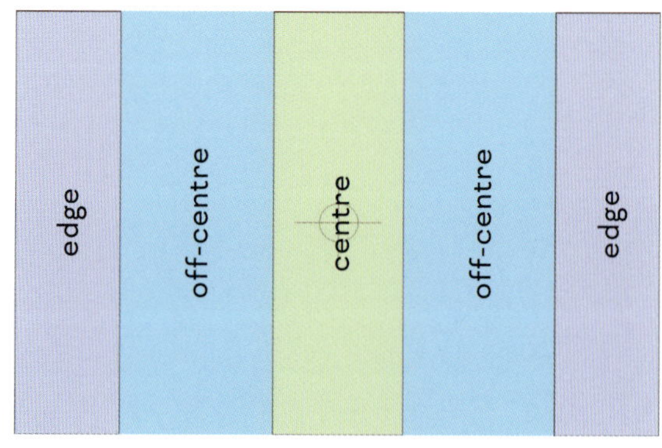

To simplify things, there are three basic zones: in the middle, off-centre and way off-centre, and there's often no reason to be any more precise than that. The zones drawn in the illustrations are not intended to be exact by any means. The size and shape of the subject influence the choice. In the picture of the farmer carrying a sack of millet, he fills the frame top to bottom, so can slide only left or right – centre, off-centre or edge. With a much smaller subject the choice is much greater, and it makes sense to subdivide the extreme zone into edges and corners. The corners of the picture frame are graphically strong, which makes them important to take care of in general, and can sometimes suggest an interesting framing strategy, as below. We'll see more of this on pages 104 and 148. The arguments for placing subjects off-centre are to create an interesting asymmetry, and to set up a visual relationship with the setting, one balancing the other.

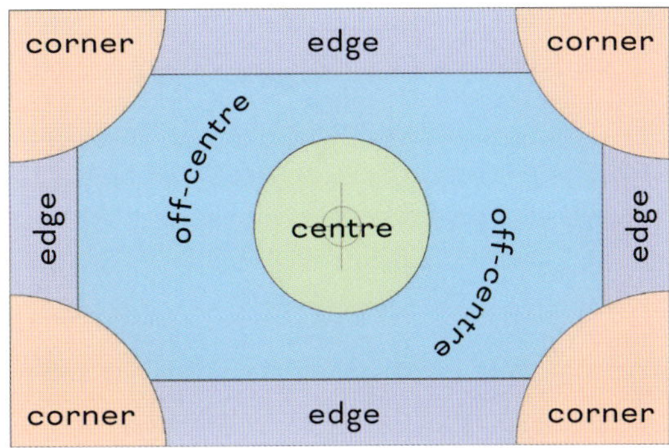

As we'll see over the following pages, there are endless relationships and dynamics possible between different elements in the frame, and very few pictures are a simple matter of one subject on an even background. All of these influence what goes where. What you see here is just the framework, and these two pictures are deliberately chosen for their simplicity.

An extreme corner placement of the man in a Nuba village, Sudan, helped to emphasize the context of the distinctive thatched houses as he faces in towards the pattern of triangles.

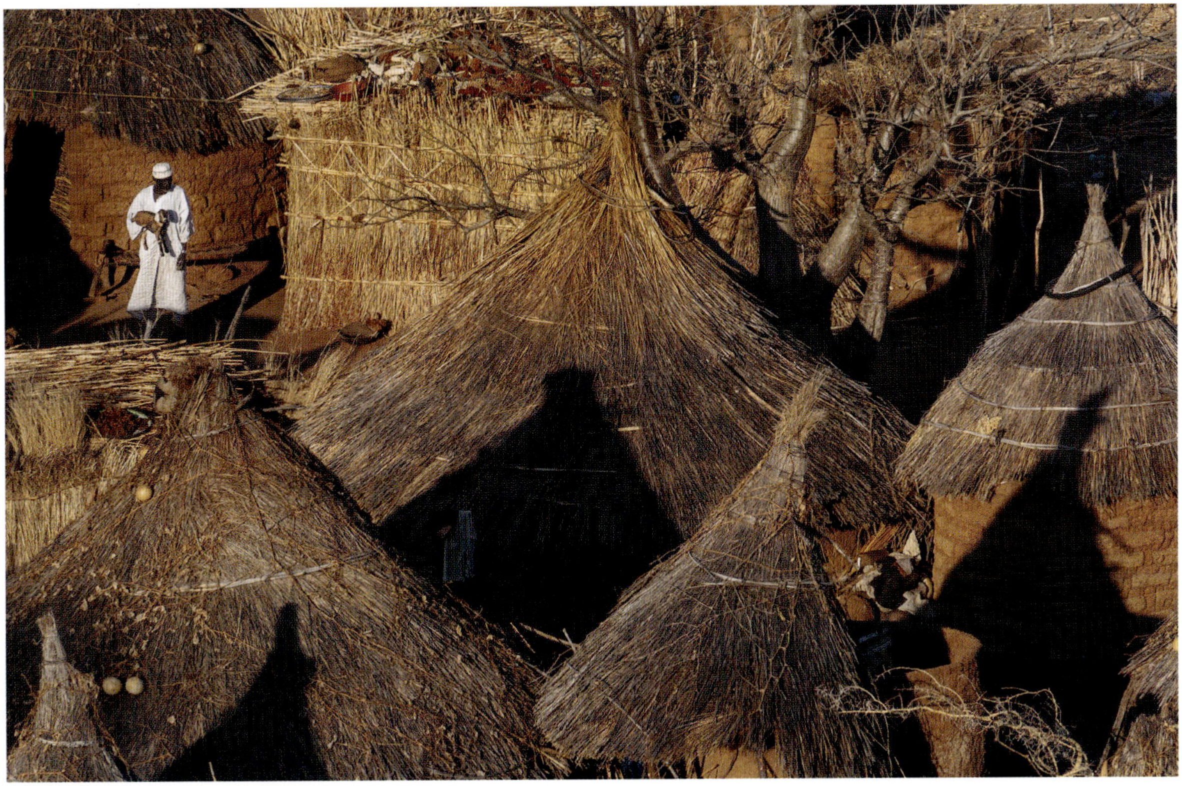

SLIMMER, FATTER

We typically take for granted the frame that the camera gives us. It's normal to just get on with it and make the composition work within that shape. But there are things to be learned by being sensitive to the proportions of length to breadth. Digital has freed up many earlier constraints in photography, and one of them is the shape of the frame.

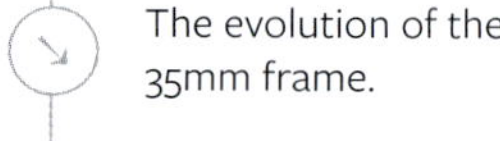

The evolution of the 35mm frame.

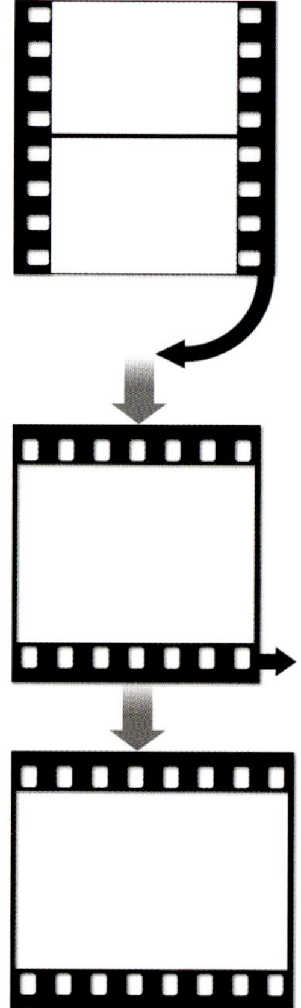

For the most part, however, we're accustomed to working within whatever constraints we're given. As of now, the two main frame shapes, or aspect ratios, are 3:2 and 4:3. Both are what people like to call legacy formats, meaning that they were invented in different eras for reasons that wouldn't apply now, but we still use them. Both, in fact, have their origins in the invention of film for cinematography. The key was to have sprocket holes on the edges of the long rolls of the film, which allowed it to travel vertically through the movie camera gate. This meant that the height of the image frame was dictated by the number of sprocket holes or film perforations. The early silent films used a four-perf pulldown, which gave a 4:3 ratio. Even though a strip at the side was lost for the soundtrack in the late 1920s, the movie industry kept more or less the same shape for the final married print, and it was called the Academy ratio.

This ruled for three decades, and audiences became familiar with it, especially through early television and then computer screens. It was reinforced in 1999 with the digital standard of Four Thirds. Conveniently, 4:3 is close enough to standard photographic prints at 10:8, and significantly, smartphone cameras use 4:3 sensors.

In the case of 3:2, associated more these days with higher-end cameras like DSLRs and mirrorless, and often called full-frame, it was an engineer and keen photographer, Oskar Barnack, working at Leitz in Germany, who saw the possibility of movie film for a light, handheld still camera by running the film sideways. The small area of film was still seen as a problem, so Barnack maximized it by extending the perforations from seven, which would give a familiar 4:3 ratio, to eight, which gave 3:2, but importantly 14 percent more picture area.

These two pictures, both face-on to buildings, show something of the difference in the two aspect ratios. While 3:2 has a sense of going a little wide, 4:3 is more compact and gives a sense of top-to-bottom depth. The differences are subtle, but when you use just one of them regularly, day after day, as most photographers do, you become sensitive to the exact proportions, and changing from one to the other may take time to readjust.

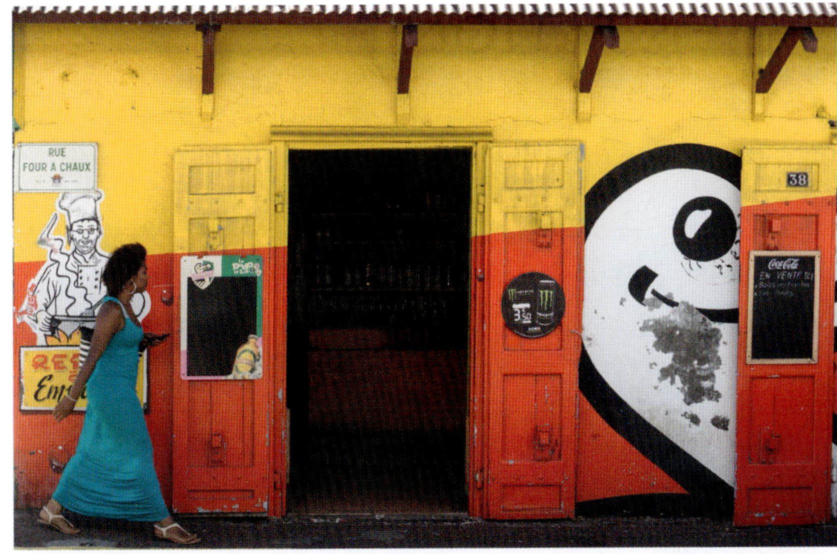

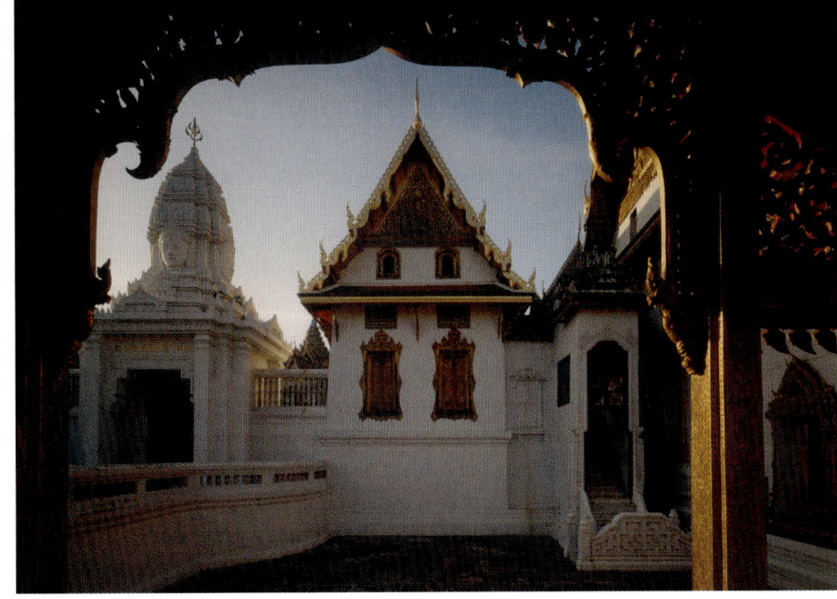

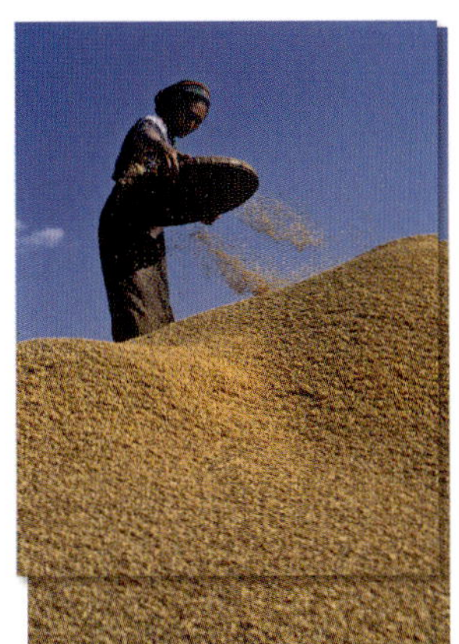

Perceptually, the differences between the two formats seem exaggerated when used vertically. As in this example, the 2:3 frame can feel unusually elongated and call for a different framing style, while 3:4 feels more conventional.

Launched in 1924, the Leica became such a success that it guaranteed the lasting acceptance of the 3:2 format, as digital SLRs inherited it. Interestingly, until digital television adopted 16:9 widescreen as a viewing format, 3:2 was for many decades an important odd-one-out in photography – distinctly wider when used horizontally, and almost uncomfortably taller when used vertically.

ORIENTATION

With both of the two main camera formats, there is always the basic choice of shooting either horizontally or vertically, but habit keeps most photographers most of the time to whatever is the default holding position.

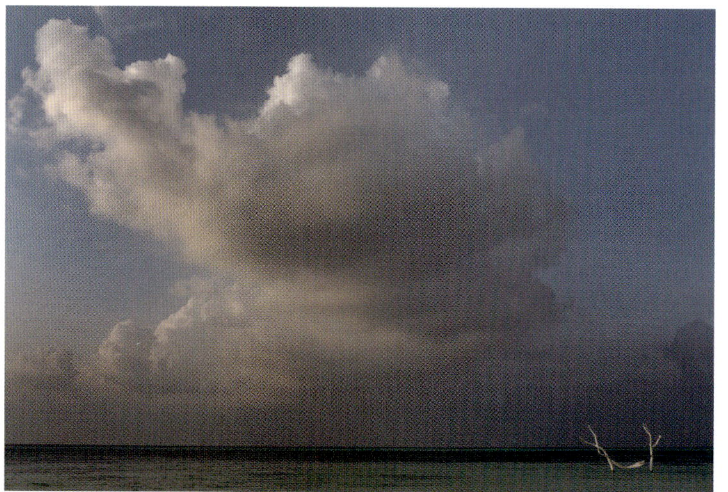

A regular camera is made to be held more easily for a horizontal shot (what's sometimes called 'landscape' in photography), while smartphone cameras are generally easier to hold vertically (also called 'portrait'). In either case, it's good practice always to consider whether the shot would be more effective if you turn the camera 90°. One reason is that the subject or scene may have verticality itself, as in the Burmese temple scene. Another is experiment, just to see what you can do with different framing dynamics. A third is how the picture will be used: is it going to be viewed on a printed page, which is almost always vertical, on a phone (also vertical), or on a laptop screen (horizontal)?

As we've just been looking at horizontal as default, here I want to show vertical examples, and the dynamics are quite different. They are more noticeable with 2:3 than with the fatter 3:4. In many situations, even most, the vertical 2:3 seems a bit too tall for comfort, and this in turn encourages placing main subjects lower in the frame – no doubt something to do with a sense of gravity at work. The series of three seascapes was a live example of searching for both horizontal and vertical framings while a brief play of light on dead branches and a hammock in the sea contrasted with a building tropical storm behind. In each case there was a connection between the white branches and cloud formations, which were changing quite rapidly. All three

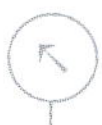

Shot within five minutes of each other, these three versions of a beach scene in the Maldives left to right accommodate to the changing cloudscape, but each attempting to relate the hammock strung between branches and the cloud formations.

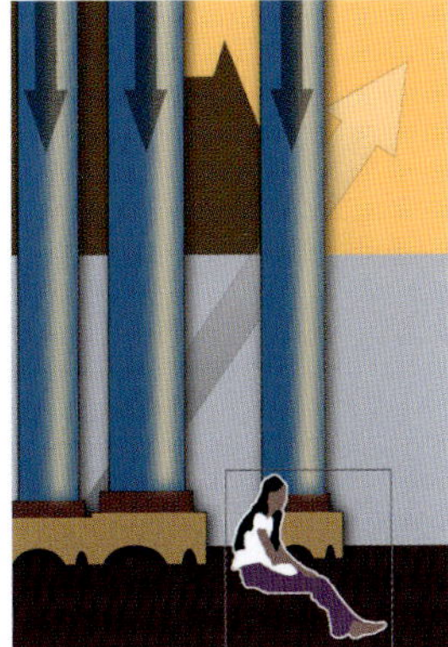

A classic vertical scene, shot in the Shwedagon Pagoda, Myanmar. Three components give it a distinct verticality: the strong pillars, the upward gradient toward the light, and the position of the girl at the foot of one pillar. More than this, the left-to-right arrangement in this framing is neat. The slimmer 3:2 format is definitely showing its height, and the result is strikingly 'tall'.

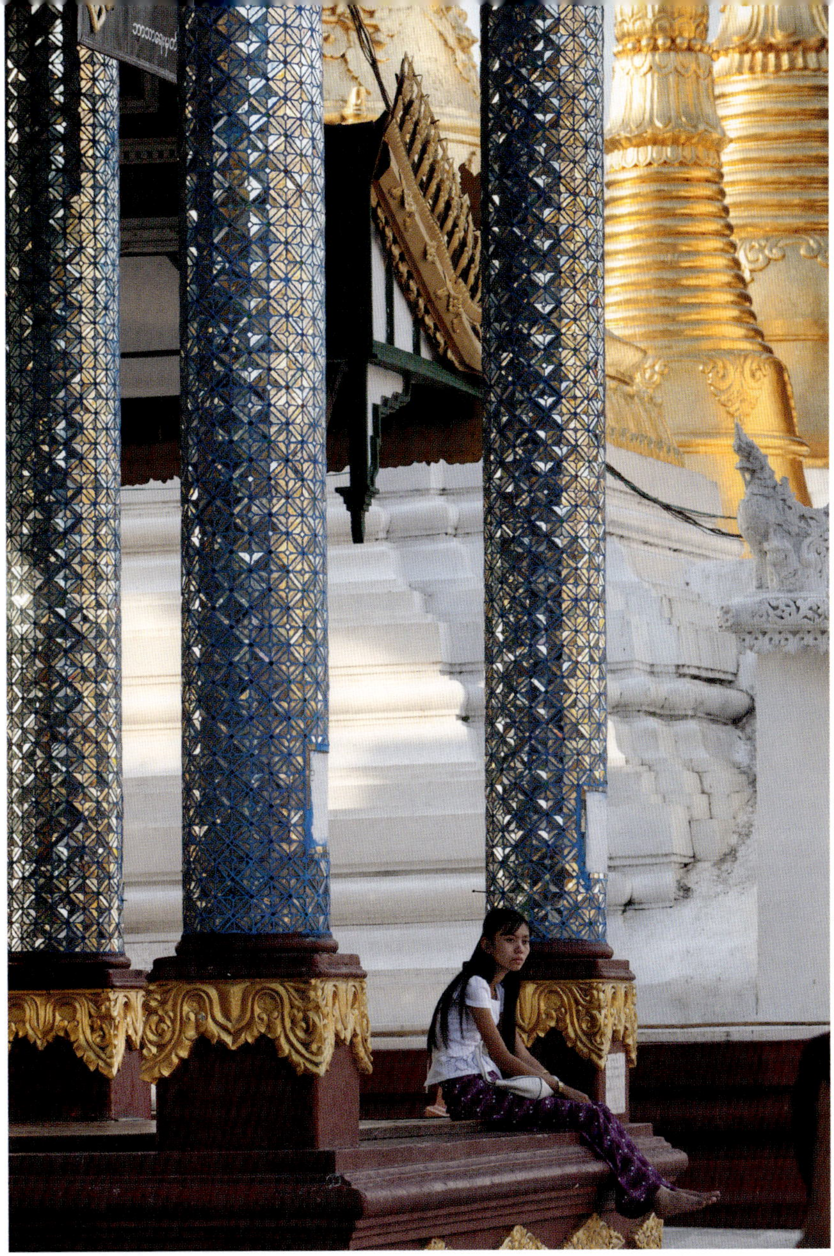

work perfectly well simply by adjusting the zoom so that the two elements fit. The right-most image makes the connection the most strongly, partly because the shape of the cloud mimics that of the branches and hammock, and partly because the precise framing forces the eye to consider the coincidence.

SQUARE

The square as a frame has never been a popular choice in any kind of image-making, yet it keeps reoccurring. Why is it unpopular? Probably by default, because slightly longer or slightly taller frames have generally been seen as 'natural' and comfortable, as we just saw.

There's no bias or direction to a square frame, and so when composing within it there's a risk of being at the same time directionless and rigid. It was hardly ever used in classical painting, to the point that when J.M.W. Turner made a series of square paintings towards the end of his life, they were famously controversial. Post-classical painters who made use of the square include Piet Mondrian, Mark Rothko and Josef Albers, all of whom were dealing in geometry anyway.

Photography, however, has had bouts of square framing, and the reasons have been technological. In other words, decided by how cameras and screen displays work rather than by what might work best for a photograph. The first was medium-format film, which for the first half of the 20th century was the most popular film size. At the time, the most reliable mechanical system for using it was twin-lens reflex, which featured a matched taking lens and viewing lens. The way to use these cameras was by holding at waist level viewing downward, and the most practical format was 6 × 6cm square, which the later Hasselblad SLR also used. For a horizontal or vertical frame, you simply cropped in the enlarger, and most of the time this was the way a square format was used. The second was the Polaroid SX-70 in its brief but influential life, and the third was Instagram, because square works best in a grid of images – and for thumbnails in general.

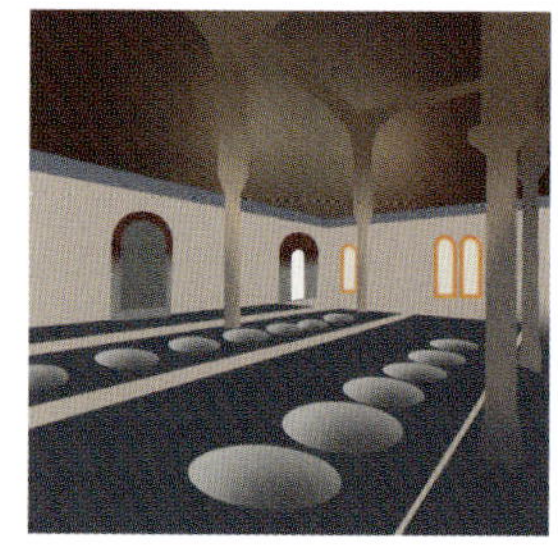

The formality of traditional architecture, here the old dairy at Frogmore, Windsor, often suits the strict regime of a square format. Note that using a wide-angle lens from a raised camera position allows a perfectly level view with no converging verticals.

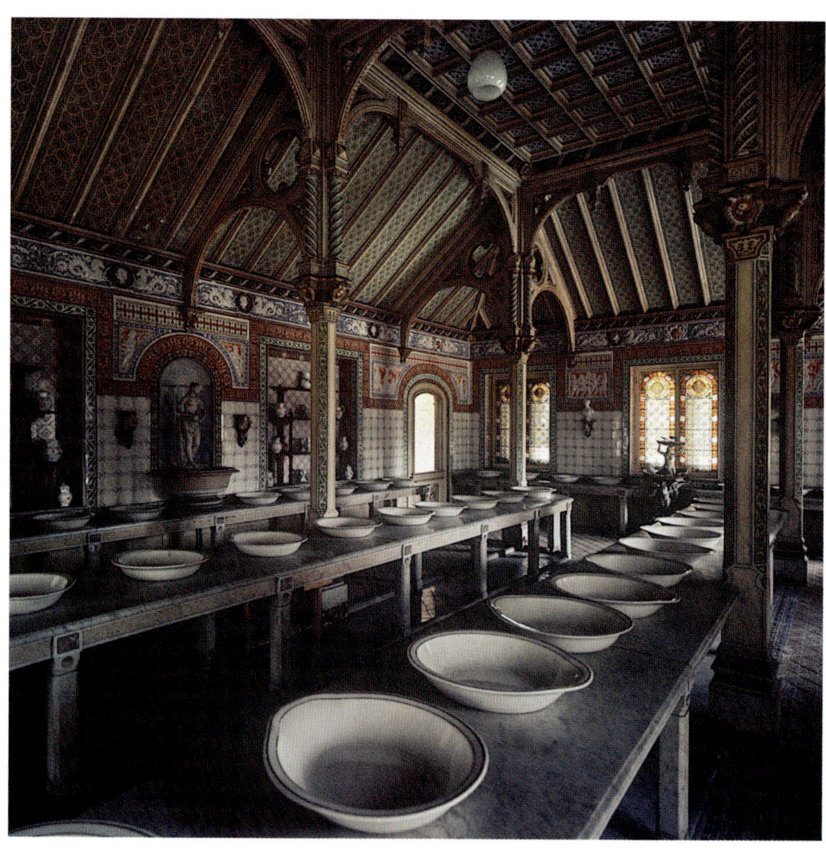

Square itself is not very sympathetic to most scenes, although very good for a limited set of compositions – subjects that fit, namely squarish or circular, symmetrical subjects, and patterns. But now comes the interesting part. There's a natural tendency to want to make a composition work in the frame that's been given to us, and it can be done surprisingly often. You can use compositional strategies to make things balance within almost any given frame. If this takes more effort and imagination, the result may be all the better for that. If nothing else, square frames prove the sheer usefulness of compositional skill.

An example of how we adapt to the frame shapes we're given, and even the distance. Square may not have a reputation for handling street scenes and the like, but by relying on an 'L' strategy shown by the arrows, this portrait of a passenger on an Amazon riverboat fits the frame comfortably, and the image has balance.

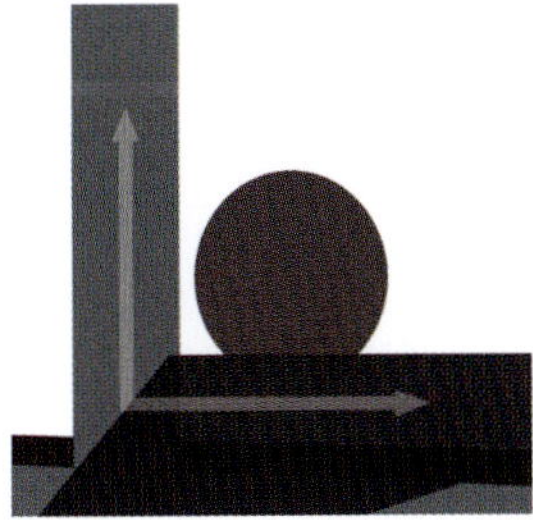

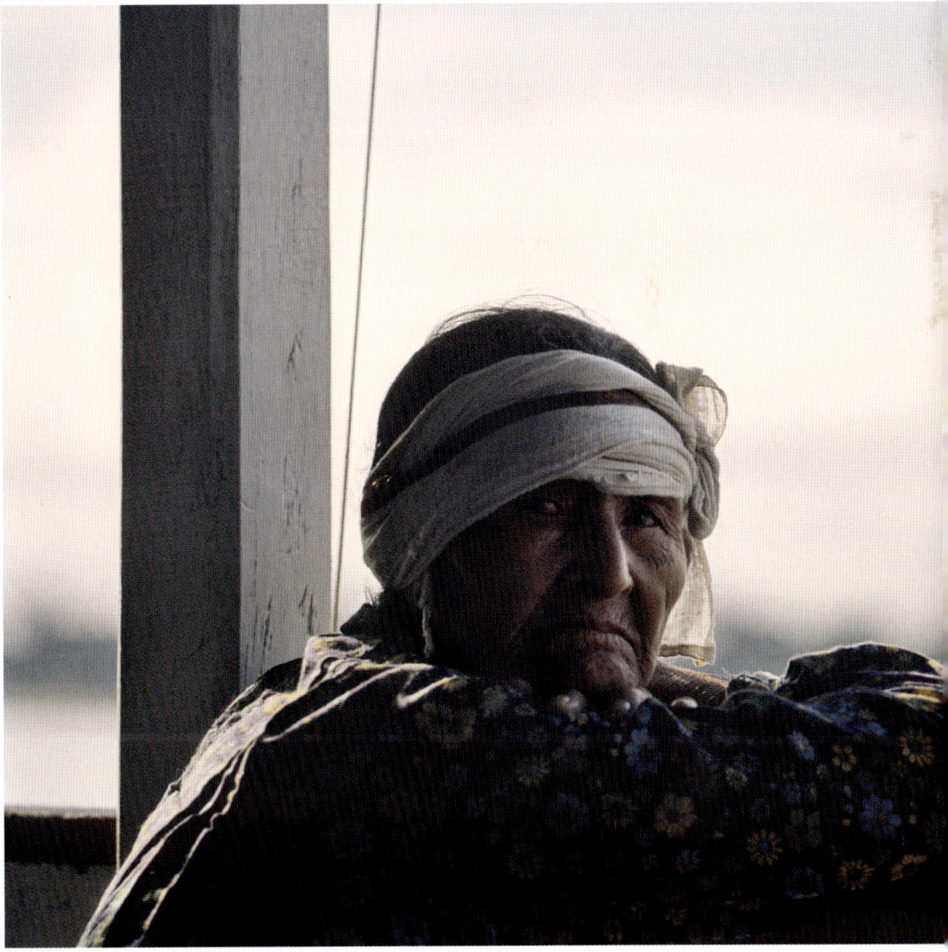

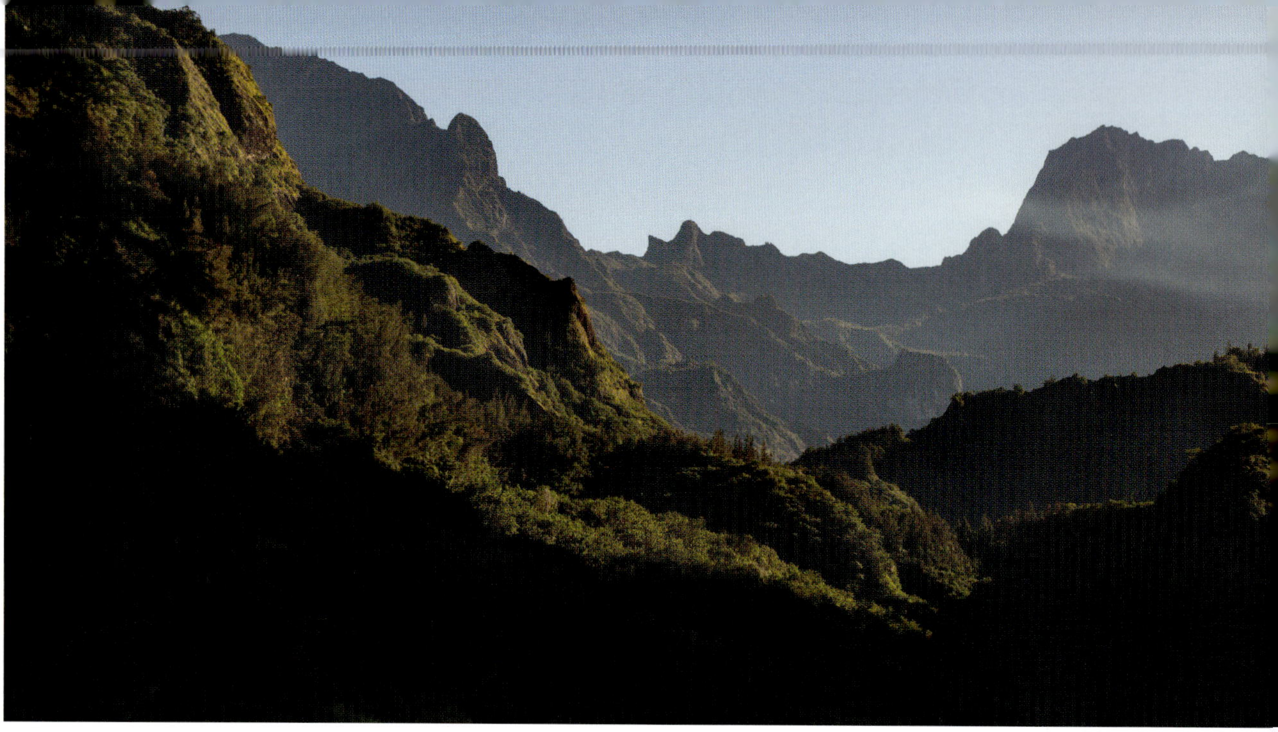

WIDESCREEN

Since 16:9 widescreen became the standard format for video, broadcast and television screens in the early years of the 21st century, it has become increasingly popular for still shooting as well, and it offers quite a different visual experience from the standard formats we've been looking at. Also, it is broadly seen as attractive by most people – a feature that merits further investigation.

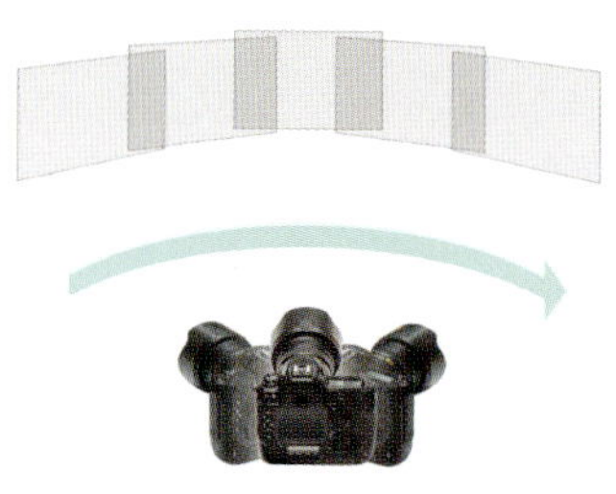

Pan-and-stitch shooting is the preferred technique, enabled by efficient software without the need for a tripod, and delivering a large image file.

Many cameras offer it as a cropping choice in-camera (camera sensors are not 16:9, so using this format always means cropping at some stage). More than that, now that pan-and-stitch is such an easy shooting option, extending the frame sideways digitally is an extra that costs no more than a few seconds in time. This is the recommended way of doing it, rather than cropping down, as it increases the file size and demands simply keeping the idea of the frame in your head as you extend it, which is a good visual exercise anyway. I'm using 'widescreen' in its cinematographic sense rather than just 16:9, which is to say anything wider than standard. Indeed, it is cinema that has the most to teach still photographers about using long horizontal formats. Since CinemaScope in the 1950s, directors and directors of photography have worked at using widescreen creatively. With a few exceptions (Fritz Lang said it was 'good for snakes and funerals, but nothing else'),[1]

1 Fritz Lang playing himself in *Le Mepris* (1963) by Jean-Luc Godard (director).

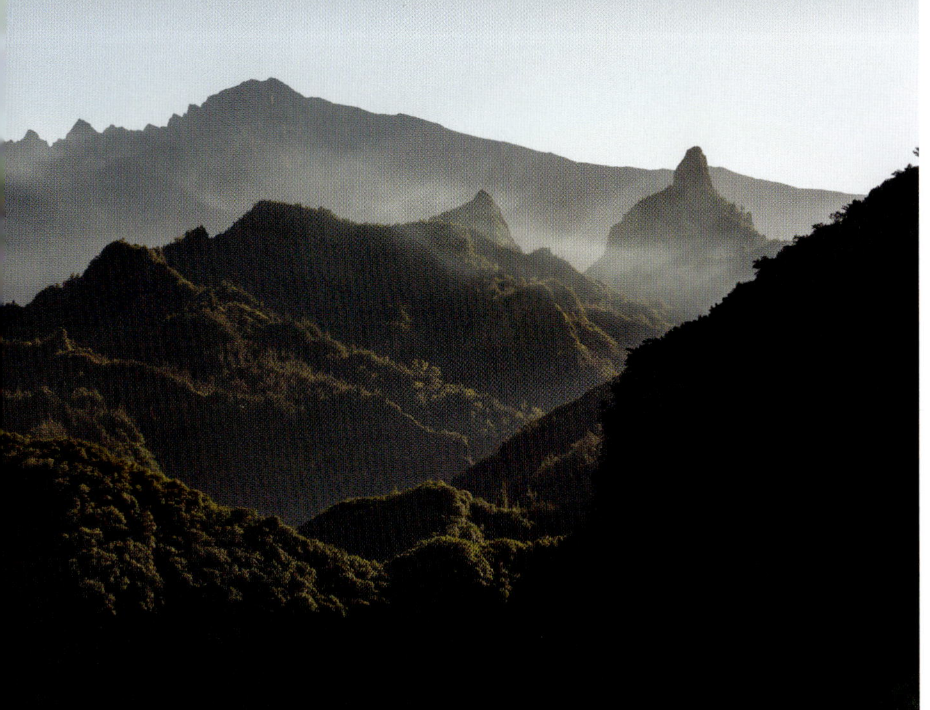

A craggy volcanic landscape on the island of La Réunion was best suited to a widescreen treatment. The undulating lines of receding outcrops were horizontally oriented, and the wider format allowed the dark foreground hills on either side to form a natural frame.

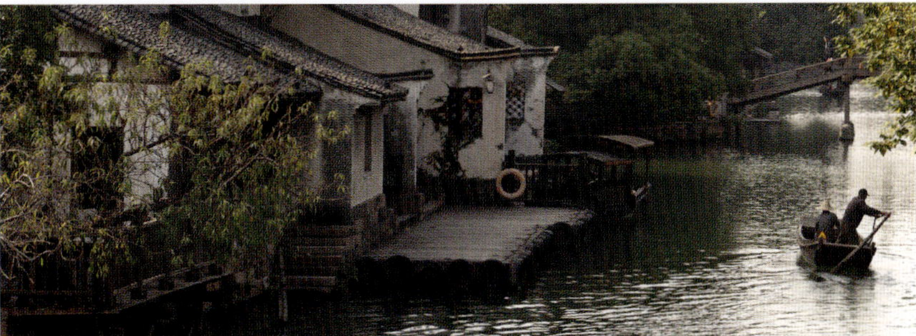

A canal in one of the old water towns of the Yangtze Delta, Wuzhen, prompted a wide framing in the style discussed in the text – action on one side of the frame balanced by architectural elements on the other side. This stretches the viewer's gaze across the frame.

most have been inspired by it, from James Cameron to Sergio Leone and John Boorman. Boorman made the point that because widescreen causes the eye to scan left and right rather than being able to take the entire picture in at one glance (when seen large), you can have different things going on, saying, 'you can direct the audience's attention to some part of the screen, and you can use other parts of the screen to suggest, almost subliminally, other things.'[2]

This prompts two different ways of using widescreen. In one, you allow the horizontal sweep to mimic the effect of standing in front of a vista, where the expanse itself is its own justification. This obviously works well with many landscapes. The other way is to occupy the frame with elements such as by filling it up with things side by side (see page 156), or setting up a counterbalance between subjects at either end (see page 150).

2 John Boorman in *CinemaScope: In Praise of Widescreen*, BBC, 1992, via YouTube, www.youtube.com/watch?v=QtLUy9l1a44.

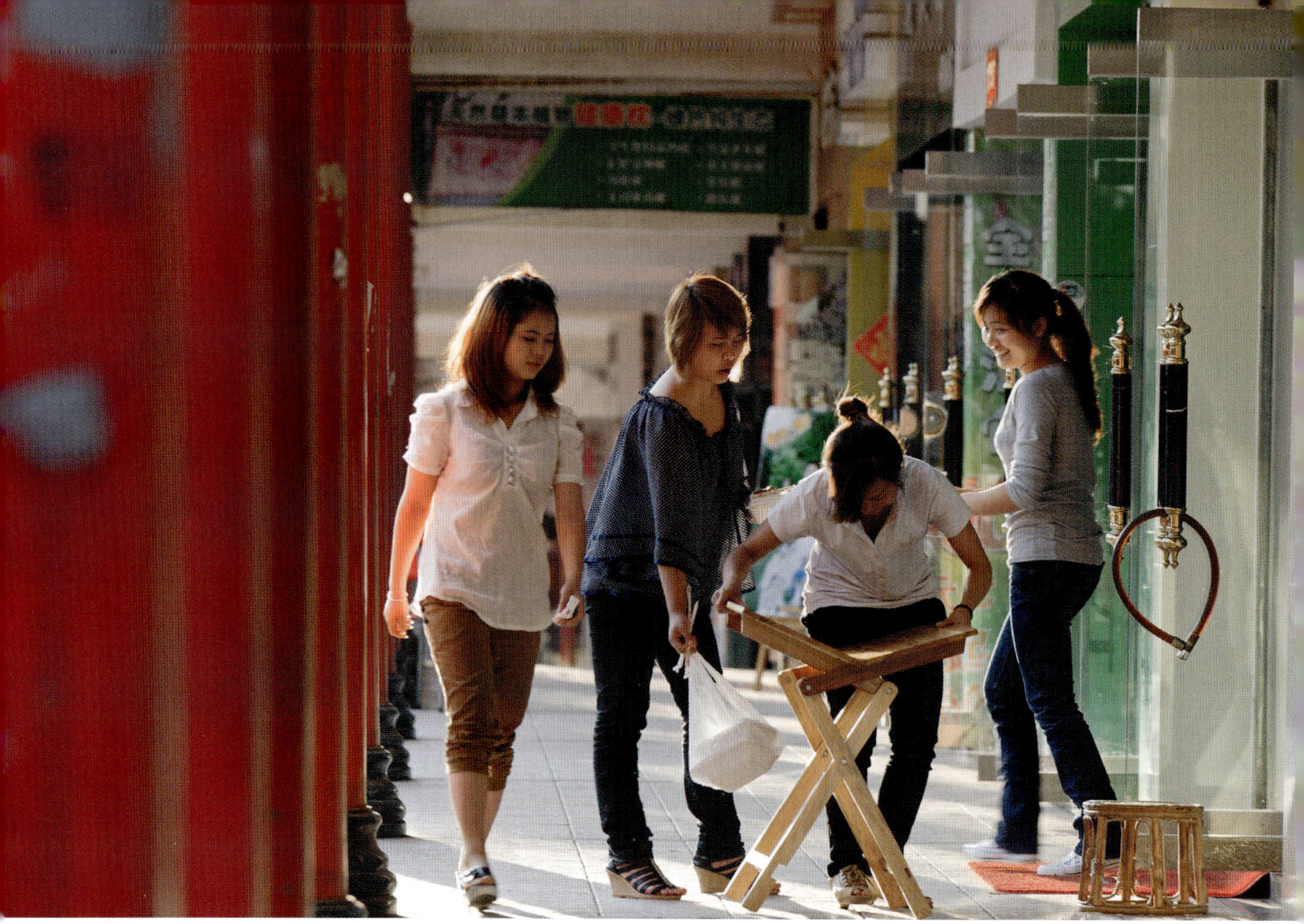

BASIC DIVISION

Not every picture needs division – one subject may fill the frame, or it may be a field of many objects (see page 156) – but when you have two neatly separated areas, such as land and sky, then you also need to decide where the dividing line should go.

Horizons are probably the most common frame dividers in photography, but there are others of all kinds. How important they are to an image typically depends on how contrasting the two areas are on either side, and that could be contrasts in brightness, colour or texture. It could also be a content-driven difference, which happens a lot in architecture, with walls, doorways and in the case of the picture here, pillars (but also a contrast of colour). As with placing subjects on pages 52 and 53, there are many possible influences on moving a dividing line up or down, or

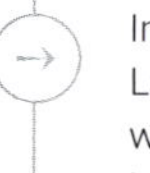

In this helicopter view over Lake Mead, Nevada, there was sufficient topographic interest to want to keep the horizon as high as possible.

In this small-town Chinese scene, the line of red pillars is cleanly divided from the main action, helped by the green complementary colours. The girls joking are the main event, but the division is an extra feature. As the schematics underneath show, the useful limits are from a narrow red strip to one taking up over a third, simply by panning a little to the left or right. The final choice was between these two.

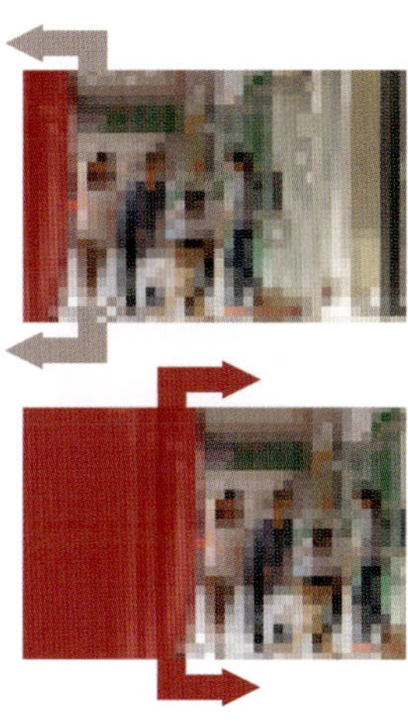

left or right. I've given my reasoning for the examples here to give something of the flavour of the decision-making process. As a general rule, the cleaner the break, the more it draws attention to itself.

The horizon is special because it's a constant in our lives and experience, so there's a general expectation that it should probably be somewhere near, but not exactly on, the middle of the frame. Over time, this has inspired a surprising amount of discussion and argument over where the horizon line 'should' go. In reality, with so much else going on in landscapes, it is not the most critical of decisions. It does, however, provide the opportunity for being different by choosing an extreme position, high or low. Of course, the further the horizon departs from a clean straight line, the less relevant it is.

Apart from horizons, frame division can vary from subtle and understated to so strong that it becomes a major feature of the composition, even at times seeming to create two separate pictures that just happen to be stuck together. This is something you can choose to do or not do, and this tends to follow another kind of division – between photographers who are drawn more to the content of the scene and those inclined to explore the graphics.

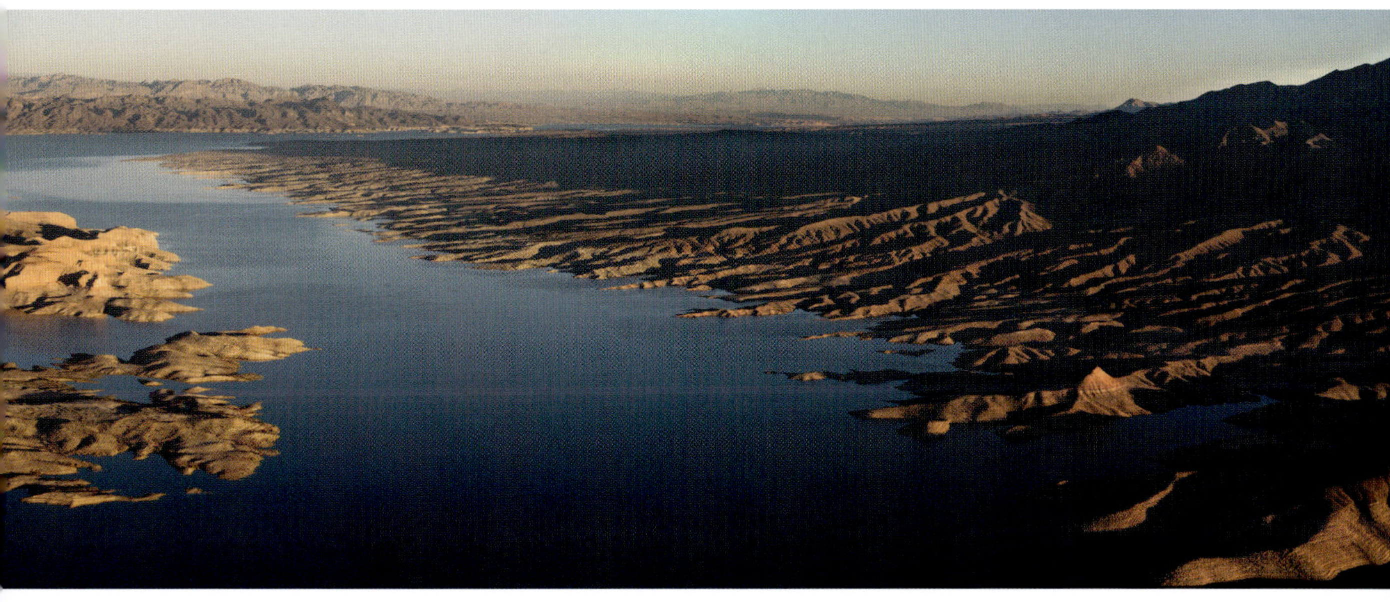

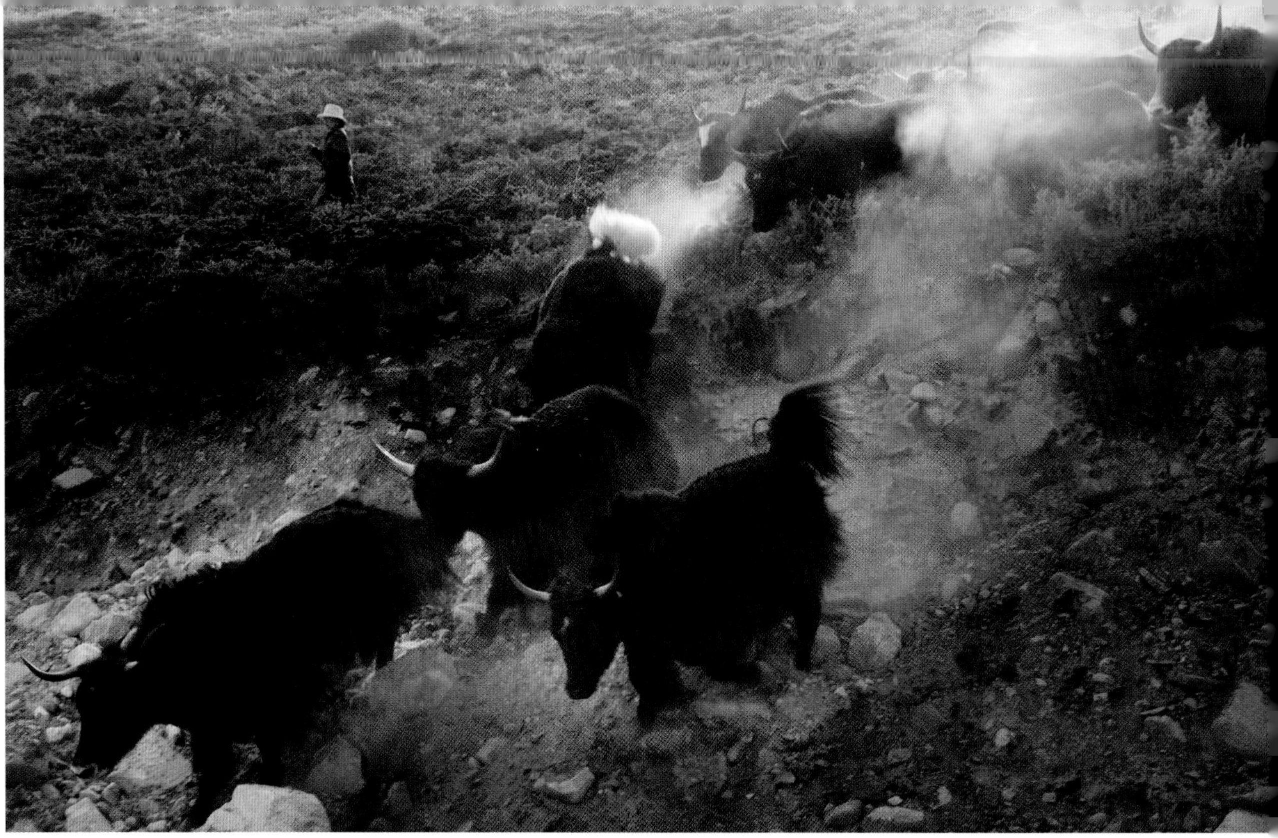

DIAGONAL DIVISION

For the simple reason that most photographs are shot with the camera level, most frame divisions are either on the horizontal or vertical, and these have come to be seen as somehow normal.

Standing out all the more then are the much fewer occasions when we're offered a division on the diagonal. This is not the same as simply having prominent diagonals, which we'll look at in the next chapter (see page 88). For an actual division, the areas on either side of the dividing line need to be meaningfully different. In fact, while a two-part division divided by a corner-to-corner line is a possibility, the right-angled triangles on either side tend not to look such coherent areas as do the rectangular divisions we've just been looking at. Triangles simply don't look quite so self-contained as squares and rectangles. For this reason, a thick central band works the most strongly, ideally at the angle set by two opposite corners of the frame. It not only conforms to the frame, but it is also opposed distinctly to the horizontal and vertical edges (shallow angles don't look decisive).

All this seems to limit the opportunities for a diagonal division, but it also makes it more interesting when you do find a situation that offers it. The Tibetan yaks

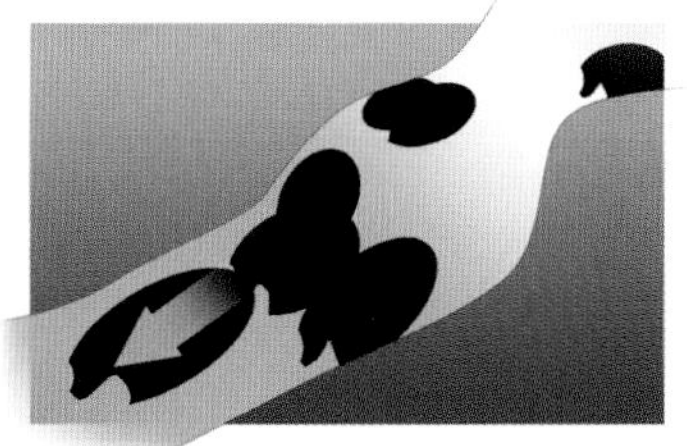

As described in the text, the action here on a hillside in Sichuan, China developed quickly, and from this viewpoint the natural framing, using the zoom, was corner to corner. It was the dust kicked up and brightened by the backlighting that created the higher contrast band, dividing the frame.

In controlled conditions such as a studio or interior, it's obviously easier to manipulate a scene into the relatively unusual diagonal division. Here in a contemporary Japanese tea house serving sweets for the tea ceremony, the viewpoint and diagonal banding energizes what could have been a static arrangement.

rushing down a slope qualify for this reason. The diagonal band that the yaks and the dust they were kicking up created was not only short-lived, but depended on the eye of the photographer. A couple of seconds earlier or later and their mass wouldn't have stretched fully across the frame from top right to lower left. Framed like this (with a 24–70mm zoom lens and the zoom being racked backward and forward constantly to search for the neatest composition), the herd has been channelled into an energetic, flowing band.

In fully controlled studio photography, the same kind of division is much easier to make, and it can be a useful device either for grouping different units in a still-life shot or, as in this example, for making a structured setting to place a subject – in either case, it adds a graphic energy.

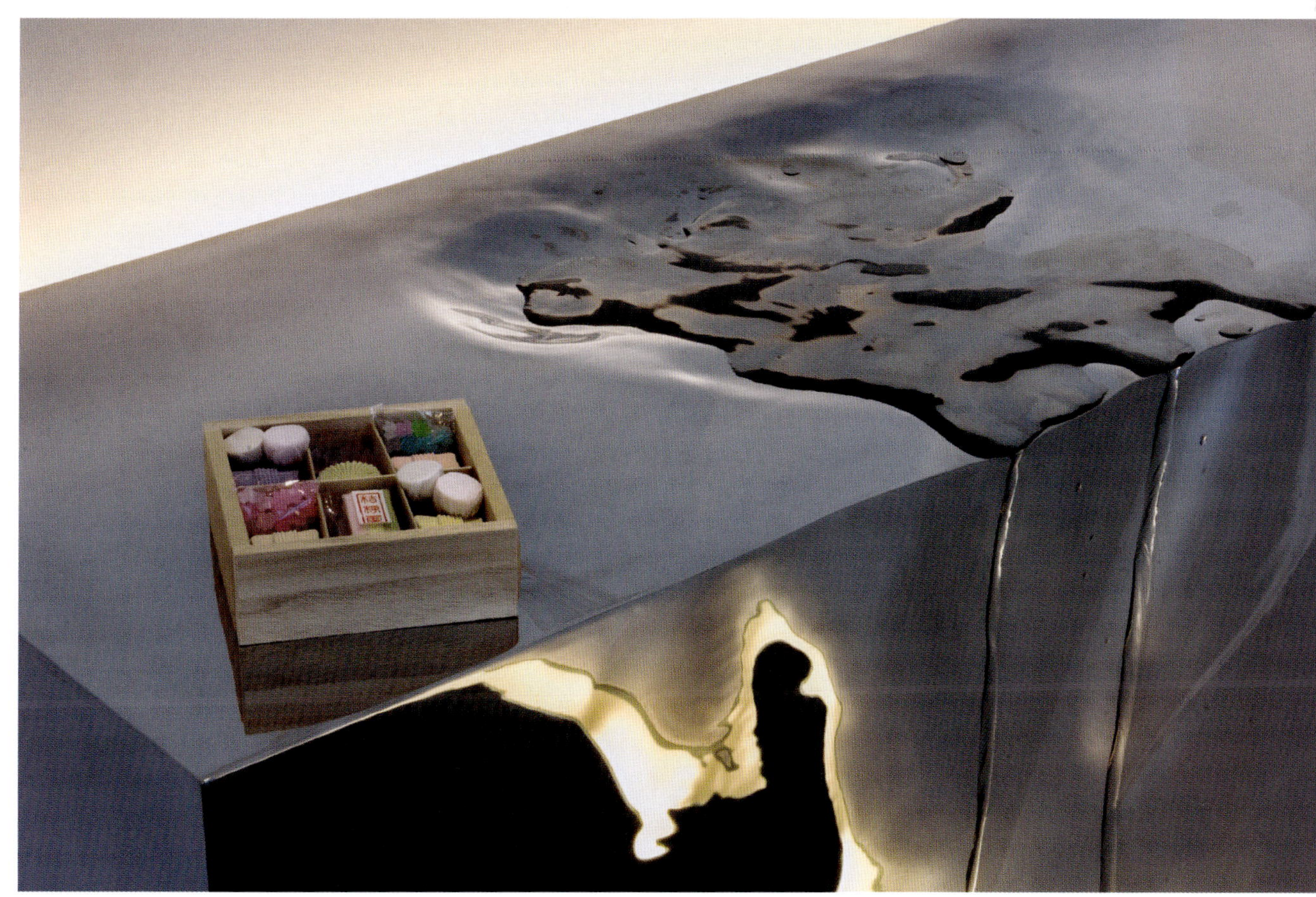

CHAPTER

4

SECRET GEOMETRY

Geometry, with its calculations and exactness may seem ill-suited to the way in which photographers put their images together, given that shooting is usually rapid and situations often fluid. Henri Cartier-Bresson thought otherwise, and he certainly shot in a fluid, rapid manner. He used the word frequently, and for him it meant something instinctive, not calculated, an underlying 'rigorous organisation of visually perceived forms.'[1] In a successful photograph you could see the geometry later, but of course you could use only intuition and experience to apply it at the time of shooting. In that sense, the geometry of composition happens behind the scenes. It also did in classical painting, but painters had time to plan and organize and, often, sketch out the framework before painting. This underlying pattern and arrangement is sometimes called the armature. In fact, photography has inherited all the thought that centuries of painting inspired. Some of the design ideas are more useful for camerawork than others because most shooting has to be rapid, but all are interesting and worth exploring.

1 Cartier-Bresson, Henri, *The Decisive Moment*, New York: Simon & Schuster, 1952.

The idea of implied shapes is common knowledge, and it's usual to talk of triangles, rectangles and circles as the variations. What is less often acknowledged is that there is a huge difference in their frequency and usability. Triangles are naturally the simplest, needing only three points, which are easy to find almost anywhere. Rectangles and circles, however, operate differently. Actual rectangles are way too common to be interesting because they're so basic to the built environment, and so need a different treatment if they are to have any surprise value, while implied rectangles that happen by chance are rare. Circles and other rounded shapes also need to be unexpected and by chance if they are to be interesting and worth using, and situations that give rise to them are uncommon.

Why bother? On a purely organizational level, because a simple shape gives order and structure to an image, and while there's nothing to say that you should have this, it helps the 'competence' of a photograph. There's also another reason at another level, because graphic structure acts as an extra layer of viewing, and audiences generally appreciate this.

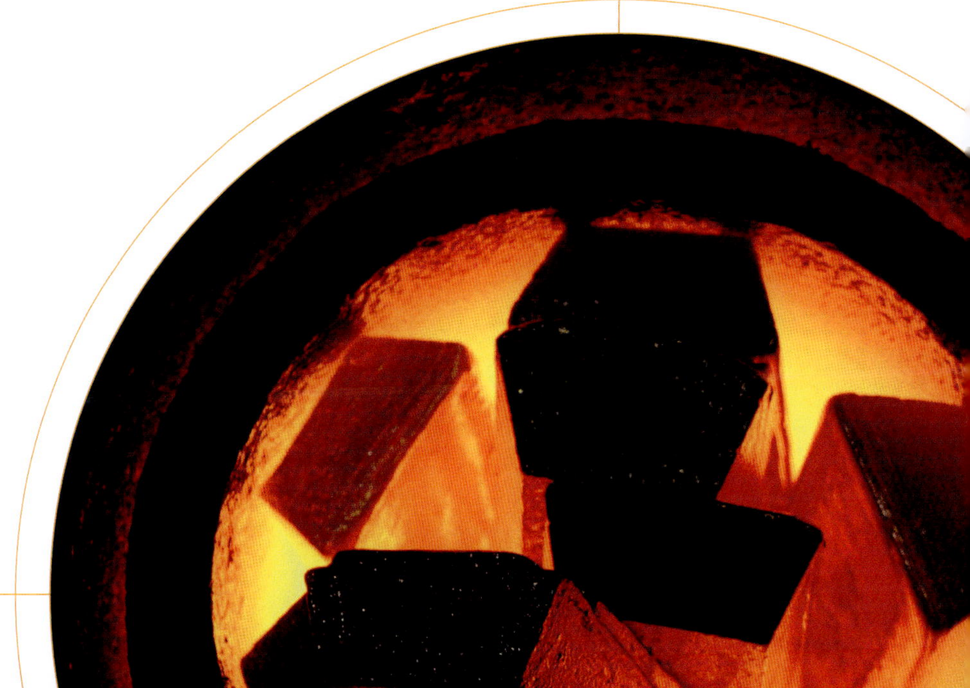

RABATMENT

This is a painter's term, borderline obscure, but a very common practice in classical painting, used by artists including Giotto, Nicolas Poussin, Eugène Delacroix and Georges Seurat, among many others.

With more time to consider a still life of a Chinese statue, rabatment of the vertical 2:3 frame gave two squares overlapping vertically. Diagonals between the corners of these squares and the corners of the entire frame give a set of intersection points, which located two vertical lines (pale blue), and the statue was aligned with one of these.

That already sounds way too far from photography, but the simple idea of rabatment – rotating in the mind's eye the short side of the frame onto the long side – turns out to be very practical indeed for regular shooting. All those painters, of course, had time to plan and work out the armature of their canvas in advance. That meant the network of lines and intersection points, and the very simplest starting point was rabatment. As the illustration shows, if you rotate the short side down onto the long side, you have a square. Two overlapping squares, in fact, and how much they overlap depends on the shape of the frame. I'm showing here 3:2, so they overlap by a third. Ordinarily, calculated divisions are of little use to most photographers, as we have to shoot immediately. But in this case, it's simple, because we can all judge a square instantly on the left or right, and that can be a way of enclosing a main subject, as in the picture opposite below.

For a classical painter, that was just the start, because he could then draw several criss-crossing diagonals, which gave rise to intersection points. These in turn could be used for positioning a subject off-centre yet with some logic. This is less easy to judge by eye for photography, and more useful for still life and other static subjects that give you time to think, but as the division stays the same for any given frame shape, it's not too difficult to memorize. The value of templates like rabatment and the Golden Section (which we'll see next) is that they offer a reason for placing the division in the frame. Not everyone thinks it's a good enough reason, but it has credibility.

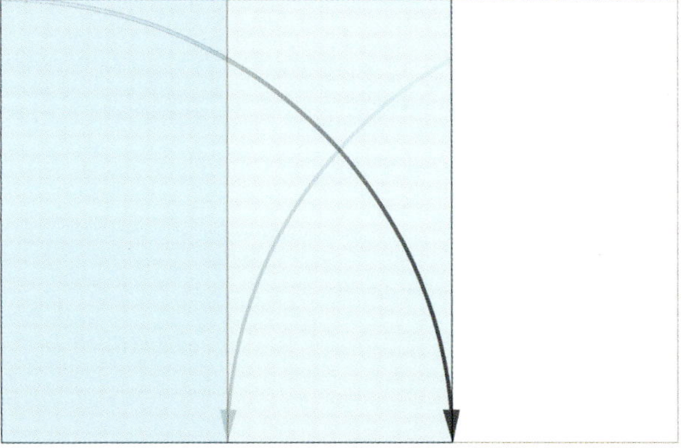

Basic rabatment of a 3:2 frame. The two verticals are rotated down 90°, giving two overlapping squares.

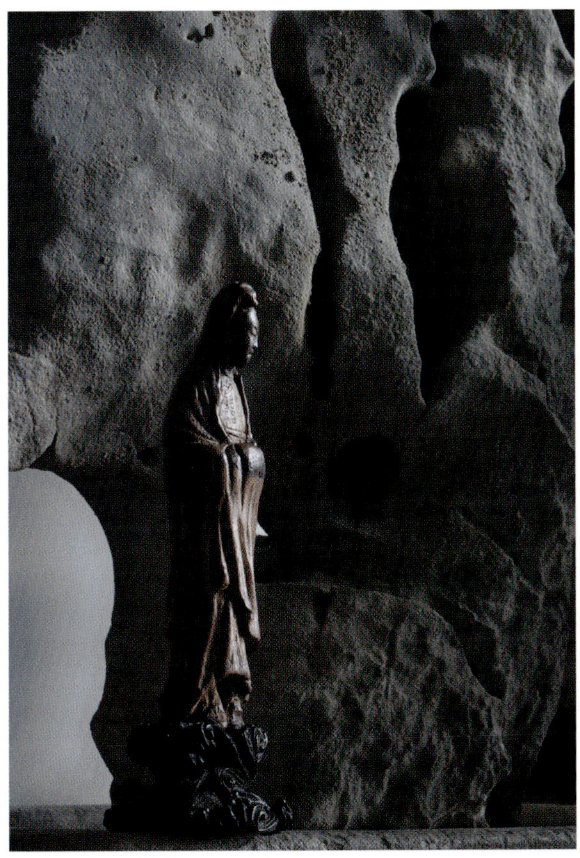

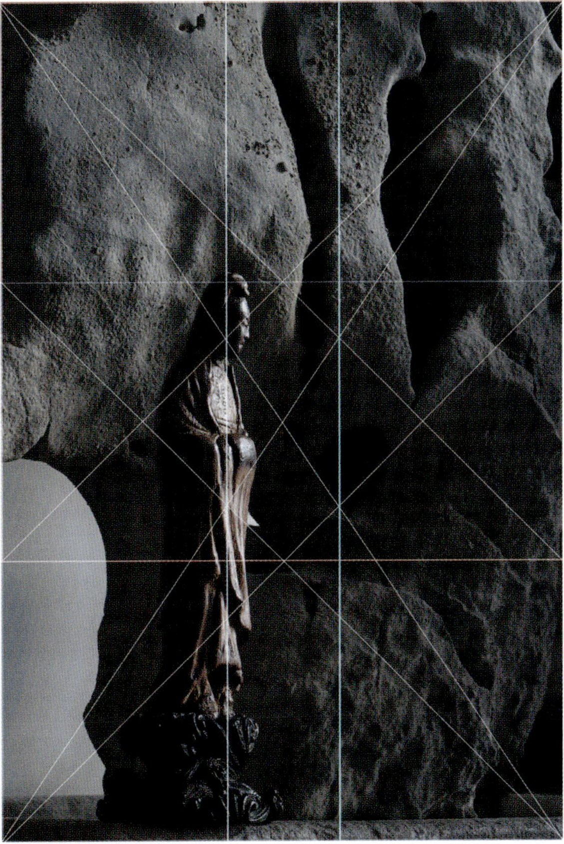

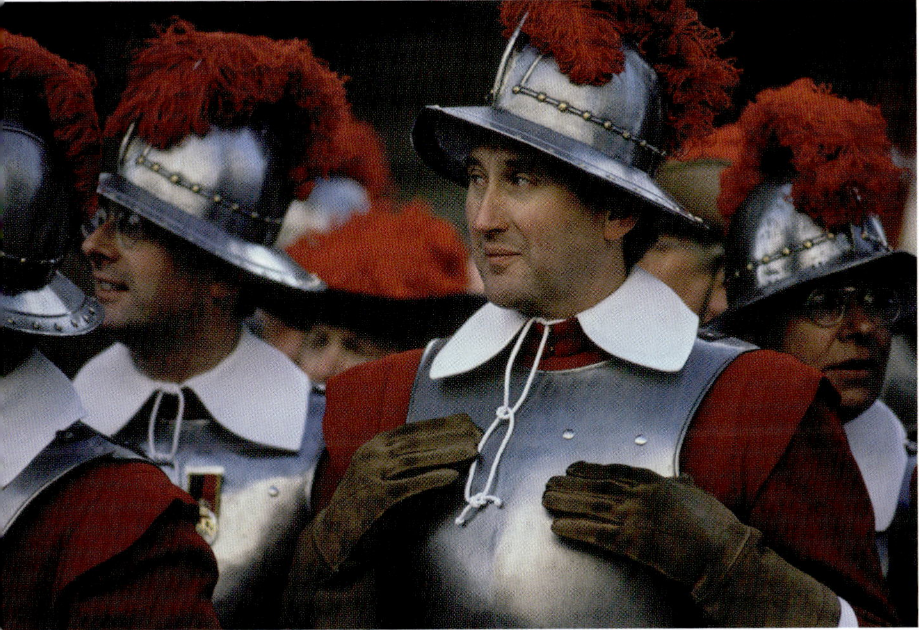

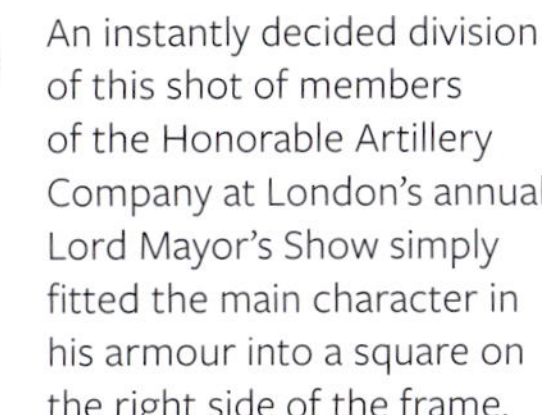

An instantly decided division of this shot of members of the Honorable Artillery Company at London's annual Lord Mayor's Show simply fitted the main character in his armour into a square on the right side of the frame.

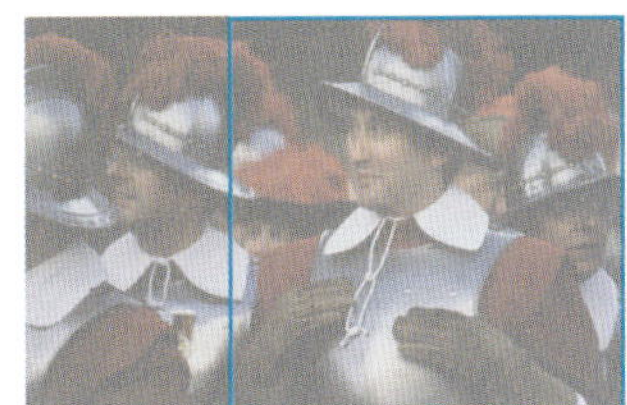

GOLDEN SECTION

One idea that informed classical painting at different times was that of special proportions that would give some sort of perfect arrangement. One of the earliest and most well-known was the Golden Proportion or Golden Section or Golden Ratio.

It was a way of making a main division of the frame so that the relationship between the smaller part to the larger is the same as the larger part to all of it. Numerically, this is 1:1.618033989, or mathematically Φ (*phi*).

You can divide any frame in either direction like this, and because the divisions are linked in a unique way, in painting in the Middle Ages it came to be seen as divine and mystical. Since then it acquired a reputation for being almost magically harmonious.

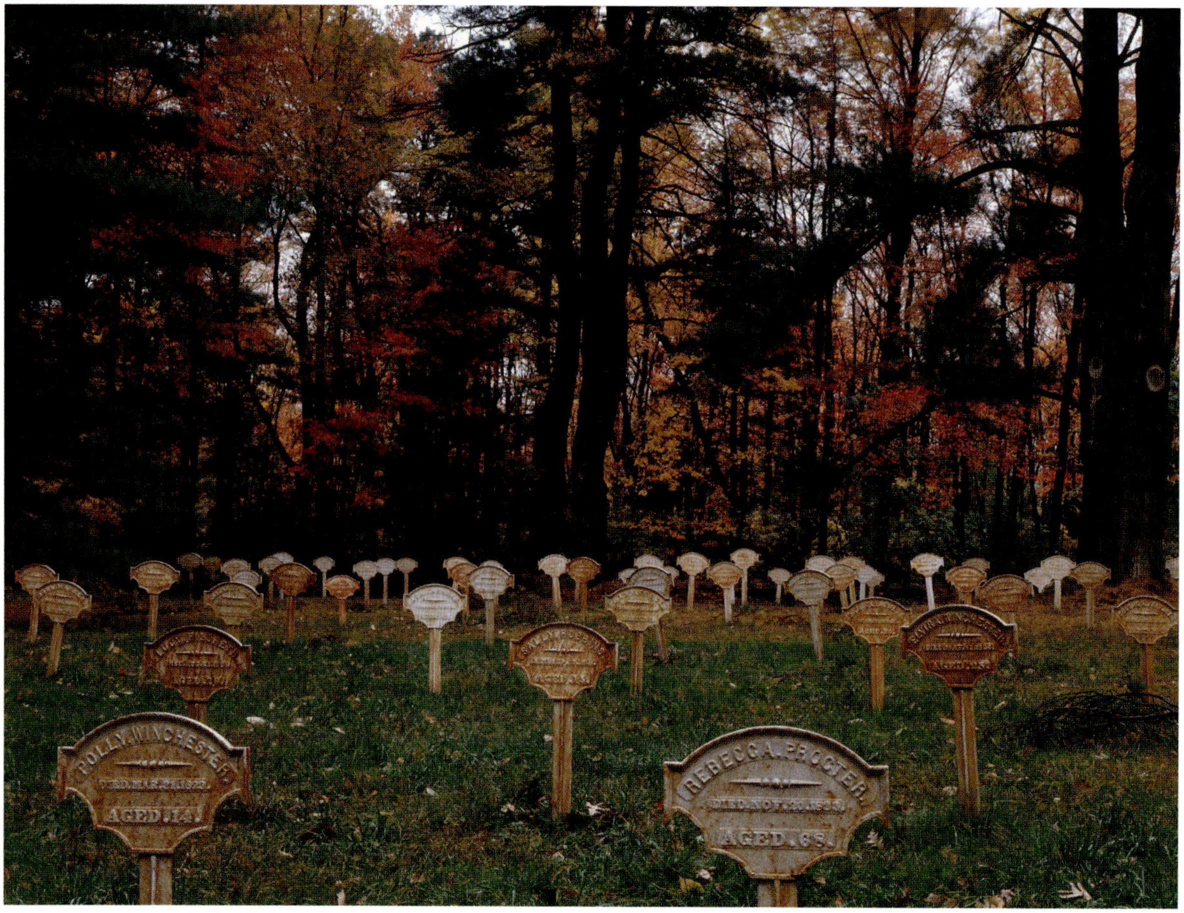

This shot of a Shaker cemetery in New England demands a division, yet there are no special subject needs to push it one way or the other. The Golden Section here is simply a comfortable way of doing it.

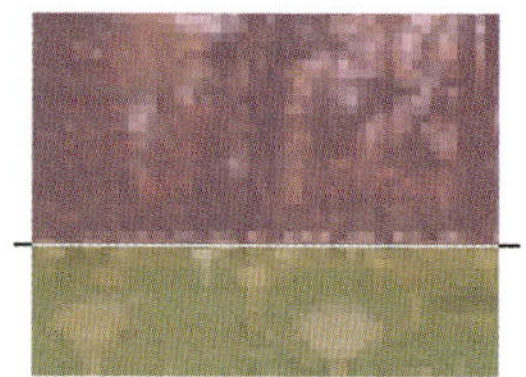

The jury is still out on whether such 'golden' proportions really do translate into a harmonious effect when we look at an image, but it has its supporters.

Using it for most photography, however, is more of a stretch than for painting, for the simple reason that very few of us have the time to calculate like this, even if we wanted to. Painters have time to construct, but most photography is about capture – and quite rapid capture at that. However, it's just about useable with a large or medium format camera on a tripod when you have a very formal subject like a landscape or a studio set. In fact, once you're familiar with the way this special division looks, it's easy enough to figure it out intuitively and quickly. Both of these pictures are divided on the Golden Section – one of them twice, horizontally and vertically – but of course neither were calculated or measured. They just seemed at the time a comfortable and satisfying division.

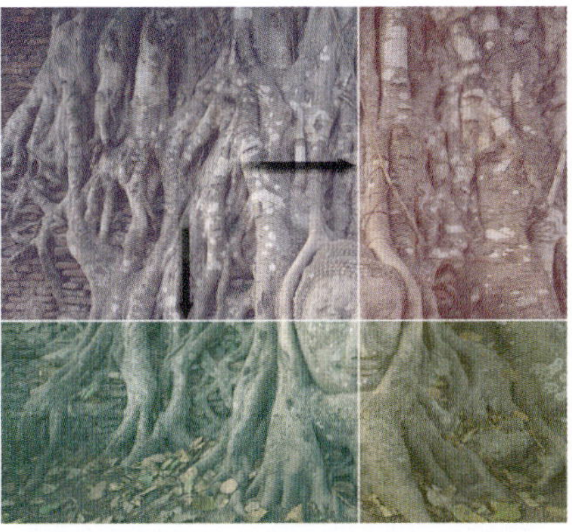

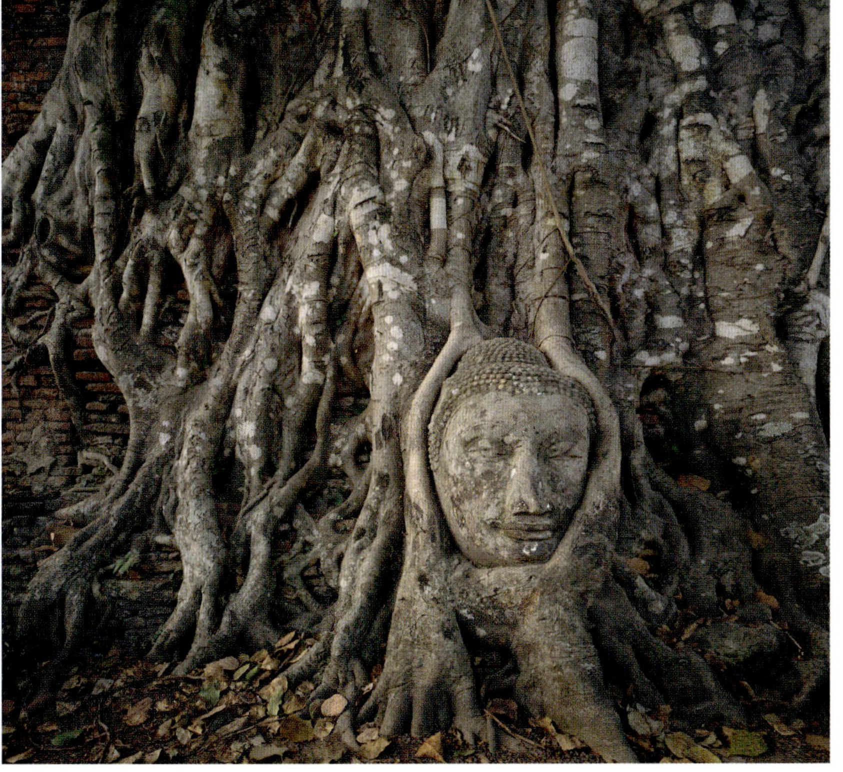

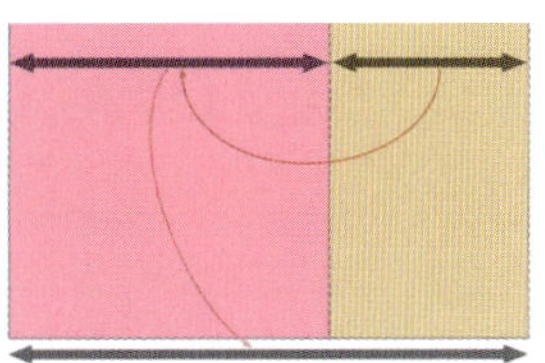

The proportion of the smaller (pale yellow) to the larger (pink) is the same as that of the larger to the entire frame.

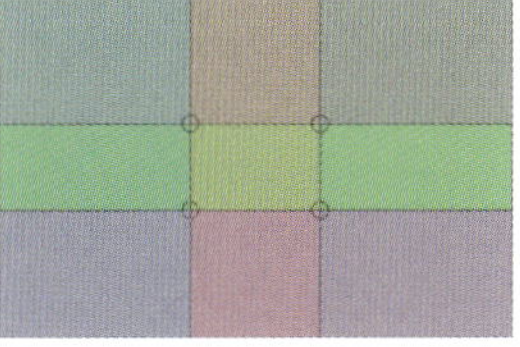

Also potentially useful for placing an isolated single subject are the Golden Points at the intersections of the four possible divisions.

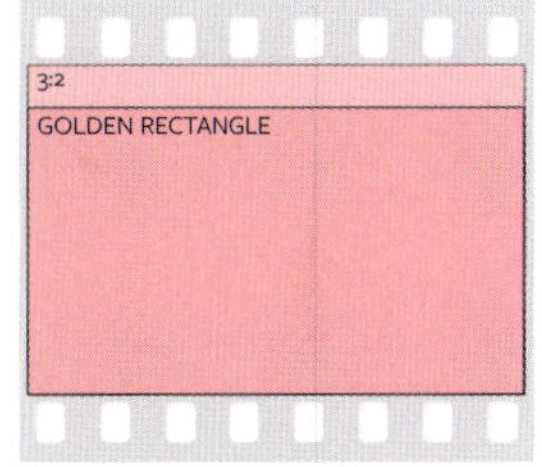

While any frame can be divided according to the Golden Section, the most 'perfect' is arguably the Golden Rectangle, itself in these proportions. There's a possible case for cropping a 3:2 full-frame image to this.

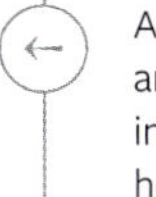

A two-way division, left-right and top-bottom, gives an intersection location for the head of an ancient Buddha statue that over centuries was caught up in a multi-rooted ficus tree.

FIBONACCI POINTS

Closely related to the Golden Section that we just saw is the Fibonacci series, and it has occasional use in photography, though less than some people would like to claim.

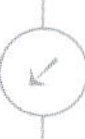

The golden spiral is logarithmic, growing by Φ, the golden ratio. Approximately, you start with a square on one side of the frame (like rabatment, page 68) with a quarter circle on it. Then repeat for the rectangle remaining from the square, and so on. The centre of the spiral is a Fibonacci point.

Named after the Medieval scholar who made it popular in science and art, it's a progressive series of numbers in which each is the sum of the previous two (0, 1, 1, 2, 3, 5, 8, 13...). Turned into geometry, it creates a special spiral that never changes shape however much it extends, and its most famous appearance in life is as a spiral shell, particularly that of the nautilus. In fact, it occurs throughout nature, in plants as well, not surprisingly because it allows things to grow without changing their shape (useful if you're a mollusc). Not quite so useful for shooting, however, even though you'll find attempts on the Web to overlay this spiral on photographs. What may have some justification, however, is the point that a spiral in a frame converges on, as shown here. And if you look at the divisions used to calculate it, going from left to lower right to upper right and so on, they are remarkably close to the Golden Section.

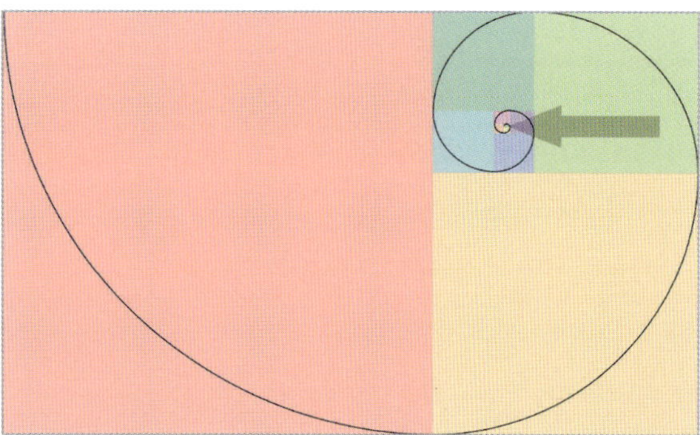

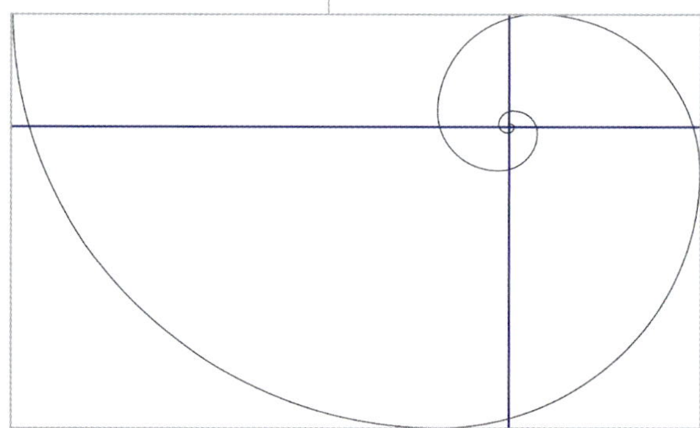

Here we're at the quirky end of composition, though at least there's a rationale, as there is for the Golden Section, as opposed to the tiresome rule of thirds, which has no basis other than an observation by a painter and engraver of little note, John Thomas Smith, about Sir Joshua Reynolds's paintings (Reynolds said nothing about this). Ultimately, such calculated divisions and points are just suggestions, alongside all the other influences in this book that can push or pull a composition one way or another.

A kung fu master meditating in an ancient Buddhist cave in Chongqing, China. Fibonacci points are more eccentric than Golden Points, which suits this vertical scene in which we want to see something of the height of the cave.

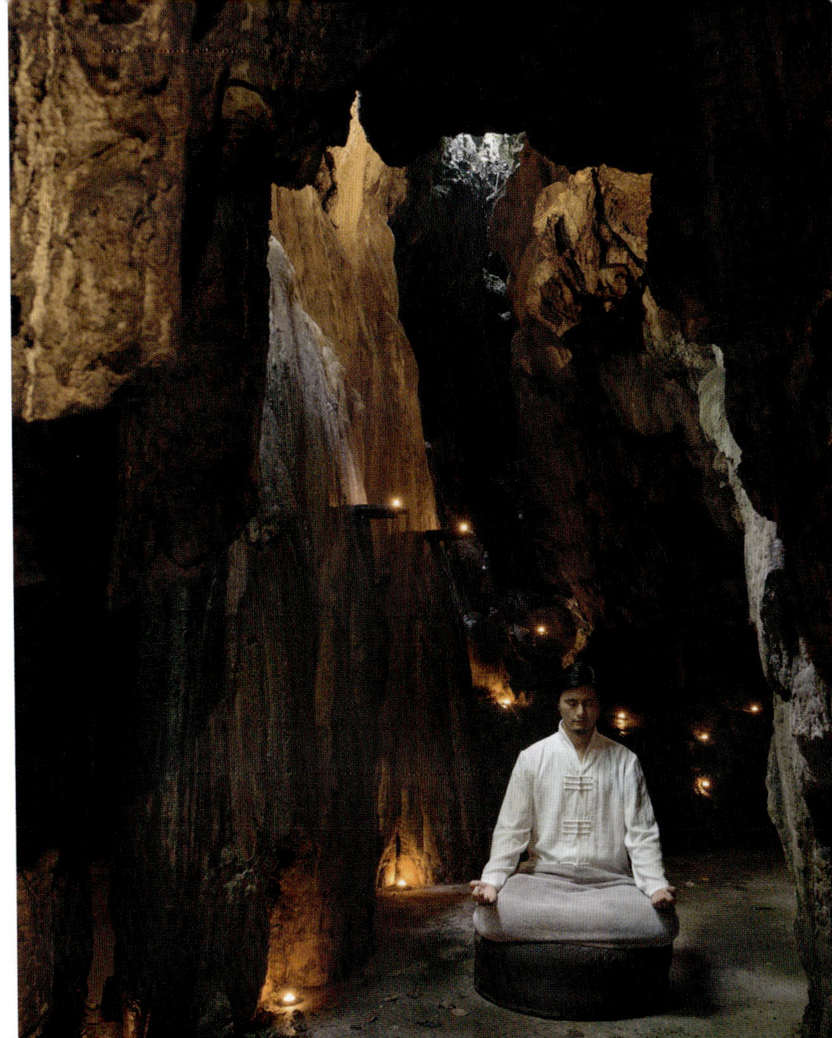

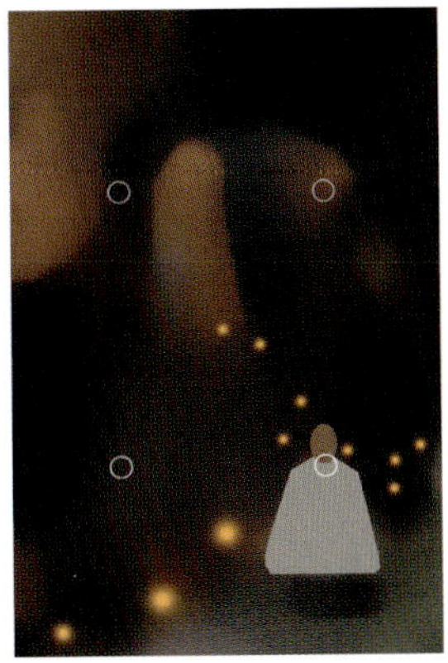

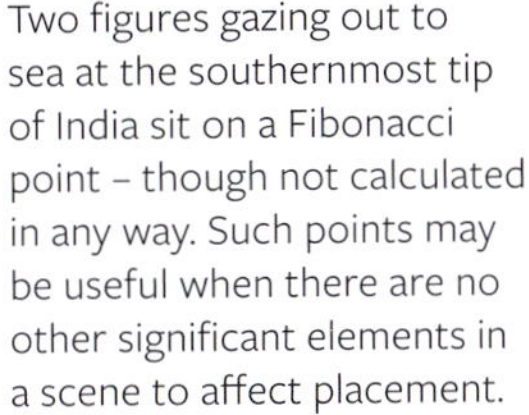

Two figures gazing out to sea at the southernmost tip of India sit on a Fibonacci point – though not calculated in any way. Such points may be useful when there are no other significant elements in a scene to affect placement.

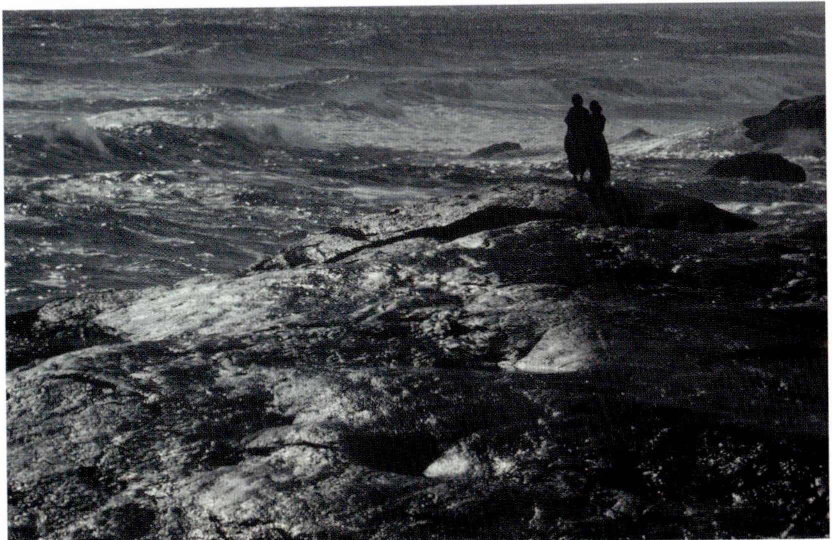

MUSICAL HARMONY

If the Golden Section and Fibonacci points seem a little obsessive, there is yet one more line of exploration inherited from painting, and that is music, unlikely though it may seem for image-makers.

I'll say from the start that I know of no one who has used this idea to its full extent in photography, given how complicated it is; however, there are many examples from Renaissance paintings. If we're looking at image-making that can be planned and constructed, it's intriguing and not completely off the wall. It goes back to the Renaissance architect Leon Battista Alberti, who suggested that the proportions responsible for musical harmony would also be harmonious visually, in particular the octave, perfect fourth and perfect fifth. These are musical intervals between notes that generally sound pleasing. Alberti was interested in the positions on a string that produced them – their pitch ratio: an octave is 2:1, a perfect fourth 4:3 and a perfect fifth 3:2. There's not much of interest that can be done with 2:1, but the other two can make extended shapes with special divisions. And, of course, the meaning of 4:3 and 3:2 isn't lost on photographers. Alberti's method was to 'double' them, as the illustrations show, and the results are a wide frame of 9:4 for the perfect fourth, and 16:9 for a perfect fifth – lo and behold, widescreen! Moreover, the divisions were interesting: 4/6/9 and 9/12/16. This sounds hopelessly theoretical for imagery, but for Italian painters of the time, like Sandro Botticelli and Andrea Mantegna, it was practical. Botticelli's two most famous paintings made use of them: *The Birth of Venus* is based on the perfect fourth doubled and *Primavera* (below) on the perfect fifth doubled.

Perfect fourth

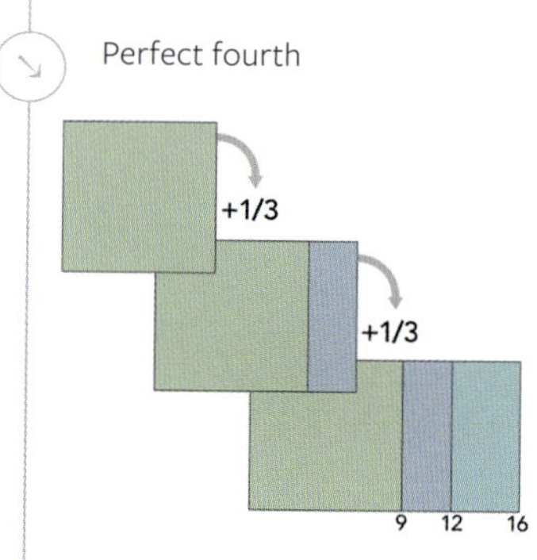

Perfect fifth

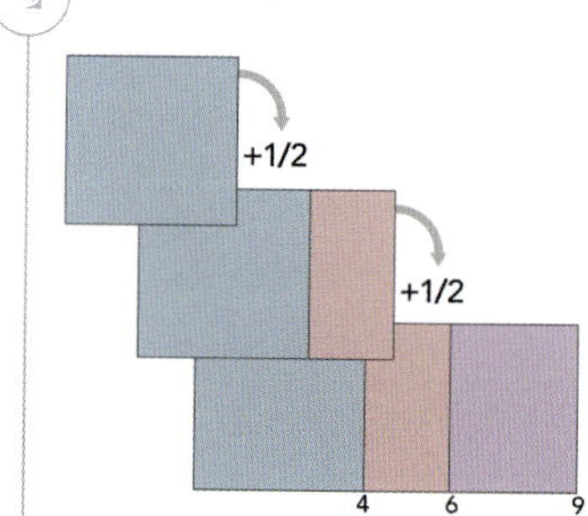

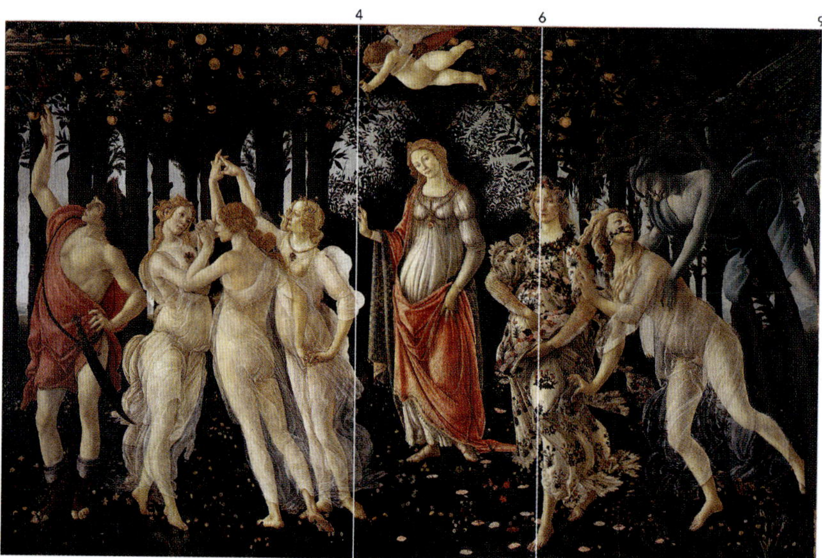

Complex though it may sound, there's an easy way to make both of these divisions by starting with a square. At top, for a perfect fourth, add ⅓ to the square and then add ⅓ to the result to make a 16:9 frame divided 9/12/16. For a perfect fifth, as above, add ½ to the square and then add ½ to the result to make a 9:4 frame divided 4/6/9. The frame proportions are less important than the division, and Botticelli's painting is less stretched.

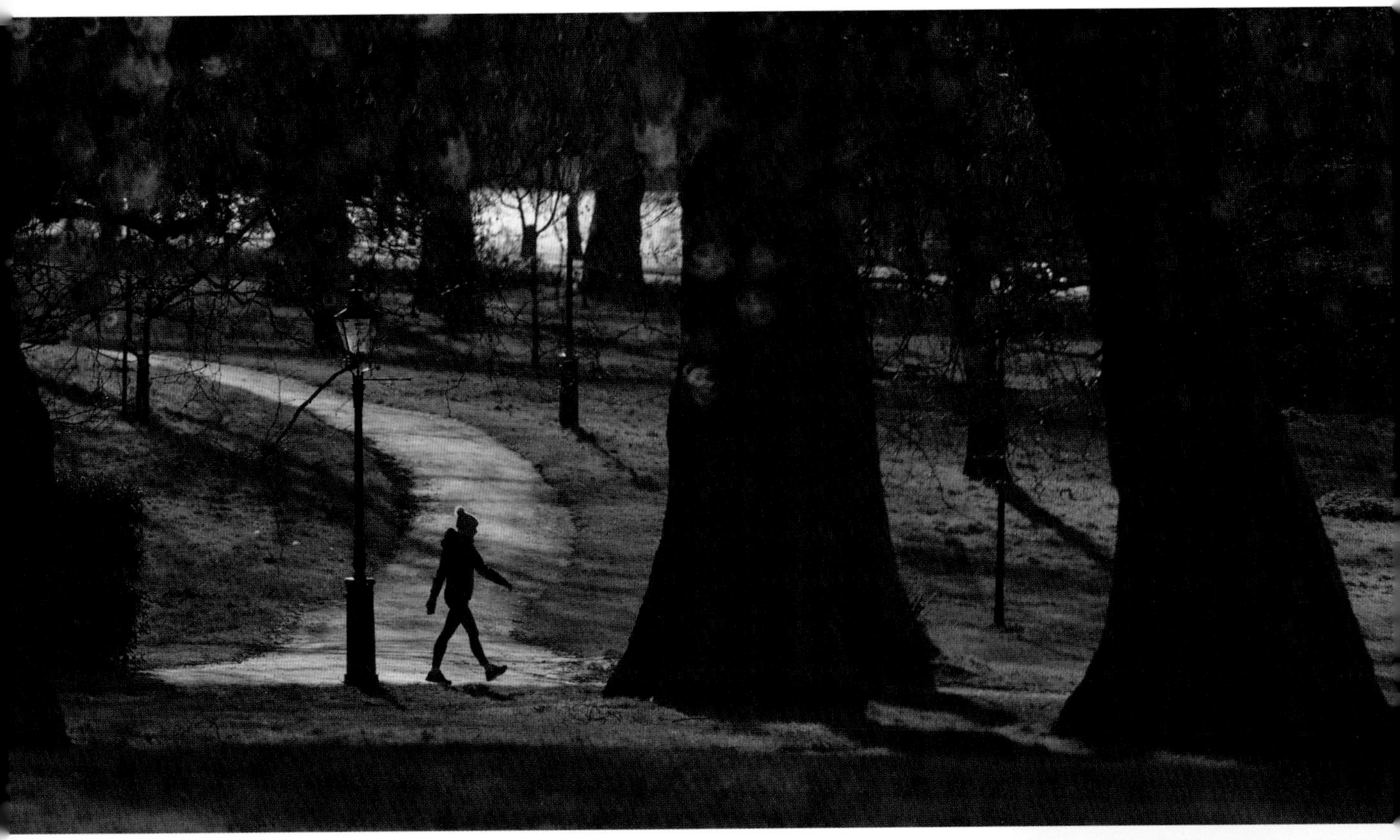

Fascinating stuff, but is it really practical for photography? Not in the way I just described because of the time it would take to work it out, so only possibly, perhaps, in a studio. However, if we put precision and calculation to one side, the perfect fourth and the perfect fifth make three-way sandwich-like divisions that have some value for composition. All three segments are different. The central band is the thinnest, and it's offset to one side, and the largest division is a square. So, if you have the kind of scene that's open to being divided into sections, this can work very well, with enough asymmetry to keep it interesting, The square on one side (just as in rabatment, page 68) is easy enough to visualize, and the small middle section is well-suited for putting a key subject of interest. Or, if you like, instead of treating the frame divisions as spaces into which to put things, you could take the dividing lines themselves as locations for placing subjects.

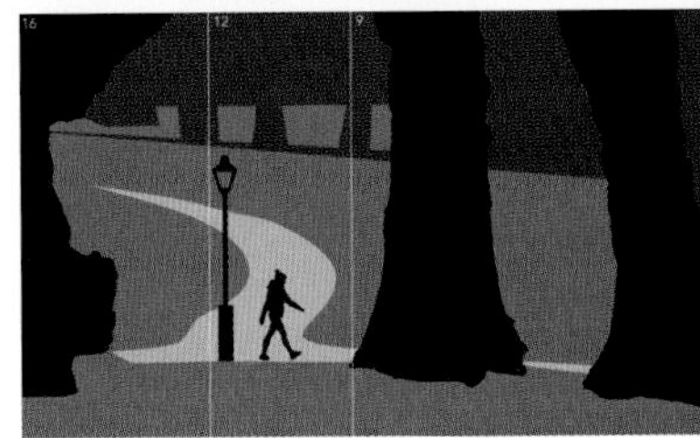

Naturally, the shot above wasn't calculated, but it turned out to be a perfect fifth, shooting to 16:9 widescreen, in the reverse of the upper diagram at left. The intuitive composition was to place the bright band of the path off-centre left and wait for the walker to enter that space. On a 16:9 frame, the right-hand block is a square – a kind of rabatment.

THE EVER-PRESENT TRIANGLE

Working an implied triangle into an image is one of the most basic ideas in composition.

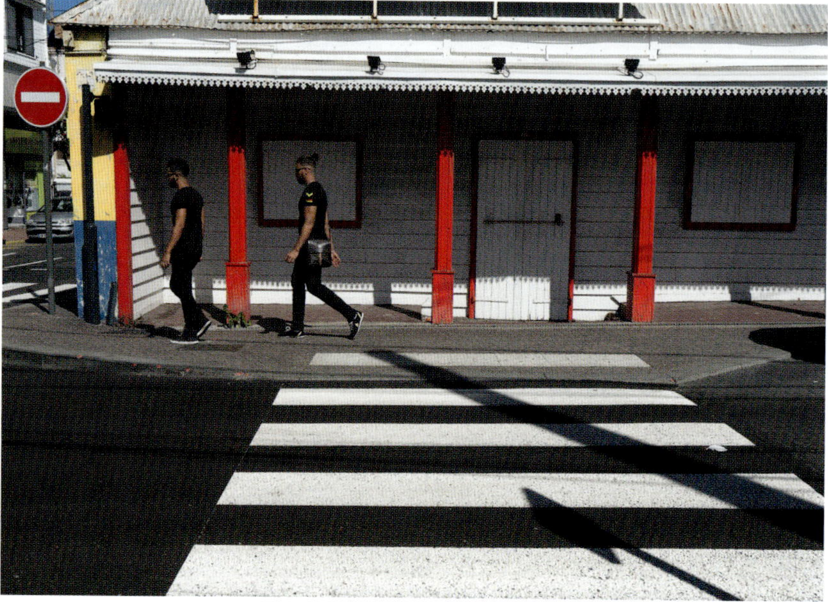

The sharp diagonal shadow of the lamp post (which was out of frame to the right) suggested a possible triangle when added to the left edge of the crossing and the bottom of the frame, but it needed a figure at the apex to become worthwhile.

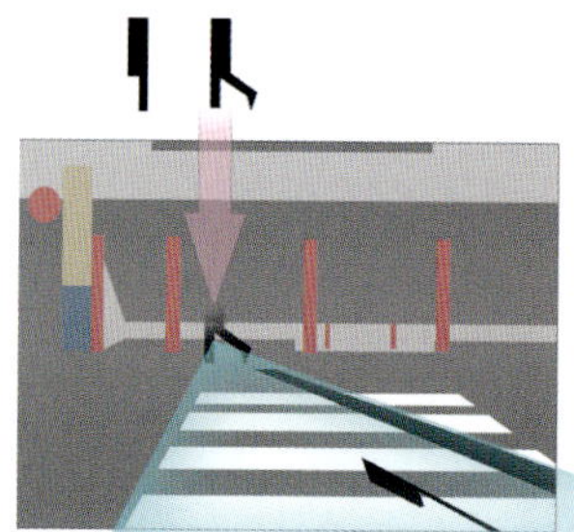

It's the simplest of all shapes – three corners and three sides – and any three prominent points suggest a triangle, unless they're in a straight line, because we have an innate tendency to 'see' them given only a few visual clues.

As I'll introduce in the next chapter, this visual urge is usefully explained by Gestalt psychology, and it's surprisingly widespread and strong when it comes to triangles, much more than with any other shape. More on the reasons for that in the following pages, but the trick, if there is one, is to make your suggested triangle interesting. That tends to mean unusual, or unexpected, or coming together in a clever way. Complete triangles offer nothing to discover graphically and are simply subjects in their own right, but encouraging the viewer's eye to imagine a triangle from a few clues adds an extra small layer of experience, and it makes the image that bit more enjoyable.

The street scene from the island of La Réunion shows the process of finding clues and then using them. What first attracted were the bright splashes of primary colours on a stark pattern of white and dark grey, made all the more structured by this frontal, squared-up view. What raised the image a notch was the diagonal hard shadow of the lamp post, which went most of the way to adding a triangle as a graphic overlay. It needed a passer-by to complete it, and this might have been a predictable moment were it not for the coincidence of the second man's stride. As he reaches the apex of the almost-triangle, his legs neatly complete it. And both men are in black.

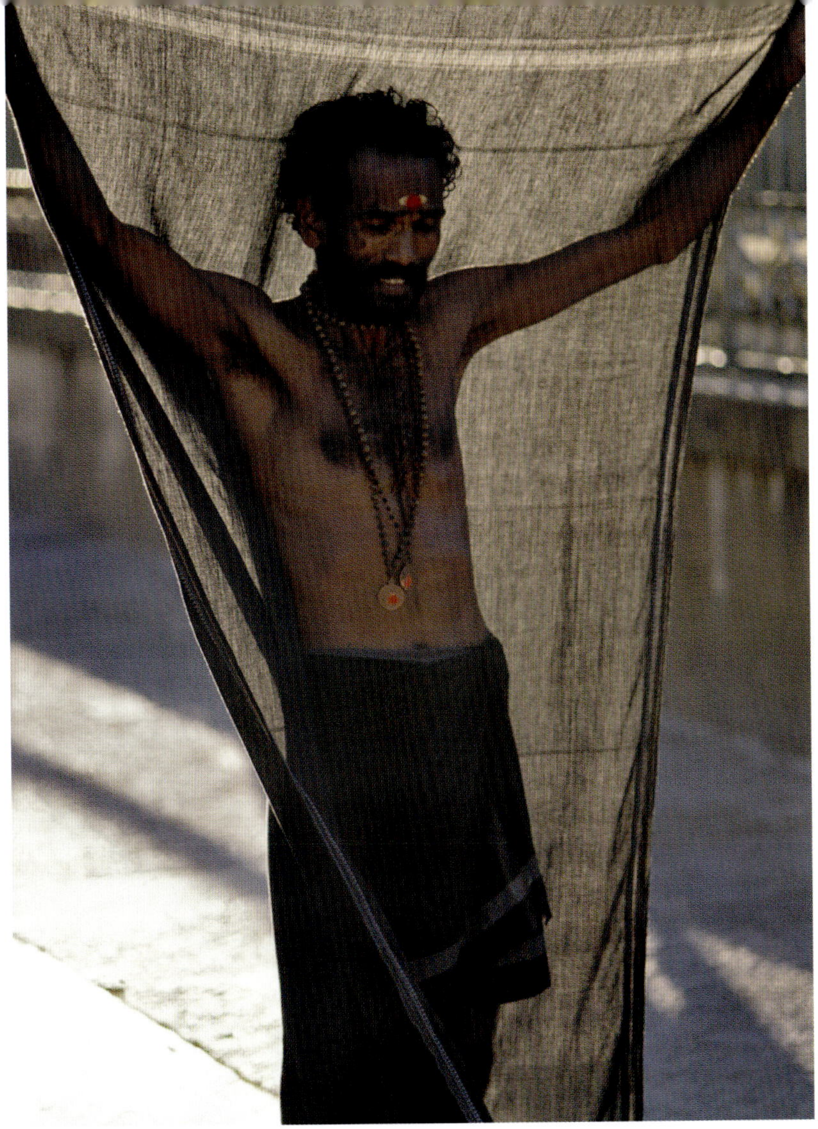

Although the apexes of the curved triangle are outside the frame, the shape is clear and well-defined, reinforced by the curve of the man's upper arms and shoulders.

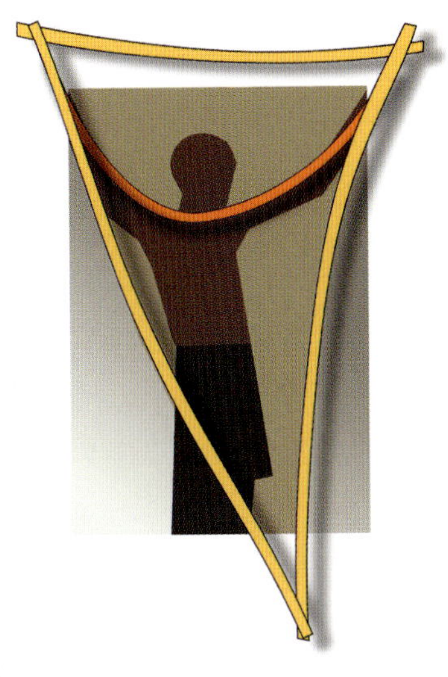

The other example is perhaps more straightforward and more obvious, but the curving inverted triangle adds a strong structure to this backlit shot. Indeed, simplification is what makes this image work. The man is a worshipper at a Hindu temple in southern India, and he's raising and stretching the cloth to dry after bathing in one of the *ghats*. At just this single moment and with this framing, all is simplified, his wrists and the corners of the cloth neatly located in the upper corners, with two clean sweeps of cloth edges converging downward. Outstretched arms have religious connotations in any case, and though the reason here is practical, the man's pose and expression contribute to the moment.

THE UNCOMMON CIRCLE

While the idea of implied shapes is well understood by most photographers, there's a general assumption that the basic shapes – triangle, rectangle and circle – are somehow on an equal footing.

That's true enough in classical painting, but most photography has to put up with what's available in front of the camera, and they're not at all equal. Yes, there are some situations when you can arrange, and of course in the studio that's part of the skill and art, but in the available world of shooting, circles-by-suggestion are rare. This means that while it's often possible to fall back on locating and using triangles if you want a shape structure, when it comes to circles it usually means taking quick advantage of a lucky find.

As with all use of shapes, you score the brownie points by finding them where they're least expected. With circles there are few, if any, prescriptions for this, although it's not a complete coincidence that my examples here are overhead shots looking almost straight down. Circular shapes and patterns are not entirely uncommon, but we don't often see them from our normal viewpoint. I'm not going to get into crop circles, but one reason from them has to do with gathering and enclosing, and that's partly what's happening opposite, as two tea farmers empty fresh leaves into a pile. It's the unexpected additions like the arc of the man's shadow that make it work. Additionally, while it works in its original 3:2 format, I think that cropping it to square enhances the circle a little by virtue of the equal sides to the frame.

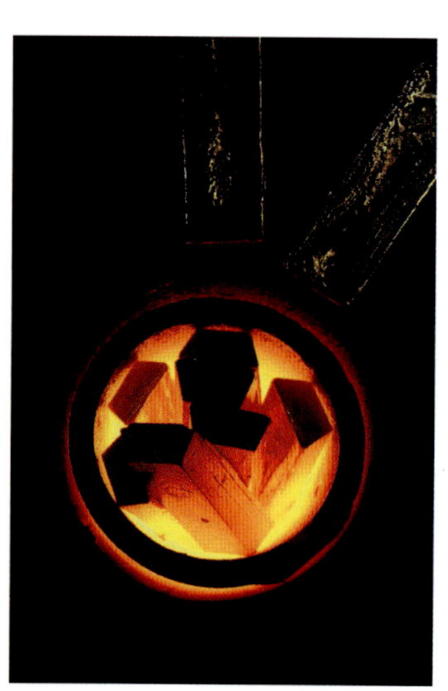

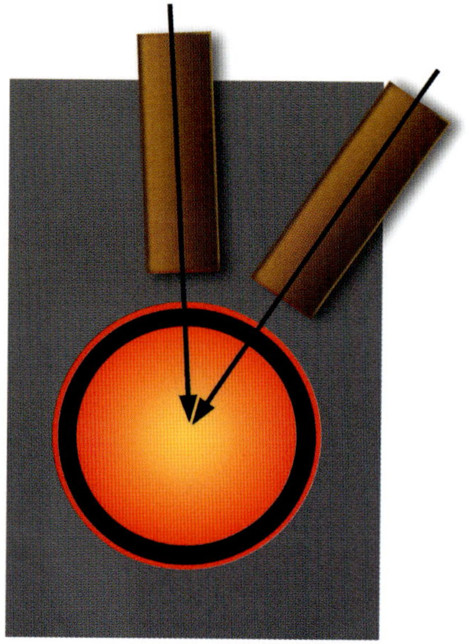

← A kind of a 'guess-what' image, looking vertically down onto a gold-smelting crucible filled with 20kg ingots, lit only by the molten gold inside. The unusual scene emphasizes the role of the geometry – a circle with dimly lit rectangles of two ingots pointing to its centre.

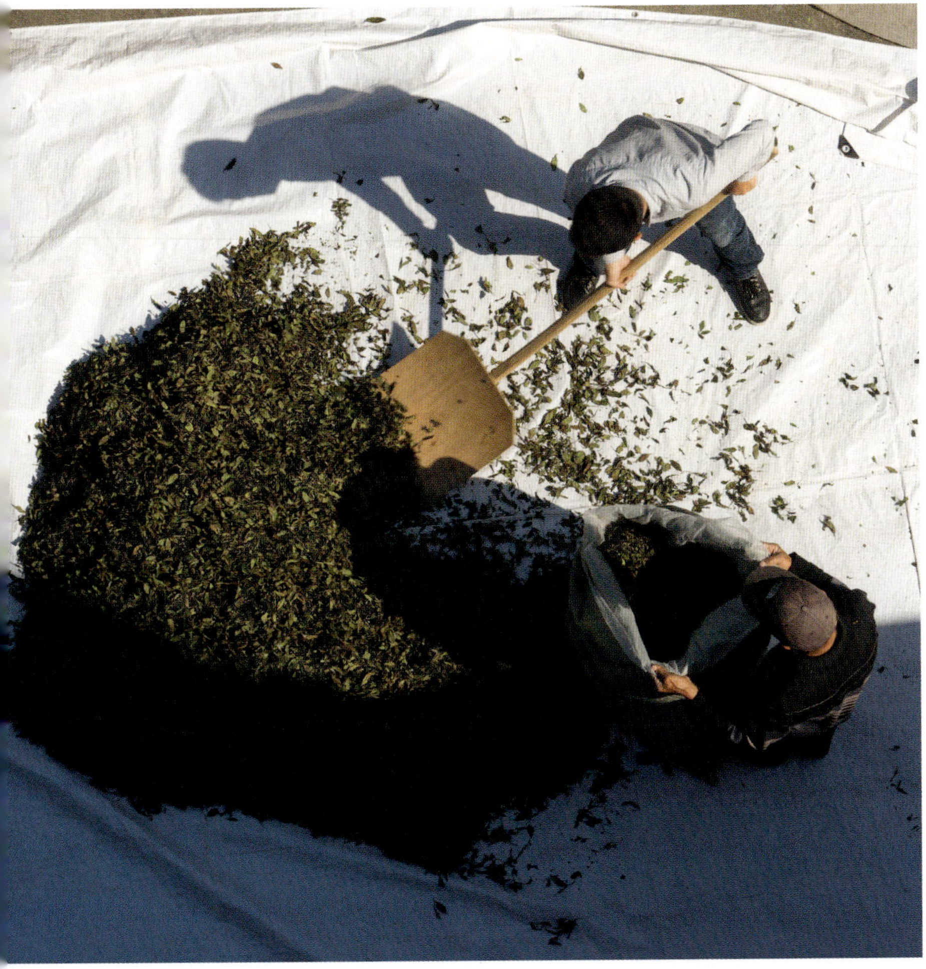

In Fujian province, China, two men were scooping up tea leaves that had been drying all day in the sun right below a three-story building, which offered a different vantage point from usual. As the pile of leaves got smaller and rounder, and the man at the top moved in closer and his shadow started to complete a circle, aided by the eyelines of the two men facing inward (and of the shadow, which in effect became a third person from this view). While there was also the suggestion of an oval, cropping to square eliminated this and focused on the circular arrangement.

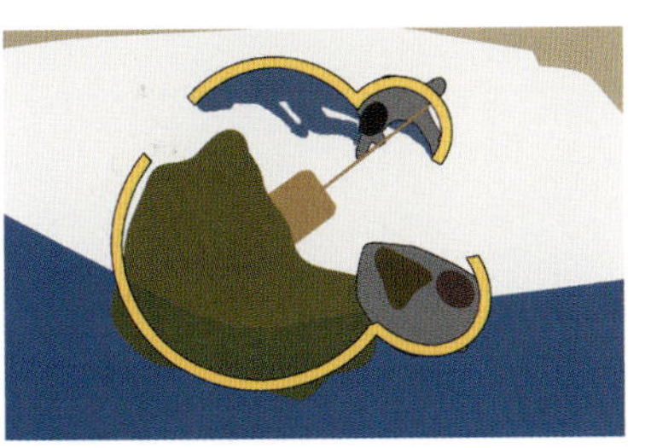

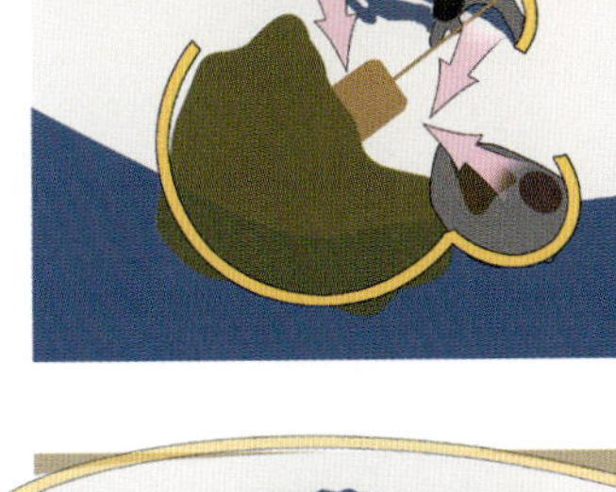

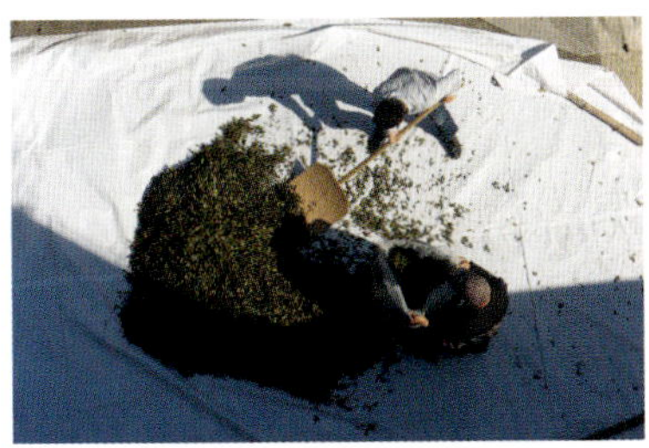

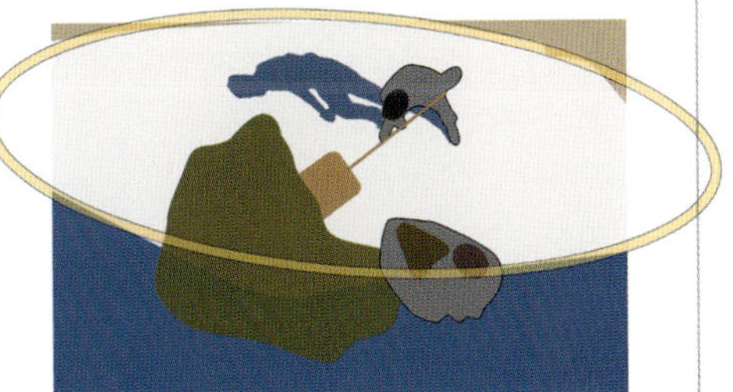

REPEATING RECTANGLES

The problem with making interesting compositions with rectangles is that they are the most common shape we know – the basic unit of construction, from windows to doorways, to building façades, boxes and cupboards.

The list is endless. We're surrounded by them, and there's little point in suggesting them because there's no surprise. For rectangles to play a useful geometrical role, there needs to be some repetition, some interlocking, repetition or other way in which different rectangles relate to each other and to the picture frame. The latter goes without saying: rectangles demand alignment, and that means shooting them squared-up and face-on (see page 42). We're talking, in other words, about a full-on rectilinear theme and style, and this is always going to be stiff and correct. In fact, it's hard to escape an approach that is obsessively precise, so it helps if you embrace this. It may not be a style that appeals to everyone, but it's inevitable.

Architecture, as you might imagine, offers more opportunities for this than most subjects, but because rectangles are by far the most common shapes in buildings, it's important to work even harder on finding special situations. Here, let's look at one subject – American Colonial-era clapboard barn walls – with slightly different treatments. There are two here, although very similar, and they share a rigorous formal symmetry. The tall shuttered windows have multiple panes, which extend the rectangular repetition, and are themselves arranged in a rectangle of four. One of the barn shots was used twice for a book – on the cover and an interior spread – in which the designer

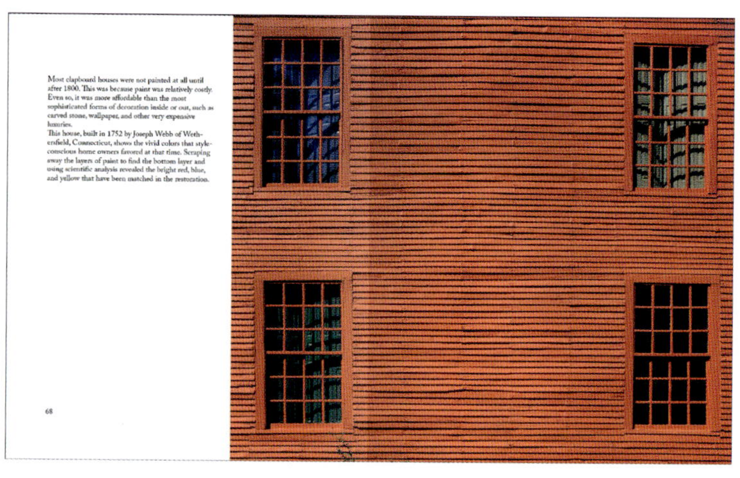
Most clapboard houses were not painted at all until after 1800. This was because paint was relatively costly. Even so, it was more affordable than the most sophisticated forms of decoration inside or out, such as carved stone, wallpaper, and other very expensive luxuries.
This house, built in 1752 by Joseph Webb of Wethersfield, Connecticut, shows the vivid colors that style-conscious home owners favored at that time. Scraping away the layers of paint to find the bottom layer and using scientific analysis revealed the bright red, blue, and yellow that have been matched in the restoration.

68

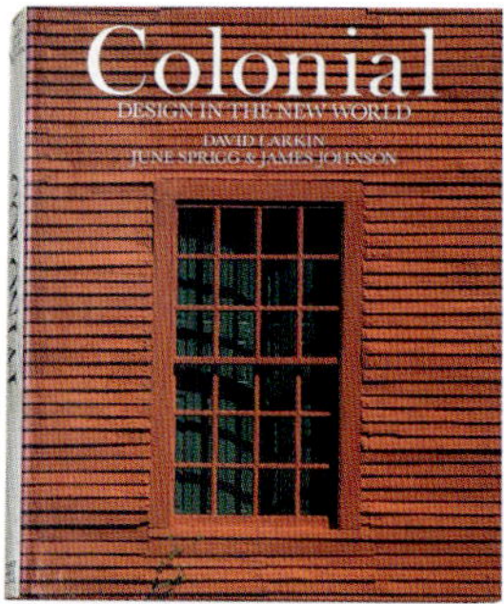

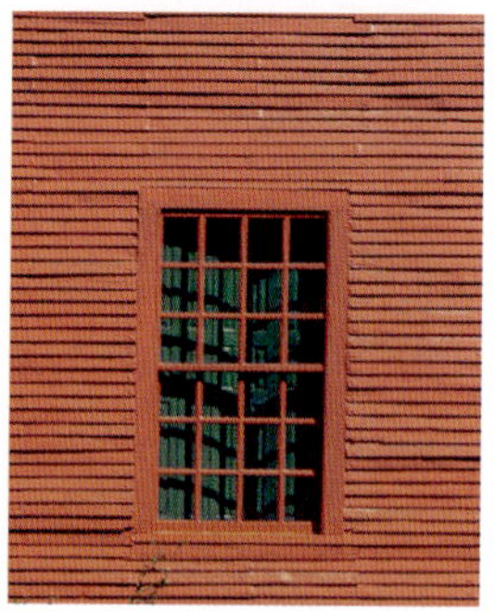

For a book on US Colonial architecture, the decision was taken to embrace the rigidity and formality of ordered rectangles rather than to find a way around them or turn them into other arrangements. That meant precise squared-up shooting and full-on repetition – as in the original architectural aesthetic of the period.

picked up the rectangular theme and extended it in the use of the typography. On the spread, the picture is cropped to reinforce the rectangle by placing the windows in the corners, and then the entire picture is given rectangular prominence on the double-page spread by running out to the edges of the pages and contrasting with the white rectangle on the left – and on top of this, the block of text is run as a rectangle aligned with the upper windows.

With the second barn, the picture has been cropped so that the four windows occupy a clean rectangular position lower left, and the roofline was positioned to create a precise triangle of sky. This emphasizes that the theme of the picture is geometric simplicity.

A Shaker cemetery in New England, unusually lit by a low sun from behind the camera in extremely clear air, casting a pattern of dense shadows that interlocks with the rectangles of the plain headstones.

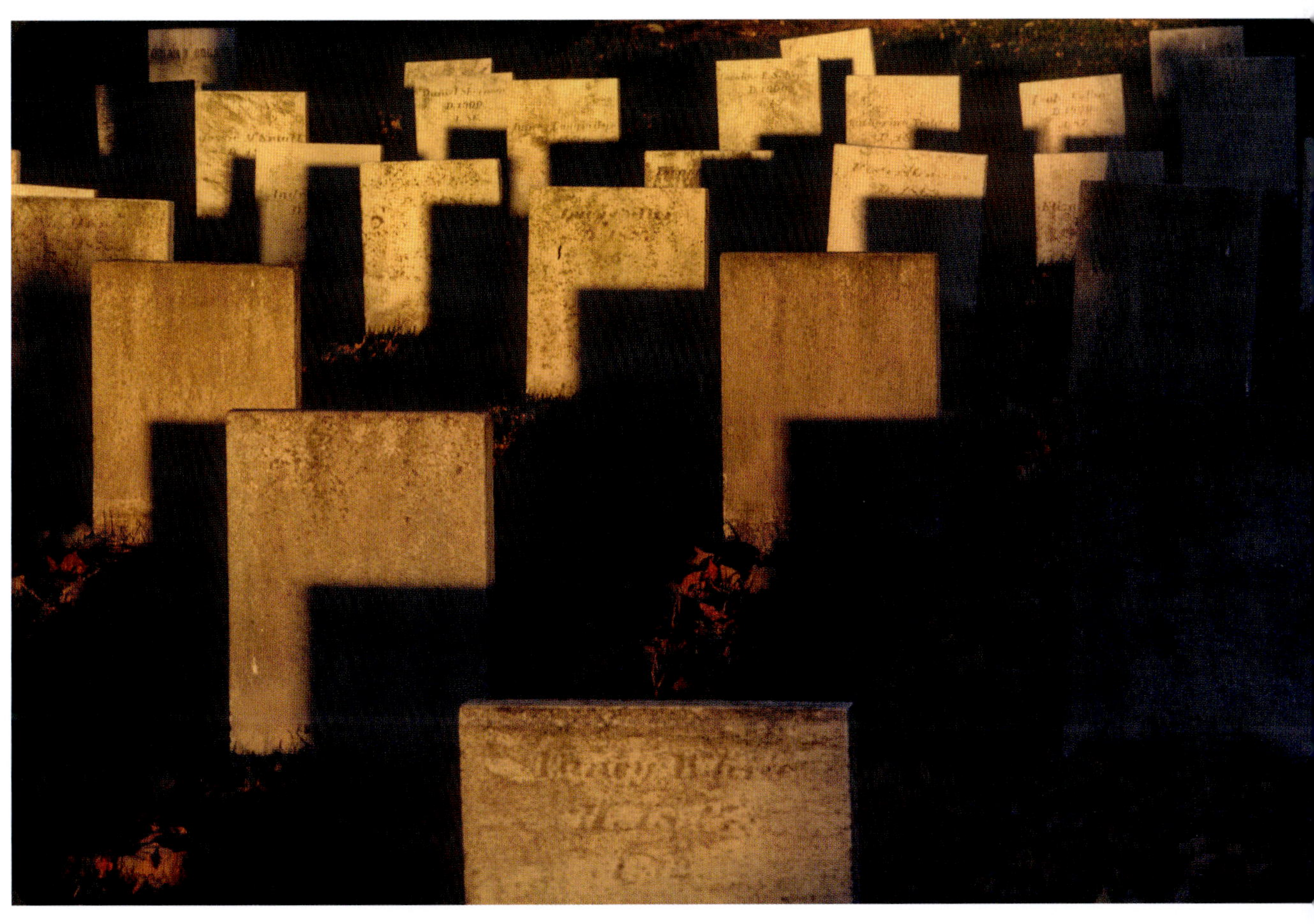

MONDRIANESQUE

Piet Mondrian was a Dutch Modernist painter whose work in the first half of the 20th century went on to have a huge influence way beyond the art world.

There's even a word, Mondrianesque, referring to the striking, simple and memorable style of his abstract and geometric compositions. Everyone knows them. Primary-coloured squares and rectangles set into a grid of black lines on a white background. Distinctive, strict and ordered, they get appropriated for all kinds of uses, and shooting squared-up full-frontal pictures is one of them (see page 42). Mondrian took infinite pains in his compositions, in particular the relationships in size and position between the primary colours enclosed by some of the grid lines. The closest analogy to this obsessive way of working in photography is studio still life, not the real world of fleeting capture – which is exactly why Mondrianesque composition can be so appealing on the rare occasions when you can make it work, as in these two examples. In one, an outdoor commodity exchange in Kolkata, the box-like trading booths presented many framing choices, from symmetrical to the one here. In the other, formed by the painted shutters of a market stall in Mauritius, they offered the opportunity to frame two incongruous subjects – a piece of artwork and a man's head. What both have in common is that they use rectangles as boxes to contain subjects, much in the same way that Mondrian used them to contain primary colours.

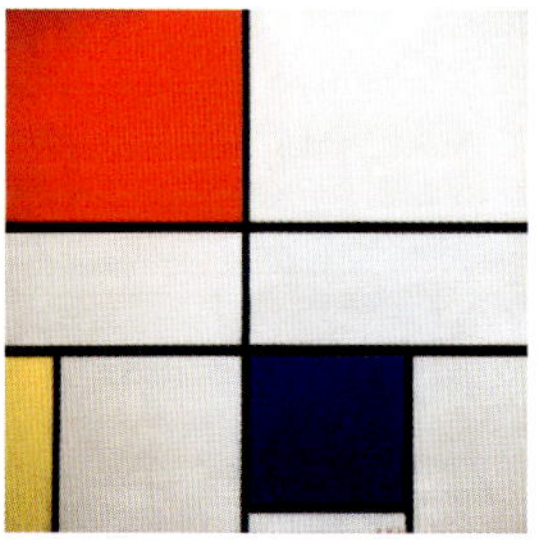

Composition C (No III) with Red, Yellow and Blue (1935) is an example of the classic Piet Mondrian style of a grid of lines enclosing solid rectangles of strong colours.

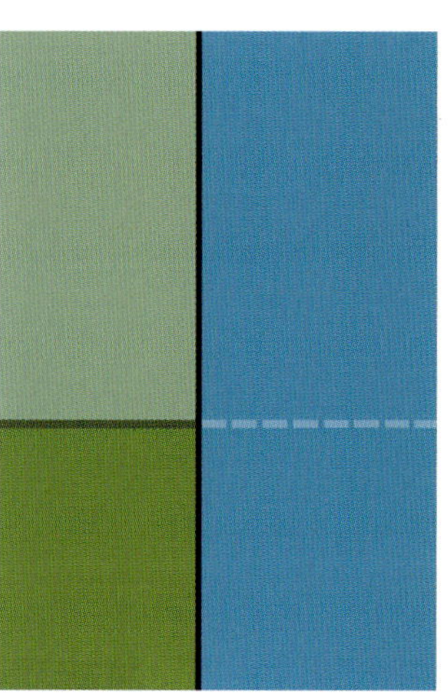

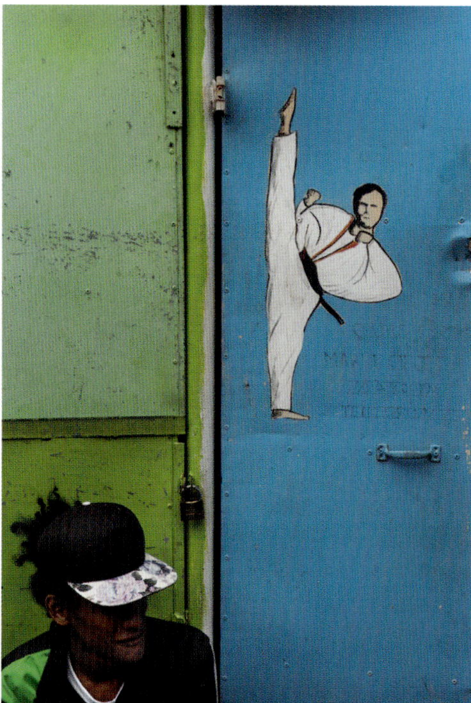

Here was a case where I started out trying to do one thing, found it wouldn't work, and then changed completely to a more unusual and very structured kind of picture. This was the weekly market in the old town of Mahébourg on the island of Mauritius, and I was after both island life and the tradition of painting buildings and frontages of different kinds with lively colours. This was a narrow passage between stalls, and I was after a candid shot of two young guys who were hanging out in the alleyway. That proved impossible, because they saw me immediately and I was just too close. Then I realized that I could do a different kind of shot by squaring up to the shutters, getting the head of one of them framed in one rectangle, and I set that against the quirky, hand-painted artwork advertising judo lessons.

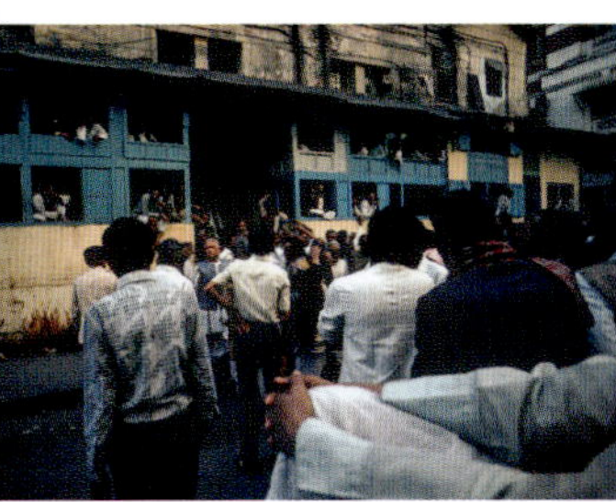

This old, almost open-air commodities exchange in Kolkata, India, was a picturesque oddity, with traders in tiny box-like booths. An animated scene, capable of being shot in different ways. What appealed most, however, was a frontal view so that the boxes appeared all squared-up and rectangular, framed so that each black space (with its inhabitant) was a different shape and size in the picture.

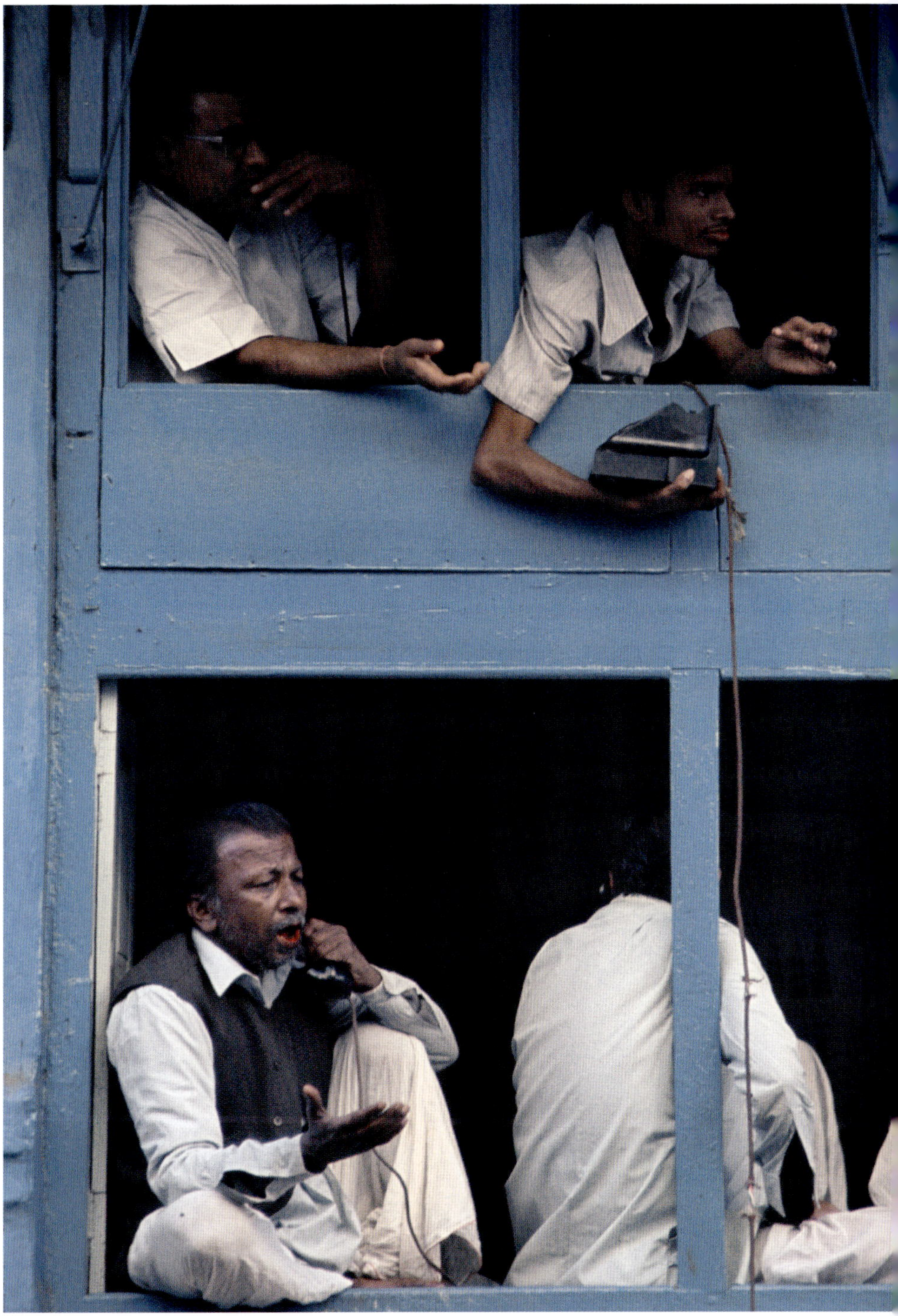

QUARTERING

Yet another riff on rectangles is quartering. It's useful for two reasons. First, it's extremely easy and intuitive to do without any actual measurement – dividing a rectangle into halves and quarters comes naturally, and there's no demand for accuracy. The quarters simply need to be approximate. Second, while an obvious treatment, it isn't particularly common, and so catches attention in an understated way.

→ For an art-directed book cover, the window pane in the door suggested a rectilinear kind of approach, which transformed easily into this simple, minimal quartered arrangement.

As both the examples here show, the technique is not simply a matter of dividing the frame into quarters but more about locating the main subject within one quarter. This is what makes it distinctive – and not so easy to pull off – because most scenes and situations simply don't lend themselves to this kind of arrangement. There needs to be a little something going on in a couple of the other 'quarters', and naturally some hint of a vertical and horizontal section. In the examples here, the necessary suggestions for dividing the frame have been aligned carefully. In the church shot, the left and top edges of the bible and the lights under the windows do the job, while in the typewriter picture, which was set up and art-directed, the desk and camera have been precisely positioned so that the right edge lines up with the edge of the glass window.

↙ An open bible on its lectern in an Oxford church. One practical reason for this arrangement was that it was being shot on square format (120 roll film) with a wide-angle lens (38mm Hasselblad SWC), and this was a way of avoiding converging verticals by keeping the camera level and relatively high on its tripod.

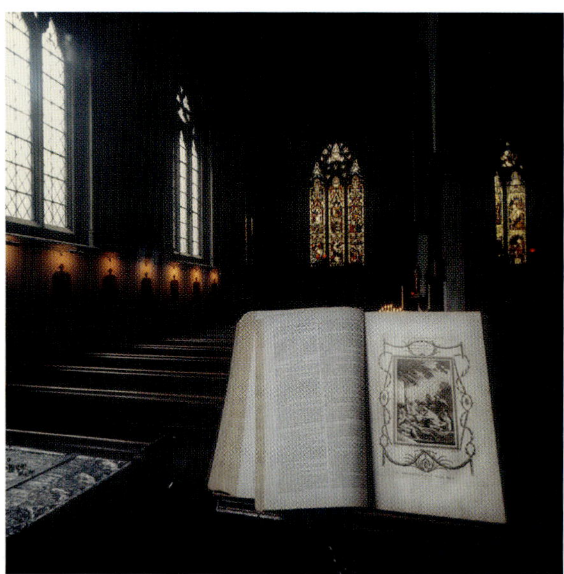

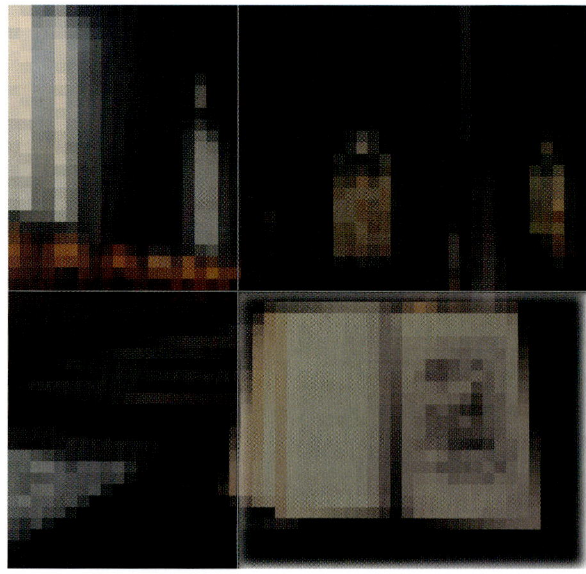

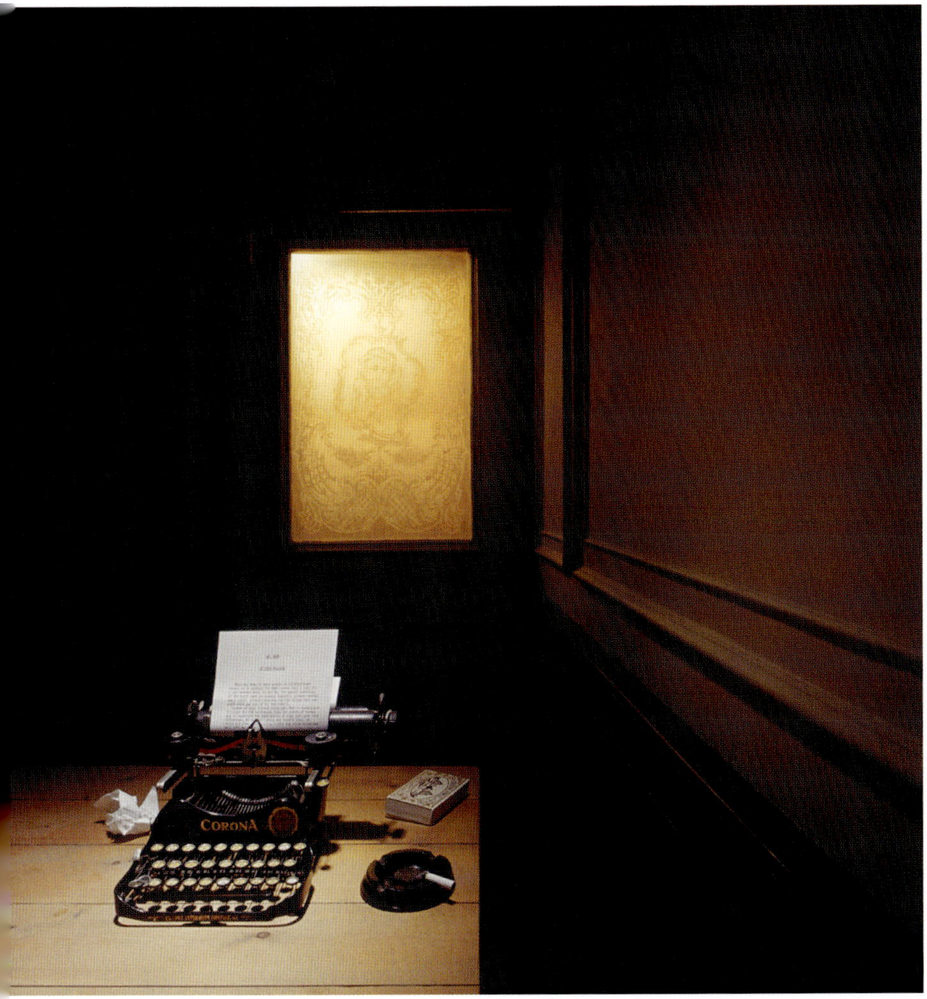

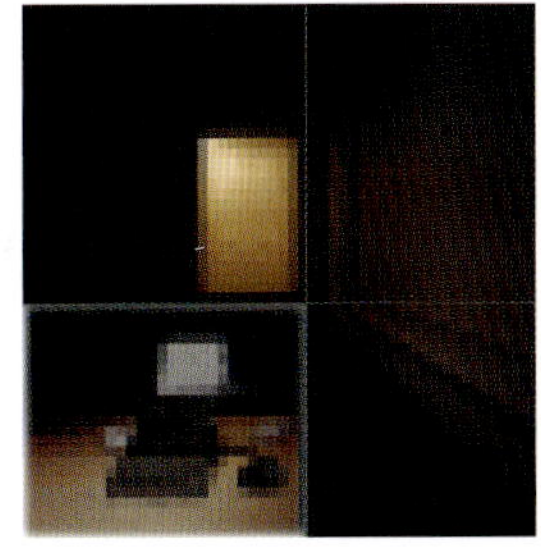

One limitation to using quartering is the absolute need for a set of horizontals and verticals. Converging verticals, for instance, destroy the idea. For the same reason of keeping things squared-up, quartering seems to work better on fatter formats, and best of all with a square format. Both of these pictures were shot on a square-format film camera with a wide-angle lens, and one influence in choosing a quartered style was to show the main subject (bible, typewriter) in its context without tilting the camera, so as to avoid converging verticals. Raising the camera, shooting level and locating the subject in a lower corner was the solution.

STATIC LINES

The shapes we've been looking at, mostly recently rectangles, are of course composed of lines, and they too have their own character. Straight lines immediately suggest man-made, and they usually are, although by no means completely.

It's logical to associate a straight line, especially if it's horizontal or vertical, with precision and design, and in the world in front of the camera this typically means architectural. But then, there's the horizon, and in flat terrain that's often the dominant line, and there are also rows of things, and long shadows from a low sun (by stretching the shape of whatever's casting them, they tend to straighten out).

Horizontal and vertical lines are by definition precise. A degree off and they have an angle, and because every image takes place inside a rectangular frame, we're very sensitive to this precision. The eye automatically compares them with the edges of the frame, and the closer they are to the edges, the more critical we are. The eye naturally expects and demands them to be accurate. For these reasons, horizontals and verticals have a sense of rigidity, exactness and control. They're locked inside the frame. This can be a positive or negative quality, depending on how you treat them, and also on what a viewer's basic expectations from the subject are. The negative side, simply put, is boring and predictable, a common issue with architectural photographs.

While the scene at this Yunnanese Buddhist monastery was unpromising on arrival – cluttered and disorganized – the situation gradually resolved itself in an unusually ordered arrangement of rectangles and a circle, equally spaced, from a frontal viewpoint.

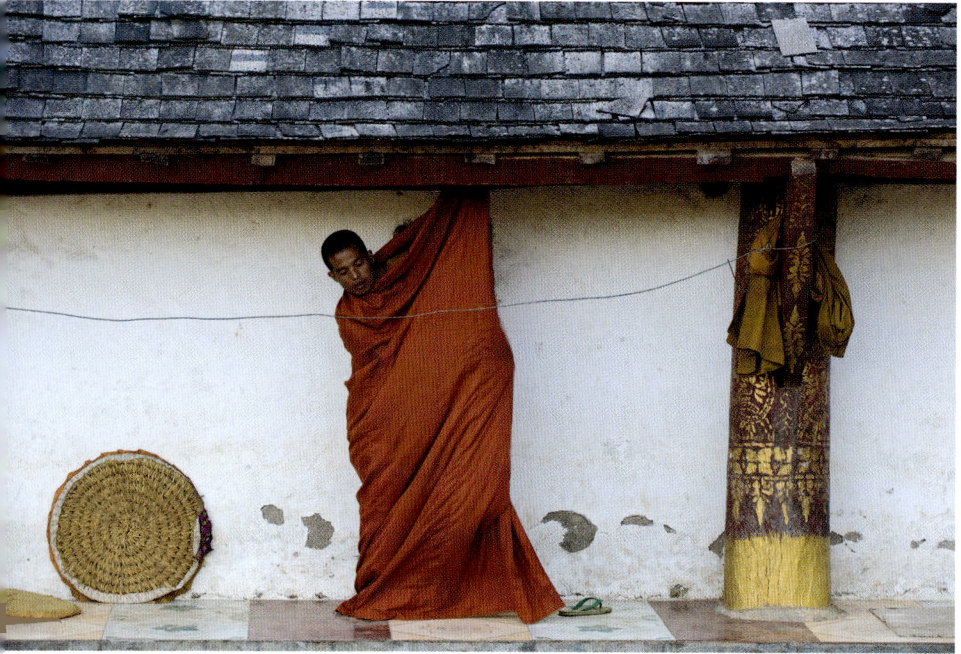

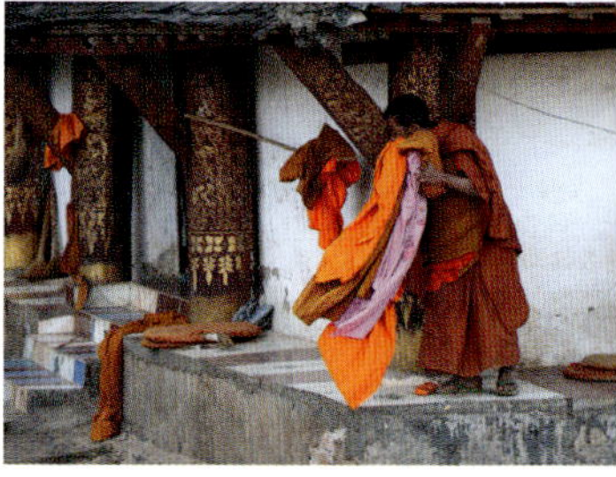

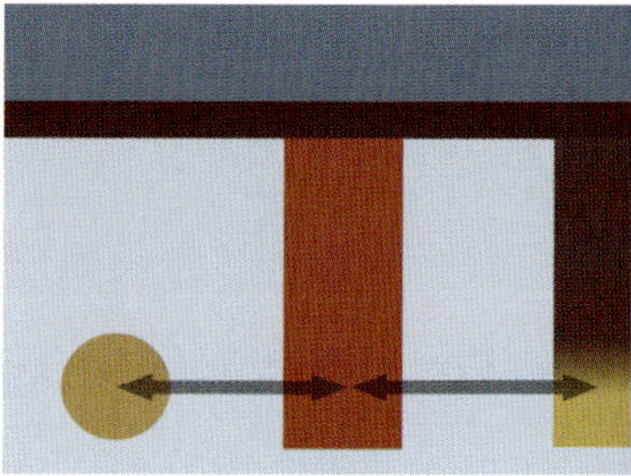

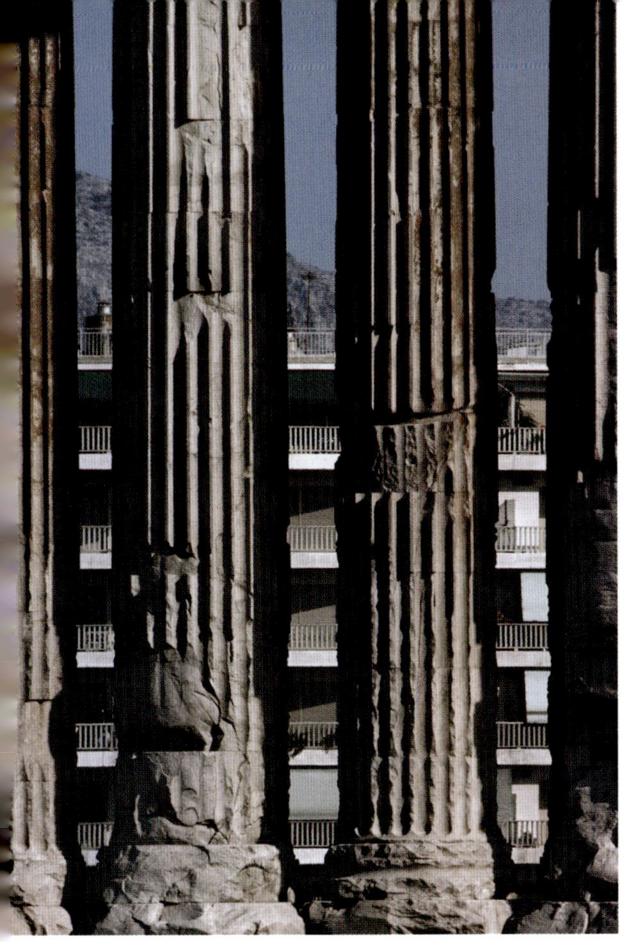

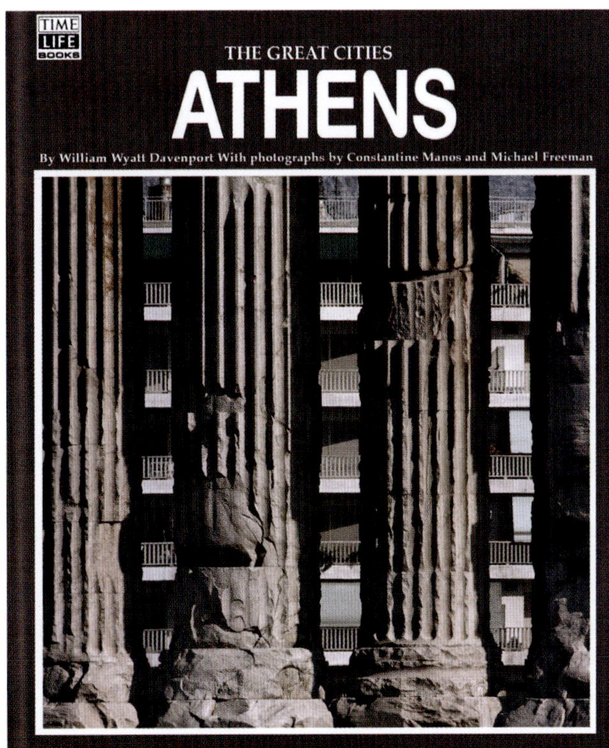

There are two escape routes. One is to exaggerate and double-down on the precision and rigidity, the other is to find the precision in situations where you wouldn't normally expect it. The two examples here show this difference. Amplifying the precision means, for example, finding repetition and also closing in to eliminate any other lines, and that's exactly what happened in the picture of the Temple of Olympian Zeus in Athens, which was shot for the cover of a Time–Life book on the city. This was an art-directed shot designed to contrast antiquity (vertical columns) with modernity (horizontal apartment balconies). At the other end, there are scenes that you can sometimes turn into horizontal-vertical structures by timing and viewpoint, as in the case of the rural Buddhist monastery in southwestern China. The situation didn't seem to have much structure at first, but with luck and perseverance it came together, and the lines – or rather, bands – made it unexpectedly graphic.

↑ The overlay of verticals (the columns and spaces between) and horizontals (the façade of an apartment block behind), met the art director's needs for a statement of contrast between old and new for this book on Athens.

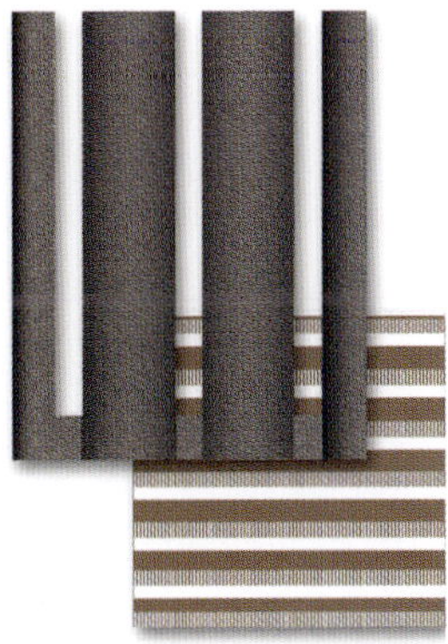

ANGULAR ENERGY

If horizontals and verticals aligning themselves with the picture frame give out a sense of being grounded and ordered, diagonals challenge and energize. This is partly because they simply differ from horizontals and verticals, and partly because of associations with movement.

There's no need to take these associations literally, any more than treating a horizontal as a real base or a vertical as actually rising, but somewhere in the background of perception, the notion of gravity creeps in slightly. Diagonals carry some sense of a slope, with a hint of rising or falling.

When there's the opportunity to vary the angle, as in both of these examples for instance, one key decision is how strong to make the diagonal. This is basically a matter of degree and length. If the shape of the frame were not an issue, the most diagonal degree – meaning the most different from horizontal and vertical – would of course be around 45°. However, the aspect ratio matters because of the corners. They can play a special role with diagonals, not only because corner-to-corner is the longest, and therefore strongest, diagonal possible, but because 'pointing' into a corner is a natural compositional fit, as you can see on pages 10–11, 12 and 64. This does not mean that there's any obligation to aim for the corner, but it helps if you're trying to bring order to the image. If you're shooting with a normal full-frame 3:2 ratio, then the strongest diagonal will be 33° (clearly, precision to the degree isn't the issue). A more extreme technique – more a style, really – is tilting the camera when shooting horizontally, and I'll come to that in the last chapter (see page 160).

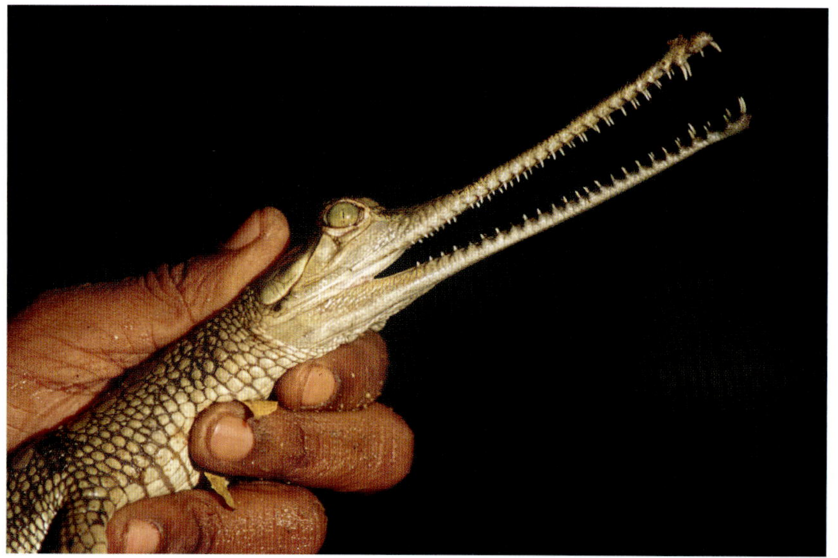

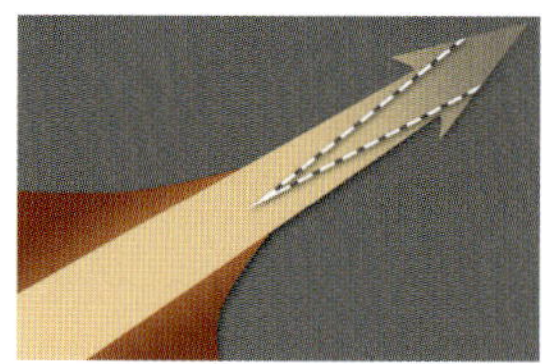

← A young *gharial* at the Madras Crocodile Bank held by one of its keepers. The corner-to-corner framing was a natural, but the slim reverse triangle formed when it opened its jaws doubles up on the diagonal theme.

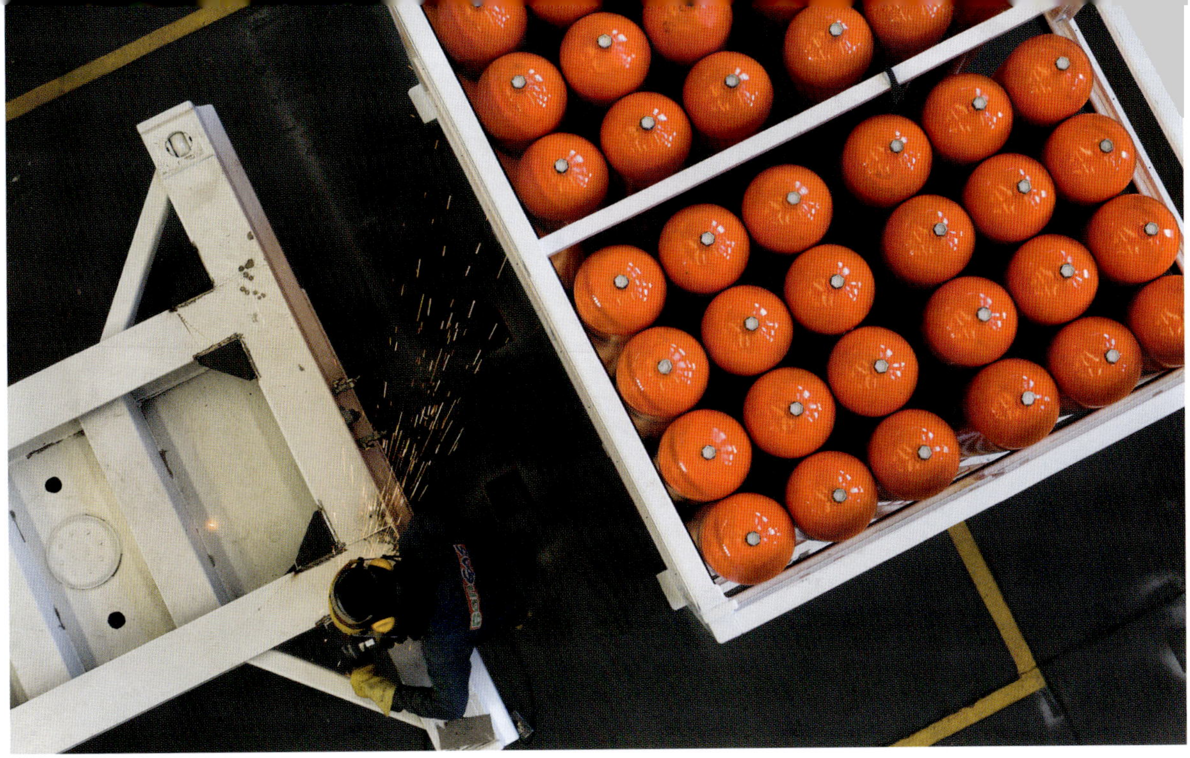

Multiples of diagonal lines usually reinforce each other visually, as you'd expect, and if they're parallel, that's fairly straightforward. However, if they're at different angles, and particularly if they diverge or converge, there's a much stronger sense of movement and of drawing the eye, as we'll see in Chapter 7 (see page 142).

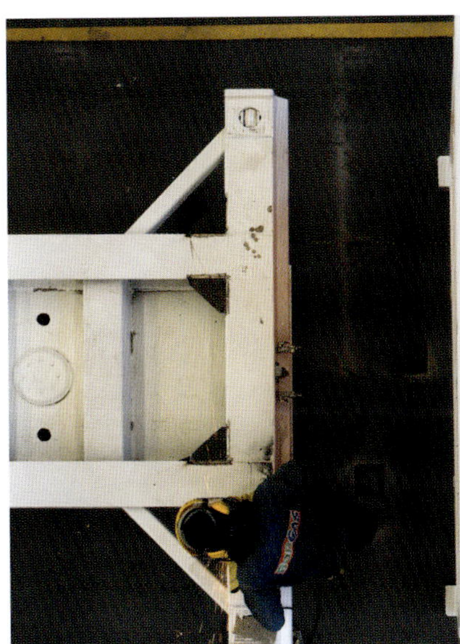

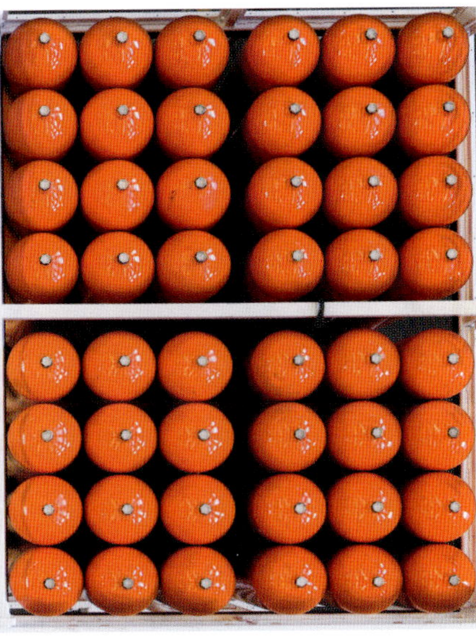

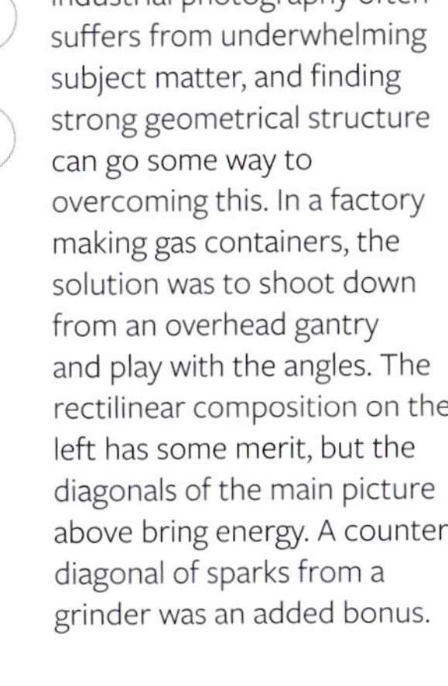

Industrial photography often suffers from underwhelming subject matter, and finding strong geometrical structure can go some way to overcoming this. In a factory making gas containers, the solution was to shoot down from an overhead gantry and play with the angles. The rectilinear composition on the left has some merit, but the diagonals of the main picture above bring energy. A counter diagonal of sparks from a grinder was an added bonus.

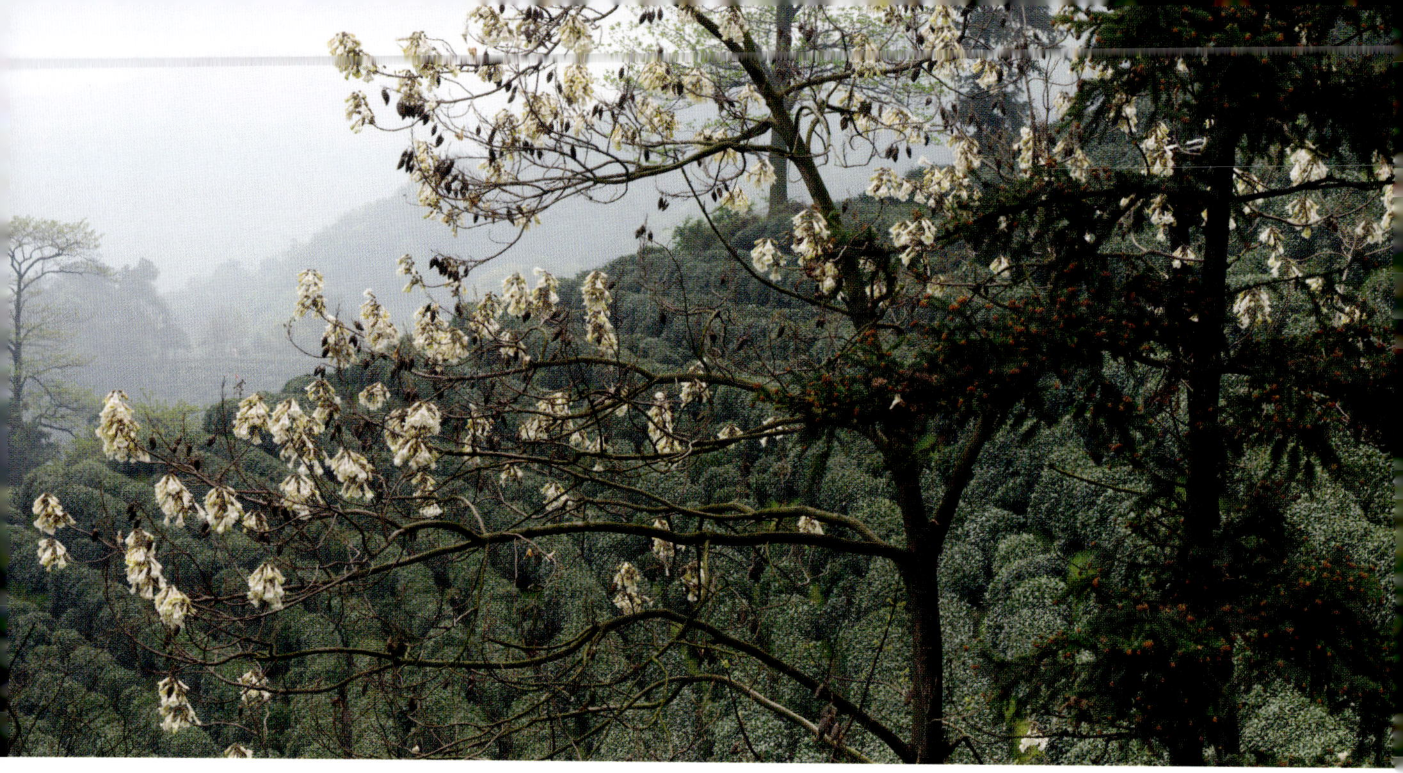

THE FLOW OF CURVES

Curves work differently from any kind of straight line, not just because they are less common and so catch more attention when they do appear, but because they are almost always seen positively by viewers.

They seem to be inherently attractive, and this may be because they invoke a sense of flow, continuity and smoothness. They also play a useful part in containing parts of a scene, as we'll explore on pages 94–5. Straight lines are much more characteristic of man-made things, are simpler and generally come with angles at the ends. A curve, on the other hand, is defined by its smoothness and absence of kinks or irregularities. The problem with curves-by-suggestion is that while three points can suggest a triangle, and three or four can suggest a straight line, curves need several to many. As a result, most curves that are compositionally useful for photography tend to be the edges of rounded things.

As with all the graphic elements that we've been looking at in this chapter, curves become interesting for photography when they are not ready-made, but when the photographer has been able to find or suggest them by some effort, such as viewpoint or juxtaposition, and when they are at least slightly unexpected. In real-life shooting, they're hard to plan for. The tea-picking shot here is a good example of this. The main curve (dark green line) is a coincidence of the slope of the hill and one

↑ The repeating curves of tea terraces, hill outline and flowers on branches elevate this tea-picking shot by creating an unexpected, yet also understated, structure to the frame. The small picture (below) is from lower down the same hill looking up, showing the importance of viewpoint in creating the curves.

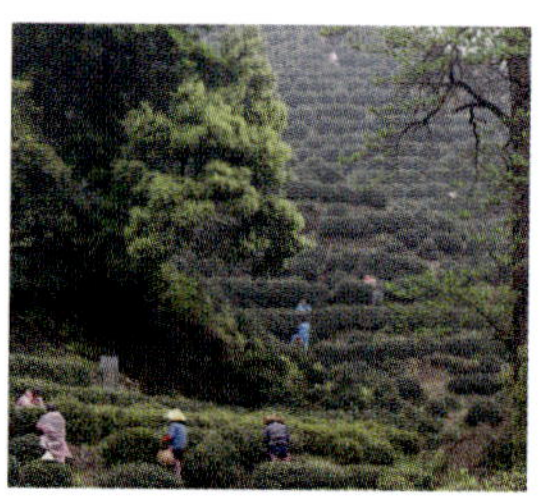

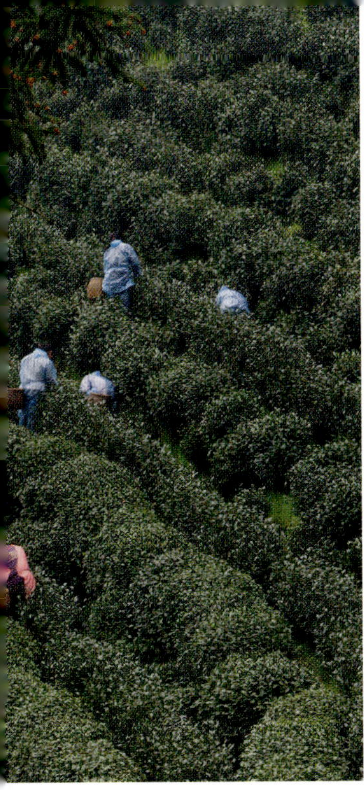

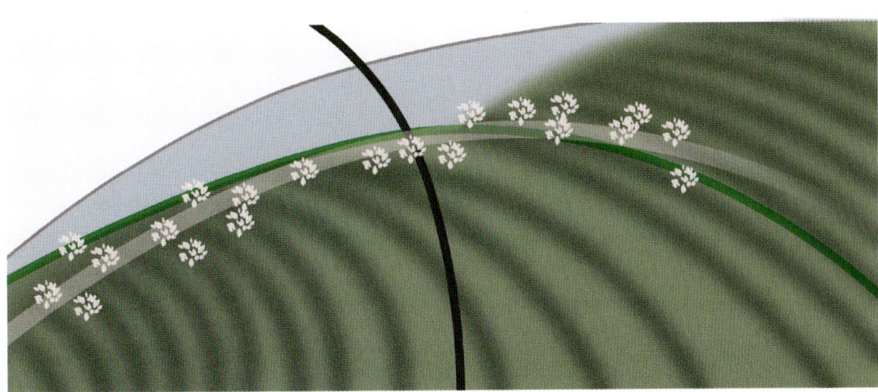

or two of the rows of bushes, and it exists only because of this viewpoint and some branches obscuring the 'join'. The view from lower down the hill has none of this. The graphic theme is then picked up by the repeating curves of tea bushes up and down the slope – again, these are purely a matter of viewpoint. The curve of the distant hill and of the slender tree trunk in the middle are happy extras, but the real bonus is the pattern of Paulownia flowers forming a curved arc over the scene. This also shows that curves in multiples reinforce each other and are more special compositionally.

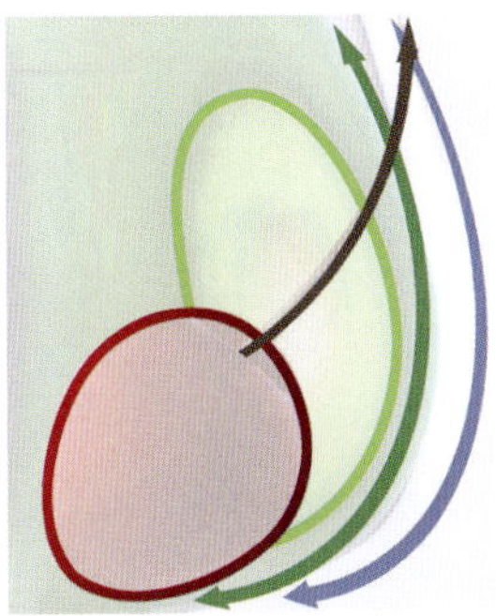

More repetition of curves in a still-life close-up. The curves of the glass, the cherry and its stalk are further picked up by refraction in the liquid, which creates a kidney-shaped highlight.

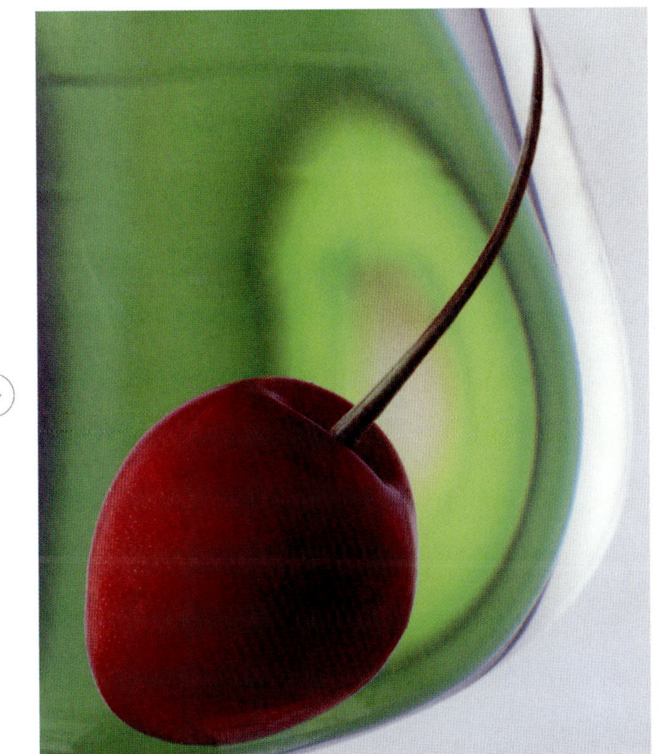

CHAPTER

5

HIDDEN INFLUENCES

For the most part, up to now I've been trying to show what to do with the design of a photograph in order to achieve a particular effect, but the world of predicting or guessing how viewers are going to react is ultimately built on people's subconscious and unconscious visual habits. When you purposefully – let's say mindfully – look at an image and examine it, you're using cognition. But that demands attention and usually also some inspiration or motive for doing it. At other times, when you're simply taking in a picture without any intensity, a number of hidden influences are at play, and these are what I want to look at now, starting with salience, which is the quality of standing out and drawing attention. Once again, I'm invoking the help of eye-tracking research to show how our eyes naturally go to certain subjects and graphic combinations, how long they stay there, whether they revisit, and so on.

I introduced the idea of Gestalt to photography with *The Photographer's Eye* back in 2005, when it seemed a slightly oddball theory. Since then it's become mainstream – but for web design. At least now it is reasonably well understood, and I'm emphasizing it in this chapter because it underpins so much of the way we react to composition, both as photographers making a photo and as viewers looking at it. There's even a risk that because so many of the principles of Gestalt seem so obvious once they're pointed out, that they discourage taking any action. By that I mean that they can fall into the category of 'I'm doing that already. Why should I do anything different?'

Indeed, Gestalt isn't worth much if all it encourages is nodding the head and treating it as a theory that explains what we already know. Being practical about it is much more interesting. Photographically, there are two ways of using Gestalt principles. You can act to reinforce them or you can turn images around to challenge expectations, and it's this second technique that can be powerful. Gestalt is, indeed, all about expectations, which is why in the following pages I'm giving them the titles of 'need to do this' or 'need for that'. There are several principles (they used to be called 'laws', but that's way too definite) that most people agree on, although the number isn't fixed. Most are related to each other, some more closely than others.

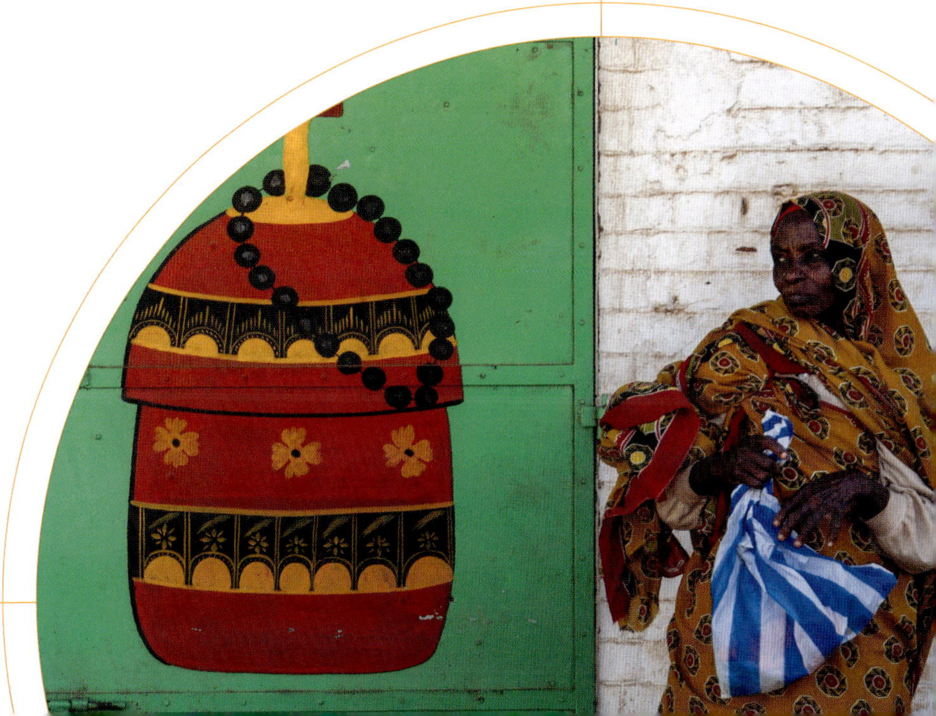

SALIENCE

Salience is how much visual attraction something has, and as we're talking strictly about photographs, it's about elements inside the picture frame. What catches attention the most?

This is all about standing out from the surroundings, so for our purposes there are two kinds of salience. One is purely graphic, like a black dot catching attention if it's in a bright patch, or a regular pattern, like a chequerboard. The other is about content, like a human face, which we're automatically drawn to – technically, this is known as semantics. Photographs often contain both, and they can compete for attention. Moreover, many photographs have more than one subject, so salience becomes a matter of what a viewer looks at first, and for how long, before moving on to look at something else. This all happens very quickly, because photographs as we view them are much smaller than the real world around us, and are framed so that we know we're going to be looking inside them (see pages 16–17),

Salience becomes interesting for photographers when you have different visual elements in the frame, either content or graphics, because they'll be competing for attention. In fact, more than just simple attention – there's the order of viewing, the time spent on each, how many times each gets seen, how many revisits, even the speed of moving from one to another. It also comes into play when your main subject is small or out of the way, as in the well-known 'figure-in-a-landscape' style, which we'll see later, on pages 98–9 and 140–1. Getting the balance right between size and salience makes pictures more engaging and interesting to look at.

I chose this picture to start with precisely because it has several points of interest, none of them central, and I was fully aware of that as I was shooting. Here was a narrow old lane in the city of Cartagena, Colombia devoted to small stalls repairing watches and, more recently, mobile phones. It's a traditional part of the fast-disappearing old city. My eye was caught by the signage, including electoral posters, and I decided to make a 'busy' image with a lot of detail but without a central main subject. I expected the viewer's eye to go first to the face of the man at left and the prominent lettering next to that, then to the face on the poster, and then to the right by way of the other signage. In other words, move around the scene, taking in different details. I also chose this viewpoint and moment with the deliberate intention of delaying recognition of the man on the right, bent over his repair work. In other words, that he would be seen only after a while, not immediately. A delaying strategy, but I hoped people would find him interesting.

→ A street scene of watch and phone repair stalls with prominent faces and lettering, in which the composition attempted to guide the viewer through the scene as shown in the diagram below, starting with the face at left, then moving through lettering and the face on a poster to the much less obvious face at right.

TERMS USED IN EYE-TRACKING

AOI Area of interest. What you as the photographer decide should attract attention.

FIXATION Where the eye halts in an image.

GAZE PATH Line showing eye movement from one fixation to the next.

FIXATION COUNT How many times the eye rests on a part of the scene.

TTFF Time to first fixation. Basically, the hit rate – the order of viewing.

DWELL TIME Total time spent on a particular AOI.

REVISIT COUNT How many times the eye went back to a specific part of the scene.

HEAT MAP Aggregate of all fixations colour-coded by amount of time spent where.

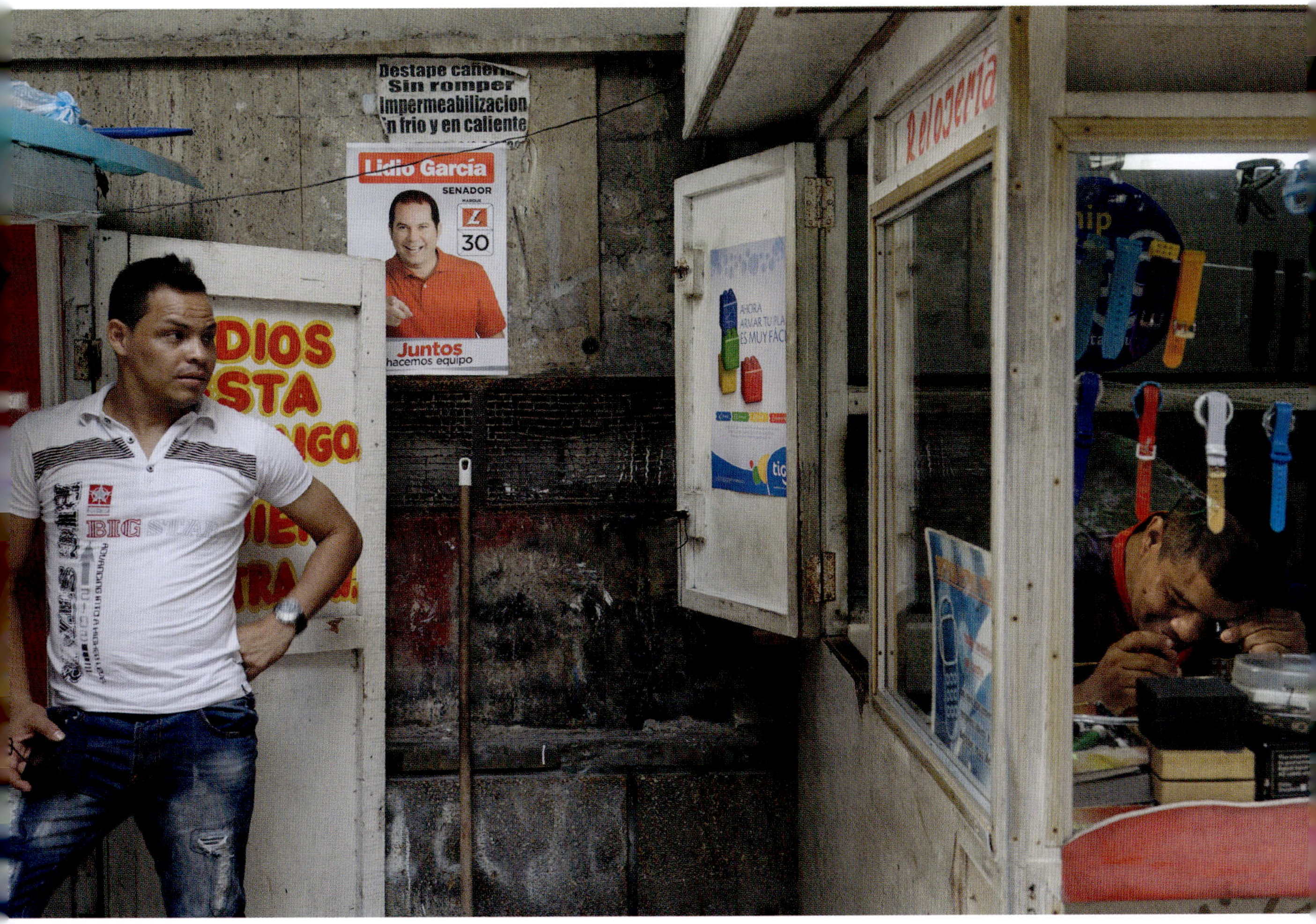

INTENDED VIEWING

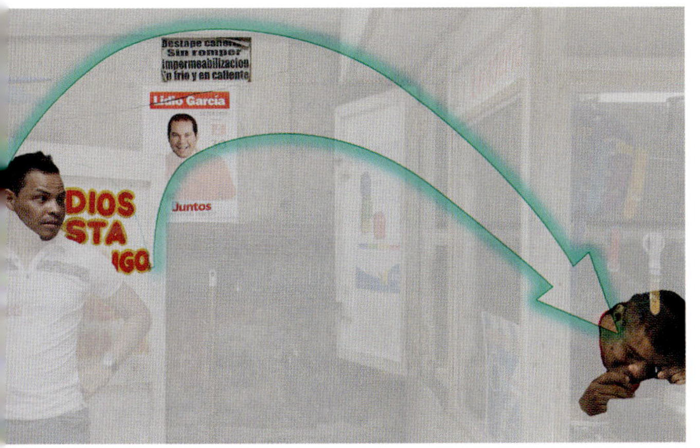

SUBJECT 3

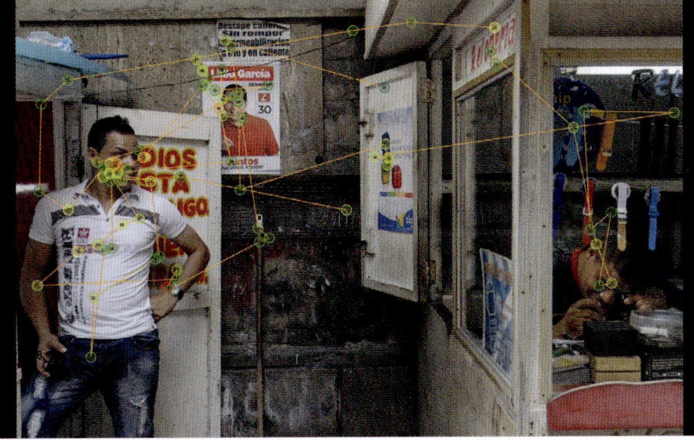

EYE-TRACKING

The team at iMotions then did their tests, and presented the viewing data in three ways. Here, you can see the gaze paths and fixations for one typical viewer, also a heat map that combines all the tests, and a hit rate of all tests combined showing which part of the frame was viewed first, then second, and so on. I was relieved that for once I'd got it right in the order of viewing. As we'll see in a few pages, under Visual Weight, faces and signage (lettering) are strong pulls – and it doesn't matter whether the face is 'real' or another photograph within this photograph. So it took on average just over 7 seconds for the bent-over watch repairer to be noticed – also satisfying was that he held the viewers' attention for longer than any other part of the scene after the poster (9 seconds to 16 seconds), more even than the man's face on the left. Only two small things I hadn't expected: one was that some viewers spent quite a lot of time on the black lettering at the top (Subject 1, below). Did that mean they were trying to read it? Could they read Spanish? And more attention was paid to the mobile phone held in the man's hand in the bottom left than I had paid at the time. In fact, I don't think I noticed it. But, as the eye-tracking of the first 10 seconds for one viewer shows (Subject 2, below right), the attention didn't even reach the watch repairer at right in the time. Now you might think this a failure, but for me it was a success because I wanted viewers to take time to get that far, and this subject did eventually, after 20 seconds.

→ A colour-coded heat map aggregates everyone's fixations, giving an instant view of what points in the picture were salient, and to what degree. It evens out the individual idiosyncrasies.

SUBJECT 1

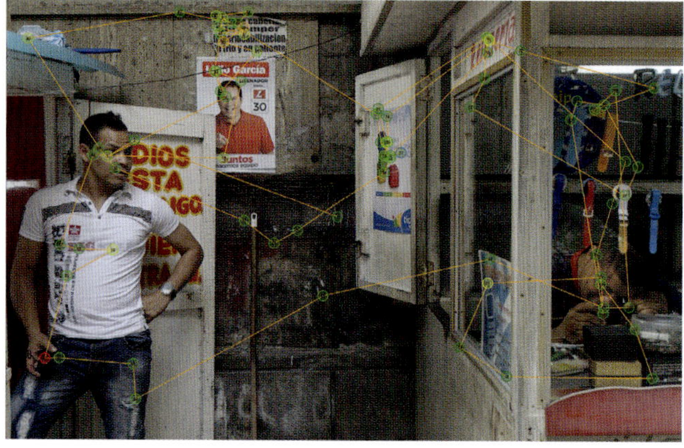

SUBJECT 2 (FIRST 10 SECONDS)

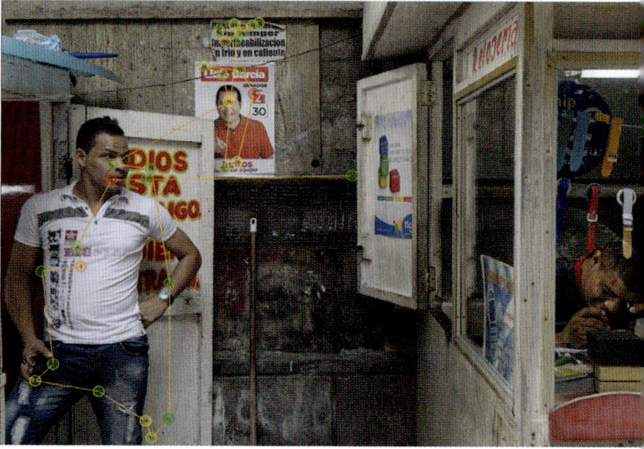

I should say at this point that salience answers only some questions about composition, even though it's impressively backed up by eye-tracking technology. With experience, you can predict fairly well how most people will look at a photograph, but then what they think or feel about it is another matter. So this is not about how successful a photograph is, however you care to measure that. I quite like this picture, though it isn't a great shot, and I have no idea what others think of it, other than by asking them directly.

→ An alternative overall view is a ranking by TTFF (time to first fixation) applied to a large grid. The rectangles are numbered in the order in which people (averaged) looked at them first.

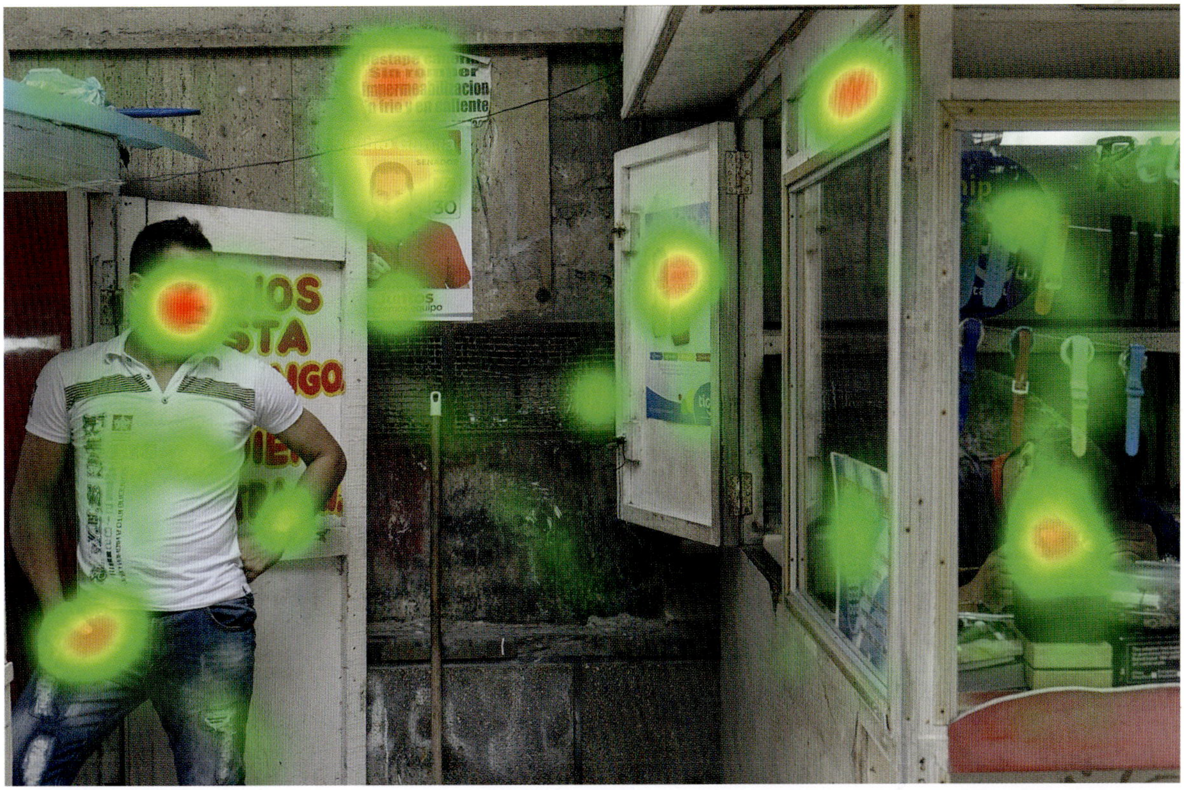

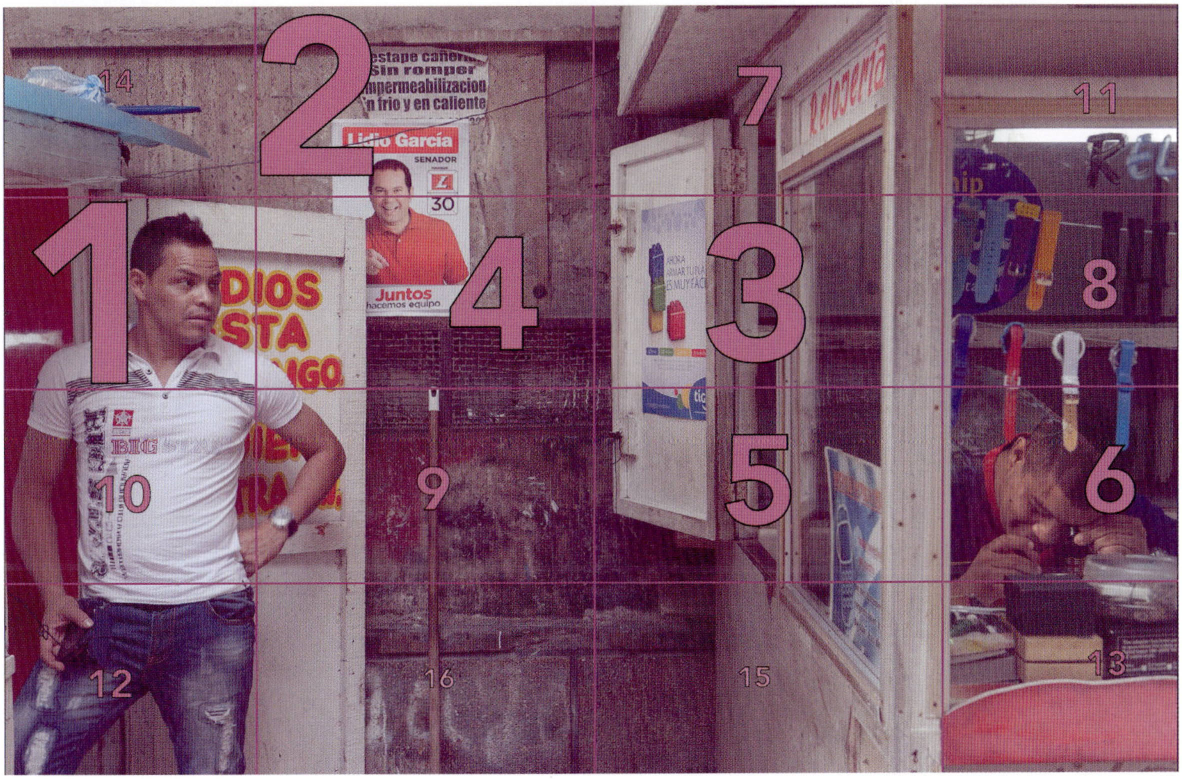

estape cañeria
Sin romper
impermeabilizacion
en frio y en caliente
Lidio García
SENADOR
30
Juntos
hacemos equipo
Relojeria
1
2
3
4
5
6
7
8
9
10
11
12
13
14
15
16

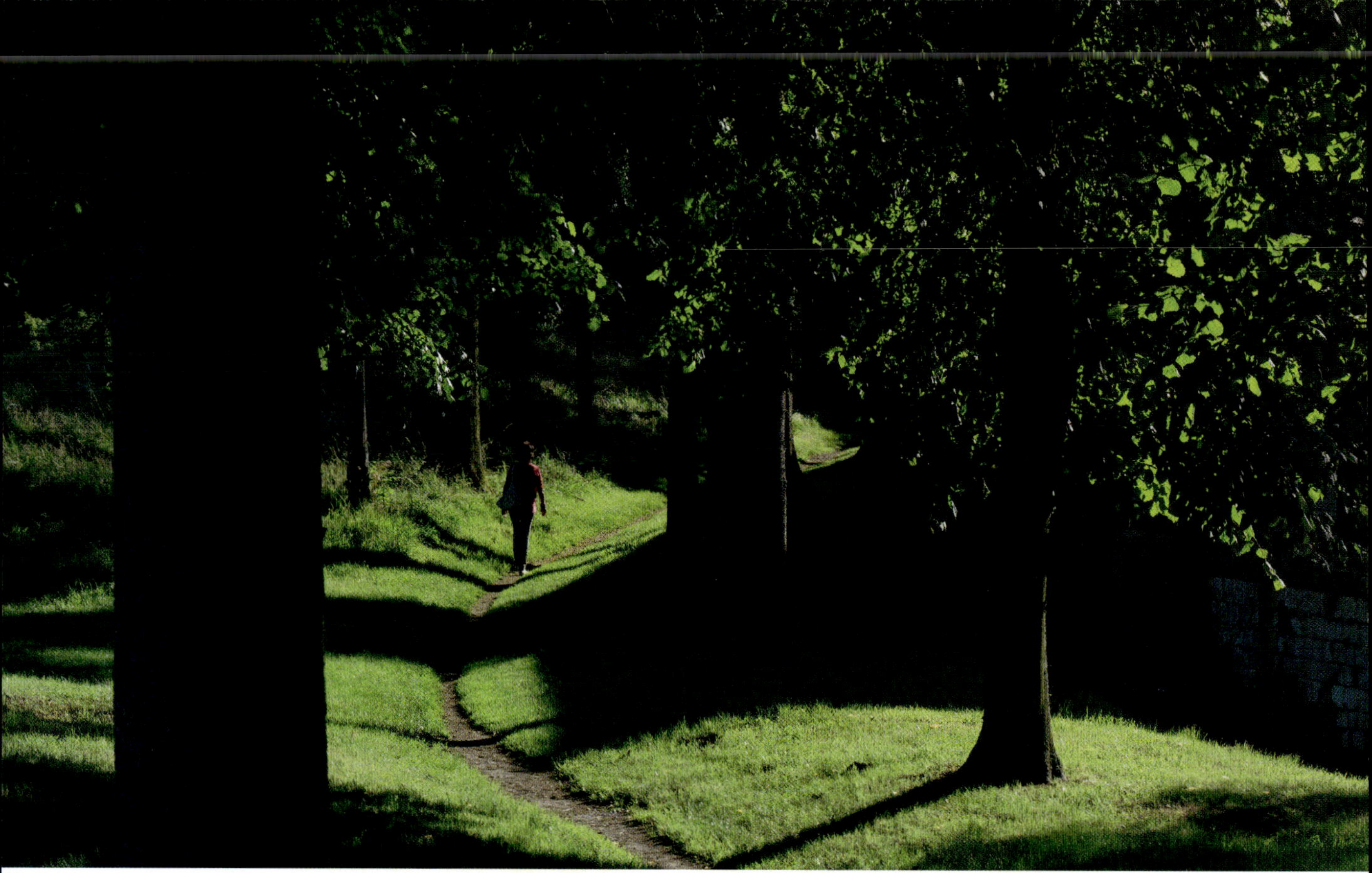

SUBJECT 1

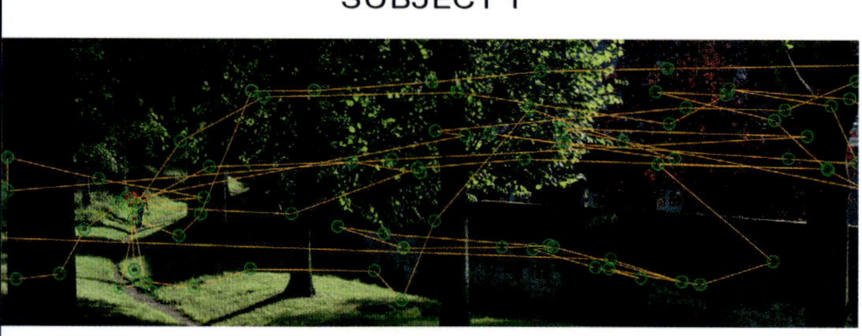

SUBJECT 2

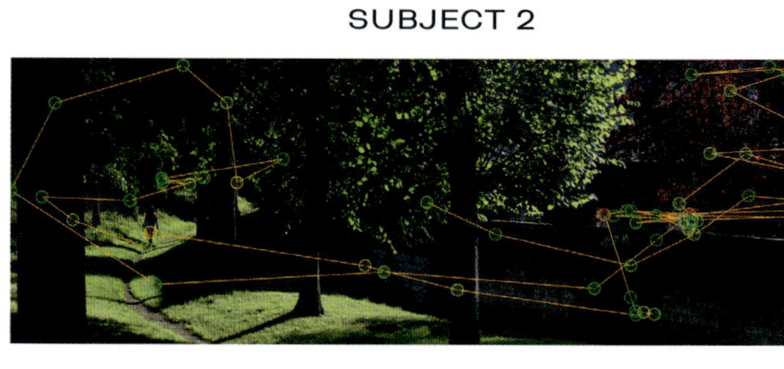

SUBJECT 3

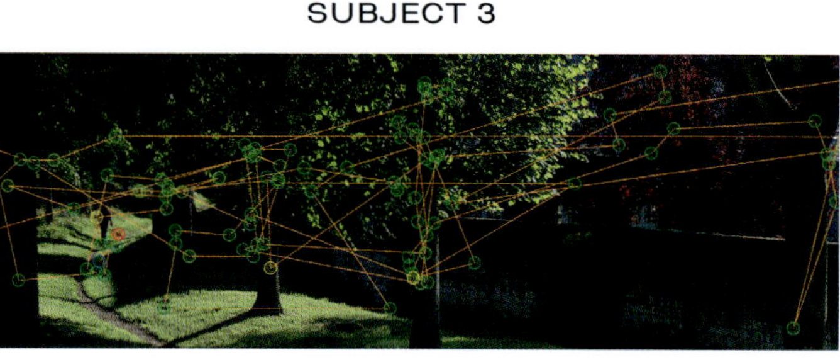

HEAT MAP

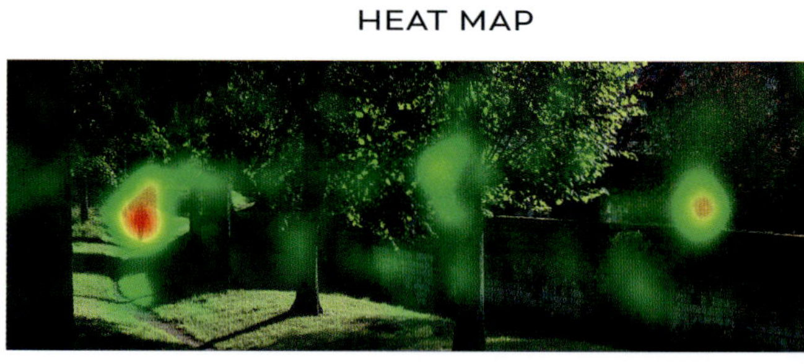

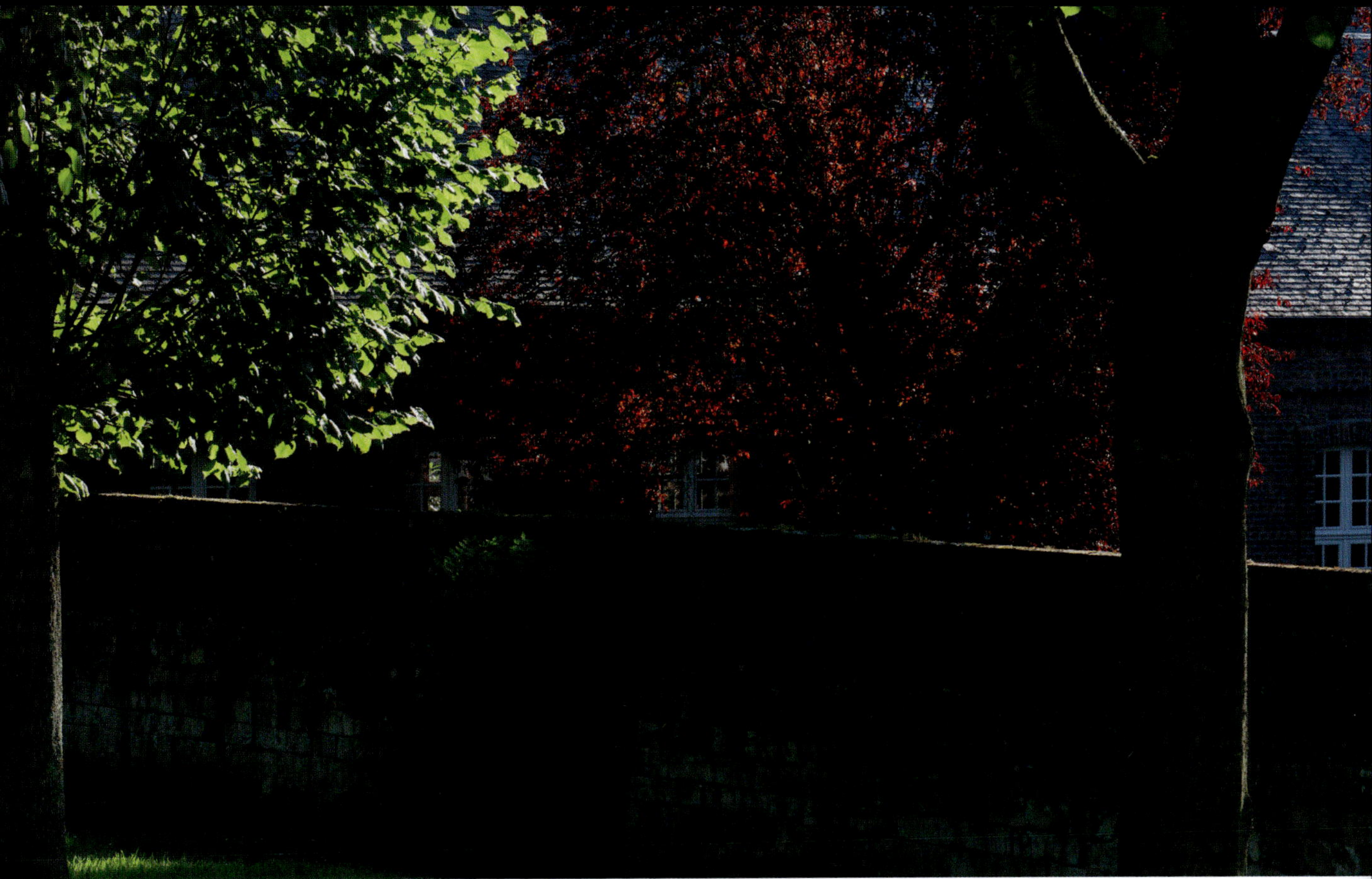

Different areas of interest within the frame between the three subjects at left show how individualistic viewers can be, but when many are added together, the average is usually predictable, as the heat map illustrates.

This shot is of a grassy walk around the complete medieval ramparts in a small French town, and the setting was the main subject. The lighting was attractive, partly backlit, and the colours rich. The wide framing followed from this – more below and above would lessen the impact of the walkway – and I wanted to include both the red leaves on the right and a space at the far left for a walking figure that would give scale and add human interest. I waited for the figure to move into that lit area for maximum contrast. I wanted to encourage the viewer's eye to move strongly horizontally from one end to the other, so I waited for the figure to reach the far left. I wasn't expecting much of a delay in seeing the figure, but I did want viewers to take in the entire scene with a lot of horizontal eye movement.

The iMotions testing confirmed this, and Subject 1 at left was typical, but also raised some other small questions. Subject 3 spent most of their attention on the tree trunks, while Subject 2 was absorbed by the windows on the right and paid very little attention to the figure. In fact, Subject 2's gaze didn't even get to the figure during the first 10 seconds. That was a reminder to me that individuals bring their own interests (or lack of) to a picture, although when all viewers were combined, as in the heat map, the spread of attention was indeed broad as hoped for. Looking more closely at how the small figure in its patch of light caught attention, it took just under 3 seconds to be noticed (for me a satisfying small delay), yet it held attention for 17 percent of the time, was fixated 8 times and revisited 4 times. All this despite occupying only 1 percent of the picture.

VISUAL WEIGHT

Intimately connected to salience is the built-in attraction of certain subjects, some of which we've just seen. Essentially, they attract the eye more for their size than do other things.

They have a kind of visual weight, and quite a lot of this is predictable, as eye-tracking proves. The most eye-pulling of all is the human face, after which the human form, then human parts, beginning with hands. Animals and other living things follow, and it's not hard to see this as a really basic evolutionary effect. Then there are words – lettering, numbers, particularly in the form of signage, which is a part of the modern urban landscape. They can even overwhelm A-list subjects, though hardly ever the human face. This even applies in a language foreign to the viewer, and that leads us on to the visual weight of graphic configurations. Areas of high local contrast have strong visual weight whether or not they coincide with a regular object. For instance, the man's striped shirt on page 18, even though insignificant as a subject, caught viewers' eyes in a controlled test, and it's wise to be sensitive to this kind of eye pull.

Lower down in the hierarchy are things that depend on the 'trainspotting' effect, where if you're very much taken up by a particular theme or interest of some kind, anything associated with that will automatically have a strong visual weighting – for you. It also depends on what else is in the frame, so just one face in a picture is stronger than several.

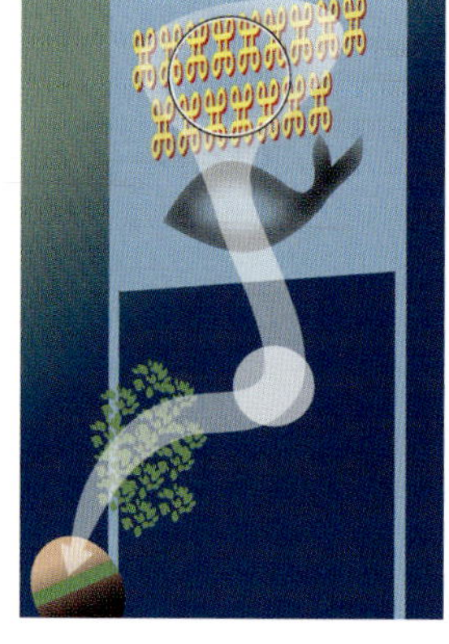

The striking signage over this fish stall in Cuzco, Peru is bound to pull the eye immediately, but by placing it at the top of the frame and adding a kind of 'counterweight' of the head of a traditionally hatted woman, the gaze path of a viewer can be encouraged to flow as shown above.

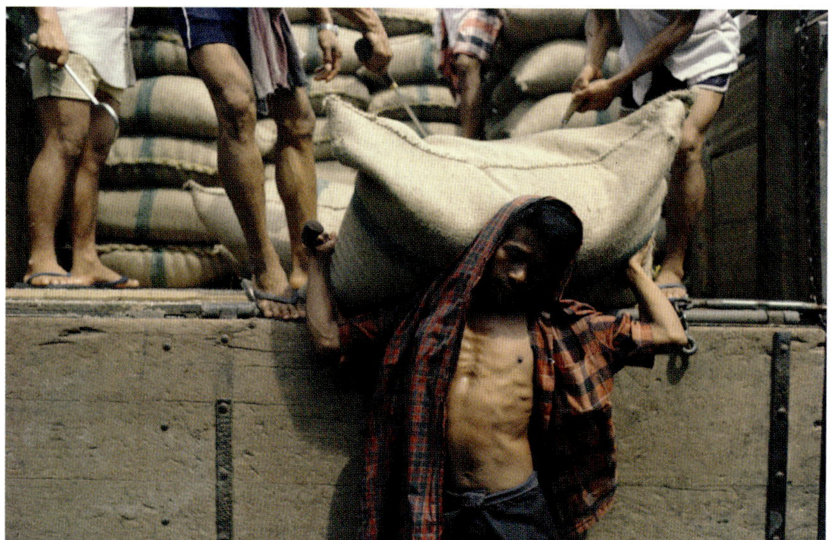

The face of a rice stevedore draws immediate attention despite lacking graphic contrast, as proved if we abstract the image by rotating it. The gaze then goes to 1: the white sack, and 2: the criss-cross pattern.

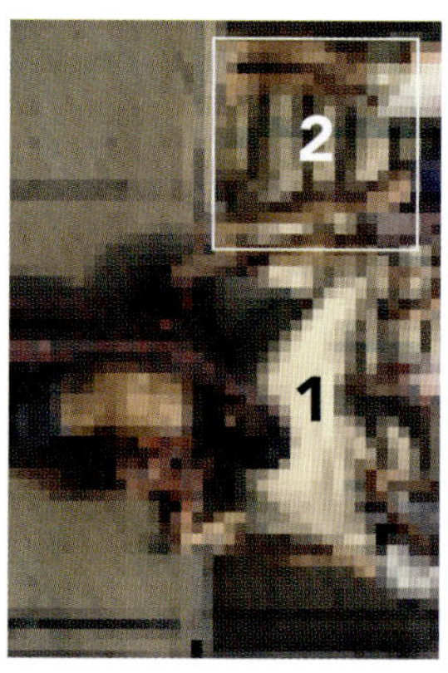

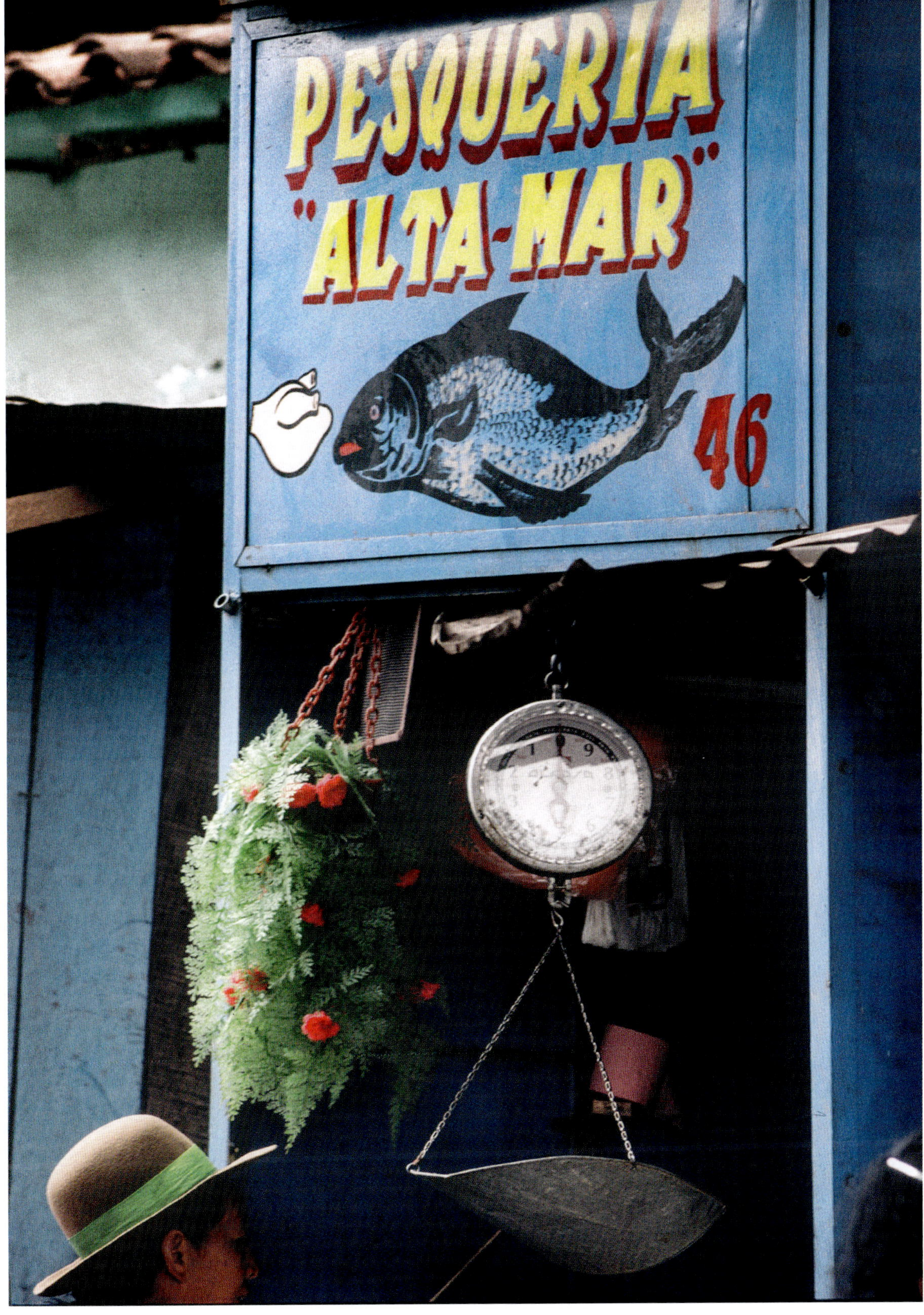
PESQUERIA
"ALTA-MAR"
46

FOREGROUND STRETCH

This method works both as a distinctive, slightly unusual arrangement and as a problem-solver. In essence, you keep the subject of interest right at the top of the frame, with a relatively featureless foreground stretching down below it. Not completely featureless however, because the foreground has a job to do, which is to lead the eye upward and connect the viewer to the distant subject. The foreground needs to have texture because in terms of picture area it will dominate the frame.

There are two dynamics at work here. One is the simple contrast between a small detailed subject at the top and a much larger, blander area below, and that can be quite striking and unexpected. The other is a steady flow from close to the camera toward the distance, and it's important that there are no breaks and that the full distance from just below your feet to the far subject is visible. This combination delivers an intriguing mixture of both contrast and continuity in the same view. There are two very different parts to the scene in both area and strength of content, while at the same time, the foreground stretch inevitably leads the eye upward. And if, for one reason or another, it's not possible to get closer to the far subject, this treatment can be a compositional solution.

This is typically a wide-angle lens tactic, and it has precedent among photographers drawn to the distorted vision of these lenses, for example Bill Brandt's well-known *Top Withens, West Riding, Yorkshire* (1945). Often, a really wide-angle lens of 24mm or less suggests this kind of view, because if you tilt the camera downward until the horizon is just below the top of the frame, then with a 20mm lens for example, there will be more than a 60° angle down from that if the framing is vertical. You can exaggerate the scale difference by shooting from closer to the ground, but there's a slight disadvantage to this in that the middle distance gets compressed. The view from a normal standing position typically works well.

It's worth noting that while this composition shares the camera work – position, angle, lens – with the kind of 'near–far' layout in which a strong foreground subject is related to a distant one (see, for example, page 41), it works quite differently. Its characteristic is the blankness of the lower main part of the picture, with nothing significant to hold attention so that the eye always moves upward.

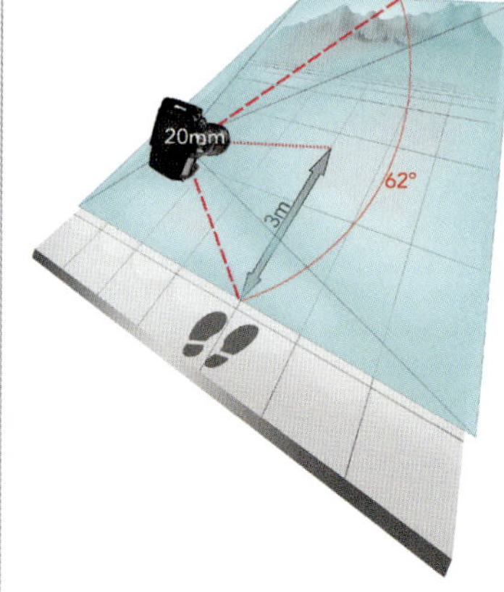

→ Characteristic of this style of shooting is that with a wide-angle lens (the example here in White Sands, New Mexico is 20mm) and vertical format, with the camera aimed downward from a normal standing position and the top of the frame just taking in the horizon, the bottom edge of the frame almost reaches your feet and the mid-point of the picture is no more than 3m into the scene. The angle of coverage with a lens like this is 62° top to bottom.

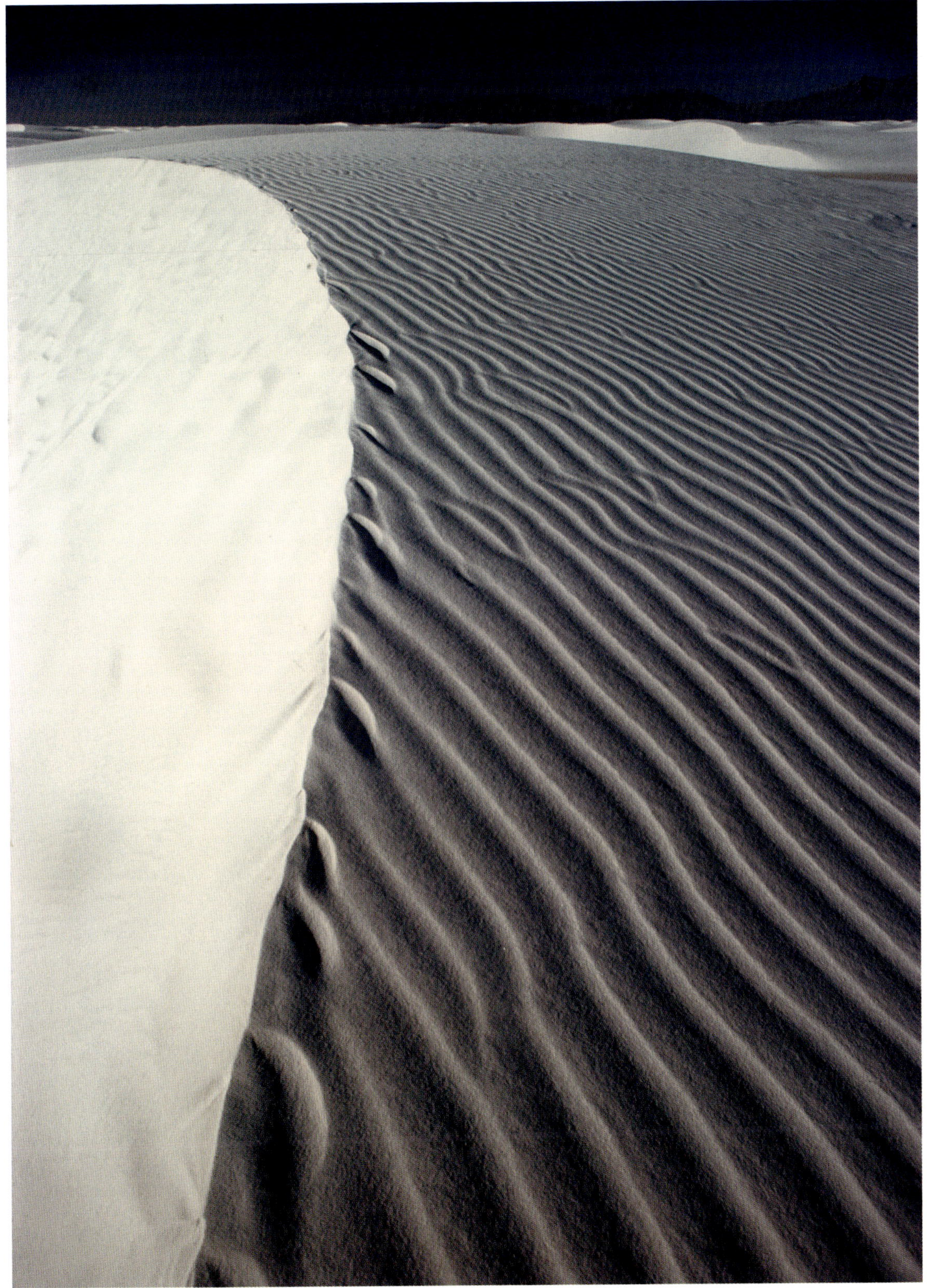

THE NEED FOR A SUBJECT

When we look at a photograph, we expect it to be about something, and that means we expect there to be a subject. Maybe more than one, but in any case an actual physical person or thing – and here's the important part – against a background.

Although many landscapes, as we saw on page 49, are exceptions, most images typically do have a subject and a background, and the eye expects them to be distinct. It's called a figure–ground relationship. This borders on stating the perfectly obvious, but it does suggest two actions that you might want to take. The first action is to reinforce the need for a definite subject by making sure that your subject appears clearly against the background, and there are indeed as many ways of messing that up as there are of helping it. It's an argument for making sure that the subject contrasts sufficiently with the background, such as by difference in lighting, or selective focus to help separate it from a complicated or similar-looking setting.

There's no surprise to being efficient like this, which is why the second possible action is more interesting – to challenge and confuse. If the eye is primed to look for a clear subject, you can sometimes use viewpoint, lighting, focus and so on to make the picture visually ambiguous. Ambiguity is something I'll be returning to in the last chapter, and it's useful if it gets your photograph more attention and more time spent looking at it. In this interior (below), what exactly is the subject and what is the background? The lighting doesn't help, nor do the vertical divisions, while the

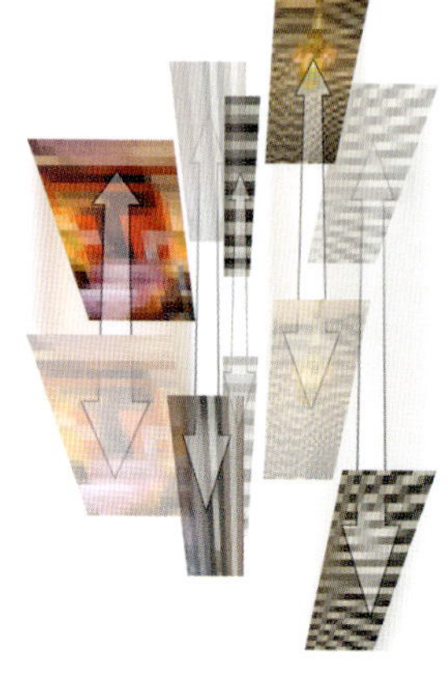

There's a sense of individual panels to this interior as the eye tries to make sense of what should stand out, and the result is a kind of forward-backward oscillation that is never fully resolved, especially for the ornate ceiling light against black-and-white stripes.

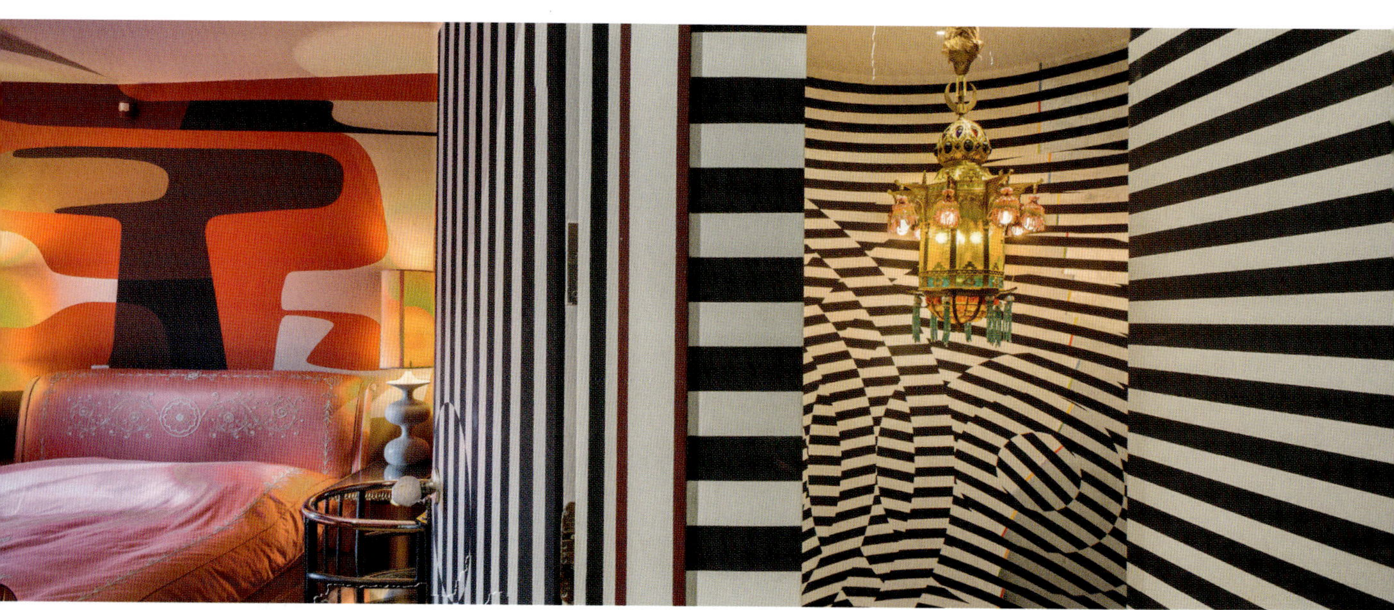

Op Art striped surfaces interfere with depth perception, as they're intended to. You might find this picture irritating to look at or intriguing, but either way it denies the viewer an easy view of figure-ground – or subject against background.

The photograph of a Burmese monk next to a *stupa* also plays on our natural interpretation of figure and ground by presenting two equally sized blocks, black and gold, with everything in focus. It doesn't take too long to work out because of the clear outline of the seated monk, but there's a lingering sense that one area ought to be larger than the other – again, deliberate. Faced with figure and ground that are in contrast but are nearly equal, the eye has a tendency to flip them.

FIGURE/GROUND

Significant elements are seen as being subjects separate from and resting on or against a background.

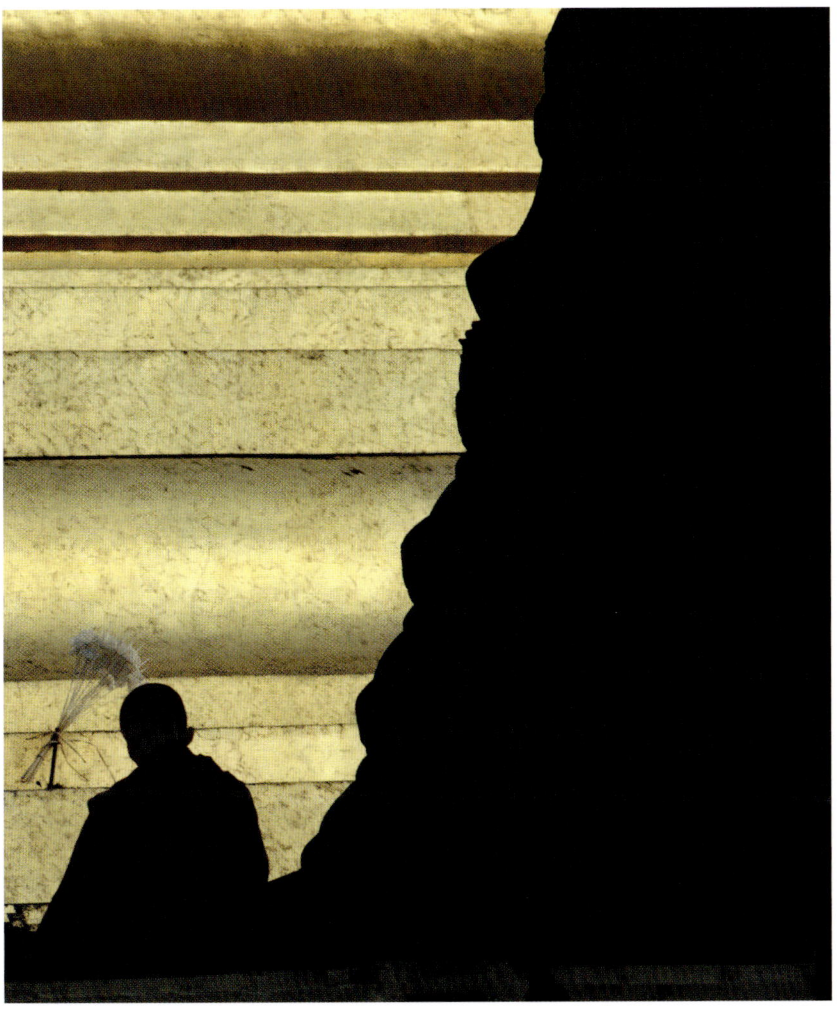

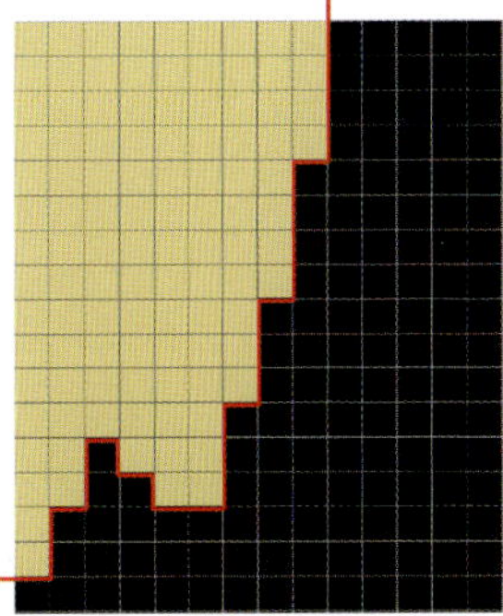

As a gridded version of this shot of a silhouetted Burmese monk shows, the areas left and right of the red line are equal, and this creates a slight vibration and flipping when looking at it.

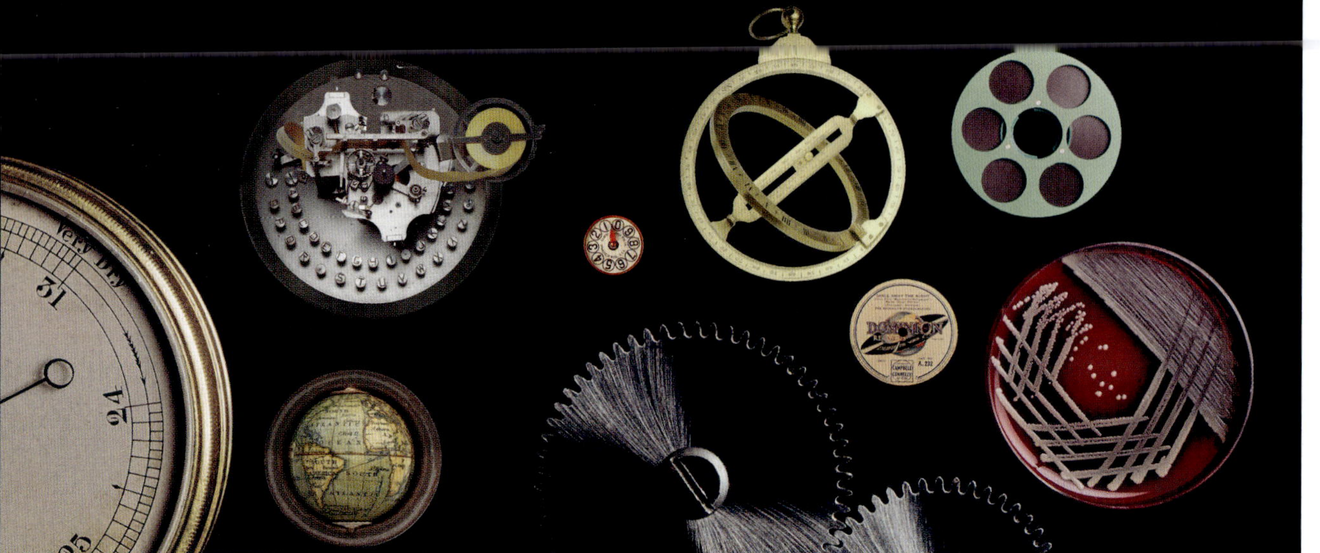

THE NEED TO GROUP

A major tendency of our vision system is toward grouping things, seeing individual elements as belonging together. As with all Gestalt principles or effects, in most cases it's also true in real life, in that what you see as a group actually is a group, and that shouldn't be surprising because, like all Gestalt principles, it's based on experience.

We expect to see what we're accustomed to see. A flock of birds is a flock of birds, and that might make a good shot for all kinds of reasons but not because they're all together in a group. That's simply a given. However, it has the potential to be interesting when it isn't true. In other words, when two or more subjects in a picture appear to be related, but in reality have little or nothing to do with each other. There are ways of using this to force a grouping. In fact, there are five Gestalt principles which share this same idea. They are Proximity, Common Region, Uniform Connectedness, Similarity and Parallelism, and they intermingle. Think of them as five flavours of grouping.

The circular objects are an easy application of the principle. Shot as a wrap-around book cover, there's obviously no question that we're looking at a calculated and arranged group of objects. There was a problem, however, which was the sheer range of subjects that the picture needed to cover (the book title was wide-ranging), and the solution was to introduce similarity in the form of circular shapes. Once that was decided, it was straightforward to hunt down appropriate and varied objects, and they could vary greatly, because the circles would be the linking element.

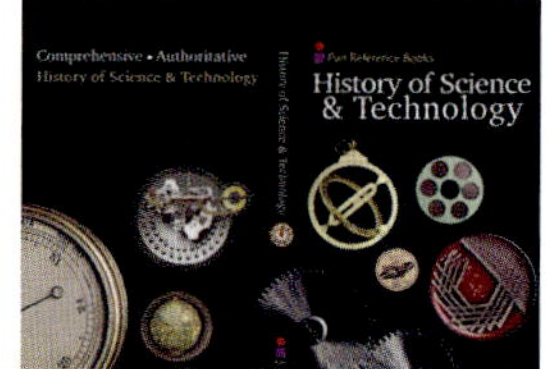

For a wrap-around cover illustrating a history of science and technology, finding circular objects within the very broad theme established the connectedness between very different items. The final selection was made from many candidates.

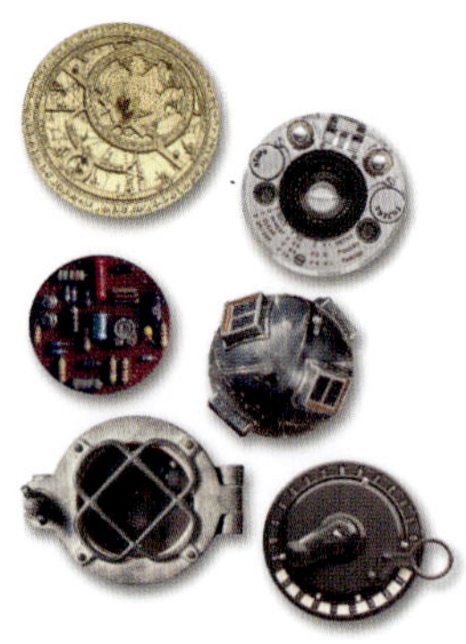

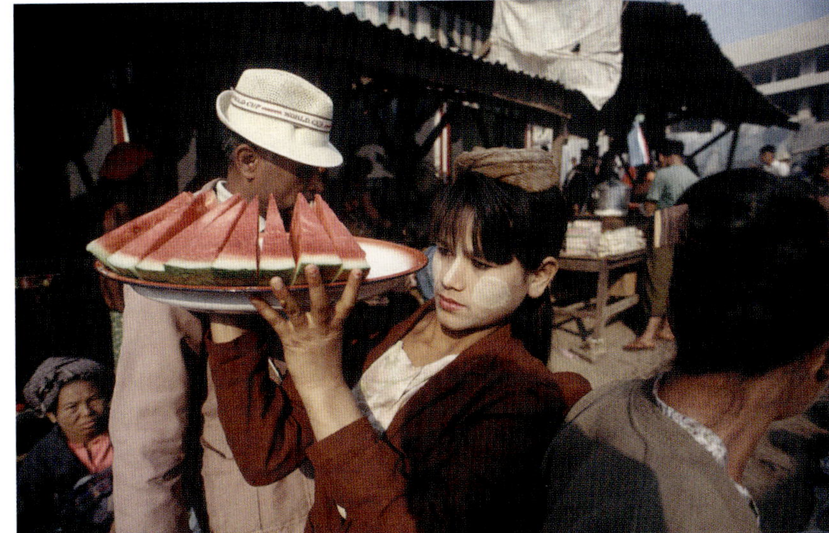

A sense of the ridiculous enters this quickly caught moment in a Burmese market by simple juxtaposition (and recognizing the possibility in the first place), a case of Uniform Connectedness.

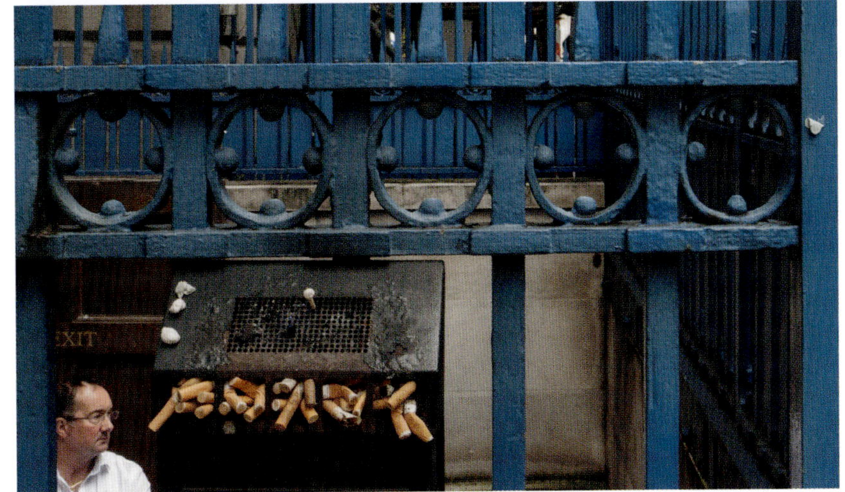

An equally inappropriate juxtaposition in London's financial district, aided by a small aperture that gives sharpness throughout and confuses the sense of depth, allowing Proximity to take over.

In unplanned real life, as with the two examples above, using this is more a matter of seizing on coincidence. It's here that still photography has a particular advantage, because each picture is a frozen moment from a single viewpoint, which opens up possibilities to align things at different distances and in different spaces, however illogical the result. Having everything sharply focused is usually one of the prerequisites, because that confuses the sense of depth.

GESTALT GROUPING PRINCIPLES

PROXIMITY Elements that are close together are seen as being related.

COMMON REGION Elements within a boundary or enclosure are seen as being related.

UNIFORM CONNECTEDNESS Elements that appear to touch each other are seen as being related.

SIMILARITY Elements that share similar visual qualities are seen as being related.

PARALLELISM (a specific kind of Similarity) Rows of elements that are parallel are seen as being related.

THE NEED TO CONTINUE

Close to our need to find groupings and connections is the expectation that sets of things will continue to do what they're doing. That can be in space or in time.

In space, the principle of Good Continuation describes our tendency to interpret objects in alignment as forming a smooth line that continues, even beyond the frame. This builds on another assumption, which is that alignment implies a relationship. In time, the principle of Common Fate states that we tend to group together objects that appear to be heading in the same direction. In both cases, we're unconsciously extrapolating from what we see to anticipate what lies beyond or what will happen.

As with all the Gestalt principles, the reality is pretty much exactly as we see, so it makes a logical explanation but leaves little room to do anything with it. A herd of cattle looks like it's walking together in the same direction. Well, it is and so what? There's no other way to photograph it. Where this expectation of things continuing can actually be useful is with multiples – lots of the same or similar things – going right to the edges of the frame.

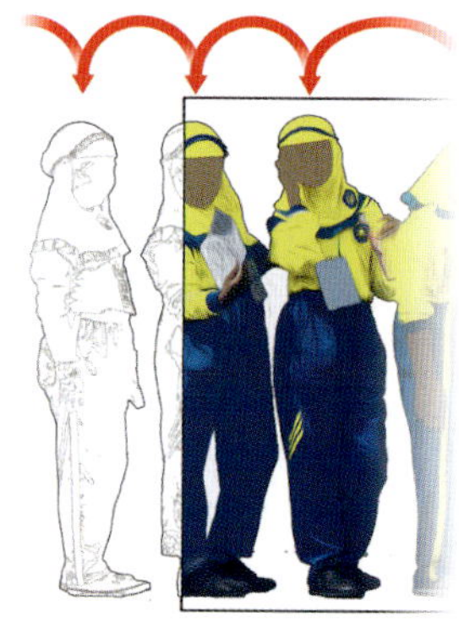

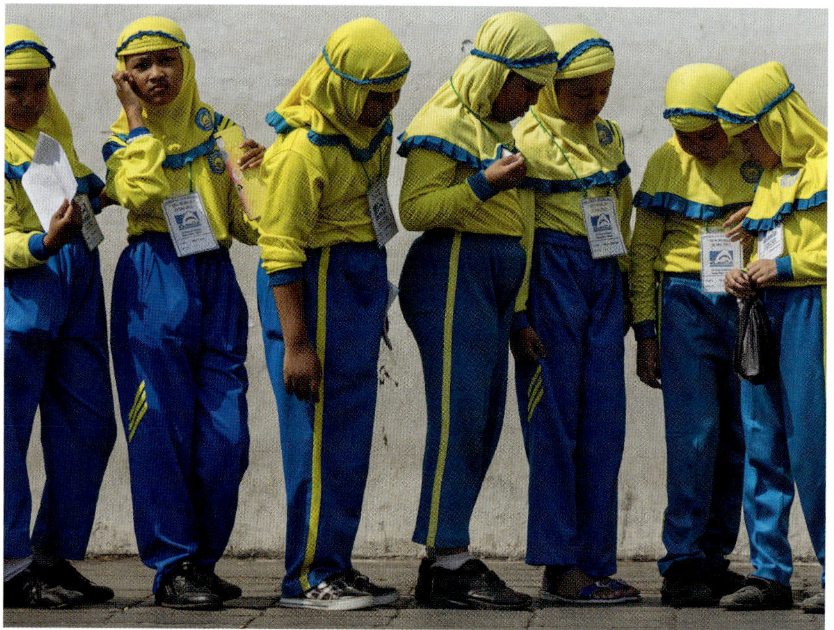

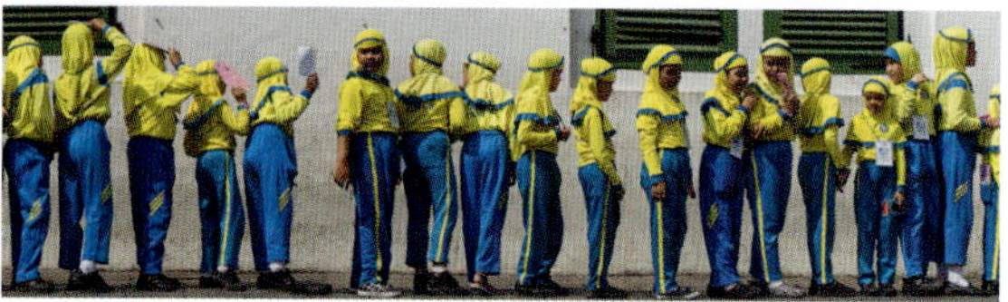

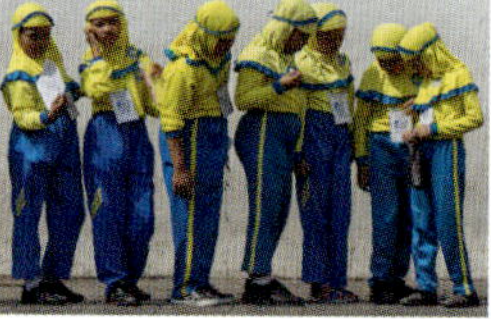

Cropping in even slightly at both sides on this line of Indonesian schoolgirls changes the image significantly. In one (bottom right), it's a neatly and tightly framed group. In the other (left), they appear as a small part of a longer group – the eye assumes a succession of figures beyond the frame. Actually, they were, as the wide picture shows. Perhaps counter-intuitively, closing in on a mass of things actually makes them seem more.

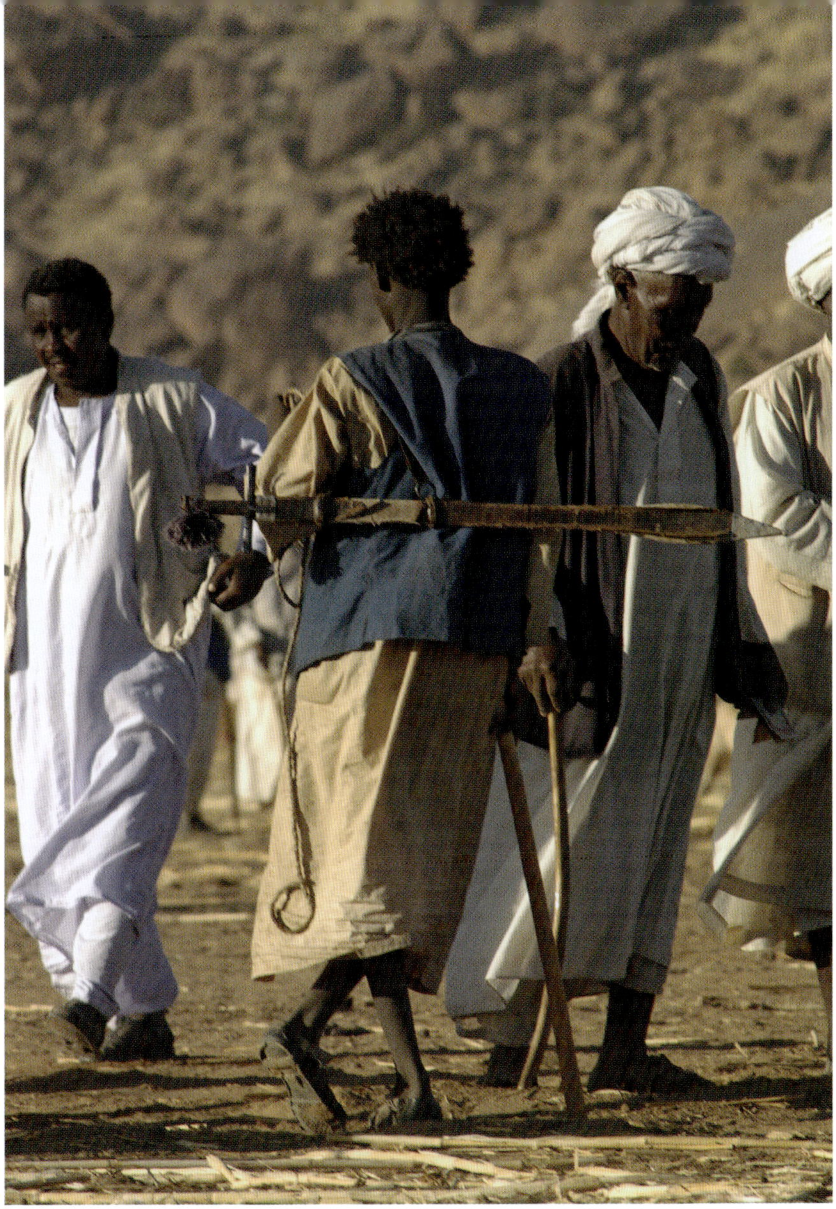

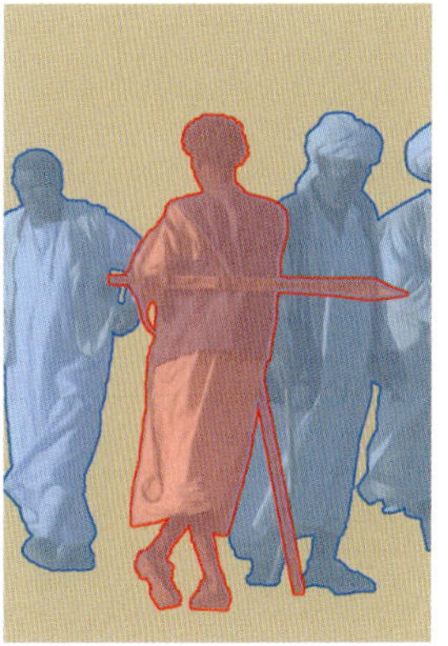

Although the three men walking forward are not in fact together, their forward movement toward us gives them Common Fate, and the man with his sword, in the centre and facing away, becomes a separate element and all the more strongly identifiable.

When multiples do this, the eye assumes that they continue beyond, possibly forever, and if the units are small and many, the result is what's called a 'field picture', which we'll see more of in Chapter 7 (see page 156). This means that if you don't really have all that many in front of you, but you'd like to give that impression, cropping in will do that trick. The shot opposite of the Indonesian schoolgirls illustrates the point neatly.

GESTALT GROUPING PRINCIPLES

GOOD CONTINUATION Elements extended in line are expected to continue along it.

COMMON FATE Elements that point, face or appear to move in the same direction are seen as a related group.

CLOSURE We look to make simple shapes out of complex or separated elements.

THE NEED TO COMPLETE

The fourth group of Gestalt principles covers our tendency to see things as complete and whole, even if parts are not visible. One of the deeper driving forces behind this is the German word *prägnanz*, which translates as 'pithiness', 'conciseness', and for Gestalt means our innate tendency to simplify.

When faced with visual complexity and disorganization, we search for the simplest forms into which this can be interpreted. This is all a part of what's called reification, which is the fundamental process of our mind filling gaps to make something whole and complete, even if we're presented with only parts of it.

This is what makes implied shapes and lines work, and is behind much of the last chapter, from the ease with which we recognize triangles (the simplest of all straight-edged shapes) to our seeing lines as converging on something meaningful. The main Gestalt principle here is Closure, or 'joining the dots' in the popular phrase. The virtual circle formed by the two men and their shadows sweeping tea on page 79 could as easily have been the example here on these pages, but the shot of the two curved prows of passing boats is a more striking version of simple closure.

Traditional Maldivian boats, called *dhonis*, feature a tall distinctive curved prow. What began as a straightforward silhouette shot of one sailing against a late afternoon sun became, by chance, a graphic construction of a circle enclosing a standing figure. The sequence shows how this unfolded as two *dhonis* pass each other heading in opposite directions. The possibility was obvious from the moment the second boat appeared in frame, and good timing immediately became essential. As explained on page 16, the human visual cortex processes part-shapes like this to complete them in the simplest way possible – as a circle.

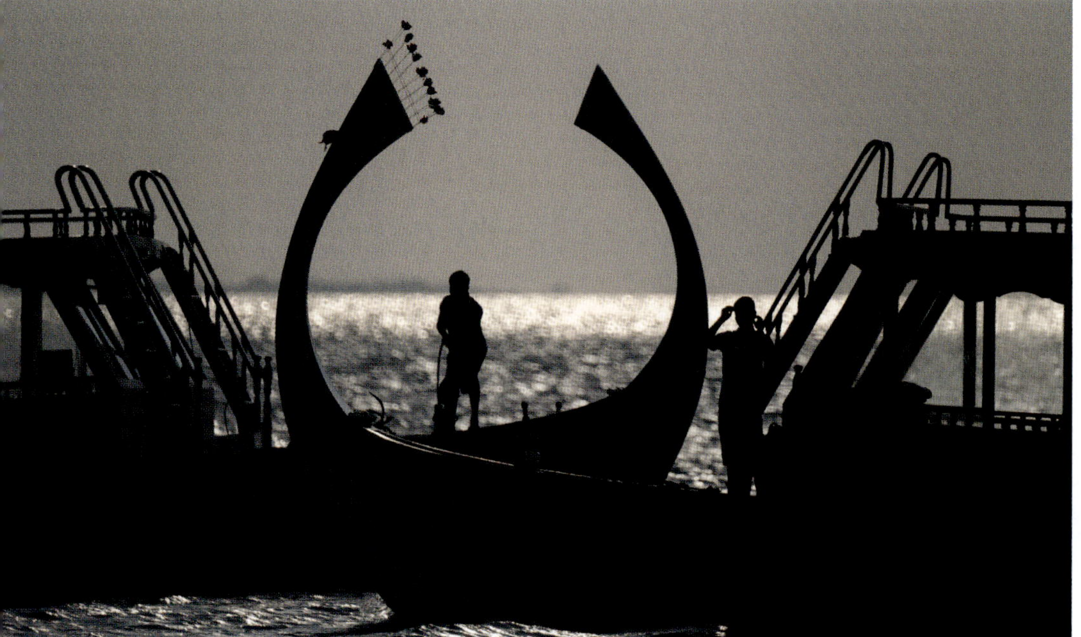

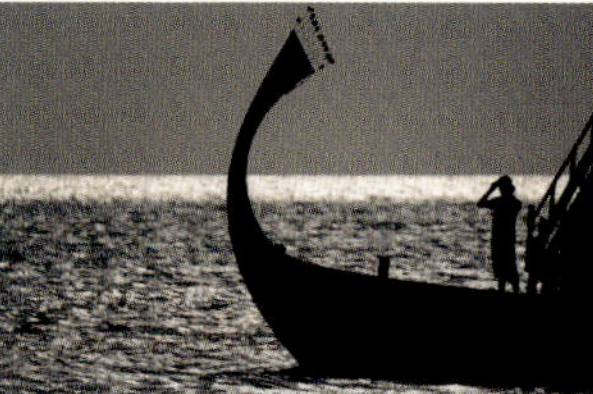

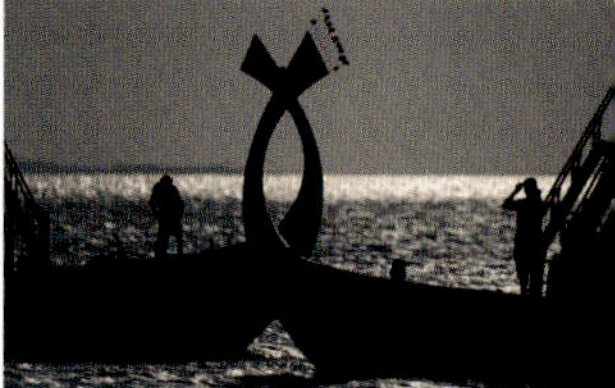

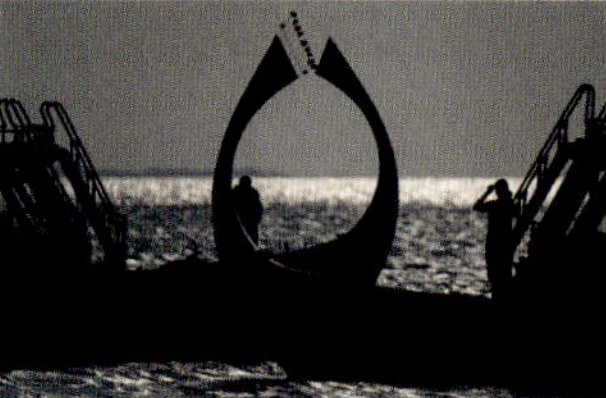

This might be a special case, but closure has some more ordinary uses. For example, it justifies slicing into objects by cutting half of them out of the frame, and this works almost seamlessly with symmetrical things and objects that we're sufficiently familiar with to be able to guess what's missing. This may not sound earth-shattering, but many photographers without much experience feel a sort of compulsion to include the entirety of single subjects in the frame when it's unnecessary, and this can just reduce the interest of the composition. The viewer can easily, without any thought, complete the rest. Tightly cropped portraits are another example, such as the Sudanese man in a yellow shirt on page 51. There's no issue in cropping the top of the head if that's what works for the overall framing. There's an economy in showing just enough to make the point.

Another way of leveraging this need to see things continue is by deliberately not showing everything – a device we'll return to in the last chapter. By showing just enough to allow the viewer to complete the picture in the imagination, there's the possibility of adding interest, as in the picture of a glass and metal office in Japan.

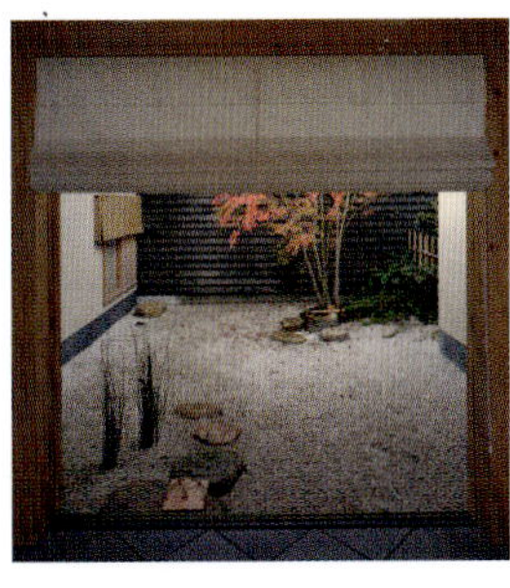

A typical Japanese garden-viewing strategy is to make it difficult, or even impossible, to see the entire view from one position, so encouraging a more thoughtful and contemplative appreciation from a visitor.

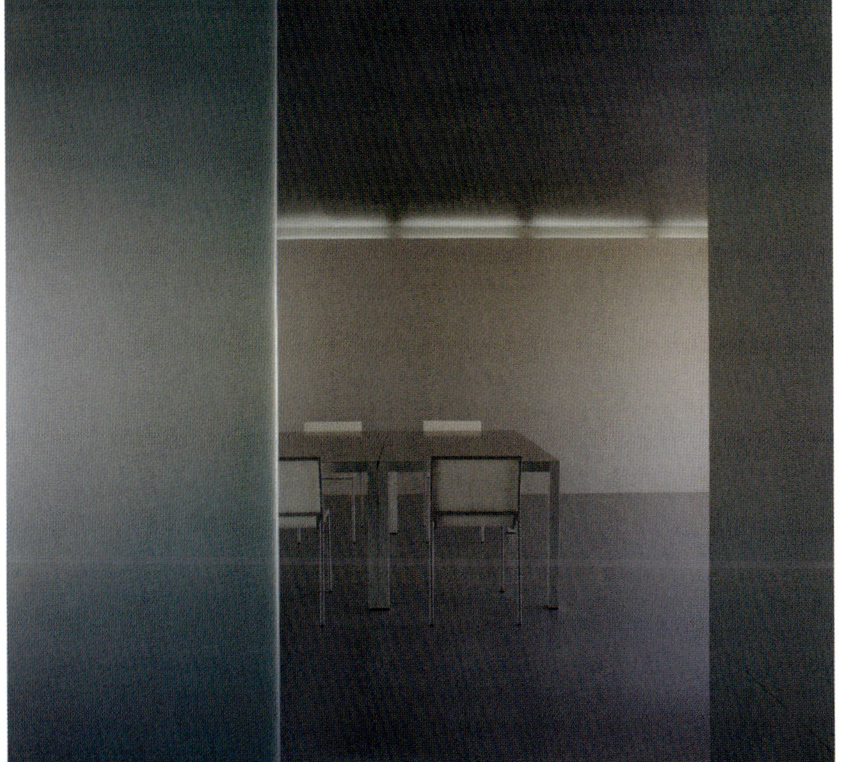

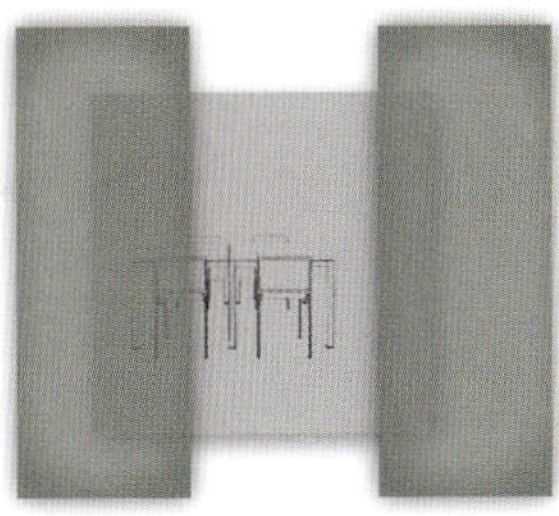

A contemporary Japanese office, designed for subtlety and softness. Incomplete views are very much a part of Japanese architectural and garden design tradition, and these are incorporated in the building design here by architect Takashi Yamaguchi. This photograph enters into the same spirit by closing off the left of the view with a sliding glass door but without loss of any significant information – we can easily extrapolate the rest of the table and chairs.

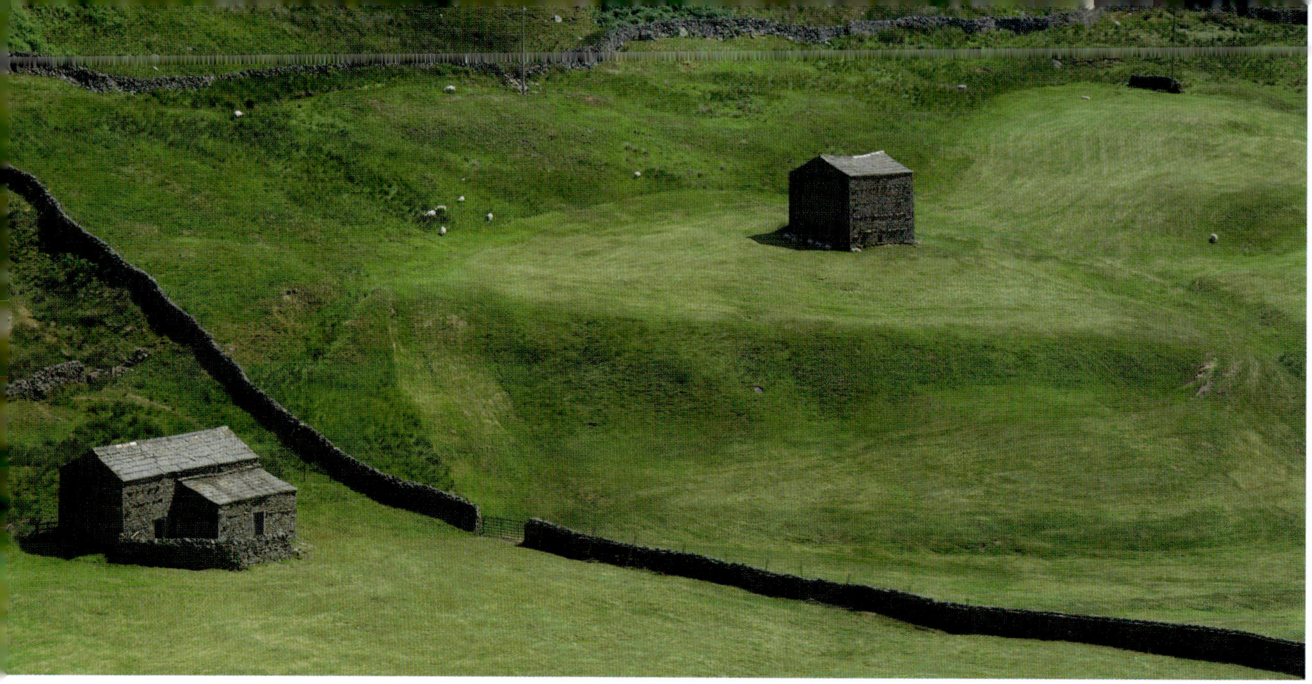

BALANCE

The idea of visual balance seems at first straightforward, but it turns out to be elusive. Most people agree that balance in a picture is felt to be comfortable and satisfying, but putting it to the test is problematic.

The simple notion of balance translates well into a kind of weighing scale, with a fulcrum in the middle – in green in the illustration on the right. I've chosen a very simplified image to make the point clear: two stone barns in green fields. In many pictures, it's reasonably straightforward to identify the elements that are going to count the most strongly, and here there's no doubt. This is just the kind of test that has been done, with viewers being asked to move the fulcrum sideways (the black triangle) until the picture seems balanced. Obviously, there are many things at work when it comes to the 'weight' of a picture element, as we saw earlier under Salience and Visual Weight, and that is why balance is so difficult to pin down.

I have two takes on this. One is that balance is not the same as liking, yet almost all tests for visual balance jump straight to asking for preference. But consider this: a picture with a single central main subject is unarguably balanced, but it can also easily be boring, hence the endless advice to place off-centre. This is not a rule and doesn't always work, but it is true that asymmetry of some kind enlivens a picture and is liked by many. Successful photographs surely stimulate, and that is not a quality of perfect balance.

How then do we reconcile the general feeling of rightness about balance with the fact that it often doesn't seem to work in making a photograph a success?

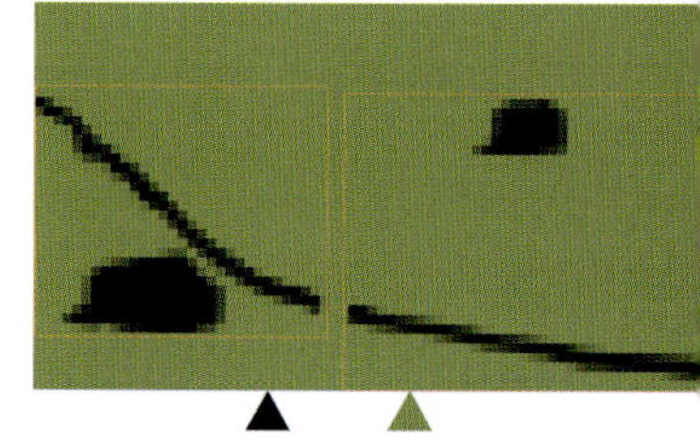

Using a weighing scale analogy with the picture balancing on a point, the green triangle is dead centre, but the black triangle is where most people tested thought the balance lay to take account of the extreme position of the building on the left.

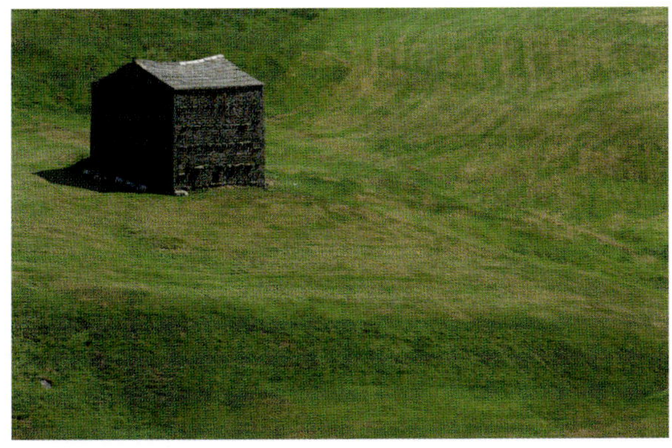

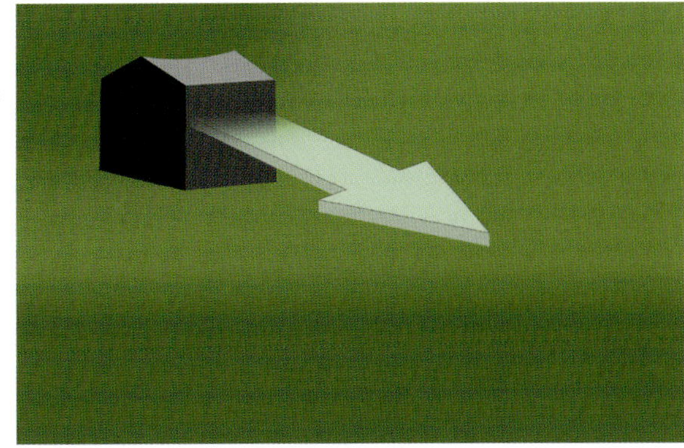

This is where my second take comes in – that people viewing pictures supply their own sense of balance, and this little bit of effort makes looking at the picture more of a pleasure. This is untested but makes sense to me. In the second picture of one of the stone barns (above) this time the placement is quite different, really off-centre. But see what happens. First, even though it's just a simple building, like a box, it seems to face into the picture, because of the angle. And because it faces towards the large area of green field, the grass becomes a kind of second subject, and it achieves a kind of balance. The way I understand it is that we derive some satisfaction from the act of searching for a kind of balance. Achieving it isn't the point. Once an image is balanced, we're less satisfied. In photography, as in all kinds of art, we get bored by having things handed to us on a plate.

It's for this reason that the portrait of a Sudanese painter works. He's on the edge of the wide frame and facing in, and so clearly set against one of his paintings, which bleeds off the edges of the frame. As a person, obviously he is highly salient, but he is offset by the strong and contrasting abstract colours.

↖ By 'facing' into the image from upper left, the stone building identifies the expanse of green as an element in its own right, so that the two of them are in an unresolved balance that is still, to most eyes, acceptable.

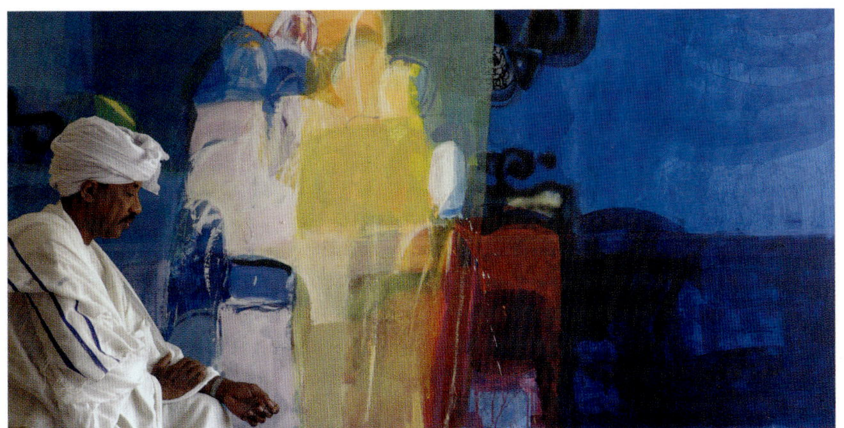

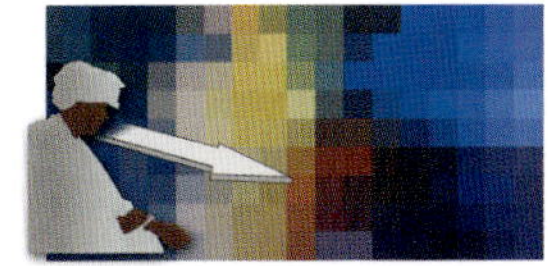

← A Sudanese painter, Rashid Diab, with one of his canvases. Even though eccentrically placed, he fits neatly into the dark blue area on the left, and faces in. His visual weight as a figure and face (see page 100) easily counterbalances the dark right side of the frame.

CHAPTER

6

THE NEW ORDER

Going back to the very first pages, I argued that composition is fundamentally useful for three reasons: to create order, direct attention and achieve interest. Probably the most basic of these is ordering – as in making sense of the visually messy and sometimes chaotic world in front of the camera. To be clear, though, order does not have to mean regimented or straitjacketed. It can be subtle, casual, loose or gentle, and it is not bound to the idea of precision. We all have different preferred styles, and the idea of order and organization is to treat the scenes in front of us so that they suit our own personality. In the pages that follow, precision does play a part, because that's my style and I set myself the challenge of getting things exactly where I want them, but you should follow your own temperament.

Many of the techniques that I've shown already, especially in Chapters 3 and 4, automatically confer some sort of order on the scene, even if only as a by-product, but here I'm going to concentrate on very specific ways of ordering – around the concepts of keeping elements separated, of fitting elements into visual spaces, and of symmetry. As elsewhere, the situations being photographed run the gamut from purely opportunistic to fully under control, but, when it comes to trying to set things in order, there's a huge difference between one end and the other in what is possible. This is one reason why I've included studio shooting in this chapter, because it tends to get less attention. However, I prefer to use the term studio for any kind of managed photography, and the space can be makeshift. While spontaneous, in-the-moment photography will always be the most practised kind, I see these days a developing interest in building up photographs from an idea, and this is ultimately what studio or managed photography is about. This has serious implications for bringing order to an image, because rather than imposing it on an existing scene, in a studio, however temporary it is, you have to build it up from scratch – from your imagination. The two approaches call for very different decisions.

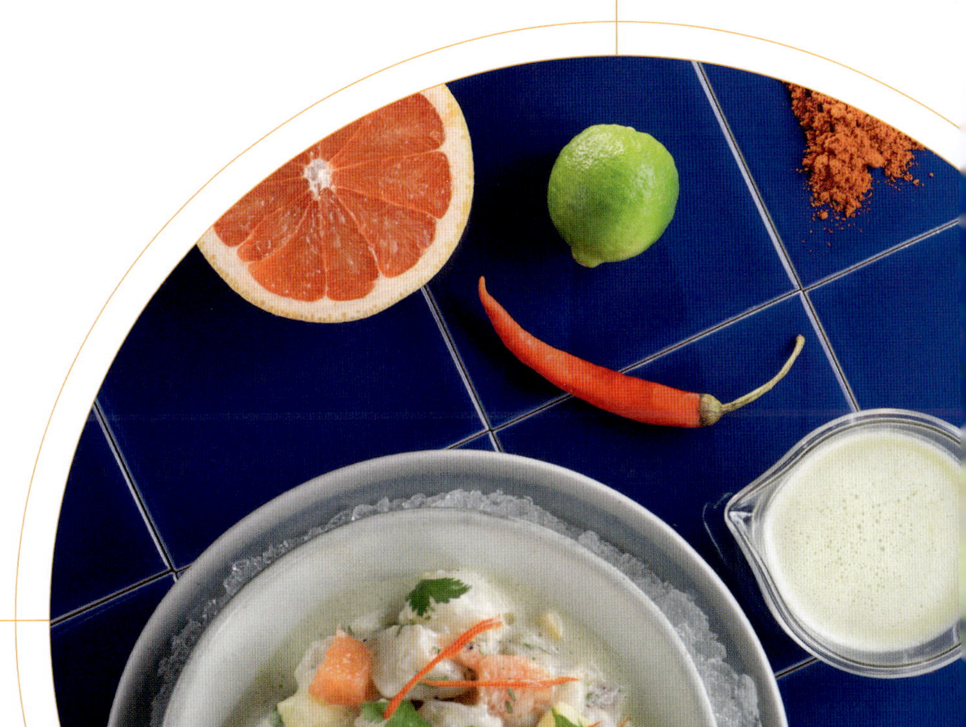

NEATNESS

I'm leading this chapter with a pretty basic concept, one that obviously goes much further than photography, and the reason I want to start with neatness is because it's the core concept of bringing order to a photograph.

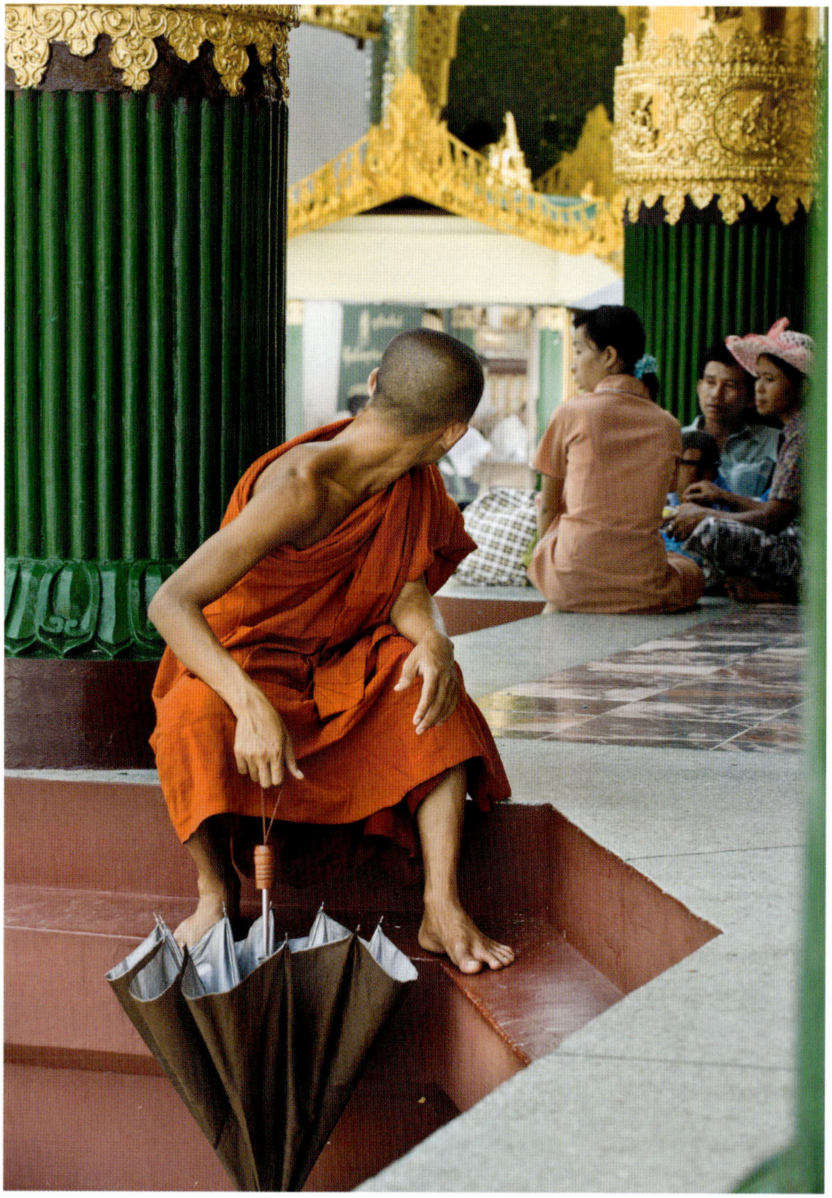

← The setting here, in Yangon's Shwedagon Pagoda, was generally busy and visually untidy. This shot achieves a kind of order by 1: separation – a gap between the monk and group of people behind, and a difference of colour between him and the pillar; 2: by making use of local geometry – squared-up green blocks, triangular umbrella and the angle of red steps; 3: by centering his turned head; and 4: by closing off the right edge of the frame with a sliver of defocused green.

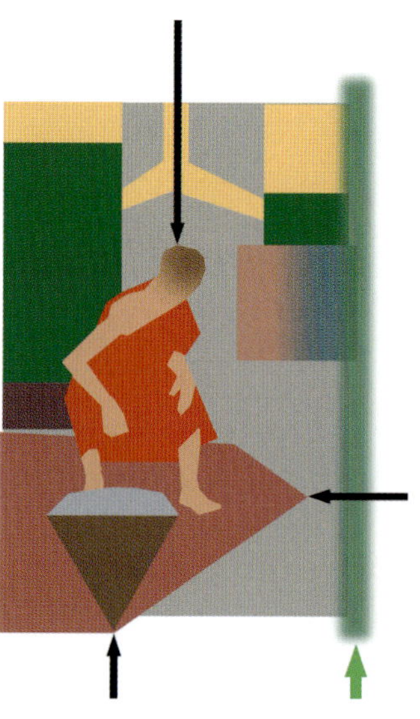

All the techniques in this chapter, and many of those elsewhere in this book, involve some form of tidying up the image. It's a basic kind of compositional housekeeping, whatever kind of photography you're doing, and it's almost unavoidable. I quoted earlier the Iranian photographer Abbas who, despite a working life dealing with all kinds of disorder, found it impossible not to try and tidy up chaotic scenes, and I think this is probably universal. When we're shooting, as soon as we have an idea of what needs to stand out and be noticed in a situation, we're already on the road to tidying. Just like tidying around the house, tidying our images involves three actions. One is getting rid of things that aren't contributing to the picture, another is straightening things up, and a third is putting things in place, just as you would if you were having a spring clean. Each of these is featured on its own elsewhere in this book, but these two pictures are examples of these kinds of tidying at work.

The shot of the Burmese monk is framed to cut out surrounding clutter (by walking forward), the lines and angles are quite carefully aligned, while the timing, with his head turned away, removes his face from the equation. Most of the time shooting a face is not something you'd want to discard, but faces draw attention strongly (see Salience on page 94 and Visual Weight on page 100), and without it the other elements and arrangements in this shot can breathe and interact. The shot of a roti stall in Mauritius was more focused on getting elements in place, meaning the figures, and leaned heavily on waiting for the right moment.

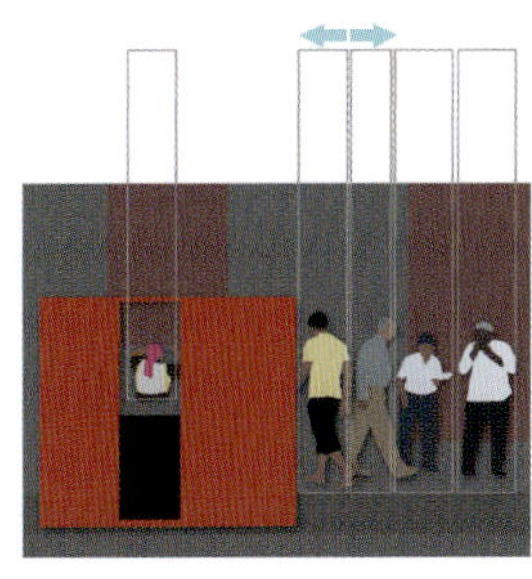

For this shot of a street stall selling roti bread in Port Louis, Mauritius, the more people the better, yet it seemed right to counter the grubbiness of the scene by keeping figures neatly separated. Having people moving is always more interesting than just standing, so the moment was when the two men walking had just passed each other, and everything was neatly lined up. As the sequence of three below shows, a fraction of a second earlier or later would have been messy.

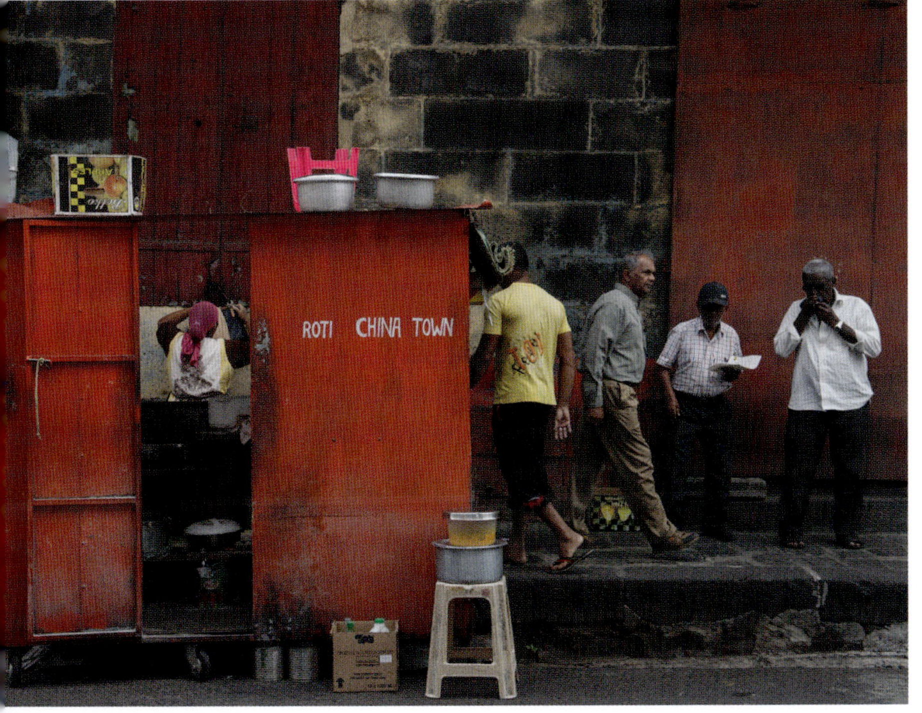

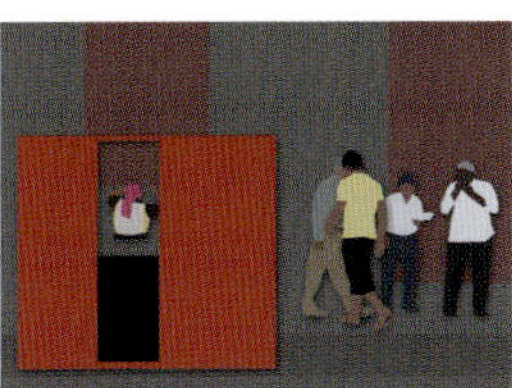

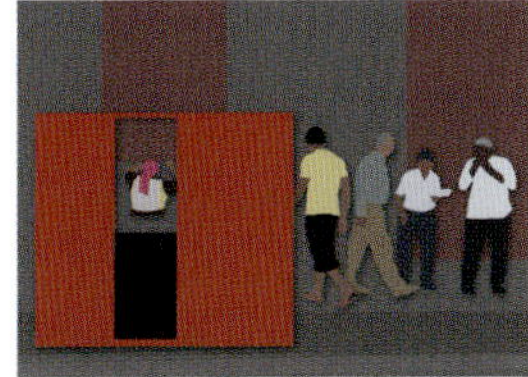

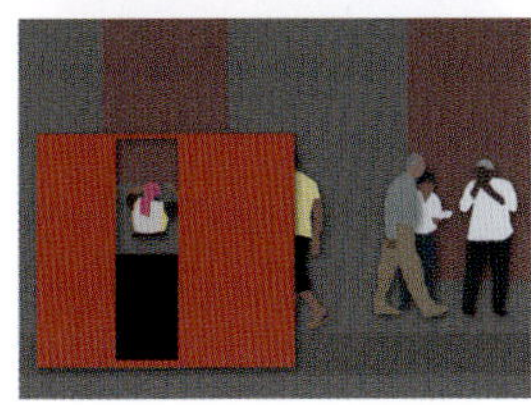

DE-CROWDING

One of the most basic techniques in composition, especially when there's a free flow of activity in front of the camera, is being able to identify the important elements and make sure they're all separated, each in its own little space within the frame. It's a very simple and natural idea.

When things overlap, they cover up parts of each other, and it tends to look messy. You might argue that life is like that, and so it's true to life, but in photography that's what a robot camera would do. Our job, usually, is to put our personal stamp on the image and bring some individually imagined order to the chaos out there.

Yet this is easier said than done when there's a lot going on and it's not really predictable, as happens in much street photography. Normally you have just two options: where you stand and the moment you choose to shoot. Viewpoint and timing, in other words.

The skill in separation is in doing three things simultaneously: anticipating how the people might move, moving to a position that might keep them distinct and apart, and reacting very quickly to split-second moments when they are.

You have more control over all of this, incidentally, if you use a wider-angle lens from close rather than staying back with a standard or longer focal length. The reason is straightforward. The closer you get to the subjects, the more of a compositional difference it makes when you step to one side. Basically, it's a matter of parallax. Even the slightest of feints left or right with a lens like the one used here (14mm) will make a noticeable difference to the positions of figures in your frame.

→ A potentially busy and messy scene, this tea-picking has five subject elements that, in order to read well and be harmonious, need to be separated from each other. The lead-up sequence shows how.

1 The starting point is not only chaotic, but has 12 subject elements.

2 Stepping to the right and aiming left is a much better idea. The four women are now separated, but the central figure is turned away and static.

3 Slightly better, though the central figure is standing, not picking, and the basket on the left is half-in, half-out.

4 Reasonable separation, but the basket is still cutting the frame, and I'm still waiting for the central figure to resume picking (and when she bends down, she won't be obscuring the far figure).

1 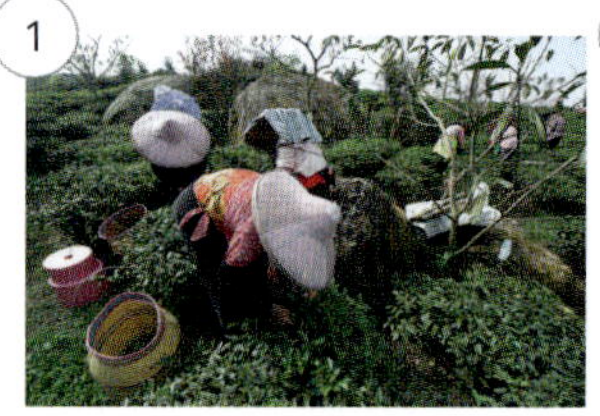

2 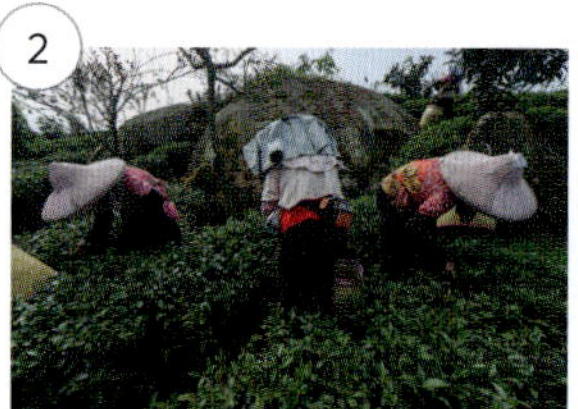

3 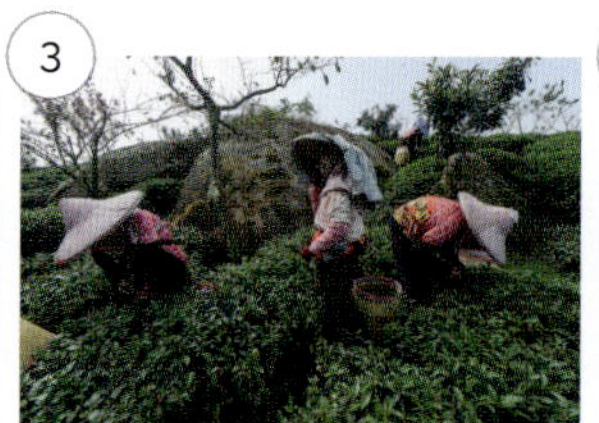

4 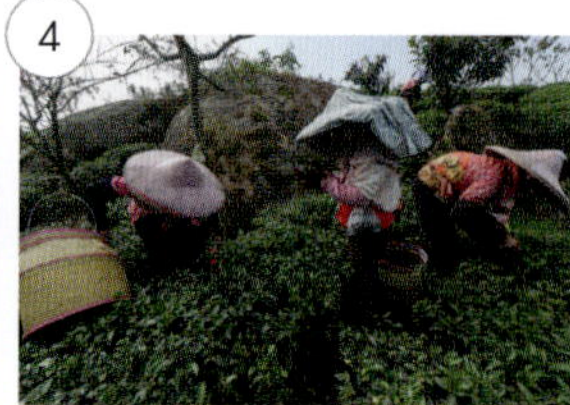

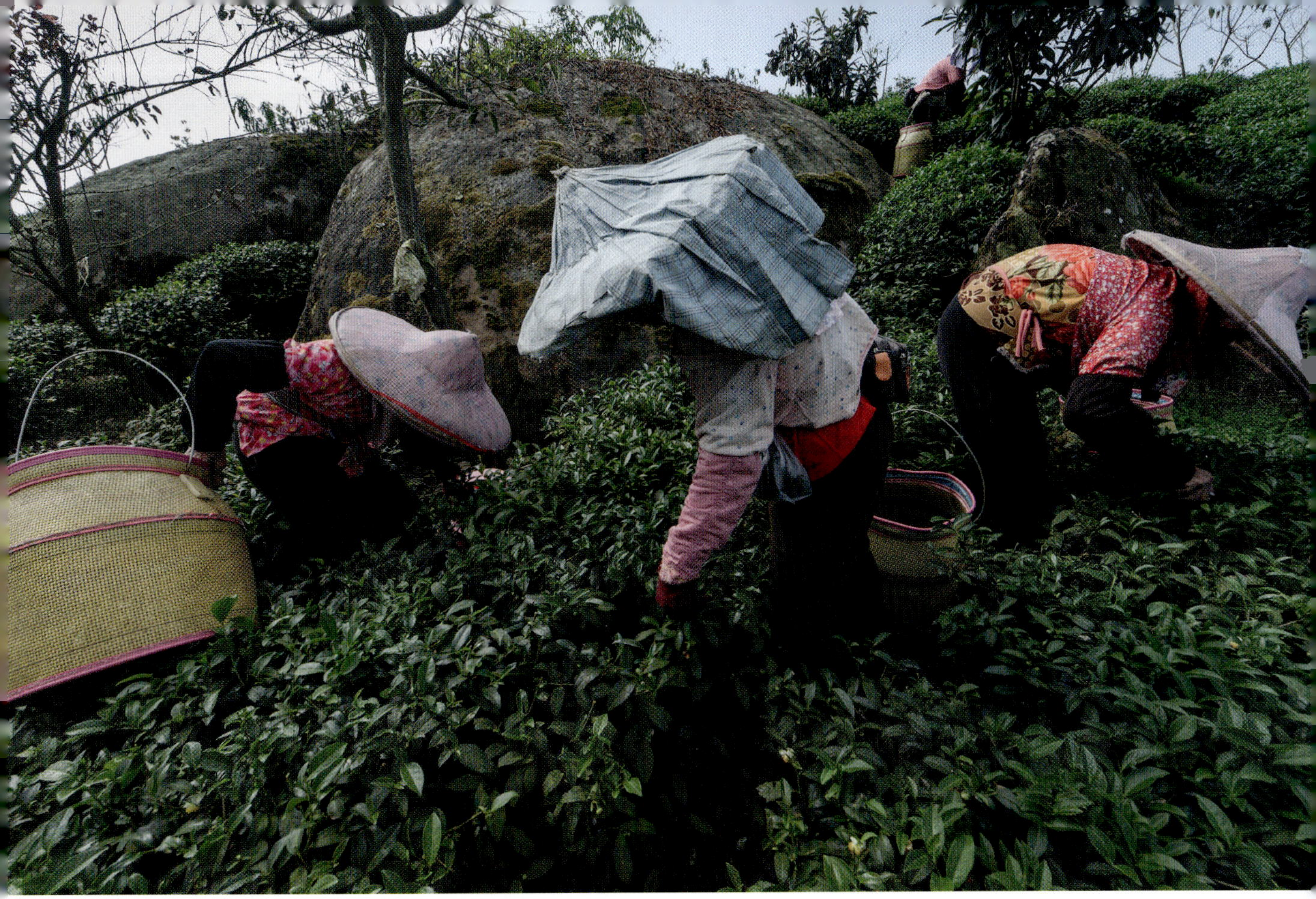

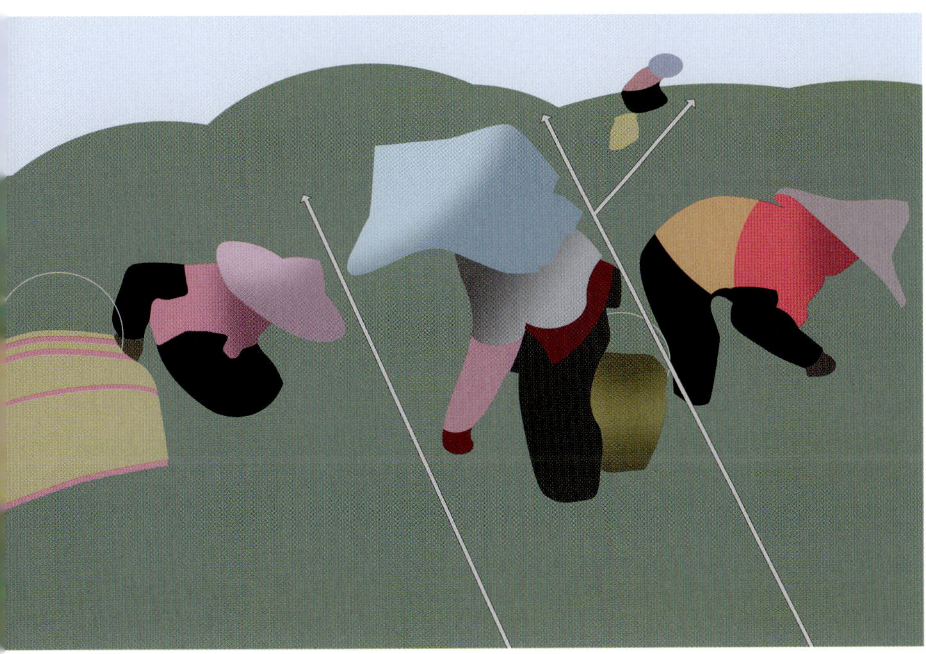

Finally, everything is in place, and all the figures are animated, picking tea. The original crowd of figures and baskets has been resolved into a neat order.

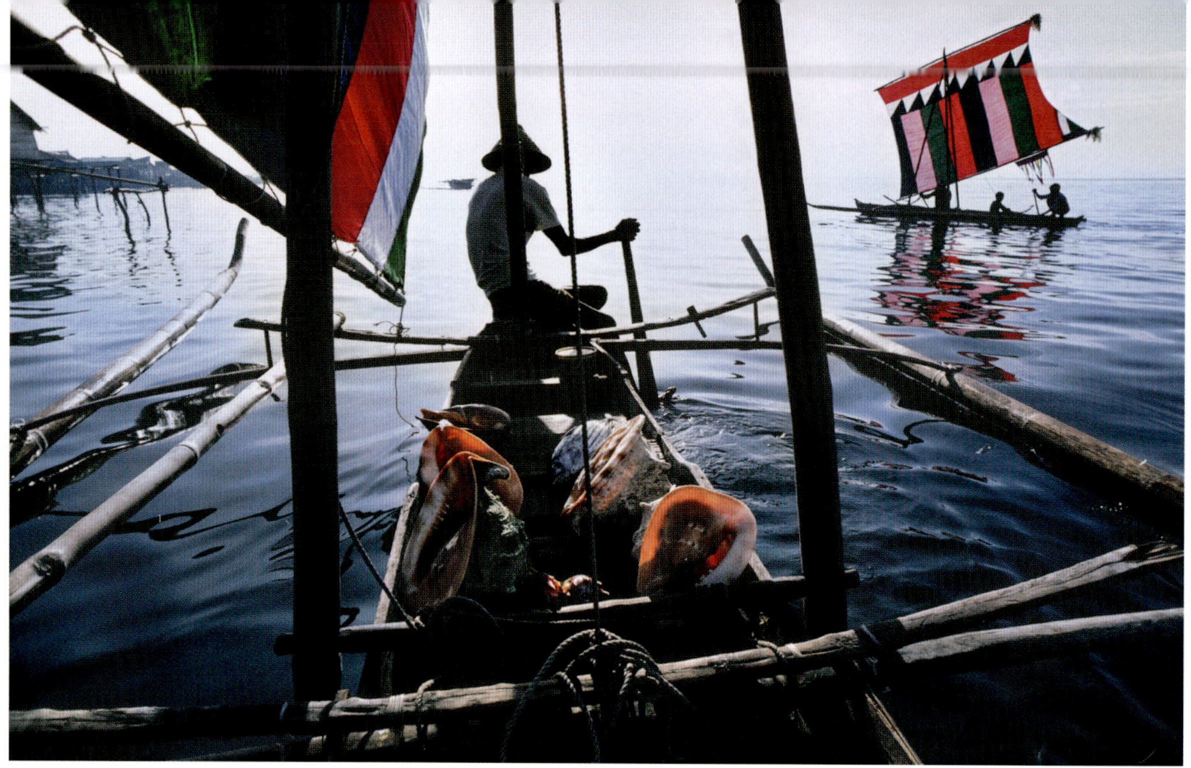

GAPS & SLOTS

Fitting things in place is a core technique for creating visual order, and I showed one example a few pages back under Neatness. Here I'd like to explore the method in more detail.

While the de-crowding approach on the previous pages was concerned with separating elements, another kind of situation not so far removed is where you start with distinct spaces in the scene. They could be spaces between things like trees, or created by light and colour, like white and dark building façades. Naturally, it's purely graphic, and the idea is to get important subjects to stand out by putting them neatly and entirely in contrasting local areas. If you go back to the placement zones on page 52, these are quite different. Those placement zones assume no other influence from the setting, while here, the setting comes pre-loaded with ready-made gaps.

In the shot above, taken on a southern Philippine small sailboat known as a *vinta*, the camera position was very restricted, with little room to move. The elements of interest that needed to be fitted were the boatman, shells, part of the sail and, very important, the second *vinta*. The principal choice was leaning left or right, and timing for the other boat. This shot was the best possible. As it was impossible to have the man clearly in any open space, I decided instead to centre him exactly behind the forward mast.

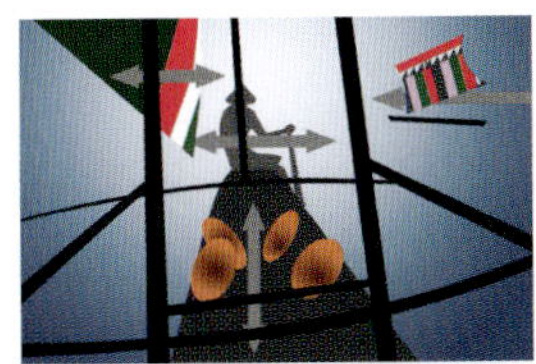

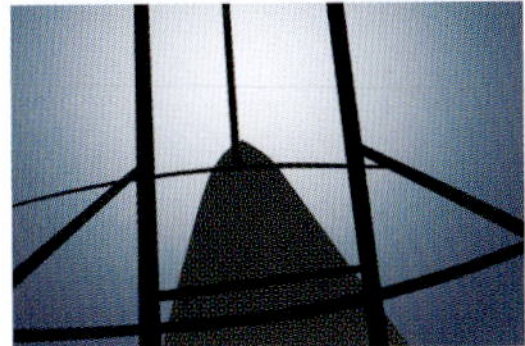

The available spaces were mainly controlled by the two uprights. The second *vinta* fitted naturally into the topmost right space (a critical matter of timing), while the shells needed to be cleanly within the two posts.

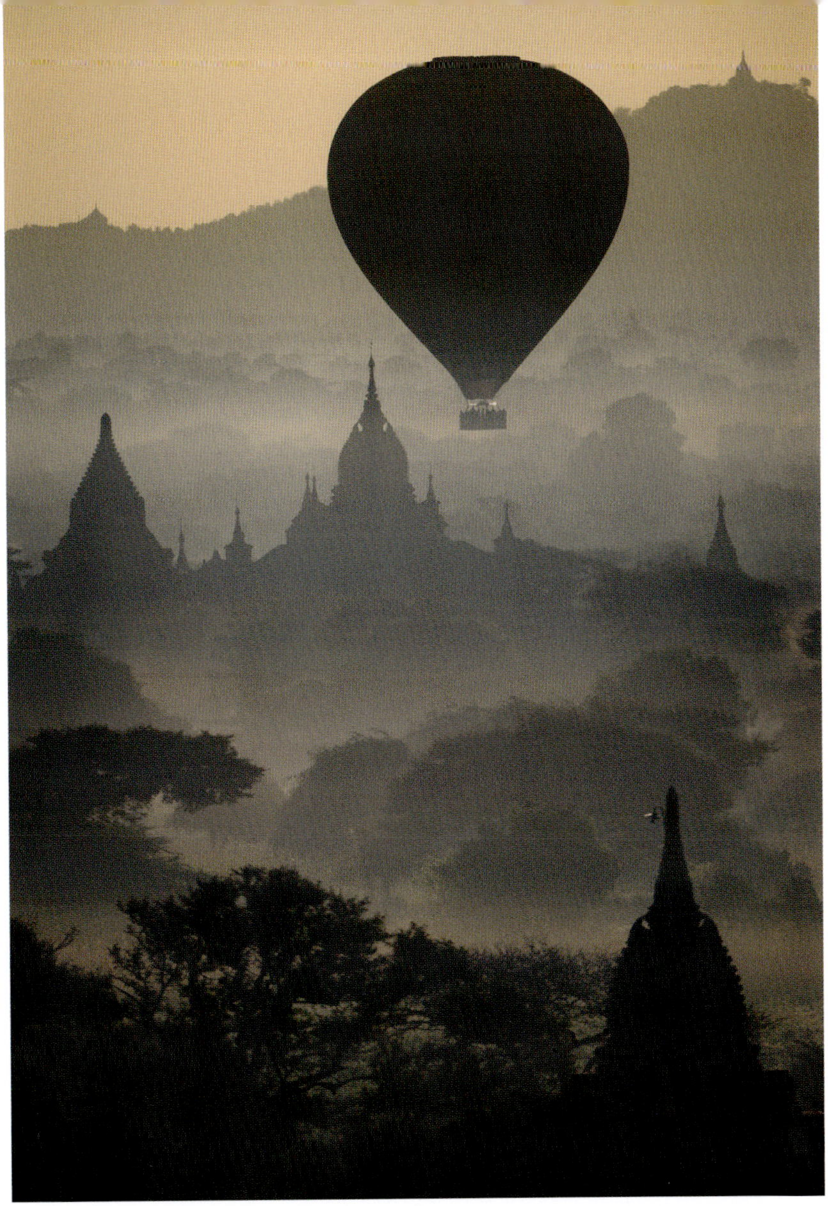

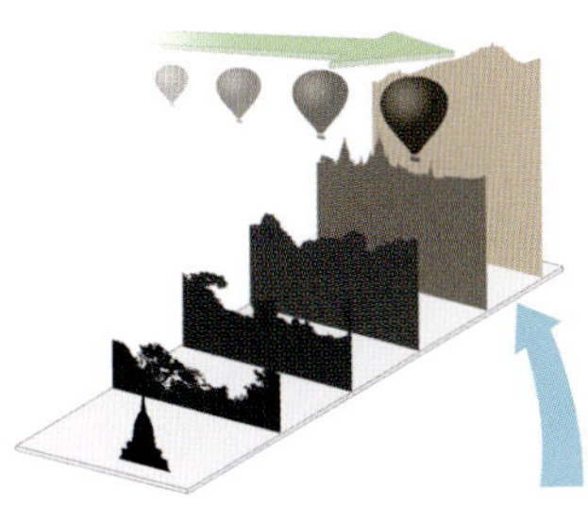

There were several minutes' advance warning of the balloon's approach – enough time to judge its height as it passed through the frame (just past the top of the middle pagoda) and to adjust the framing to make a balanced composition with it included in a clear space in the upper-right section.

The balloon shot is a straightforward example. The viewpoint was absolutely fixed – the top of another pagoda in the plain at Bagan, Myanmar, so focal length and panning a few degrees left or right were the only choices I had. The point of the shot was the receding plains of countless pagodas stretching to the horizon, nicely layered by early morning mist. And there was a balloon on the way, drifting across. The picture worked much better with the extra element of the balloon, not least because it filled an otherwise too-empty pale space.

ENCLOSING

This technique uses some part of the foreground to act as a partial frame for whatever is beyond.

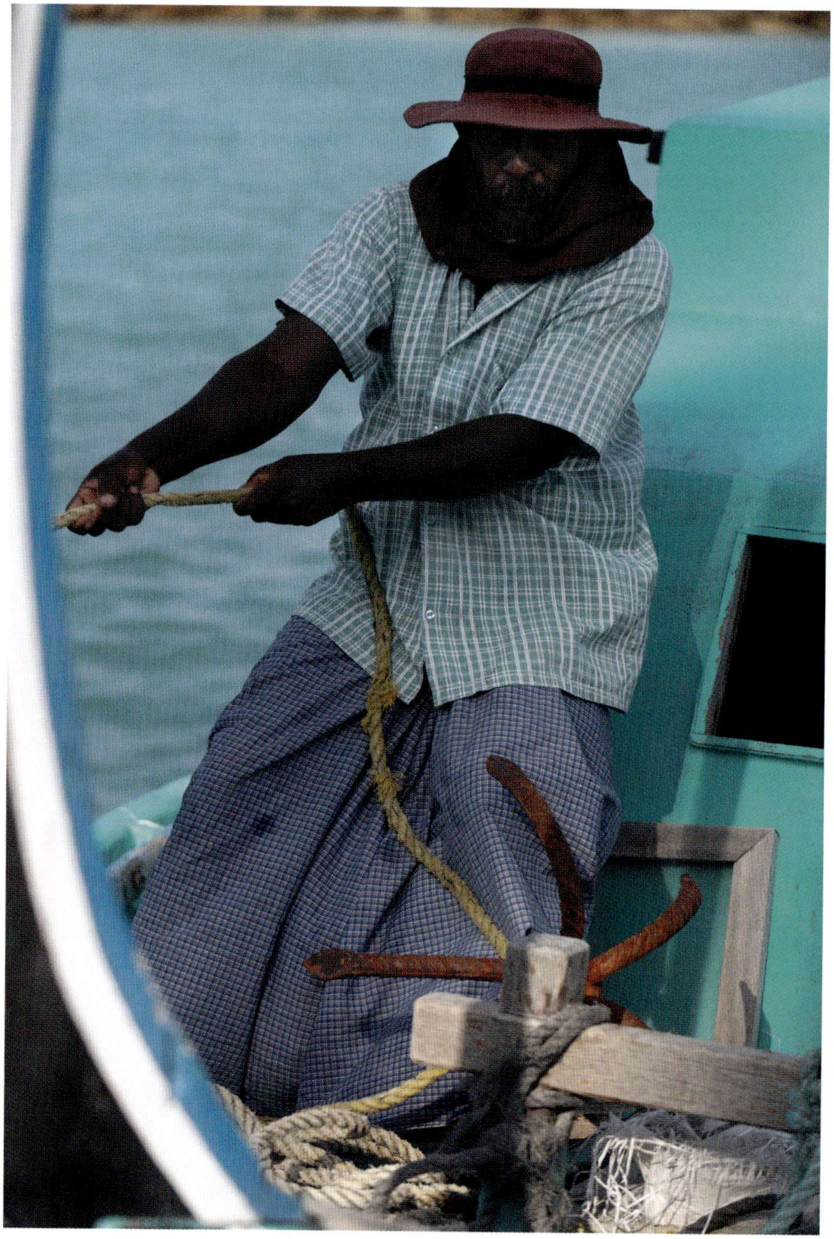

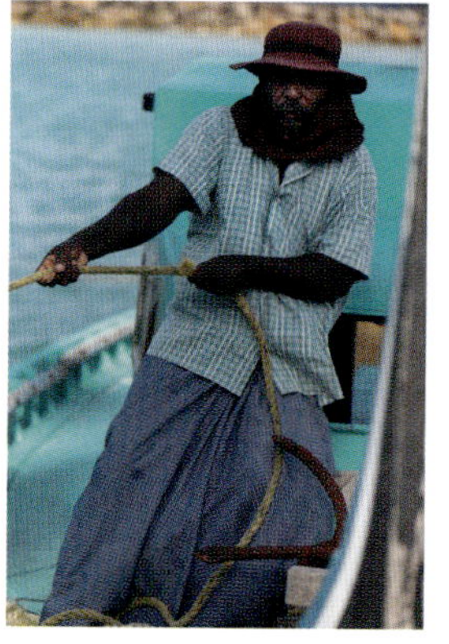

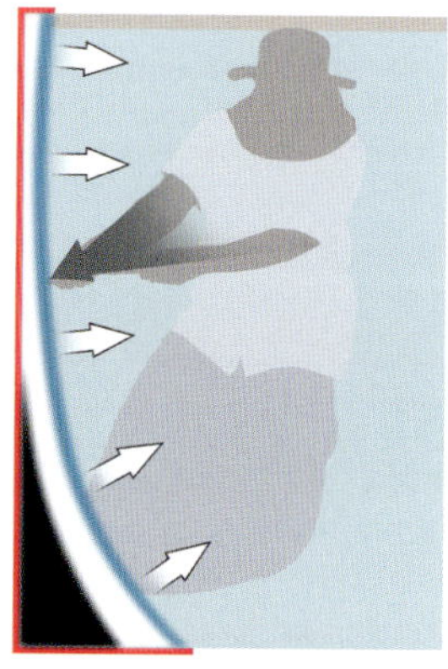

The curving prow of the fishing vessel (see the full shape in the picture on page 110) is a distinctive feature of these island boats called *dhonis*, and it made sense to include just a hint of it. The smaller version above was an earlier attempt, putting the frame on the right, but given the direction the man was pulling the rope, by stepping right I could make it work better as a stop to hold the composition (red border) and to push the attention inward (arrows).

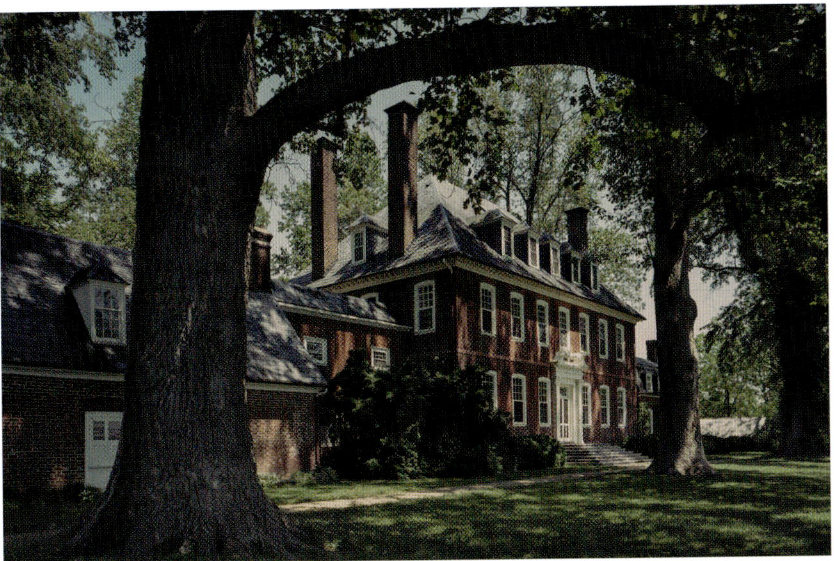

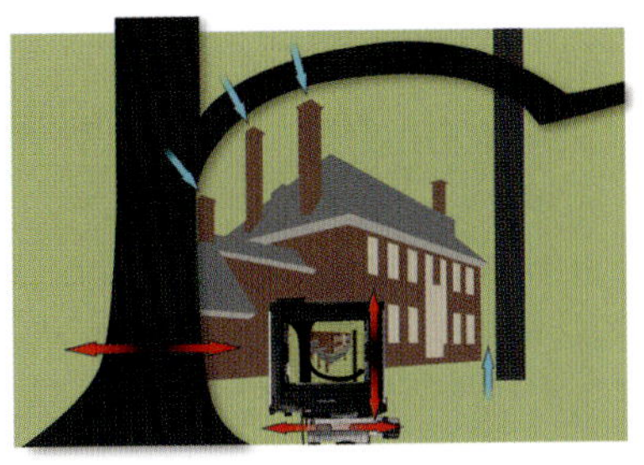

Huge old tulip poplar trees are a feature of this Georgian plantation house and its ground, and this specimen in particular offered an enclosing frame, completed by a second tree beyond, from this position. While this is a simple device in composing, the way that the chimneys could be fitted precisely to the frame made it more special. Small adjustments to the camera position and to the rising front of the view camera (red arrows) controlled the relative placement of tree and building.

I'm not promoting the traditional full frame-in-frame approach that I covered in *The Photographer's Eye*. Clear and unequivocal frames like doorways and windows have their uses, but compositionally they are hardly subtle. In any case, the frame-in-frame concept suffers from overuse and is close to being a cliché, so please proceed with caution. Here, I'm taking a looser approach, where partial framing is more suggestive than hard-edged. As these two examples show, the effect on the image shifts according to how prominent the framing – or rather, enclosing – action appears. When stronger, as in the architectural shot of a plantation house, there's a sense of creating a kind of tunnel to direct the view through and beyond. When weaker and more marginal, as in the photograph of the Maldivian fisherman, the sense is more of holding, providing a kind of stop on one side. We'll revisit this useful compositional idea toward the end of this chapter (see Anchoring, page 132). By necessity, all this is opportunistic: if you can find it, you can use it.

Both of these pictures feature an arc, and it's no surprise that curves are commonly involved in enclosing, because their shape suggests gathering and focusing inward. In the shot of Westover Plantation on the James River, Virginia, from this carefully chosen viewpoint the unusually smooth and long arc of the branch neatly encloses the main building and then connects visually with the farther tree.

The shot of the fisherman hauling on a line was a more on-the-spot opportunity, taking advantage of the tall curved prow on the left of the frame to enclose and push attention inward to the man. A tall curved prow is a distinctive feature of these island boats called *dhonis*, which was one motive to include it, but it turned out to be far more useful as an enclosing device and as a stop. Coupled with the waterline right at the top, it not only holds the attention inward, but it also adds a pleasing graphic structure to the image, all in a theme of blues and aquas.

GROUP CONTROL

There's no greater division in photography than between planned shooting and the uncontrolled real world. Most people's experience is of the real world, while many professionals' is of managed shoots, whether in an actual studio, a temporary one or a controllable situation.

In the studio – and I'm using that word broadly – rather than looking for ways to organize a scene already in front of the camera, you compose by physically laying out your subjects. The camera is often the last to come into play.

Of all the many studio scenarios, I want to focus on a type of still life that comes up frequently and calls on compositional skills in arrangement – the group shot. Typically, you need to arrange several objects that are similar in size and have some relationship to each other. And, usually, each also has to be clearly visible and look good. Given this, the core issue with a group is that it should look cohesive without being regimented or mechanical. Order, but with character.

One approach is to find a setting that offers a natural grouping space, to give some logic to the grouping and help enclose it. In the case of the gold ingot and bars, there were ten different sizes to display, and by good fortune they fitted well onto the circular iron disc of a weighing scale. The scale is a prop, certainly, but one that belongs in the bullion vault where the shot was made. An alternative, in the absence of something as neat as this, is to build a space by choosing appropriate

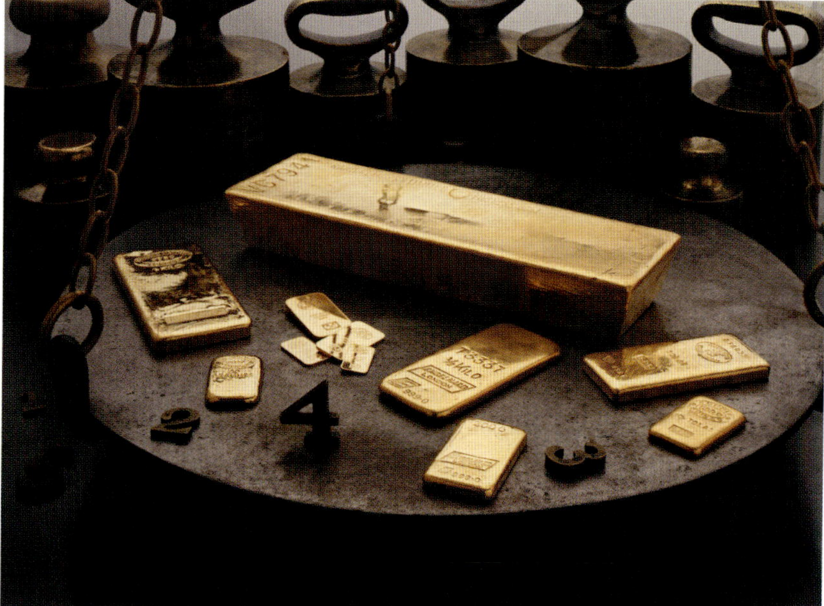

A circular iron scale provided the logic for grouping the dozen different gold bars (see also page 106 for more on the Gestalt principle of Common Region). There were two arrangement needs 1: from the viewing angle, to separate all the bars visually, and 2: to avoid a regimented look. The angle of each bar viewed in plan was made different, with the largest behind, then the positions were fine-tuned from the camera view. Cut-out iron numerals used in the vault were added to fill gaps.

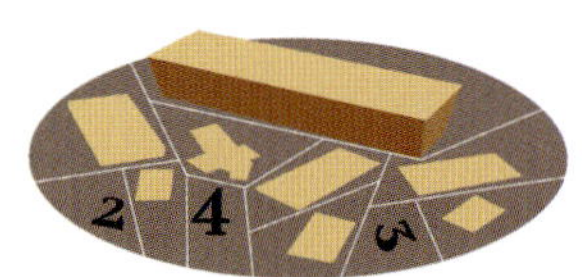

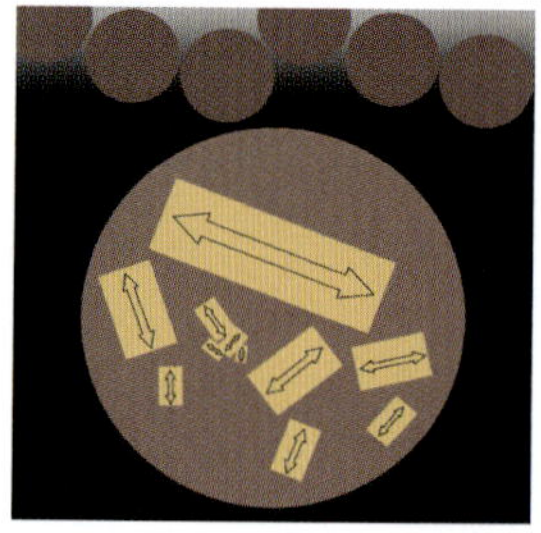

props stacked at the sides and behind. The brass measuring weights in this shot do that job partly by closing off the back.

There are countless ways to arrange, but one theme that occurs over and over is the desire to balance order with naturalness. Structure and logic are needed, but usually you don't want absolute ruler-and-compass precision because that looks stiff and artificial. Striking this balance is never easy, because the viewer knows that you're arranging in the first place, and yet the ideal arrangement is one that no one notices. This can take a long time to achieve. The key to the gold grouping was to make all ten placement angles different. With the cocktail drinks, which had to be in three groups – two decanters with two cups/glasses each and one stand-alone glass – the solution was to use the angle-to-camera to conceal the orderliness.

The three groups of cocktails (3-1-3) were part of the brief and, together with their reflections in black perspex, they needed to be visually separated. Arranging them diagonally in plan (as shown below left) translated into a seemingly more fluid grouping from the camera angle. Fitting the foot, bowl and reflection of the central glass neatly between the left and right groups was fine-tuned through the viewfinder.

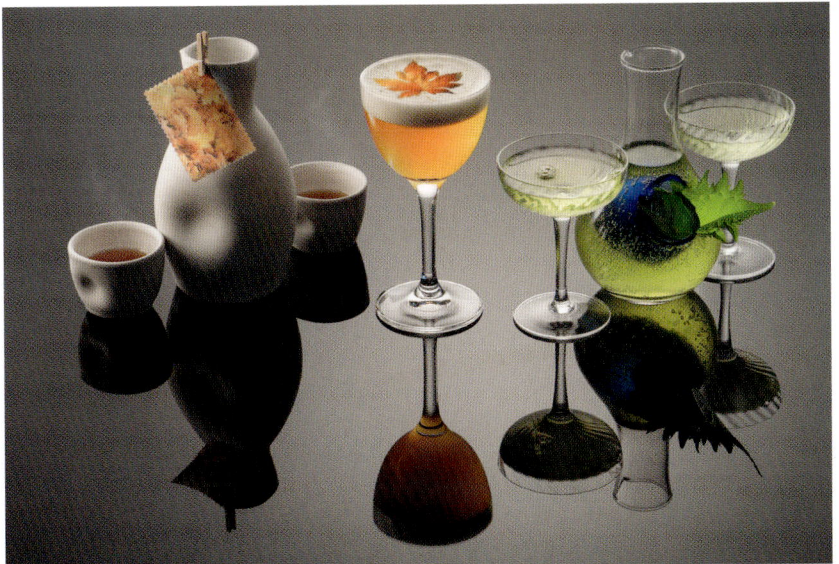

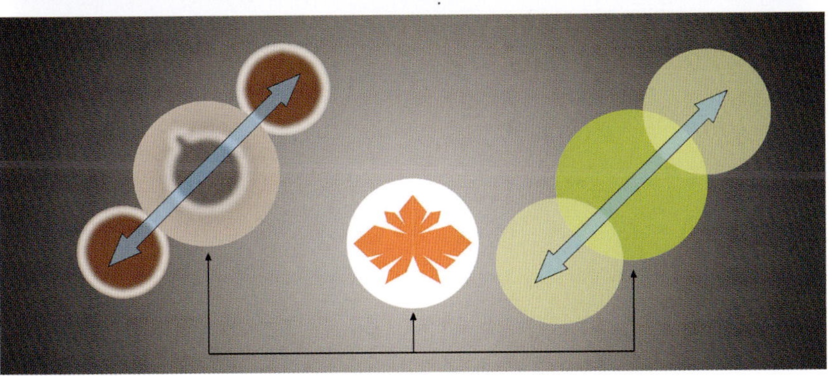

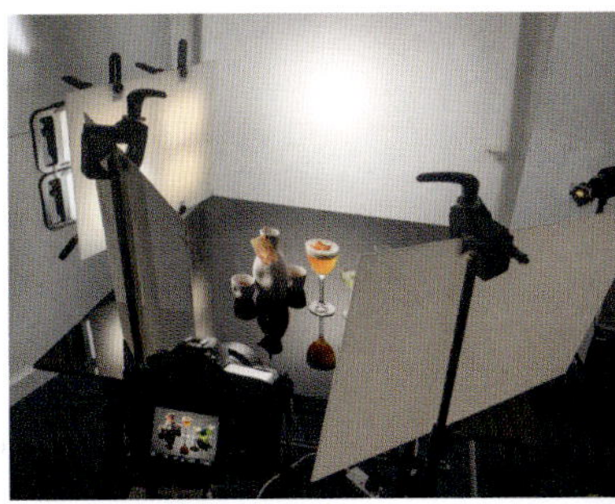

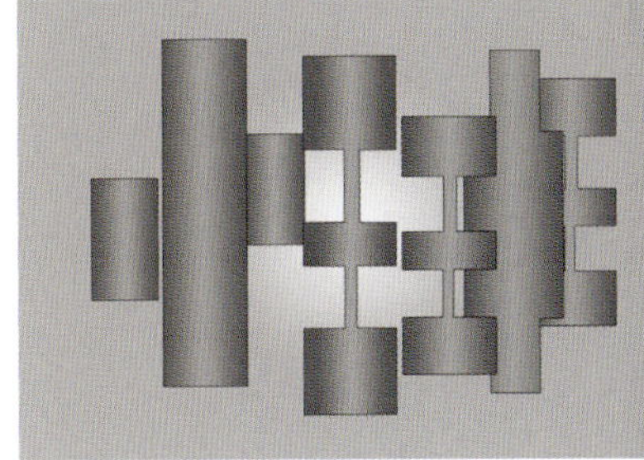

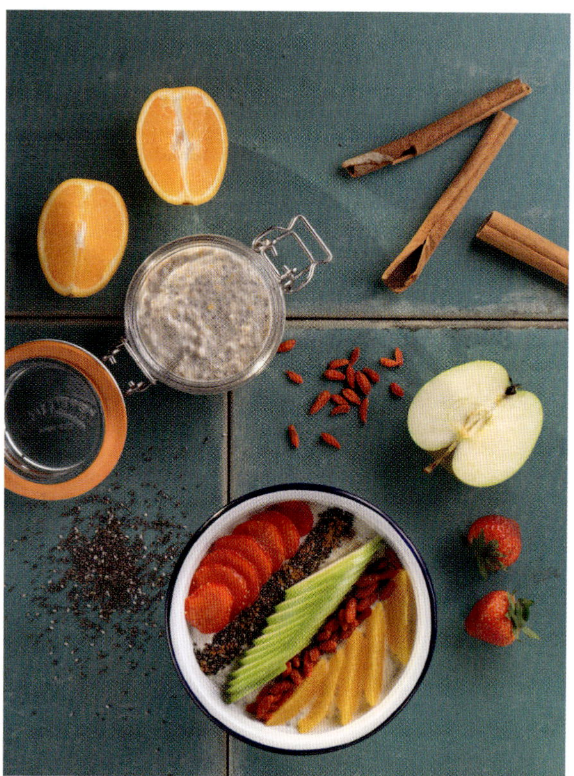

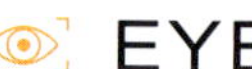

EYE-TRACKING

Arranged scenarios are intended to deliver information to the viewer, so explanation is more important than mood and atmosphere. This has to be planned for in the composition, and it can also be measured in the result. Here's an example from a cookery book; the images not only needed to present the finished dishes attractively so that readers will want to eat them, but also had to work hand in hand with the accompanying text to show the ingredients and method. All the images also need to fit together visually as a series. That means applying a consistent style but including visual variety within it.

Here, the decision was taken to shoot them as what's called 'top shot flat lay', which is self-explanatory, mainly for time reasons. Everything had to be completed in a week, and this style has the smallest and most easily changed background (the lower the camera angle, the deeper the background, which becomes time-consuming to alter between shots). The tiles were a design feature of the resort and restaurant for which the book was being made, and these were changed between shots for variety, as was the position in the frame of the finished dish. The style chosen for the entire series was the dish as served, plus the ingredients. We hoped readers would spend at least half of the viewing time looking at the dish, with the other half of the time briefly looking at the ingredients, which were included to help explain the recipe. One concern was that there might be an imbalance of attention between dish and ingredients; in particular, with this shot, I was worried that the bowl might have been placed too low the frame to get full attention.

One of a series of 80 shots with varied tile backgrounds. This arrangement was tested to see if the very low position in the frame of the finished dish would result in less viewer attention.

We ran an eye-tracking test to see if the composition decisions had been right. Here are gaze paths and fixations from the viewers tested, each spending 30 seconds looking. Everyone looked at all the ingredients and the bowl, and importantly, kept returning to look at the bowl two or three times, so we judged it successful, although there were individual differences such as the oranges and glass lid drawing extra attention from Subject 3. The heat map, however, which aggregates all viewers' time spent, spells a failure that I should have anticipated. The bright muesli close to the centre draws the most attention, which it shouldn't, and takes away from the finished bowl, which is too far away from the centre. Perhaps it's not a real failure, because everyone takes in all of the elements as hoped for, but it suggests a reordering.

SUBJECT 1

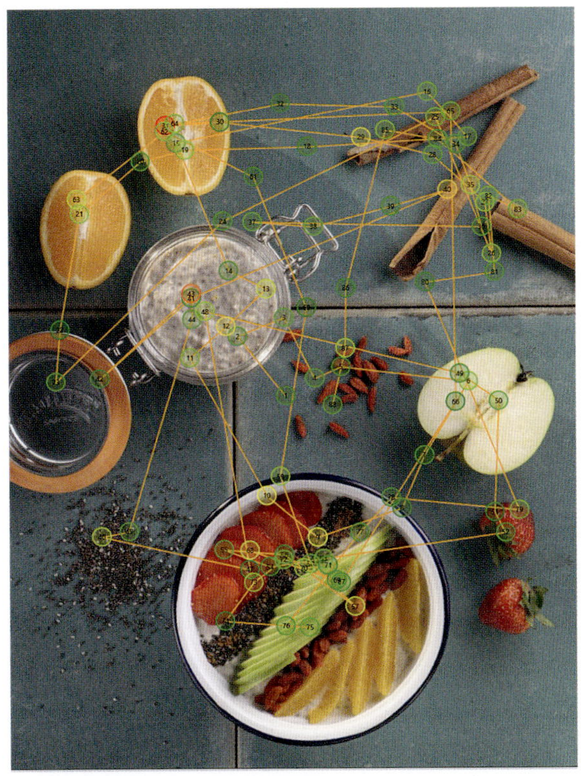

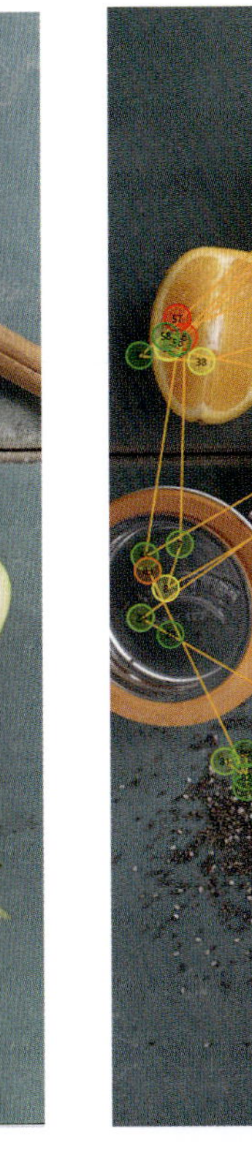

SUBJECT 2

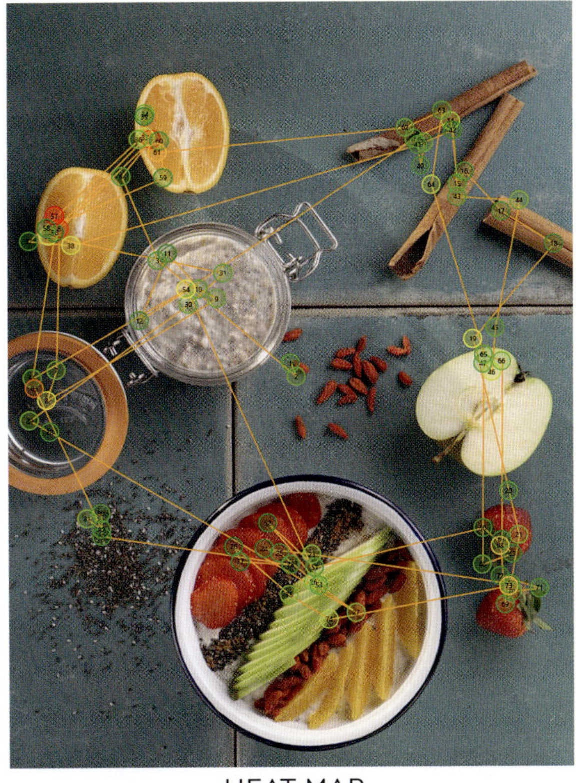

SUBJECT 3

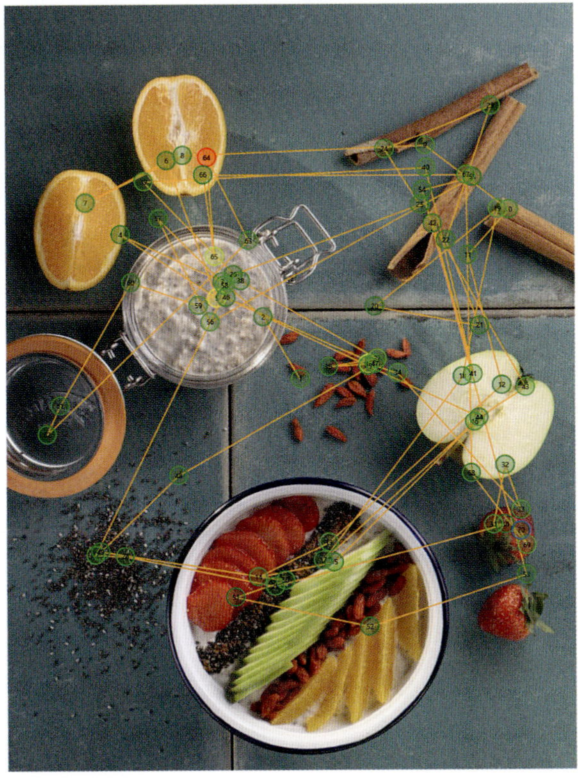

HEAT MAP

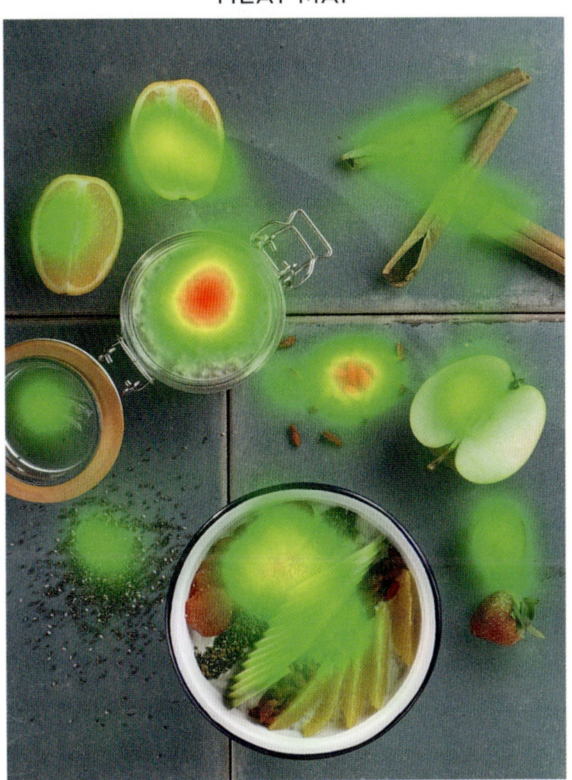

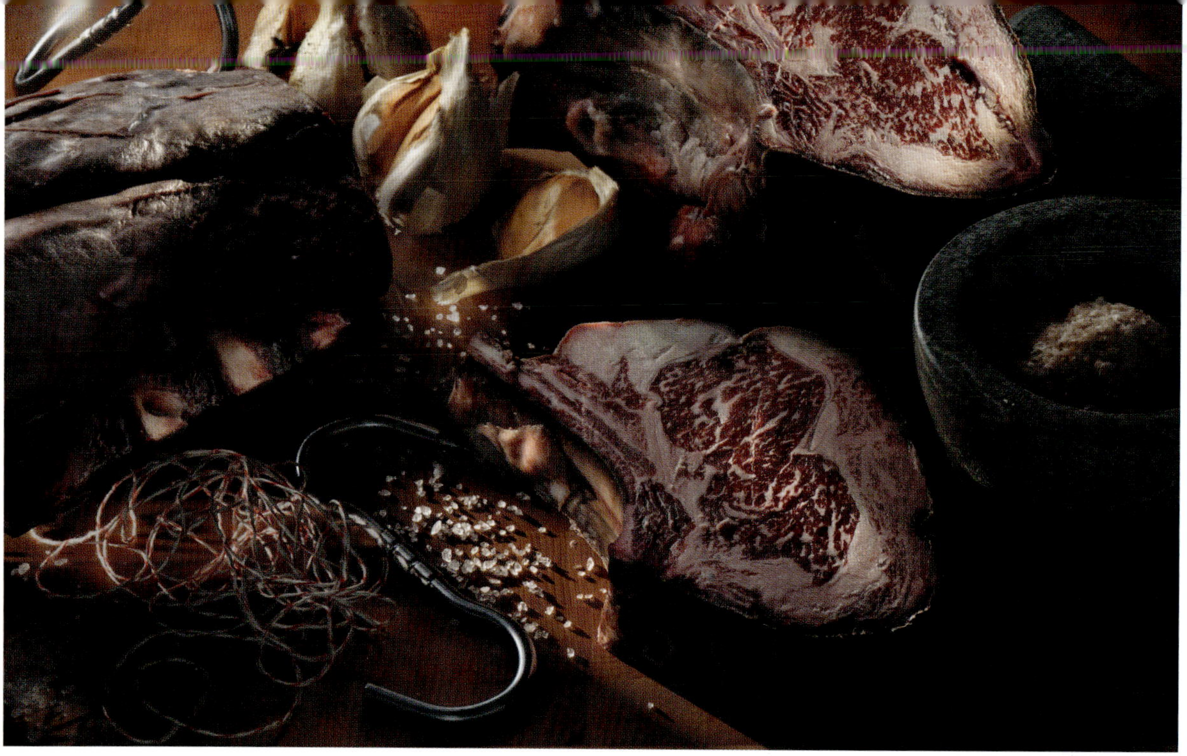

FULL ARRANGEMENT

It may seem strange to use the art word 'tableau' – an arrangement of a number of motionless figures to tell a scene from a story – for a studio still life, but this is as close as photography today usually gets to what was a staple of classical painting.

More than that, the compositional challenge is identical and intricate. Just study the most famous of all tableau paintings, Rembrandt's *The Night Watch* (1642), below, to see how complex it is to fit two dozen characters into a frame. On top of that, to have all their faces visible in an arrangement that's lively and connected without looking like a stiff, monotonous group portrait. It might be cheeky to compare that masterpiece with a still life of meat, but they both take time and a lot of thought. First, the frame needs to be filled, which means that some of the objects have to run off the edges yet without concealing any important part. The corners pose a particular problem because they can't just leak off emptily. Here, three of the corners are occupied with objects

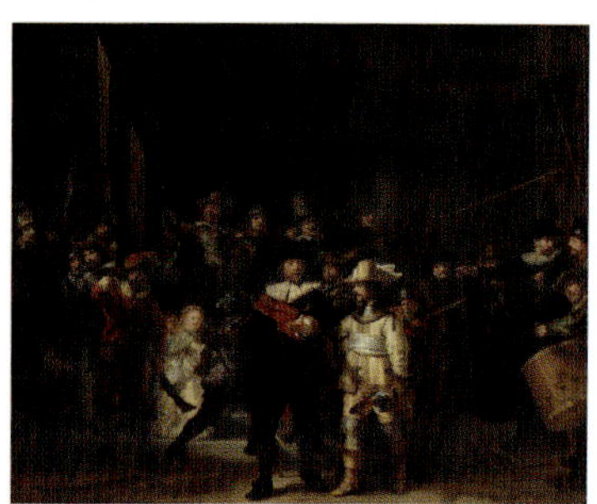

↑ The core of the composition is a triangular arrangement of the three steaks (1 to 3 in red below), around which the secondary items (4 to 10 in white) were fitted. The corners are always important in an arranged shot and need to be managed or covered in some way to keep the overall composition tight and structured.

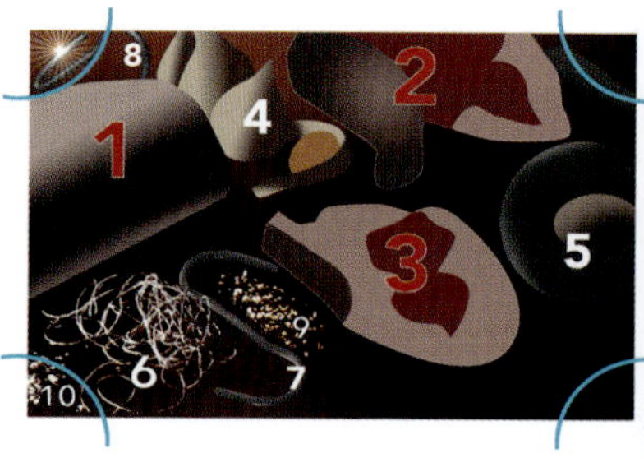

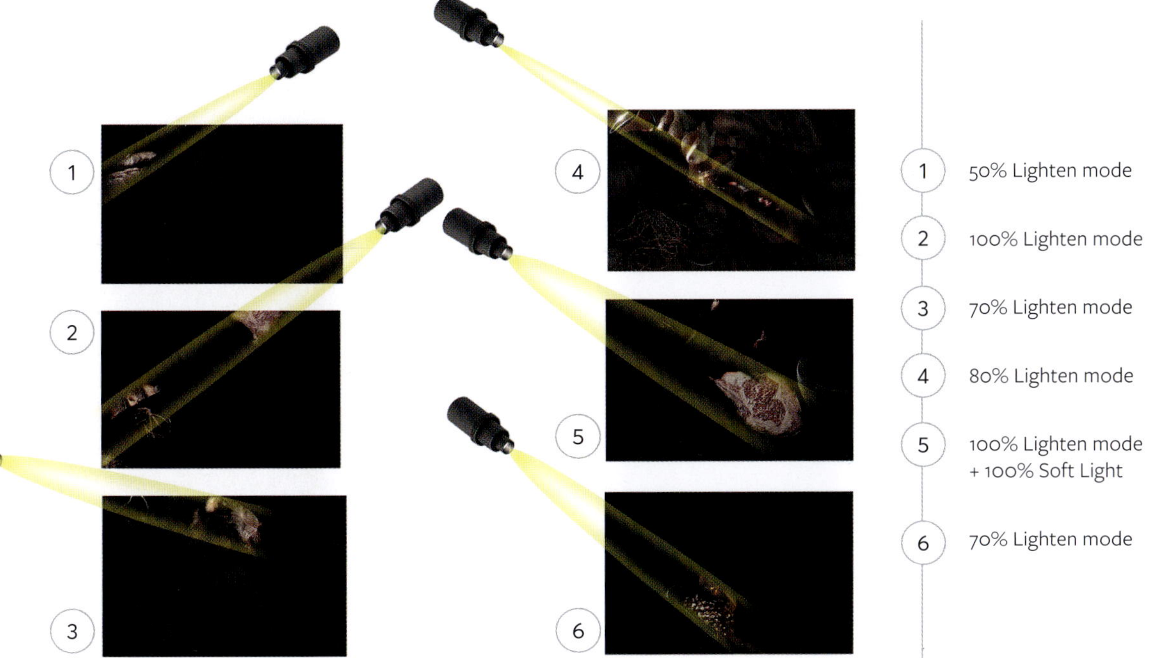

(and a glow of light) and the fourth goes black. Second, objects need to be arranged in order of their importance. Here, there are three main characters – aged tomahawk steaks – and a supporting cast of secondary foodstuffs (garlic, salt) and utensils (hooks, string, pestle and mortar). All must fit together. Third, there needs to be some overlapping to integrate everything, otherwise simply placing them side-by-side would look flat and unlinked. Finally, careful lighting picks out what's important while creating the necessary shadows, and in fact much of the composition is actually controlled by the lighting, which gives prominence to some areas and lets others sink back into shadow. The lighting technique was a set of tightly focused spotlights directed at different compact regions, and they were later combined as layers, which allowed the brightness of each to be fine-tuned in post-production.

↑ On top of a softer overall illumination at a low level, six individually separated spots aimed from different positions around the set controlled the balance of lighting, and therefore viewer attention. They were combined at different percentages and modes as shown above.

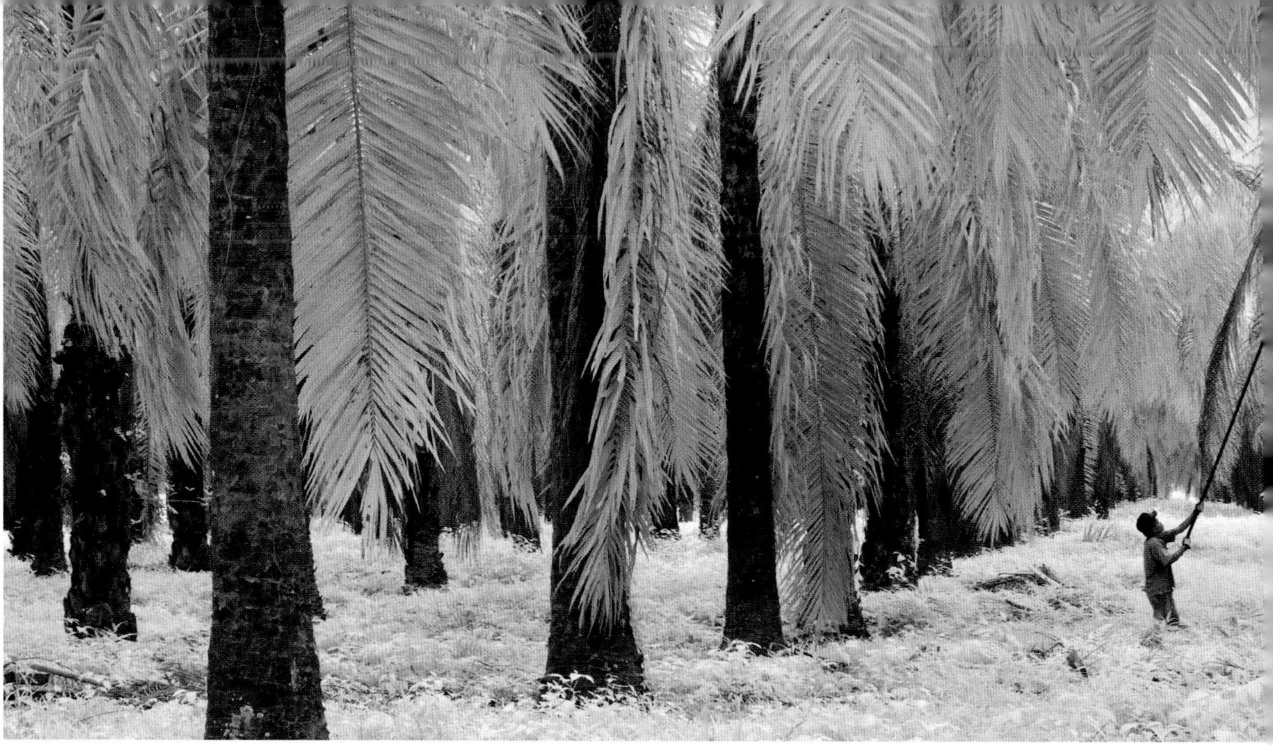

MIRRORING

Despite the many techniques for escaping the bad reputation of bullseye dead-centre composition, there are of course occasions to celebrate it and enhance it, and as long as they do stay occasional, they can be striking. Mirroring is one of these, and as the name suggests, it relies on one half of the image being almost a mirror image of the other.

Actual mirrored surfaces, like still water and shop windows at a very sharp angle, are possible candidates, but they usually suffer from being too obvious – the real point of a successful mirrored shot is that it should have some element of surprise. This doesn't need to be major, but at least it should be a little unexpected or unusual, and typically that means finding symmetry in more natural or casual situations. Architecture, for example, is full of symmetry, and that makes it less interesting because we see examples of it every day. Most people, however, are unfamiliar with large plantations, which makes the regimentation of trees seen from the centre of an aisle, as in the oil palm picture here, striking.

↑ Shot in infrared, the view straight down between rows of oil palms is strikingly symmetrical, but to make it a little more interesting compositionally, it was offset to the left in this pan-and-stitched photograph. Versions with the man in a different positions and absent (below) were less effective.

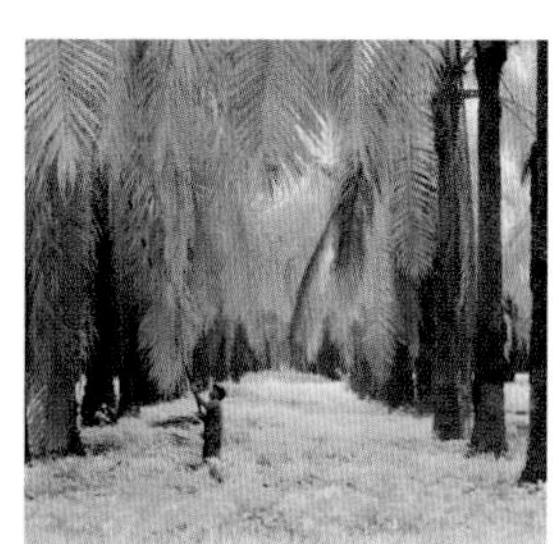

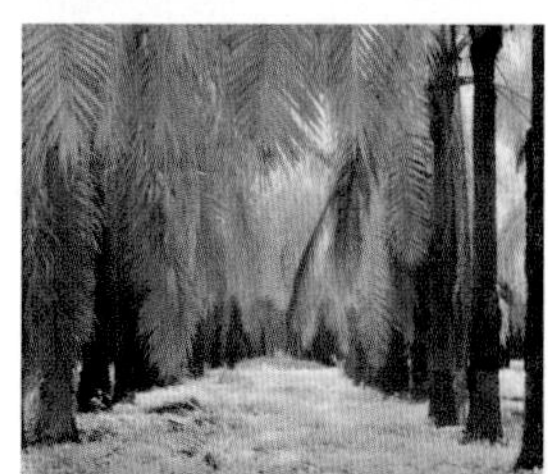

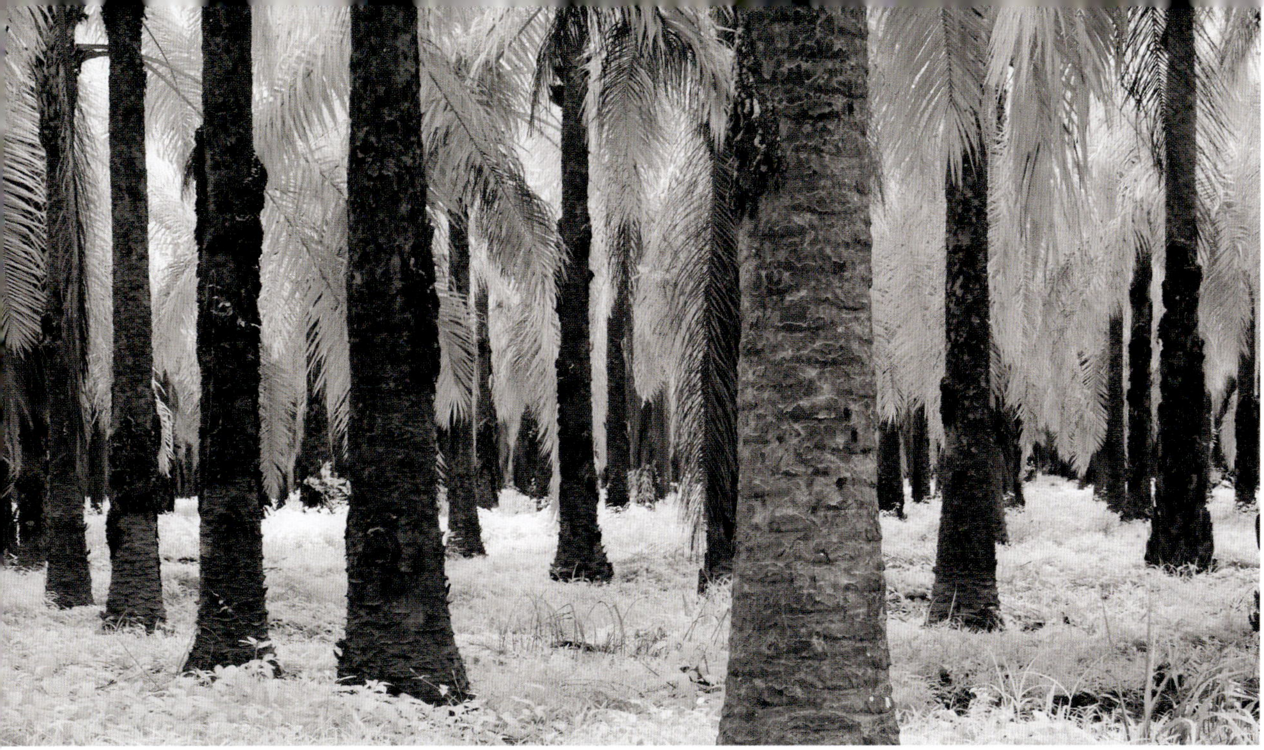

A strong part of the orderliness of mirrored images is the division of the frame into two, and there's a certain unexpectedness in seeing what looks like two pictures not just side by side but butted up against each other. If the division is right down the centre of the frame, as in the case of the Greek fishing boat, it seems in defiance of the more thoughtful and subtle frame divisions we looked at in Chapter 4, like Rabatment (page 68) and the Golden Section (page 70). It's cruder, but as I said earlier, if it's occasional, it can make a strongly graphic image.

A telephoto lens gave the compression that flattened this view of a Greek fishing boat, while the colour accents of red on the rigging and yellow on the hull play a key part in pointing up the bilateral symmetry.

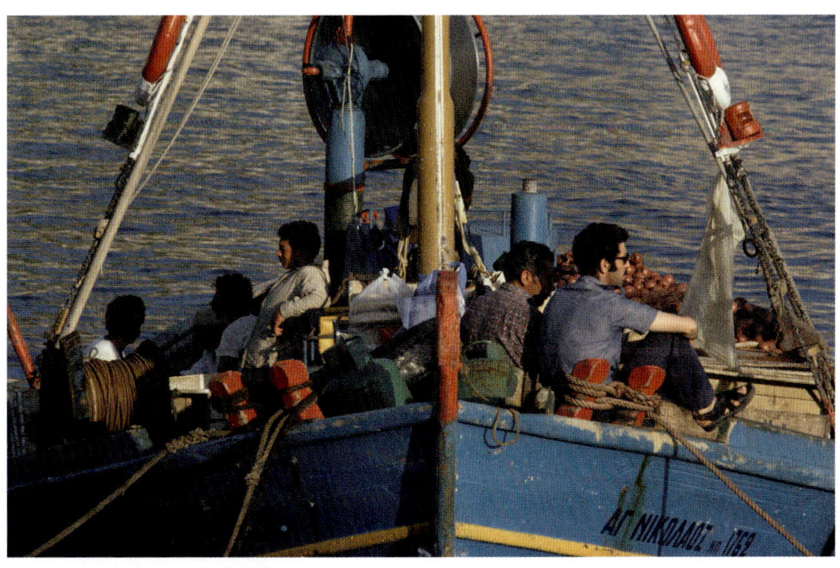

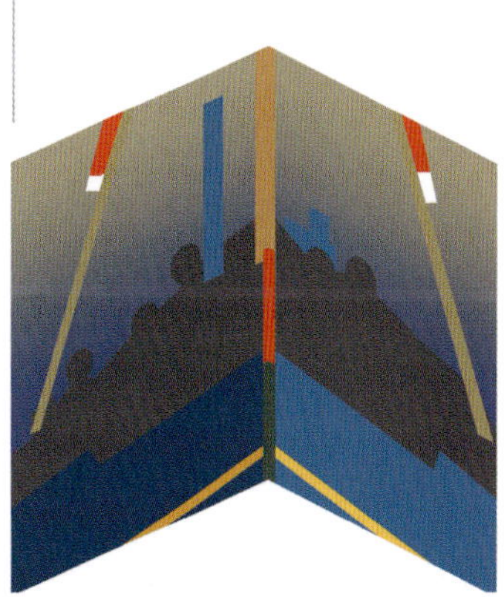

ANCHORING

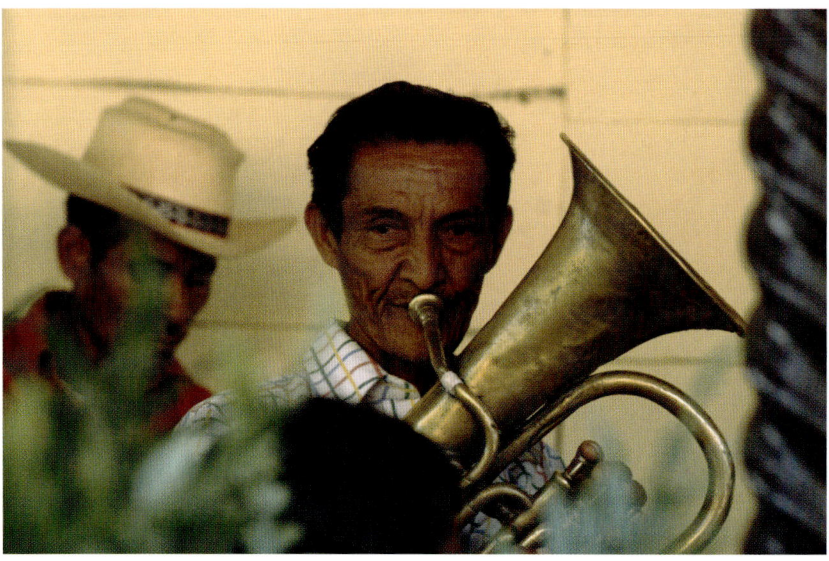

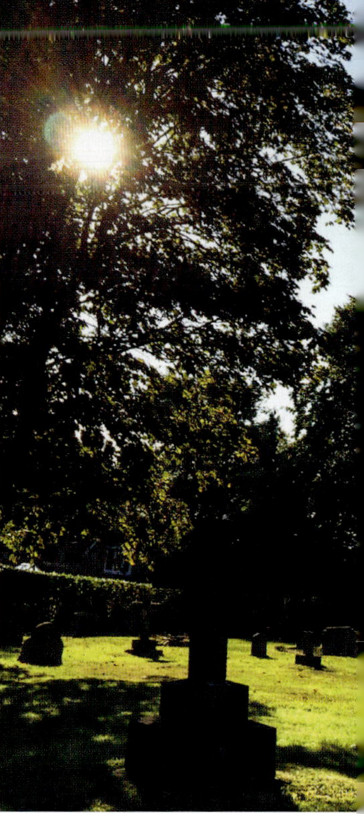

In some picture situations, there's a case for blocking off or 'holding' frame edges as a way of giving a kind of solidity to the scene, locating it firmly. In particular, it helps to stop the eye drifting off and out of the frame, and can even, if you have two or three such anchors, help to enclose the scene and draw attention gently inward.

Like almost any other compositional technique, it's a style of its own, and it appeals to some people but not to others. It is, in any case, a definite way of ordering the picture. And it's almost always opportunistic – a matter of taking advantage of whatever is available in the scene. The picture here of a player in a small brass band in Colombia is a straightforward case. The original camera position was a fraction to the left, with the yellow wall showing at the right edge of the frame. This slightly weakened the composition as the right edge drifted off, aided by the way the tuba's bell 'points'. Moving slightly to the right brought the ornate pillar into frame, adding some of the character of the farmhouse and anchoring the right edge.

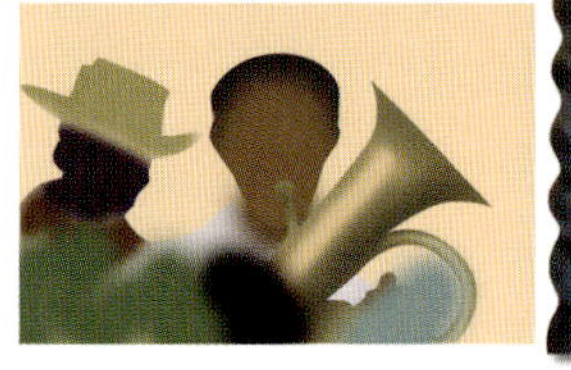

An unfocused spiral pillar solves the problem of an otherwise weak right edge to this photograph of musicians playing at a Colombian ranch. The left side of the image already has a man and foreground foliage, equally unfocused so that the attention is firmly on the man playing the tuba in the centre.

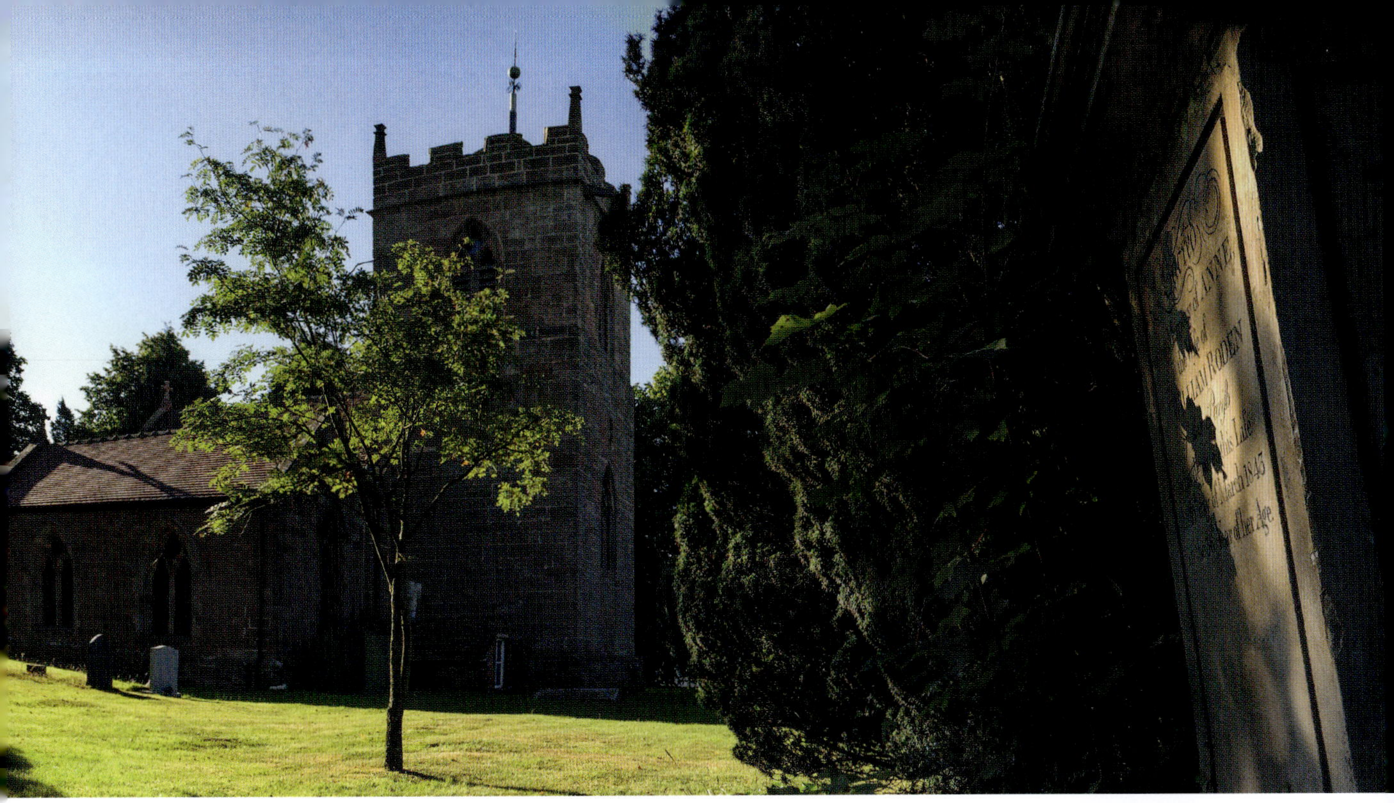

Two opposite masses provide the anchoring stops at left and right of this widescreen shot of a Shropshire church and its grounds. Although different – a foreground gravestone and a distant tree – they are related to each other graphically, as each is dark with a bright centre. This coincidence helps them to enclose the scene and direct attention inward.

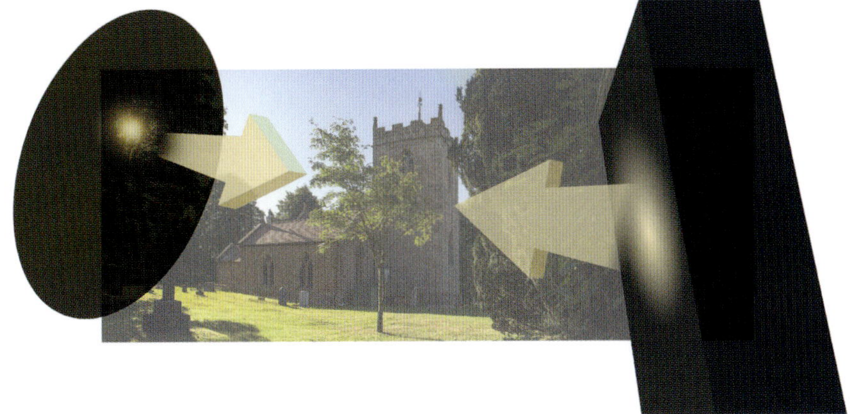

A more proactive use of anchoring is in the widescreen shot of an English country church. Sunlight filtering through leaves onto an old gravestone is not only an attractive motivation for making this the foreground, but it provides what widescreen framings often lack – a stop at their sides. Widescreens are enjoyable and satisfying to use because of all the possibilities they have for including different subjects, as we saw in Chapter 3 (page 60), but they have a typical problem in that they let the eye wander sideways. Left and right anchors solve this.

CHAPTER

7

THE DIRECTOR'S CHAIR

These last chapters are essentially devoted to the three jobs of composition that I introduced right at the start. The previous chapter addressed order out of chaos, the last chapter will deal with creating interest through unusual design, and this chapter is about directing attention. This is clearly ambitious. With video, for example, your audience is firmly under your control (as long as it chooses to sit and watch), and wherever the camera goes, the viewers do too. A still photograph is a completely different matter.

Viewers will look around a photograph as they wish – usually rapidly. Moreover, as we saw from the eye-tracking tests, individual viewers also bring their own interests and quirks to looking. Corralling other people's eye movements is like herding cats, and the best you can usually do is to deploy devices that attract – and attract in a particular order or sequence – in the expectation that they can nudge the viewer into noticing things more or less as you would like them to. This is not an exact science by any means, but as I hope I've shown, it's possible to get to know the kinds of things that people will be drawn to.

We've already seen some effects that influence attention in a natural way. The several kinds of perspective – diminishing, linear and aerial – are strong examples of natural encouragement because they take advantage of effects that we're all familiar with and which enhance the sense of depth, so that the viewer follows them into the scene. Geometrical devices like implied triangles and circles can also push attention, whether toward an apex or inward toward a centre, as do the enclosing strategies on pages 122–3. Other techniques like quartering (see pages 84–5), and even rabatment (see pages 68–9), have grouping effects that also serve to highlight whatever they contain.

In this chapter I'm going to introduce some more specific tools for directing attention to particular parts of a photograph. Most of them are graphic, while some lean more heavily on their content, so that there is a difference between structural and semantic techniques, even though they interact. Ultimately, of course, the idea of direction in most photographs is toward the photographer's subject of most interest (and so is semantic).

We start with forging immediate connections between subjects in the frame, which not only works on attention but also stimulates engagement, and then move on to methods of taking the eye to a specific point in the picture, which sometimes might not be the most obvious or immediate point. Part of the reason for doing all of this is to ask viewers to spend more time with the picture. Especially now, in a visual world that's dominated by screens, there is increasing pressure on viewers to switch rapidly from image to image. Slowing that down has become a new measure of success in photography.

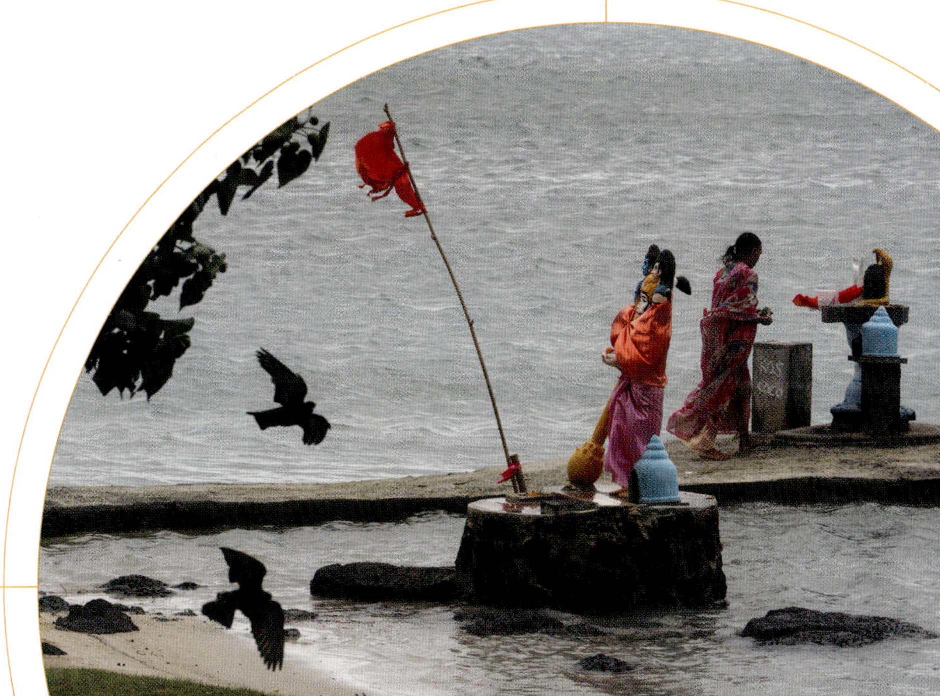

PAIRING

One disarmingly simple design principle that nearly always triggers a positive response in viewers is to find and feature pairs of things. A pair means two of the same kind, or at least similar, and close enough together that we assume they're a unit.

On the face of it this seems such a straightforward and undemanding choice – you could hardly call it an idea – that its near-universal attraction is perhaps surprising. After all, it's not as if pairs are unusual. But they do command more attention. In principle, two is not just better than one, it has a different dimension from one.

A number of dynamics come into play. One is connectedness. A pair of anything appears as a unit made up of two parts, and we naturally assume that these parts interact in some way. They have a relationship, and that might be a real relationship between the two individuals that the camera is recording, or a simple graphic relationship – and in the case of people and other creatures, both of these at the same time. In each of the images here, the pair is interacting in some way, either visually or actually, or both, and a general principle of pairing is at least one kind of close similarity, and preferable two or more. The more matching they appear, the more they qualify as a pair. A second dynamic is that a side-by-side pair simply occupies a horizontal picture frame more fully. The scarlet ibis shot demonstrates this, and this obvious arrangement lends itself to balance, centredness, sometimes even symmetry.

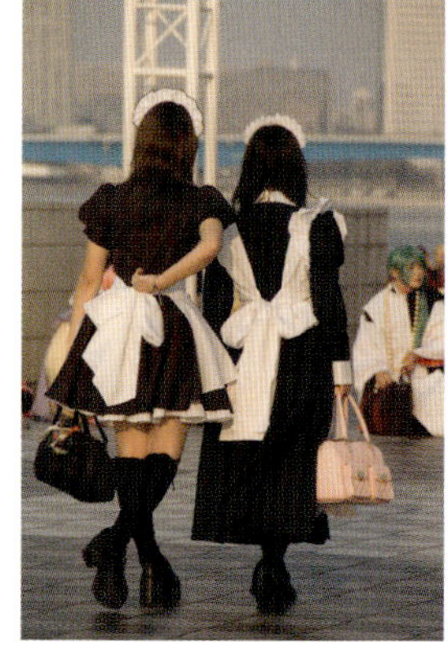

The difference between a pair and a simple couple is that pairing demands close visual similarities, the more the better. Here at a Cosplay gathering in Tokyo Bay, the quirky dress is sufficient, but it's added to by the girls walking together in step.

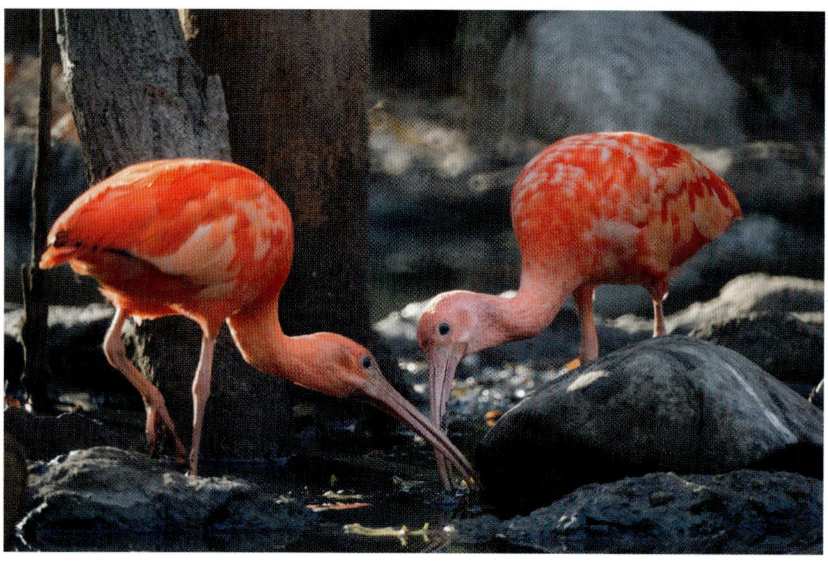

Two scarlet ibises are similar not only in shape and colouring, as would be expected, but in facing inward in similar attitudes that mirror each other (see page 130).

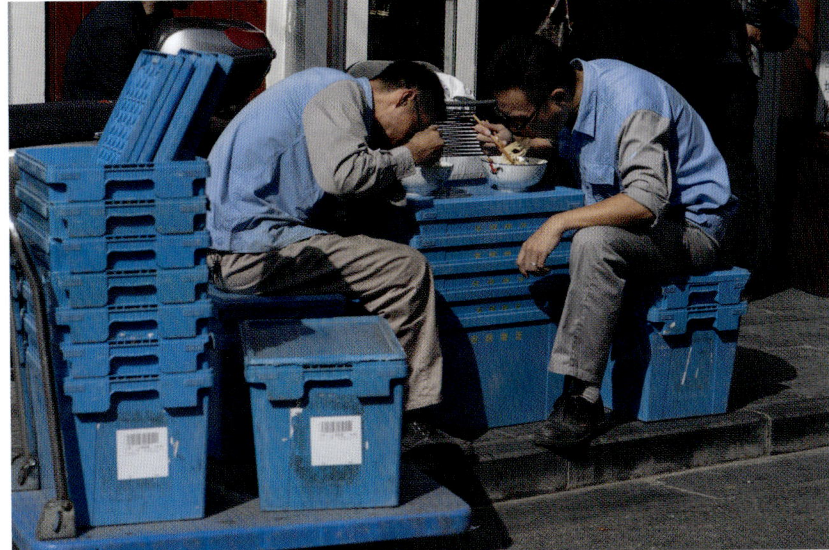

Two delivery workers in Shanghai surrounded by their crates stop for a quick midday meal, and are paired by colour, similar action and facing inward.

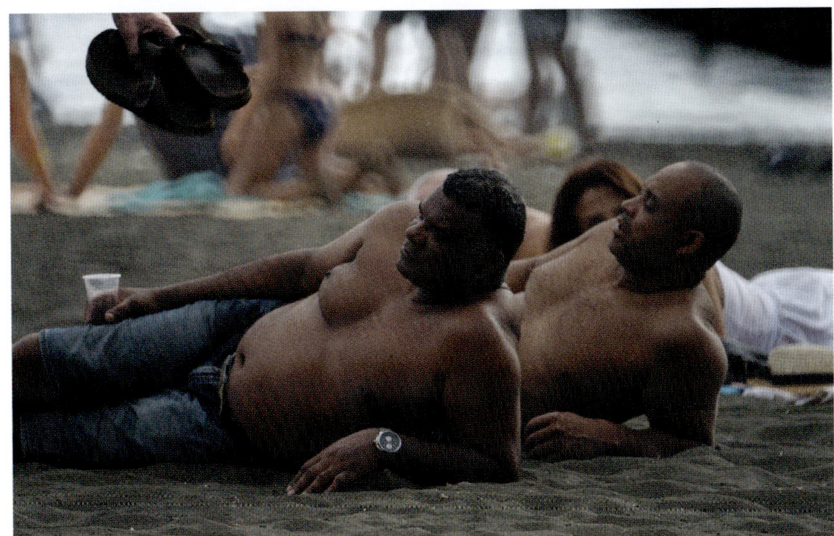

At a weekend beach concert on the French island of La Réunion, two men recline at a performance, and become paired less by being both bare-topped than by similar posture in a clear case of parallelism (see page 106).

A third dynamic is that showing viewers a pair invites a search for likeness and for difference that is very hard to escape. It's an involuntary reaction. We look for ways in which they are the same, and simultaneously for ways in which they are not. It puts the viewer in an investigative mode, so that, with luck, they engage that little bit more with the picture. All of this might be stating the obvious, and paired images don't usually have much of a wow factor, but they work. As to why we have a natural affinity for them, it's likely because we're societal animals in search of pairing ourselves.

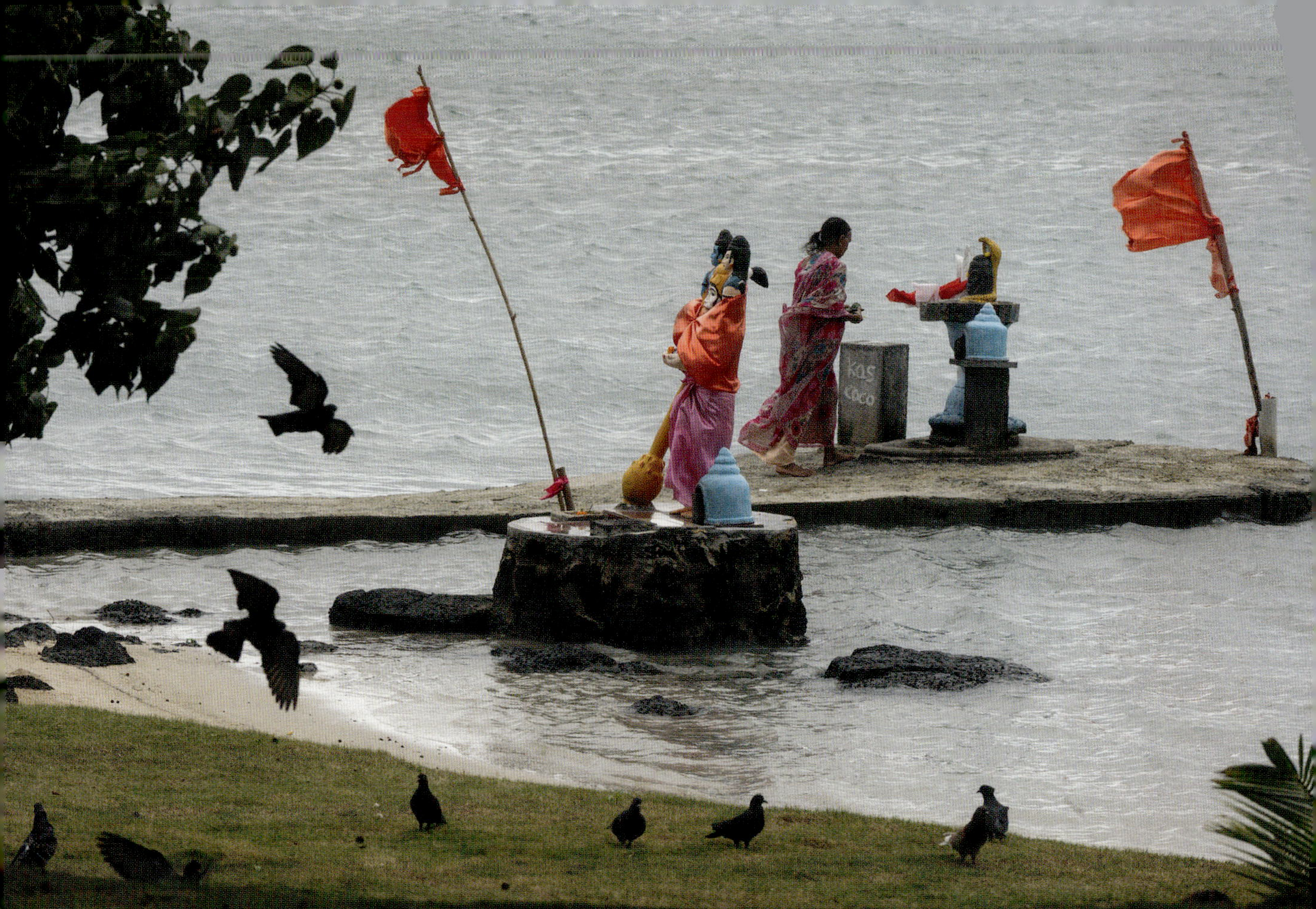

MATCHMAKING

Connections play a major role in photography, much more than in any other creative medium, because we're mainly dealing with real life and its unpredictability. That gives added value to the observation and skill in making a connection between elements in the scene.

What is it that makes two particular things go together and spark some extra thought? Juxtaposition – setting one thing against another in the frame – is the core idea. Quite simply, it adds depth to the image – depth of meaning, depth of graphic form. Often just one of these, but sometimes when we're lucky or just working harder at it, both at the same time. When it's about idea, the combinations are endless, and it's all about seeing a connection that other people would miss, but which they get once you have captured it skillfully. The skill part is crucial, because

↘ A marble sculptor in Mandalay, Myanmar, leans forward to work on a statue of the Buddha. The shadow on the Buddha's face was potentially a graphic echo of the man's face mask, but only realizable by processing in black and white and using the channel mixer to darken the purple and lighten the skin tone to match, as in the illustration.

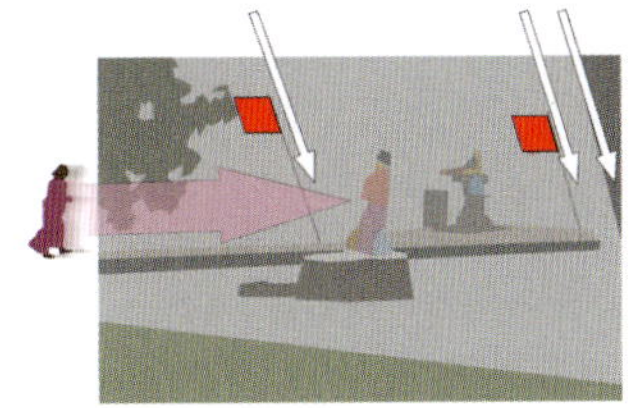

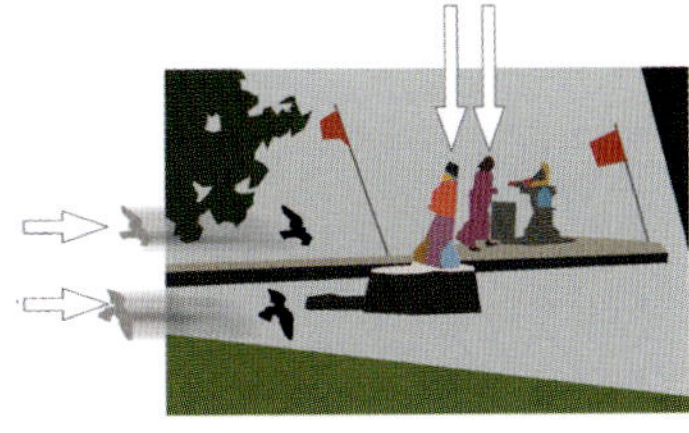

At a small Hindu shrine jutting out into the sea in Mauritius, this shot was framed in anticipation of a worshipper walking out along the stone jetty, and with luck would make a pair with the cloth-clad statue. They were framed by another pair – the fluttering red flags, and with more good luck, two birds flew into frame from the left at exactly the moment when the woman was in the gap.

getting it to work practically is not always easy or straightforward. If you just happen to come across a juxtaposition that triggers a satisfying reaction in your mind and eye, that's a stroke of luck and you need no more than a quick reaction to shoot it. If, however, you have the idea that two things might work well together but they're separated in space, the problem then is to find the magic combination of viewpoint, lens and composition that will make it work.

Matchmaking of this kind is so powerful for photography because you can't easily invent the situation without going to a lot of trouble or moving into the studio. The surprise element that a good juxtaposition needs is that two things were unexpectedly in the same space at the same time. It's also a proof that you are functioning well as a photographer: being alert and creative enough to be open to the possibilities. If you were painting or illustrating, there would be no great trick to putting two subjects together. Nor would there be if you use Photoshop to achieve it. The idea of the combination might be good, but there would be nothing special about it visually, as it's just too easy to do. This has to be in-camera. As a photographer, you have to work with what you can find, and it's only occasionally that you have the opportunity to shoot two subjects in order to make a point – even assuming you're alert enough to spot the connection. Being tied to reality makes strange and unimagined juxtapositions all the more powerful and valuable.

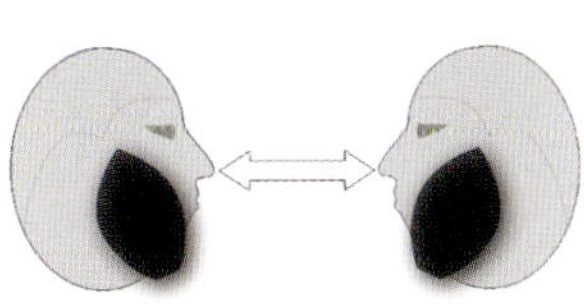

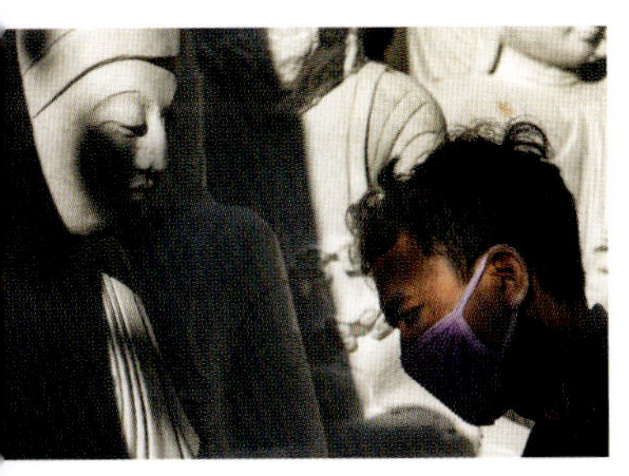

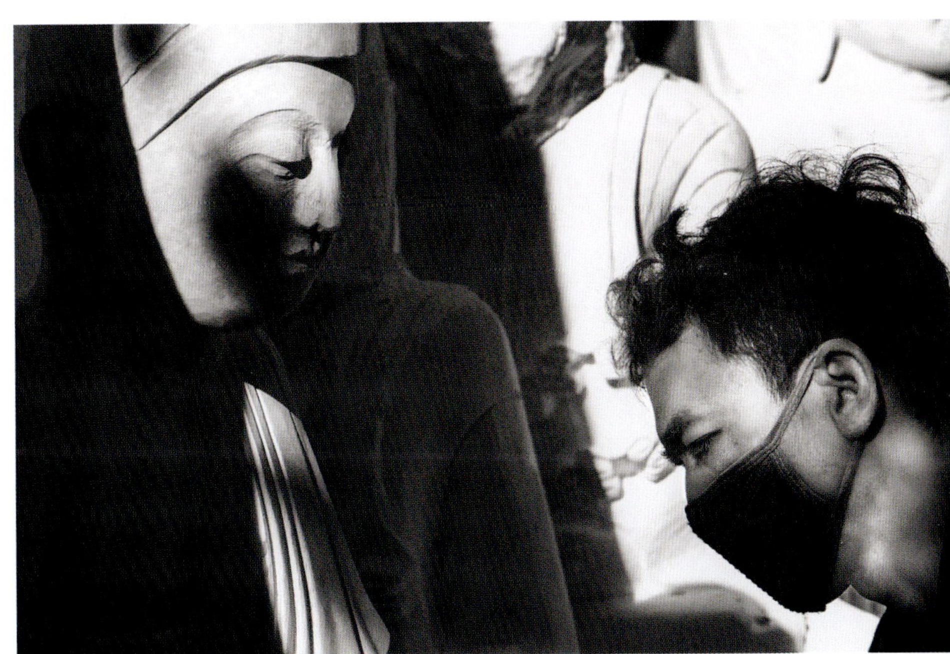

SLOW REVEAL

There's a time and a place for being clear and obvious, which is something that photography does brilliantly. It may even be what is wanted most of the time, as in spot news and in any situation where making a record is the priority. Advice such as 'move in close', 'keep it simple' and 'use a plain background' all follow this principle. Being obvious, however, has a potential drawback.

This approach feeds the glance-swipe habit that's now embedded in most smartphone and tablet users. Enter the 'reveal'. This is an idea taken from the movies, where it works more easily. Nevertheless, when you can get it right in a still photograph, it lengthens the viewing time of the image and gives it more depth. The cinematographic version has a long history and in principle is straightforward. The camera starts on one subject, or even not much of a subject, and then moves to reveal a completely different one – the real subject, as it were. The move could be a tracking shot or a pan, or occasionally a zoom, and the general idea is to surprise the audience.

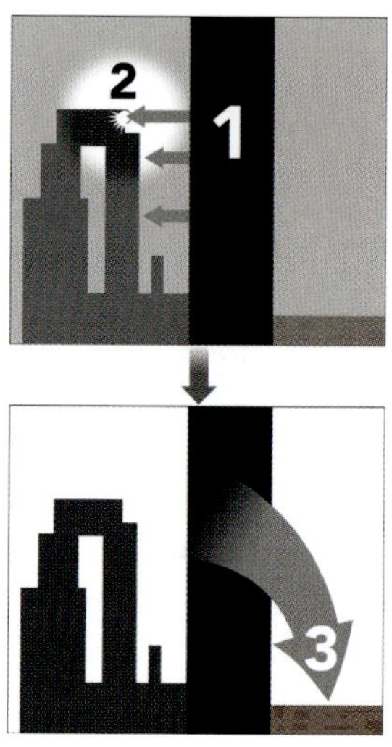

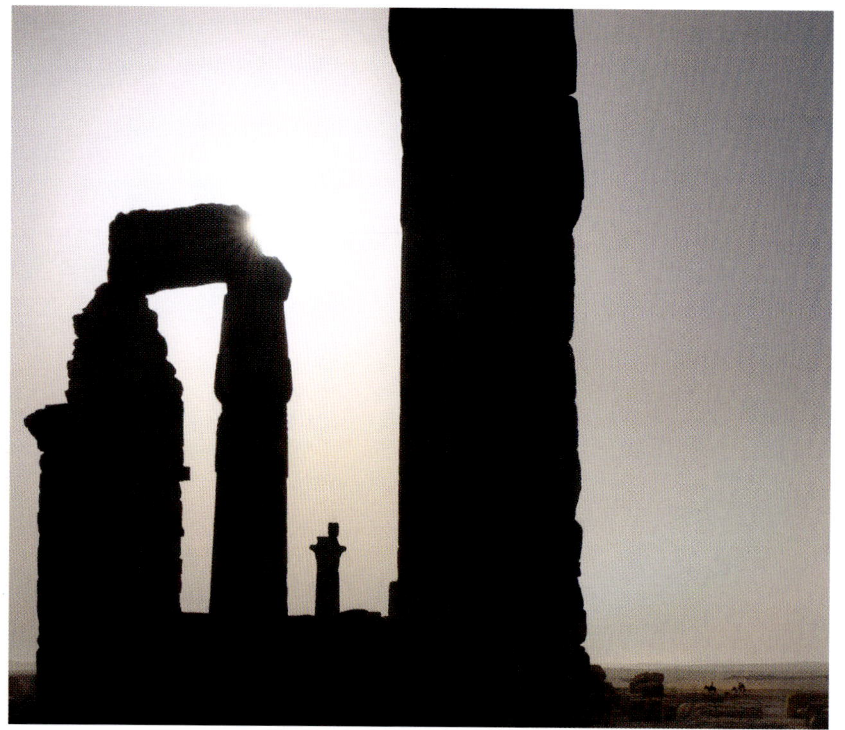

The ancient Egyptian temple of Amenhotep III in Sudan's Nubian desert, shot in silhouette. For both scale and delay, the small figures at lower right were intended to reveal slowly. The plan was to first hit the eye with the solid mass of the central pillar (1), after which the eye would go left to the sun (2), and from here to the only place remaining (3) – the lower right, the only part of the scene that wasn't a silhouette – to discover the figures.

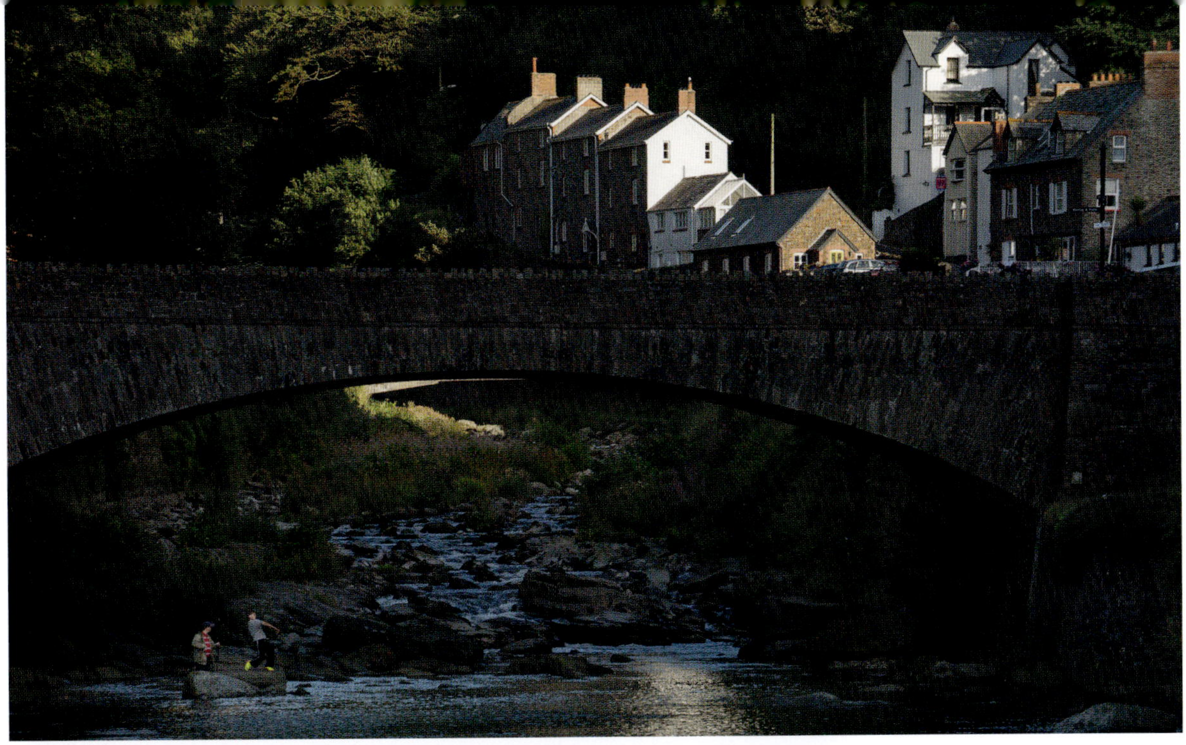

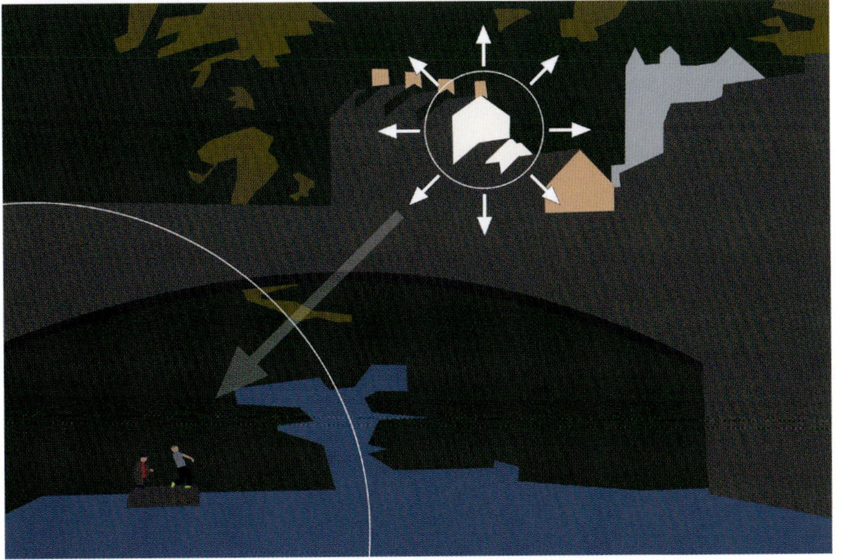

Looking upriver at the town of Lynmouth in Devon, the sunlit white end of terraced houses draws the eye like a magnet, and it's from there that the attention begins to move outward. As we saw about balance on page 112, when the obvious point of interest is way off centre, as here, the eye sooner or later goes to the other side of the frame to see if there's anything there. And in this case there is – two boys chucking stones into the river, but because of the light and the corner position, there's a slight delay

With still photography, we can't control the linear flow as in a movie, but there are techniques that give it a chance. If you pull it off successfully, you get your audience to stay longer with your photograph. The risk is that the audience won't get it at all. It's an uncertain balancing act, because if you hide the thing-to-be-revealed too well, the viewer will get bored and move on before seeing it.

POINTING

Related to the slow reveal are situations where a key subject in the picture is small or otherwise not so obvious, and you want to guarantee that it gets seen. The solution is to use graphic structures that will lead the eye toward it inevitably, without leaving anything to chance.

This is a kind of graphic pointing, and usually lines are involved. We saw earlier, at the end of Chapter 4, how diagonals and curves encourage movement along them. They act as vectors, in other words. The picture below is an example. It was shot as part of a magazine story on birds' nest soup, the exotic and high-priced Chinese dish that involves collecting special nests in remote caves in Southeast Asia. Full-length picture stories call for a large set of different images, and one of them needed to be of collectors on their way to a cave in their small boat, off the rocky coast of an island in the Gulf of Thailand. The boat had to be small yet obvious, and the schematic shows how.

The idea of intersection and convergence is developed in the architectural interior shot, where we wanted to emphasize the geometrical design while centring on the bed. Using an extreme wide-angle lens (14mm) from this angle in a corner made the maximum effect of diagonals, and as the schematic shows, the way they converge in multiple directions and intersect with the verticals visually encloses the bed, while keeping everything dynamic.

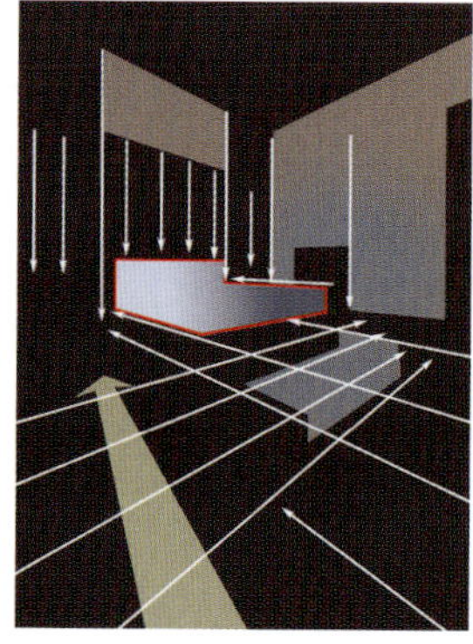

A corner position with a wide-angle lens and vertical framing guaranteed a maximum interplay of diagonals from the floor and verticals from the walls, all converging on the bed as shown above. The purpose of this was as much to show off the geometry of the interior design as to ensure that the bed remained the focus of attention.

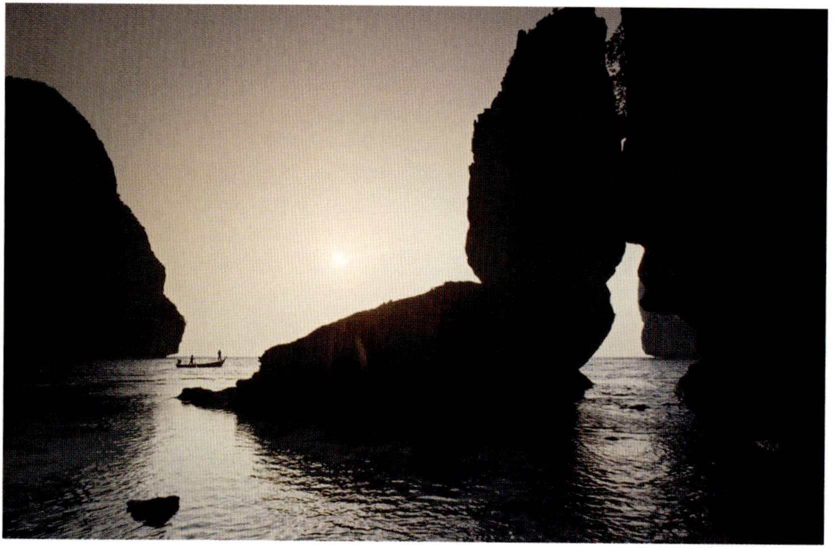

Keeping the boat this small yet immediately visible and located in the landscape meant finding a configuration of the cliffs and distinctive rocks that would automatically draw the eye toward it. Eventually this location was found, and as the arrows in the schematic diagram show, the two enclosing edges in silhouette converge on the gap of water.

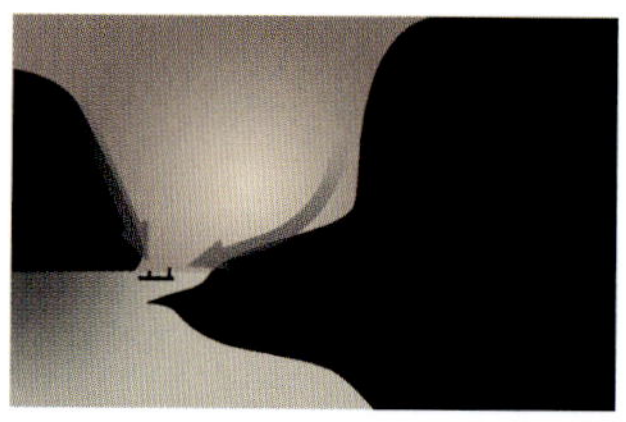

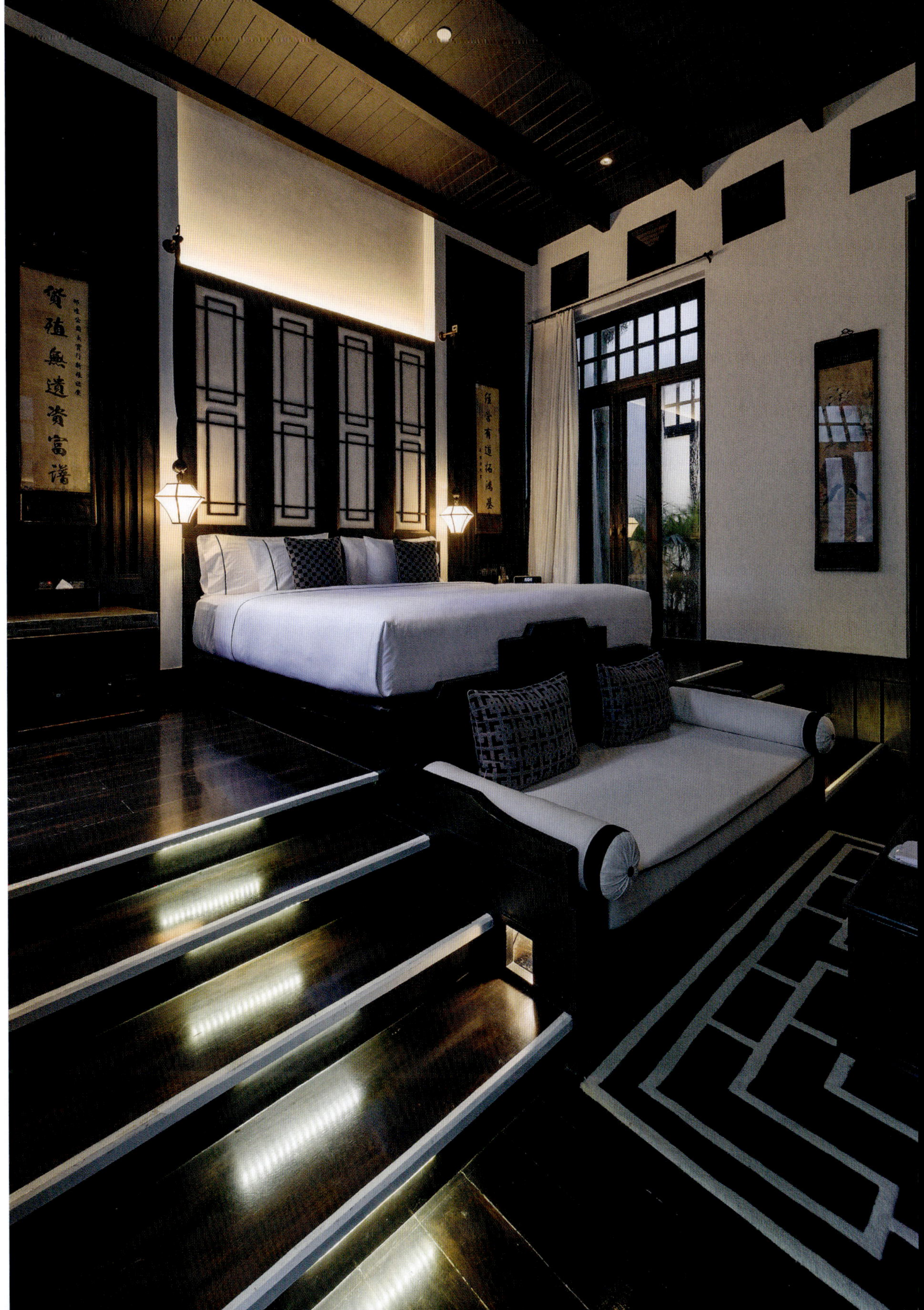
貨殖無遺資富譜
經營有道拓鴻基

FOCUS PULL

We've already seen how selective focus brings a sense of physical depth to an image (page 40), but it also strongly attracts attention. Just as the eye tends to move toward the light in a high-contrast picture, where there's blur the gaze moves to whatever is sharply focused.

This seems obvious and natural, but if you compare it with how we see the world around us, it's anything but natural. Good vision (and I include corrected vision with contact lenses or spectacles) does not 'see' blur of the kind photographers are used to with defocused camera lenses, not even in the peripheral vision that I discussed in Chapter 1. Whatever we don't focus on is hard to make out, but we can still tell whether there are hard edges or not. It isn't smoothly softened like the blur you see in the pictures here. It's called spatially imprecise.

The reason I'm making this point is that photographic blur from a lens at wide aperture has its own special quality that we don't otherwise see, and that accounts for its attractiveness. So, in addition to selective focus working to draw attention, it

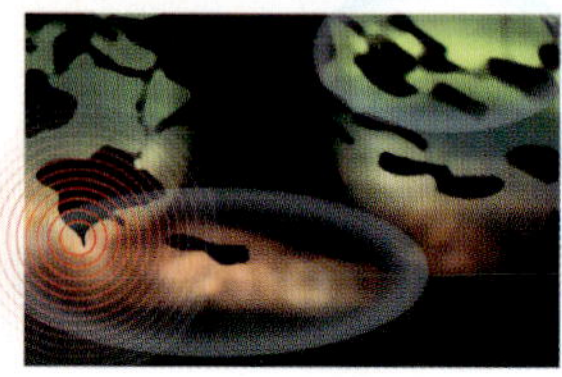

Extreme selective focus with a long lens blurred the background. Two attention-getting mechanisms are in play here: first, the two pools of light which are likely to catch the eye first, and second, the focus on the tip of the nearest leaf at left, which ultimately dominates the attention.

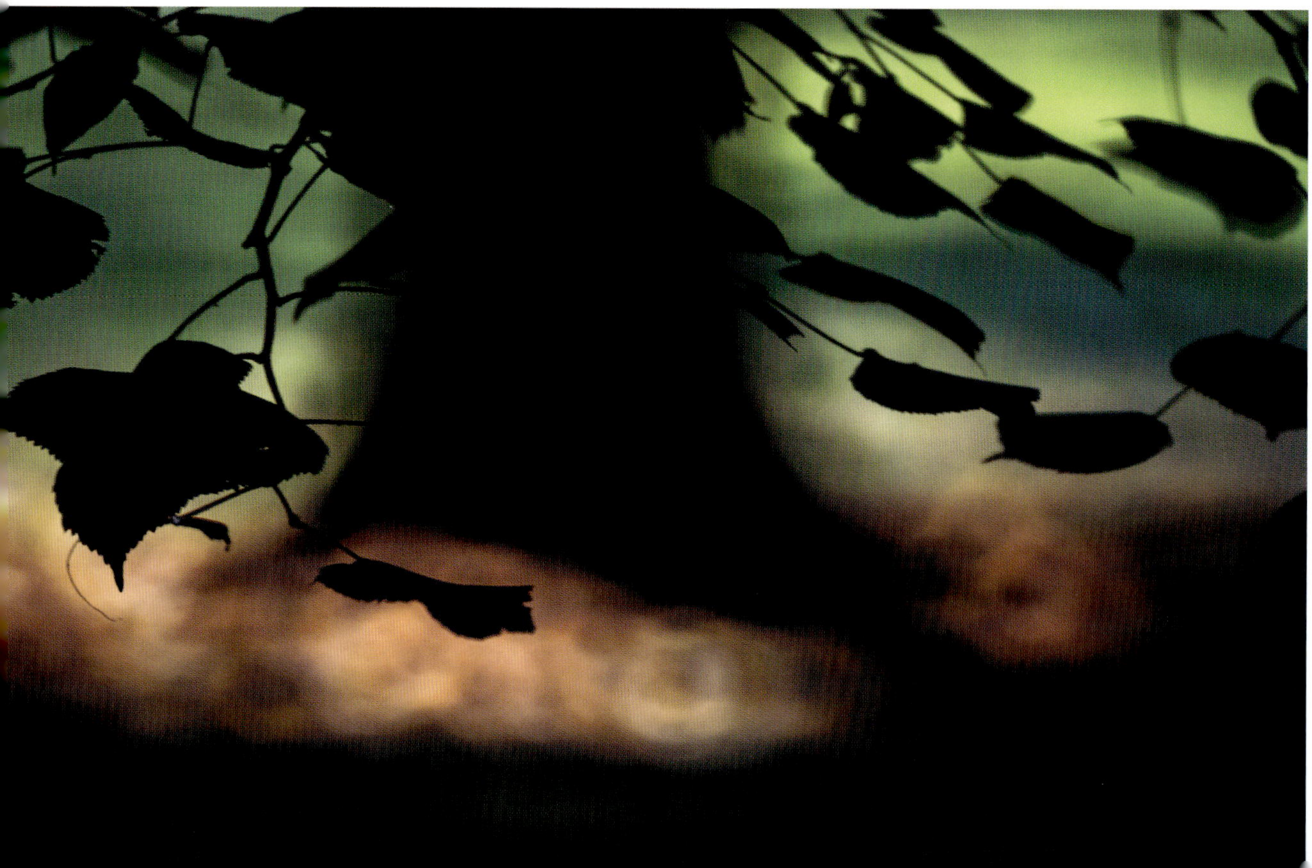

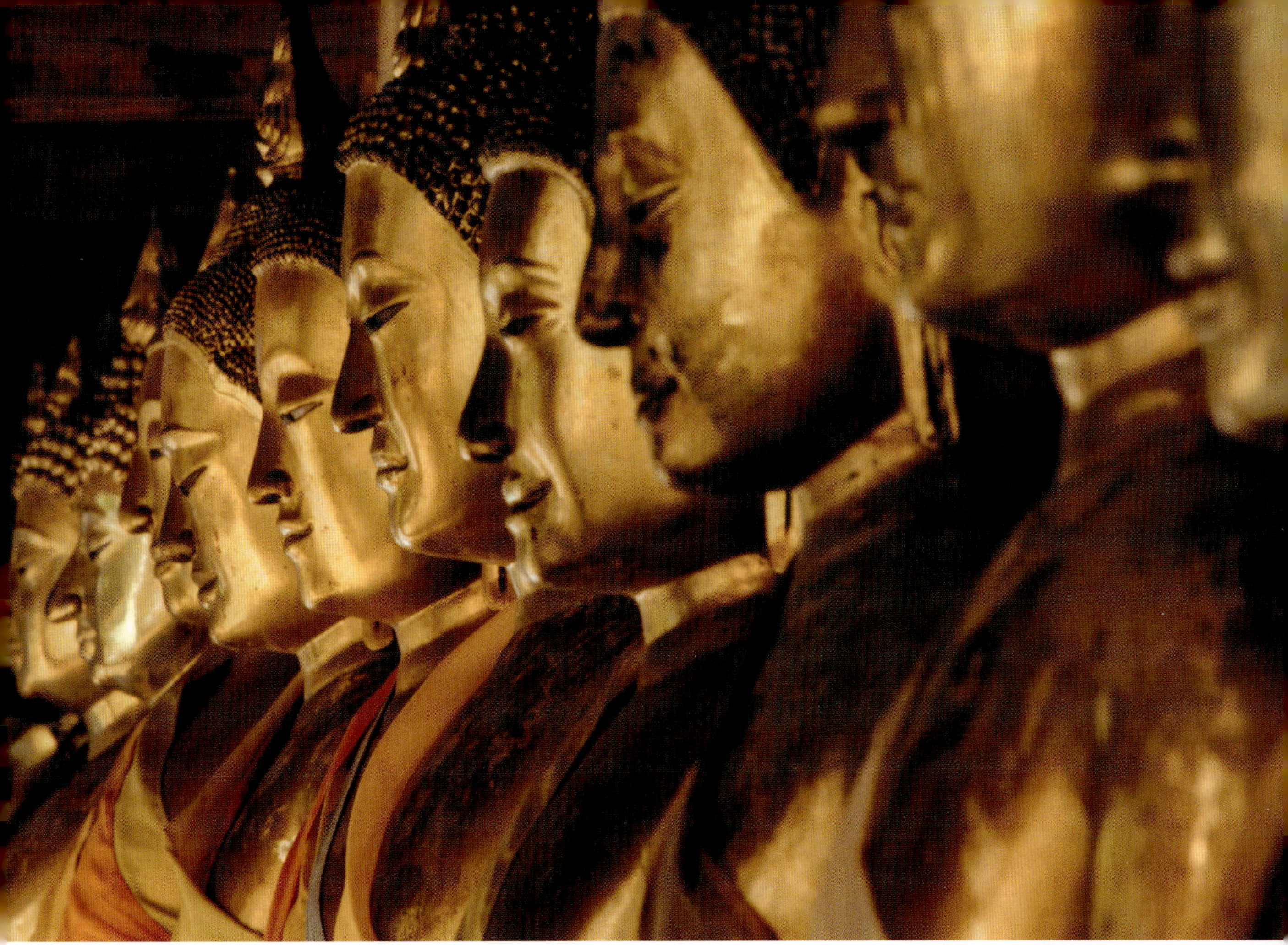

also sets up graphic contrast between small sharp point and a large blur. The quality of the blur is an essential component in this kind of picture, and lens manufacturers go to some trouble to get it smooth and artefact-free. With shallow focus, there's a difference between a focused subject that's clearly separated from its blurred background, and a focus ramp, where the focus blurs gradually away from the point of sharp focus. In the first, the eye is more likely to snap straight to it, as in the picture of the leaves, but a ramp like that in the row of Buddhas encourages a gaze that moves along it.

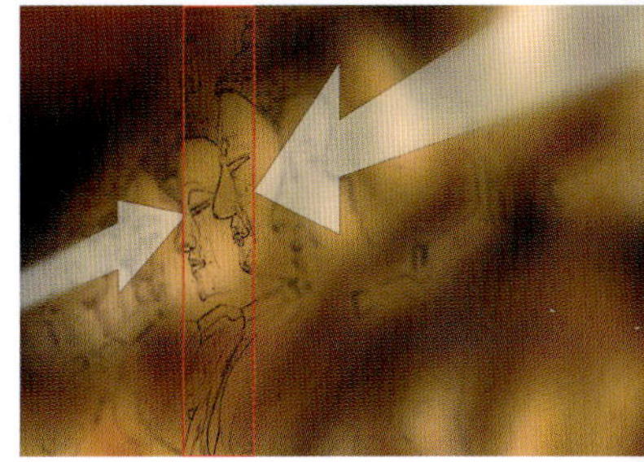

↑ Also a long focal length shot, this view at an angle to a row of gilded Buddhas is deliberately focused about two-thirds of the way in, which pulls the attention from both sides of the frame.

CHAPTER

8

SWIMMING UPSTREAM

After bringing order to a scene and directing attention around it, the third job of composition is simply to add interest. Easily said, but not actually simple to do, because it always means challenging the expectations, and there is no formula. It very much relies on imagination, and also on a sustained effort to think of different compositional ways to treat every situation you come across. To be always questioning and experimenting is not easy, and it's oh-so-tempting to fall back on tried-and-tested skills and ways of doing things. The best I can do here in the last chapter is to show a number of ideas that you might consider applying to different picture situations you find yourself in. Think of them as mini styles, if you like.

Is it possible to go too far with extreme styles and techniques? If the aim is to push the boundaries and be different, it's risky to apply limits. The history of photography, and of art in general, shows that what's radical and unacceptable for one decade can be embraced by another. Pushing the limits is what keeps any creative activity alive, even though different and experimental approaches don't guarantee better results. Far from it, the chances of going nowhere are high. There are two problems attached. One is the urge to be different just for the sake of being different, and without some good idea to back up the desire, the result can just lack credibility. The second problem is that any experimentation naturally increases the risk and decreases the hit rate.

The suggestions in this last chapter cannot automatically confer success, and they are only a small sampling from many, but we all have to keep trying, working and experimenting. Complacency is a killer, especially in composition, where it may be tempting to think that once a number of methods have been mastered, that will be sufficient forever. The American photographer Garry Winogrand, mentioned later under 'Tilt', said that if he saw a familiar picture in his viewfinder, he would 'do something to shake it up',[1] which echoes the earlier advice by Alexey Brodovitch, art director for *Harper's Bazaar* for more than two decades: 'If you see something you have seen before, don't click the shutter.'[2] He also said to photographers, 'Astonish me.' If you can astonish yourself, so much the better.

1 Garry Winogrand quoted in Caponigro, Paul www.johnpaulcaponigro.com/blog/15219/27-quotes-by-photographer-gary-winogrand.

2 Brodovitch, Alexey, *Alexey Brodovitch and His Influence* [exhibition catalogue], Philadelphia College of Art, 1972.

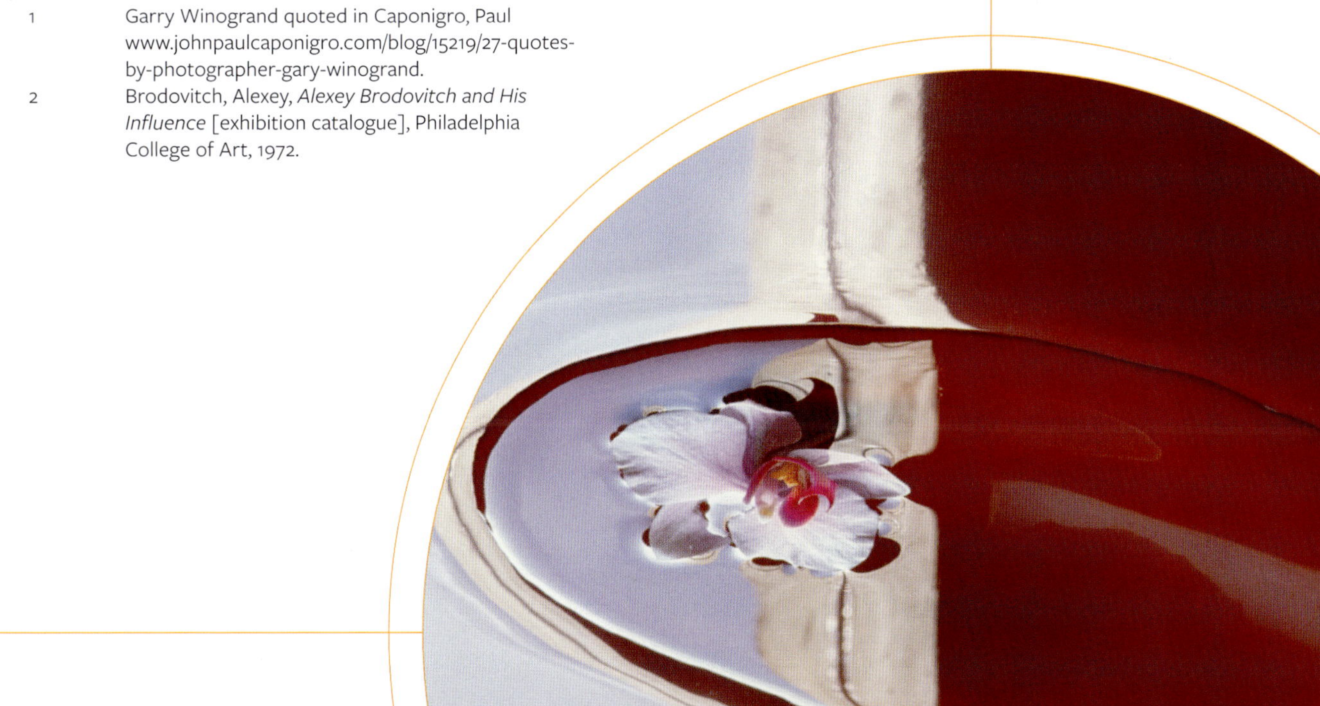

ONE-CORNER

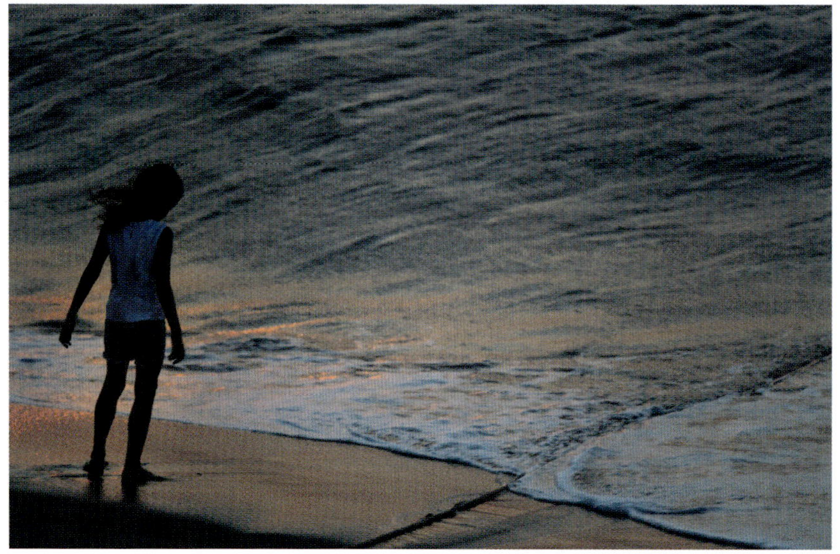

The moment and stance of this girl, playing on the waterline of a South American beach at sunset, helps to forge her connection with the water, while the long focal length (500mm) compresses the sea so that it rises up to the full height of the frame. One-corner compositions work best with a setting that we know or assume is vast.

This is a special and extreme method of composing, but it also has purpose – and history. The name is taken from the Chinese *ma yi jiao*, which means Ma's one-corner, because it was invented as a radical painting composition by the influential 13th-century painter Ma Yuan.

The subject is set in a lower corner, while the rest of the picture recedes to a misty emptiness, and no-one had seen anything like this in art before. Such an eccentric design didn't appear in western classical painting. Simply being extreme to catch attention is pointless, as I mentioned in the introduction, but here there's a good reason – in the original paintings, at least, it's about the contrast between the touchable reality of the world of senses and 'an awareness of the infinite.'[1] What makes it fascinating to use occasionally (and it can only be occasionally) is that it has some affinity with the 'figure-in-a-landscape' style that we saw on page 140, and yet the figure doesn't need to be so small. The emptiness that the figure faces into does the rest.

1 Hearn, Maxwell, How to Read Chinese paintings [exhibition catalogue]. New York, The Metropolitan Museum of Art, 2008.

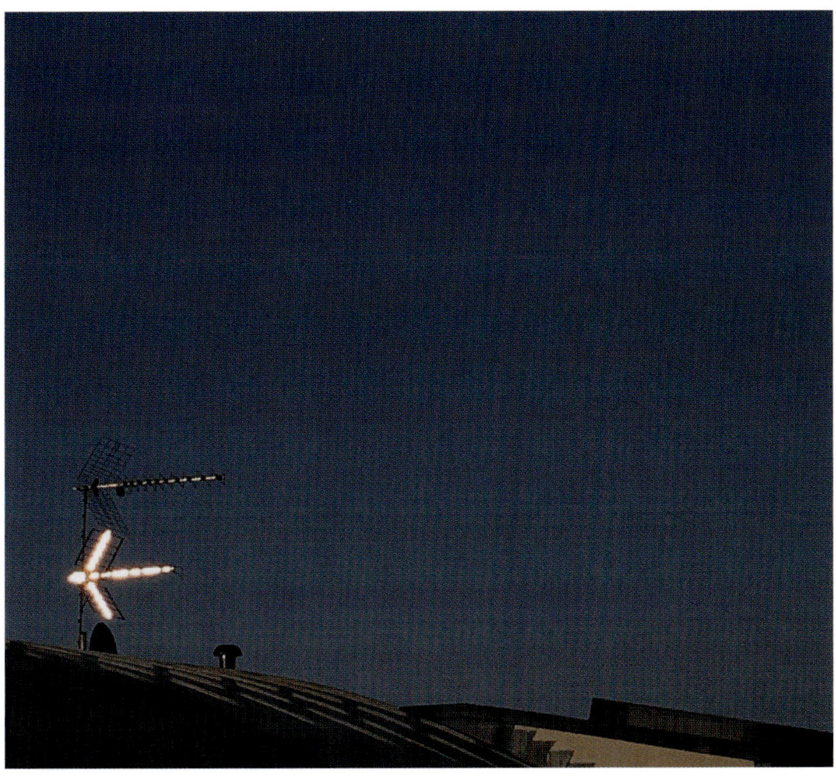

Sunlight reflecting from an aerial against a deep blue evening sky takes the one-corner style to a highly abstract direction. Again, the sky itself, featureless and endless, is a main component of the picture.

This is at the far end of the scale of offsetting a subject in the frame. Previously we've seen centred, the slight off-centredness of the Golden Points, and the more extreme Fibonacci points, but this one is as far as you can go. It draws its strength from the relative emptiness and blankness of the rest of the frame, so that sea and mist are always good candidates. Busier settings make a corner position less striking and less immediate.

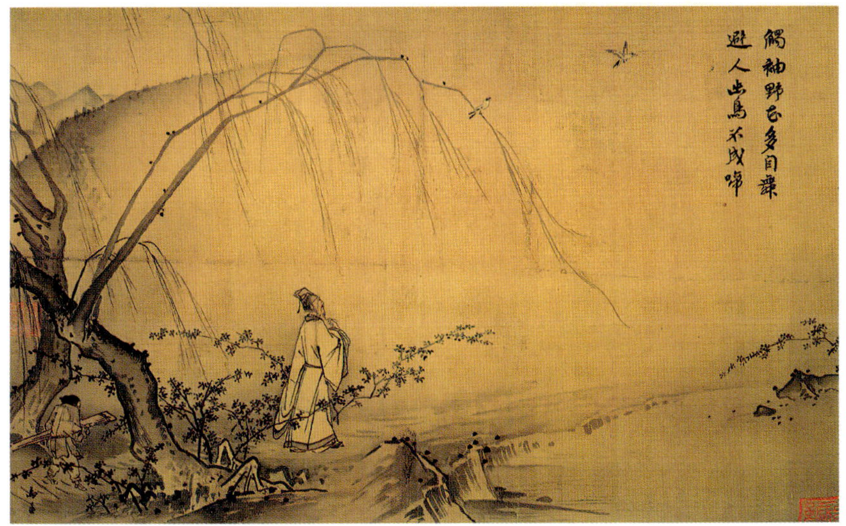

Walking on a Mountain Path in Spring c. 1160, is typical of the Southern Song Dynasty painter Ma Yuan, who invented the one-corner style, in which the active subject is pushed into a lower corner, facing the emptiness of the infinite world.

END-TO-END

The first few techniques in this final chapter are essentially about location and placement – putting subjects in less-than-obvious places in the frame. In itself this isn't particularly difficult, but it does need purpose. There has to be some point to it, ideally an underlying strategy or style. The one-corner idea that we just looked at has this – at least in its original invention.

Two subjects set up a very different dynamic, and as we've seen on pages 136–7 and 138, there's always the expectation of a relationship. Conventional two-shots, as they're called, have the actors reasonably close to each other, or at least with breathing room on either side. Applying the kind of extreme placement that we saw in one-corner compositions and putting them far from each other – right up against the frame edges (or corners) – does two things: it forces the eye to travel right across the picture, backwards and forwards, and it creates a kind of nervous energy. Moreover, if the two subjects are distinct and are not competing for attention with much else, this leaves the centre of the frame basically empty. It's neither comfortable nor relaxed, but then that's the challenge of swimming upstream.

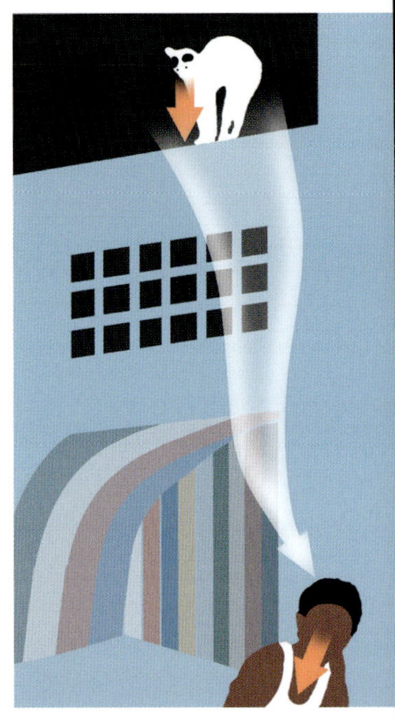

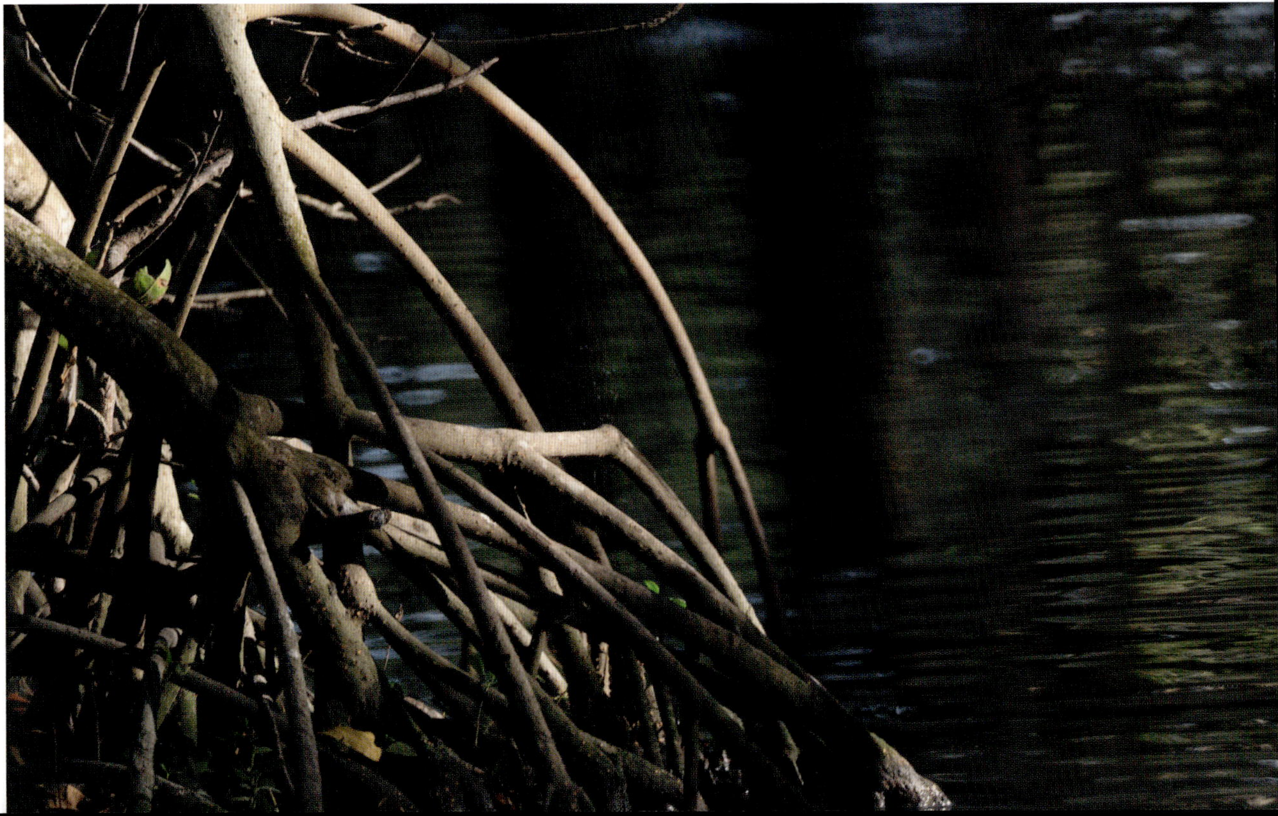

In his powerful 1967 movie *Point Blank*, the director John Boorman, quoted on widescreen aspect ratio on page 61, deliberately used this technique to manipulate the audience by injecting stress into the viewing: 'There's lots of the action taking place at the edges of the frame, and that makes the audience feel edgy. I tried throughout to create tension through composition and within this was this explosive, potentially very violent character [Lee Marvin].'[1]

Both examples here, one vertical the other widescreen, are self-explanatory, though there is in each a graphic connection between the two subjects. In the picture on the right, the gaze of both cat and man is similarly downward, while the flamingo and mangrove roots are both curving down into the water.

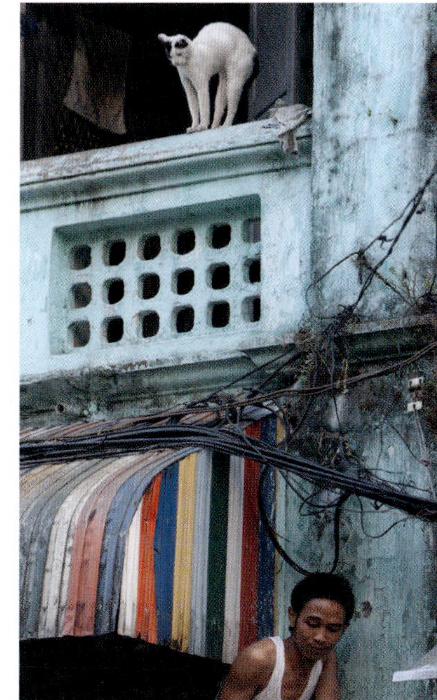

1 John Boorman in *CinemaScope: In Praise of Widescreen*, BBC, 1992, via YouTube, www.youtube.com/watch?v=QtLUy9l1a44.

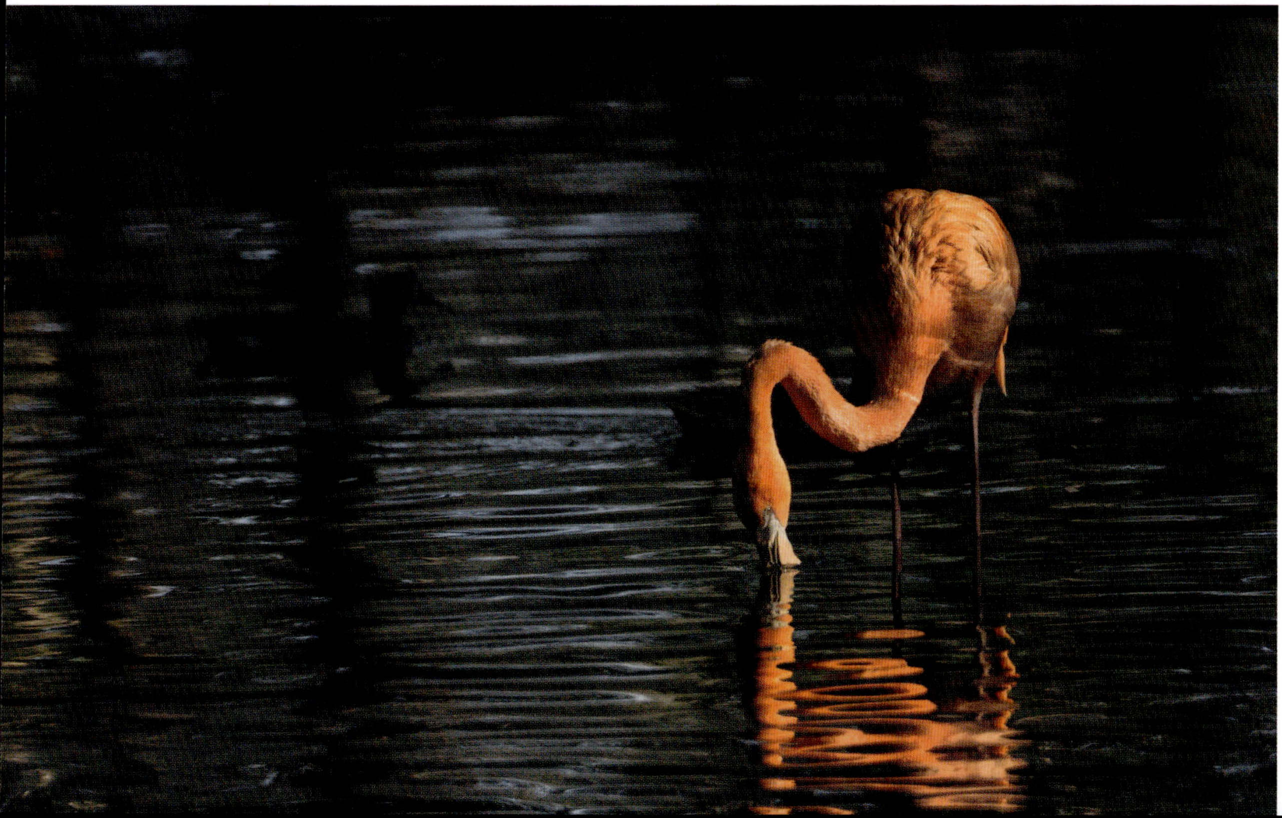

DISPERSED ATTENTION

We just moved from one eccentrically positioned subject to two, and now to several, but in doing this the viewing dynamic changes yet again. There's no longer the relative simplicity of one subject against emptiness, or the charged, slightly uncomfortable flickering from one side of the frame to the other.

EYE-TRACKING

Instead, with several points to look at, the eye is pushed to look around, but with little in the way of direction. This is a contemporary approach rather than traditional, and not to everyone's taste. It takes care to pull off, because as you increase the number of things to look at, they individually become less significant, and there's the very real risk of losing any sense of subject. You might anyway think that this seemingly unstructured way of composing flies in the face of that basic tenet of composition – bringing order – but in the spirit of swimming upstream, we're experimenting with a different kind of order.

In fact, dispersing subjects across the frame is not the same thing as unstructured, because you need to have an awareness of *how* they are scattered. Clumping in one part of the frame, for example, doesn't work. Neither does equally spaced. To be 'naturally' dispersed calls for some judgment. In fact, borrowing the eye-tracking terminology we looked at on page 94, it's probably better to call them fixations rather than subjects, because they don't have to be traditional subjects to catch the eye. Here, instead of a single main subject, the viewers are invited to look around – they have to look around, because there is nothing notable in the centre of the frame.

I would expect this image to appeal to a smaller number of viewers; others might think it had no point and no subject. What first caught my eye were the colours, and I thought I could make a relationship between the strong green, the pale yellow behind and the sharp colour accent of the red-and-white shutter. A precise, squared-up view seemed the best way to do this, but there still wasn't enough to make the image worthwhile. Then a dog walked in, and I hoped I could make it a part of this multi-subject 'dispersed attention' scene. As for how a viewer would look at this photograph, I would expect the eye to move around a lot between the following: red shutter, chair, dog, plastic bucket, windows behind.

→ This scene in the town of Entre Deux on the French island of La Réunion, shot in a deliberately face-on, flat and undramatic style, has a basically empty centre with a few possible subjects scattered around. If the red-and-white shutter, for example, had been centred, it would have taken over the image. The idea, as shown above, was to encourage the eye to move around the frame.

→ Standard eye-tracking tests were timed for 30 seconds for a sample of viewers, as previously in this book, and are shown here subject by subject, continuing onto the next page. In general, they followed what was expected, though with a few surprises.

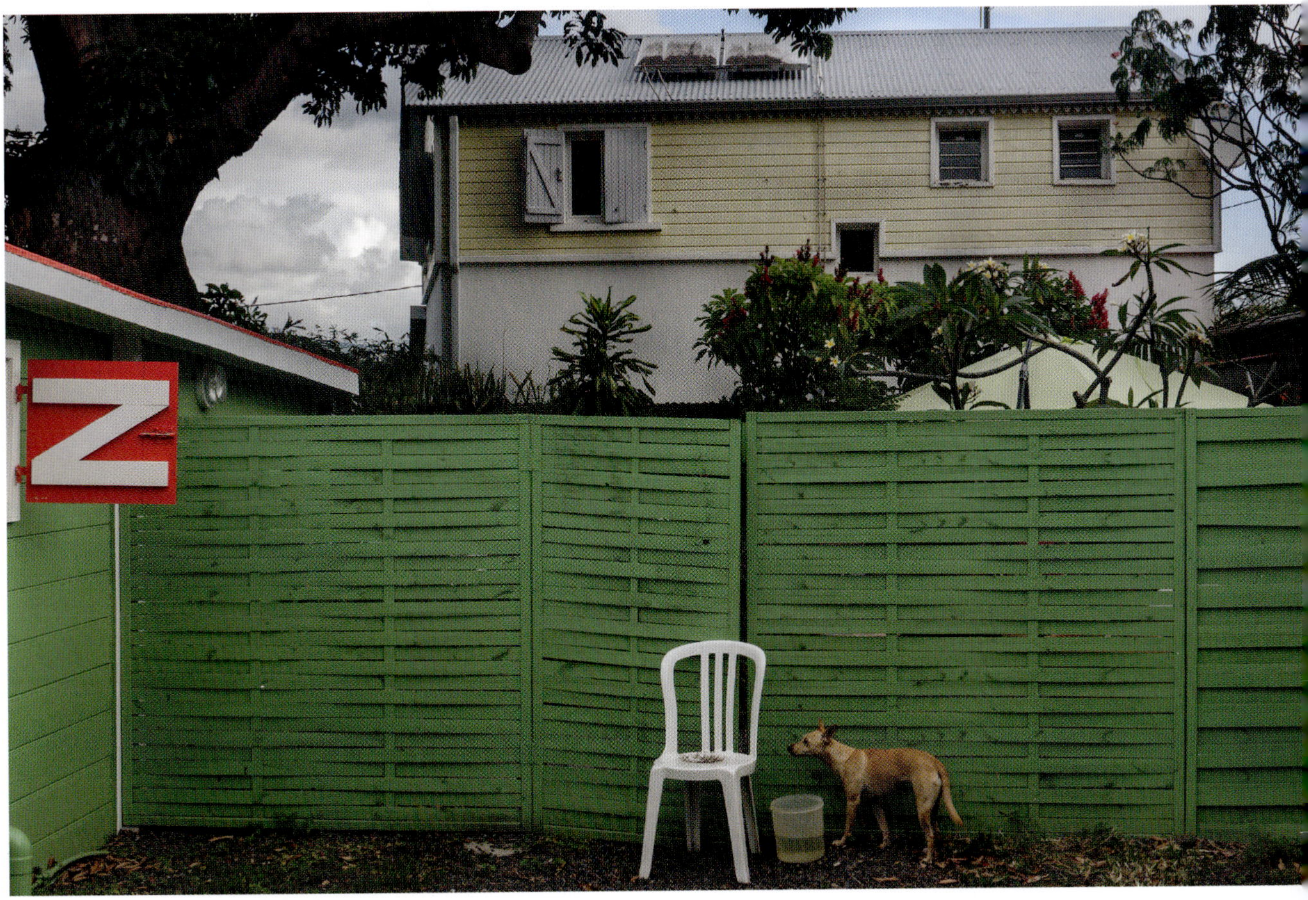

SUBJECT 1

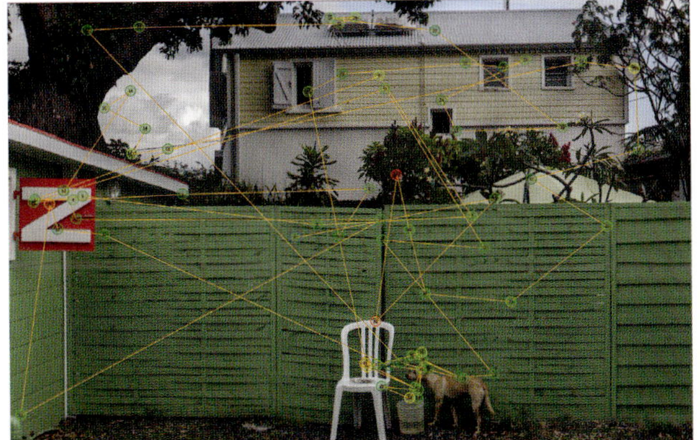

SUBJECT 2

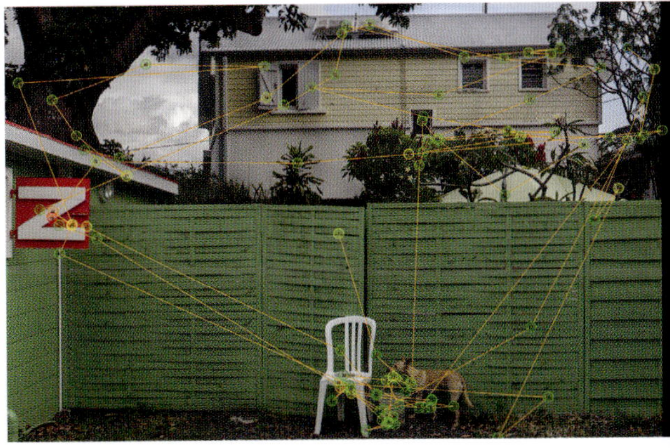

SUBJECT 3

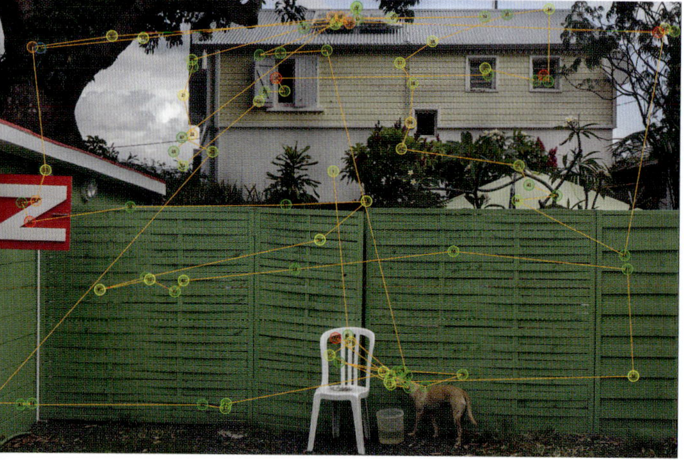

SUBJECT 4

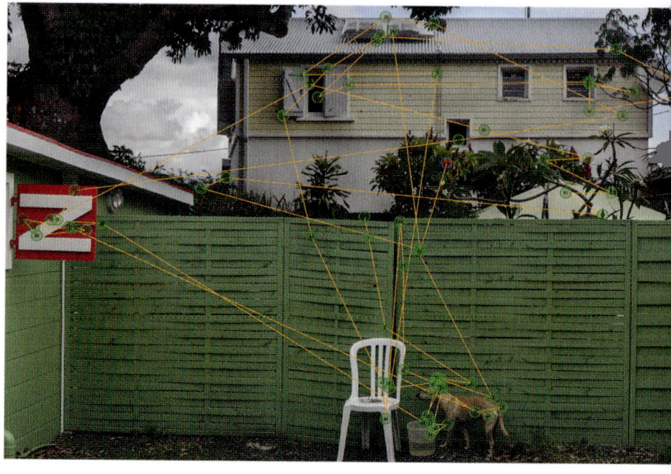

SUBJECT 3 (FIRST 10 SECONDS)

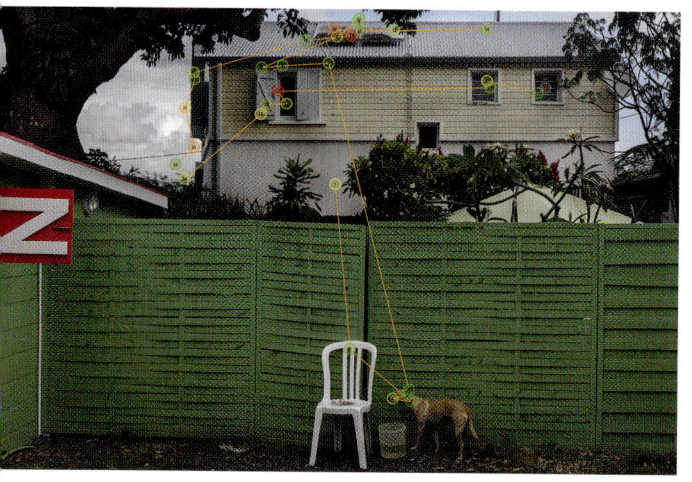

SUBJECT 5 (FIRST 10 SECONDS)

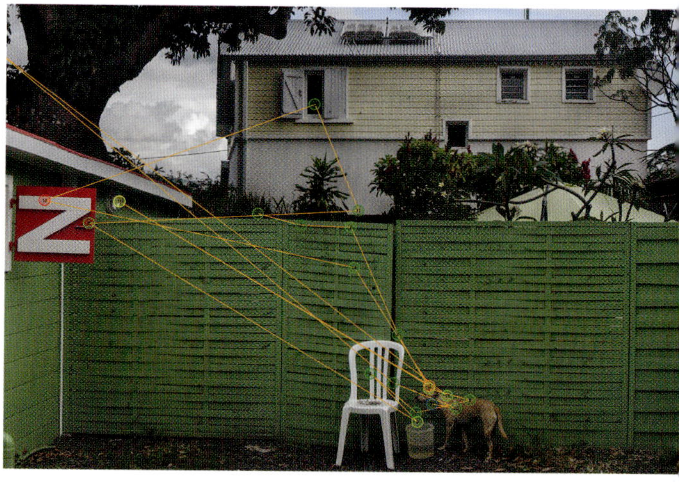

We put the picture through the iMotions testing. In general, the results were as hoped for, although the heat map shows that the dog, chair and bucket dominated attention. And as for variation, see the difference in the first 10 seconds between two viewers immediately above, one of whom (Subject 3) did not even take in the prominent red-and-white shutter, which was surprising. Also unexpected were the fixations on the featureless green wall by subjects 1 and 3 especially, though one explanation of this could be that the viewers here were using peripheral vision and simply taking in the whole dispersed scene, as described in 'How We Look at Pictures' on pages 16–17). One limitation with eye-tracking is that we don't know how much *around* a fixation point the viewer is taking in.

↖ Individual viewers varied in how they took in most of the scene, as in previous eye-tracking tests, although all of them treated the dog and chair as essentially a main subject. However, the first 10 seconds reveal even sharper differences in what first catches people's attention.

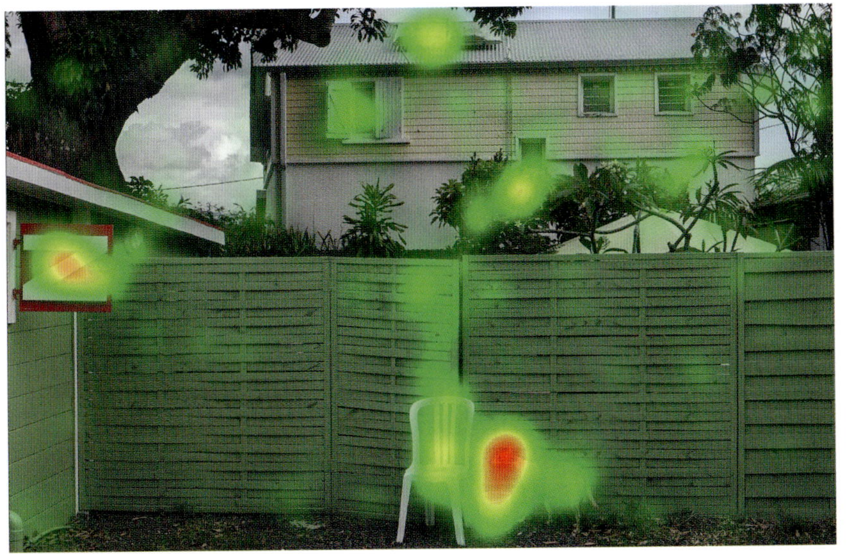

There are different ways of managing this kind of dispersal, as you can see below in the photograph of sacks being loaded in contrasty, chiaroscuro lighting. Here, it's a mixture of light and hands – bright patches and recognizable body parts, all roughly similar in size – that creates the scattering of attention.

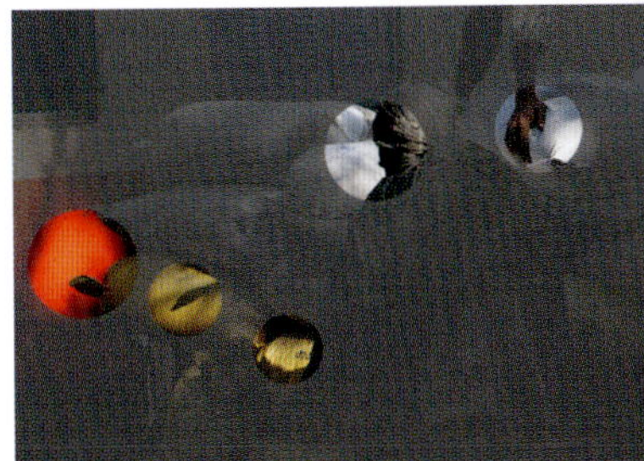

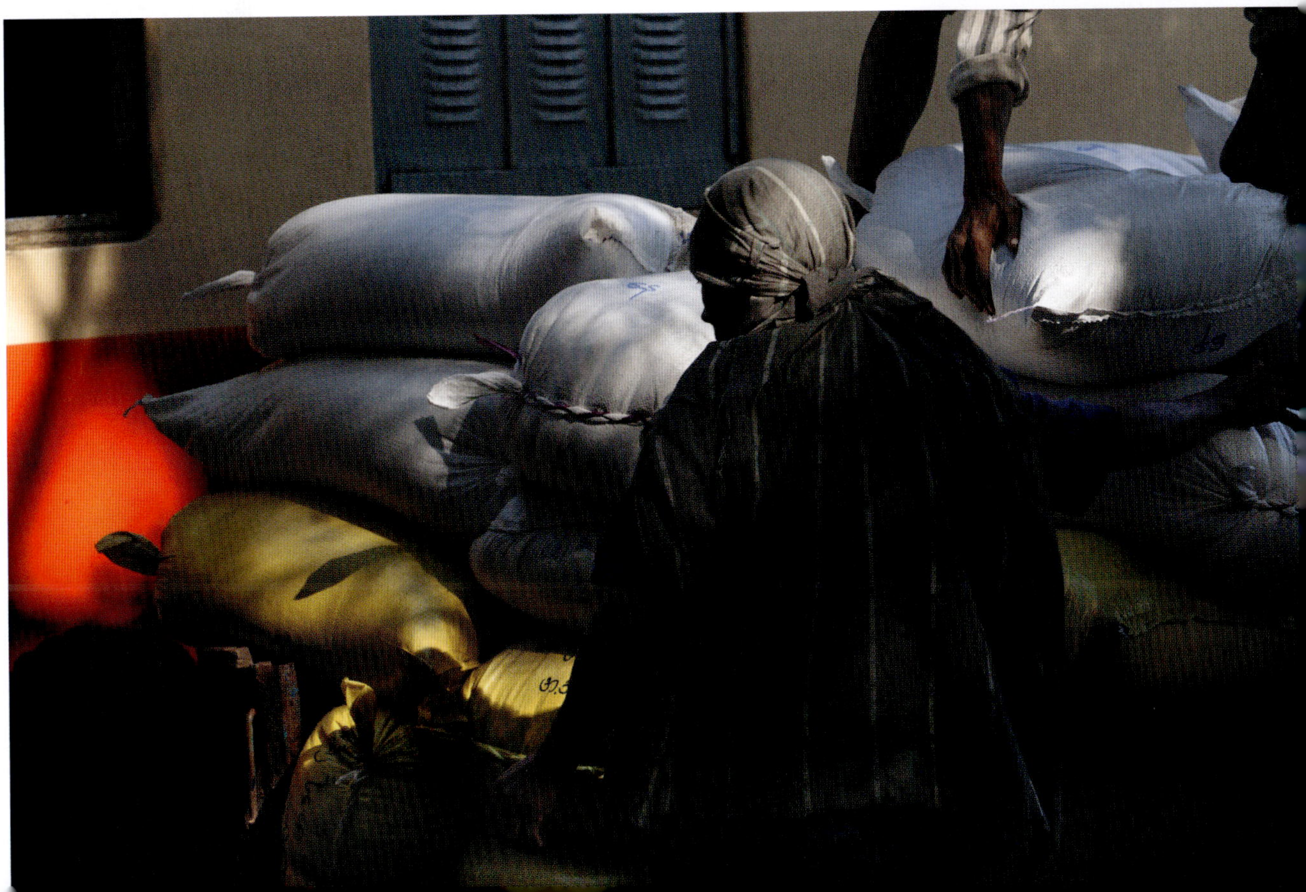

FIELD PICTURES

The next step, from dispersing small subjects to doing without them at all, takes us to what are called field pictures, where essentially you have a large area of not very much.

Put like that, this doesn't sound a particularly enticing recipe, but over in the world of painting, the style of colour field – practised by artists such as Mark Rothko and Barnett Newman – achieved fame. Like 'Dispersed Attention', this is another strategy for composition that threatens to become the 'degree zero' un-composed style that I mentioned in the introduction, and as you know by now, I don't have much time for that. However, field pictures are worth exploring for what it is that creates their uniformity – this might after all be interesting if it's a mass of repeated objects that are out of the ordinary. A large uniform area, which is the basic definition of a field picture, is composed of many similar things, usually at textural level, and it is this fine structure that justifies it or not. A blue sky doesn't work because there's no visible texture and it's too common. A body of water has texture but is still too common, as is grass, concrete, and so on. Two things work: one is when the texture of the field is made up of things that are intrinsically interesting or unusual, the other is when the field is punctuated by something else – small but different. There's an example of each here.

Making sure that the field fills the frame takes us back to the Gestalt principle of Good Continuation on page 108. As long as the texture of the field continues unbroken to the edges of the frame, it will be seen as continuing far beyond, so in shooting for this, framing, cropping and the choice of lens (telephotos are always useful) are important. In the end, however, the value of a field picture is very much a matter of taste. Perhaps most people will see it as wallpaper, which has its uses, such as on smartphone background screens. A few will see it as contemplative. Adding a breakout figure undeniably makes field pictures more popular, but you could argue that they then become something else.

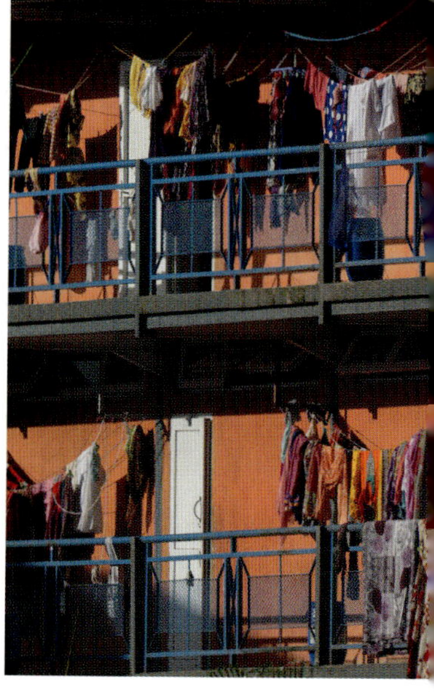

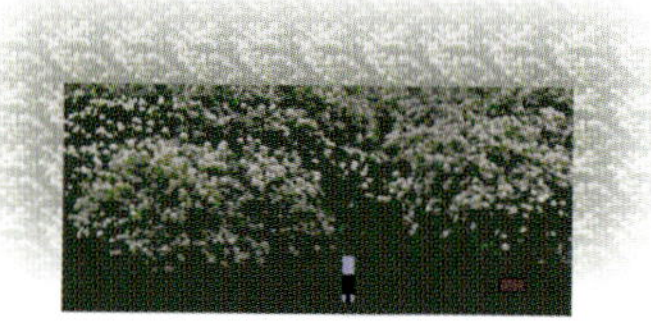

→ An example of 'field-and-point' composition, in which the figure and dog provide a contrast of scale and type with the chestnut blossoms, framed to give the impression that they extend way beyond the frame

↑ At this scale, a housing block in Mauritius with clothes hanging to dry, takes on the appearance of an almost abstract pattern.

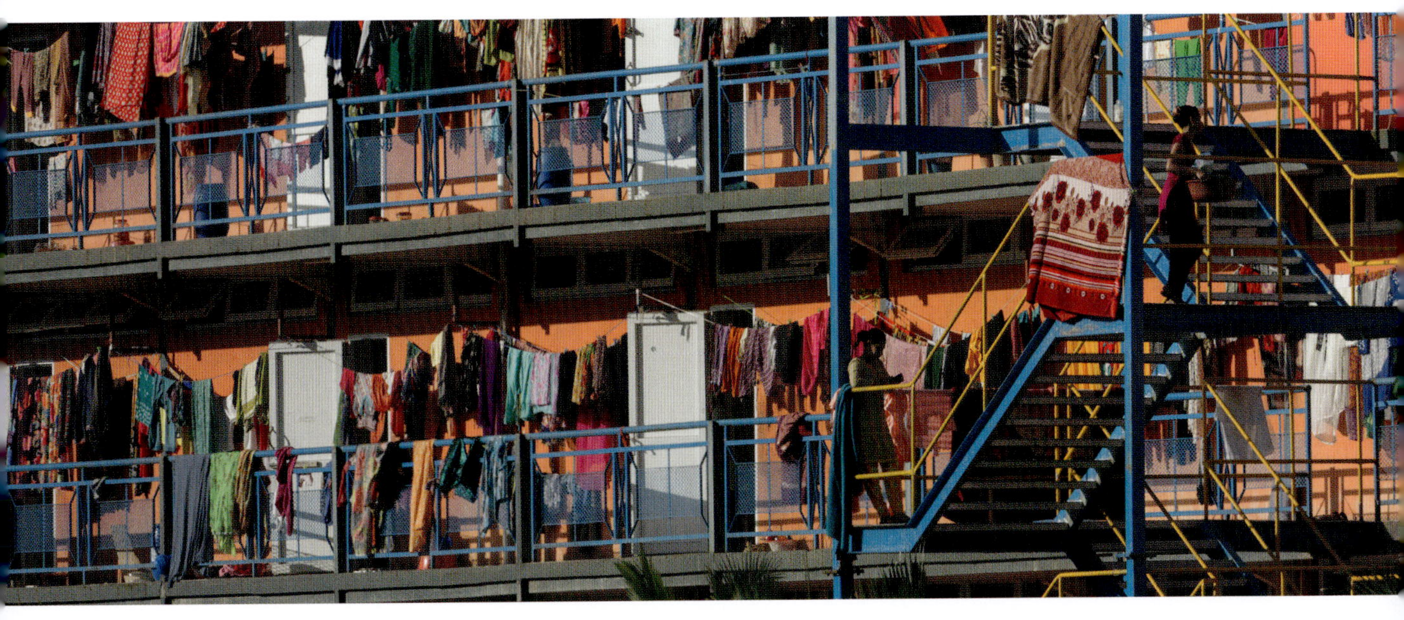

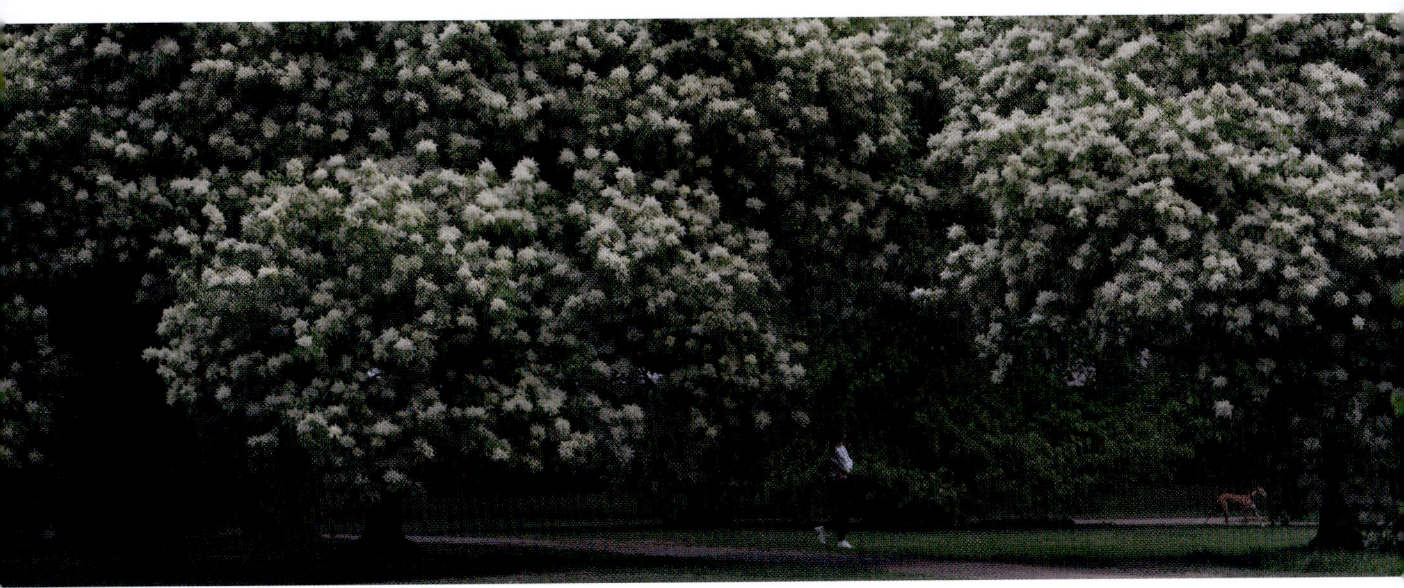

CONSTRUCTIVIST

Constructivism grew as an art movement in revolutionary Russia, and it aimed to replace the traditional art world view of composition with 'construction'.

In effect, though its aims were high and political, this meant taking a technical, hard-edged, almost engineering approach to composition. After all, as we've already discussed, composition can't actually be abolished, despite occasional attempts.

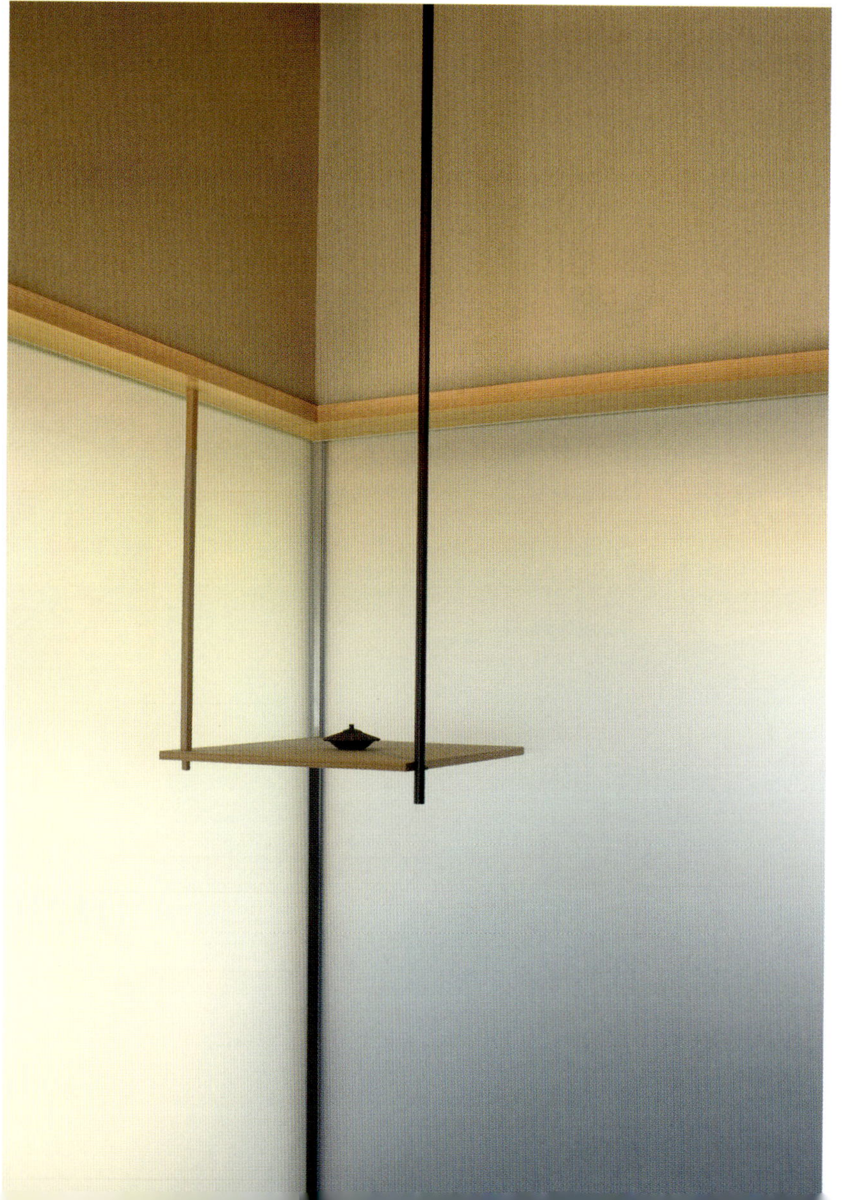

The rigour and precision of contemporary Japanese design is well-suited to this style, as in this construction featuring a miniature teapot in a glass, wood and steel tea room by Osaka-based architect Chitoshi Kihara. Constructivist photography aims to apply engineering-level precision to subjects that themselves are engineering-influenced.

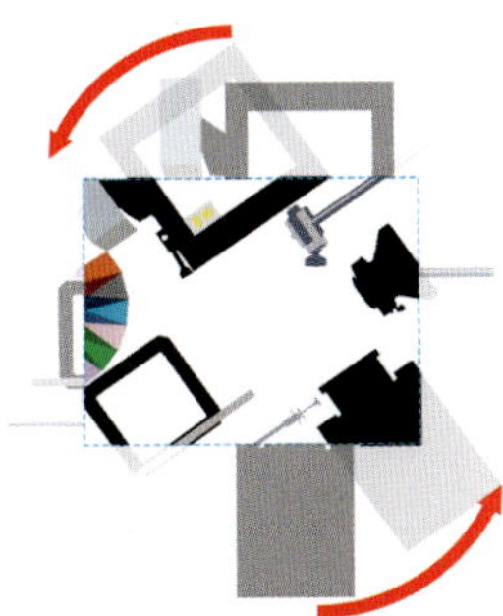

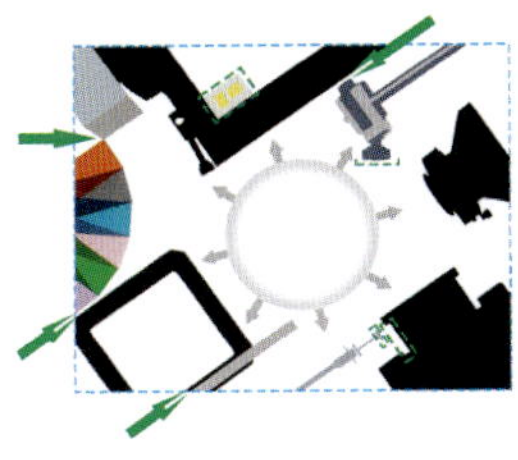

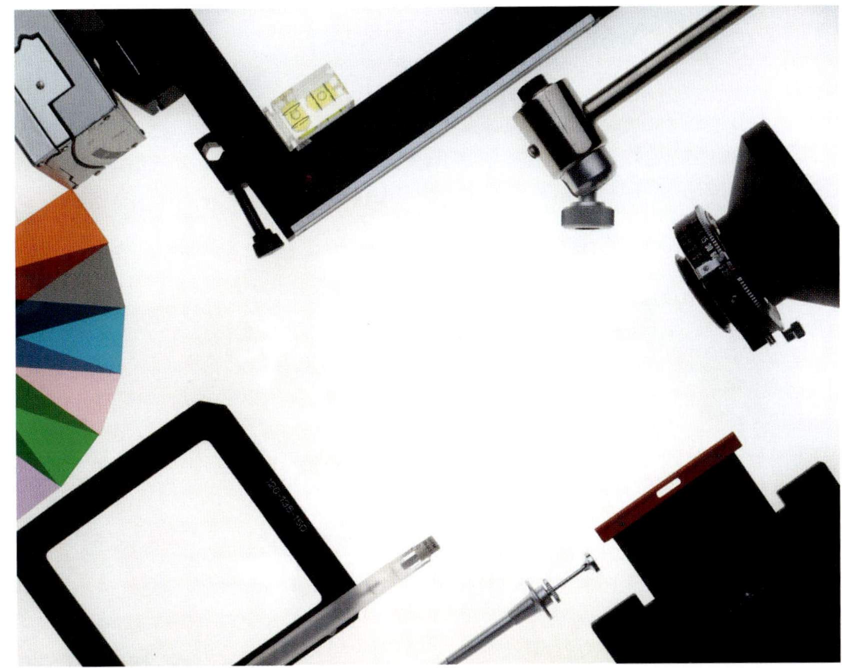

A studio still life of large-format camera parts takes an approach based on applying diagonals and triangles to the surround of the frame, leaving the centre empty: the objects follow a strict progression around the edges. As the two schematics illustrate, this involved precise adjustments to many small details. The overall arrangement involved rotating the backlit elements by 30°, and leaving an empty white centre. In detail, gaps between parallel edges were kept equally narrow (green forked arrows), with a single point of contact between two corners (green arrow). Dashed green boxes indicate deliberate arrangements and relationships.

The Constructivist approach is angular, geometric, featuring intersections and rejecting all of the traditional harmonies and satisfying relationships that we looked at in Chapters 4 and 5. It's dynamic at heart, and inevitably, elements clash with and break through edges of the frame. You can get a sense of this 'breaking apart' approach from the Italian Futurist Umberto Boccioni writing in the 'Technical Manifesto of Futurist Sculpture' in 1912: 'Let's split open our figures and place the environment inside them.'[1]

As a movement, it didn't last long in either painting or sculpture, but photography is particularly well placed to make use of it, especially in the studio, because we can easily deal with machinery, machine parts and, well, construction. In fact, there's something especially appropriate about the combination of engineering and photography. The American fashion and commercial photographer Paul Outerbridge was one well-known name from the mid-20th century, and there has been a recent revival within studio shooting. Rigorous precision is the hallmark, with extreme attention to detail, placement and alignment. Basically, this is photography as engineering, as if you were applying a protractor, set square and compass to the arrangement of things.

1 Quoted in Glueck, Grace, 'Art Review: Blurring the Line Between the Present and the Future', *The New York Times*, Feb 13 2004.

TILT

The most obvious way of injecting diagonal energy into a picture is tilting the camera to one side, and this simple action still divides audiences, even after decades of use by photographers and cinematographers alike.

As we saw in Diagonal Division on pages 64–5 and Angular Energy on pages 88–9, strong and long diagonals can make a powerful graphic statement in an image, and this is one of the strongest because the entire image is turned. Negative reactions are common, however, and part of the reason is that most of us assume that a view ought to be straight because that's normal. Another part is that a tilt is often actually just down to sloppy shooting. As a compositional strategy, then, it's suspect from the start, but it can work if you're deliberate about it and if there's at least some justification. Such justifications range from trying to include everything you want in the frame, to having one thing at least aligned to one frame edge, to making the image more energetic graphically.

One notable photographer associated with the tilt was the American Garry Winogrand, who liked to claim, when asked about it, either not to see the angle at all or that it was simply a way of including things in the frame. Indeed, street photography with a wide-angle lens from a normal standing position and the camera frame vertical, as Winogrand often shot, encourages tilting if you're close and want entire figures in frame, because there's more room corner to corner. In any case, the wide-angle lens itself introduces diagonals through angular distortion.

The tilt here began as a way of maximizing the colour green to contrast with the man's blue. Placing the left edge of the pond into the upper left corner of the frame gave some neatness and helped lose distracting details in the distance (see the setting shot a few moments earlier below). The red of the running boy confirmed the shot.

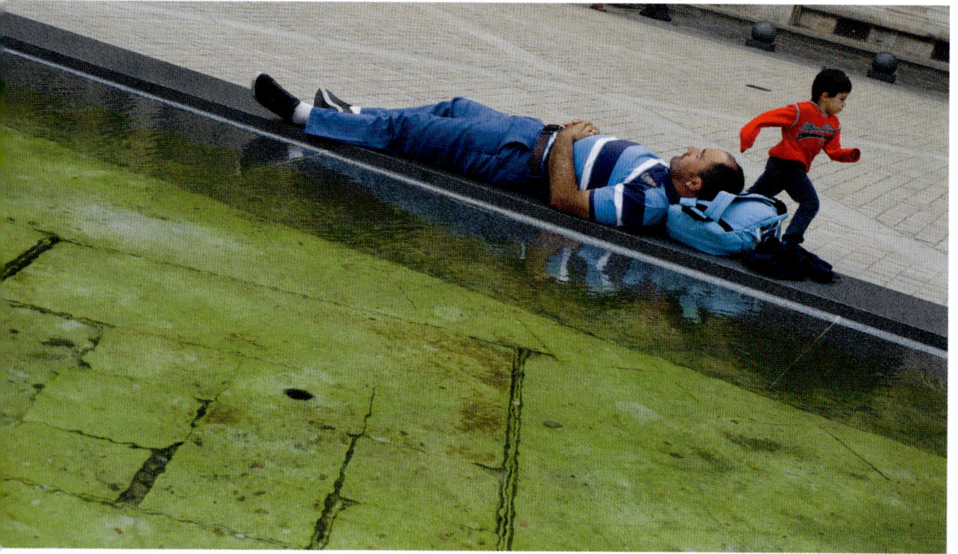

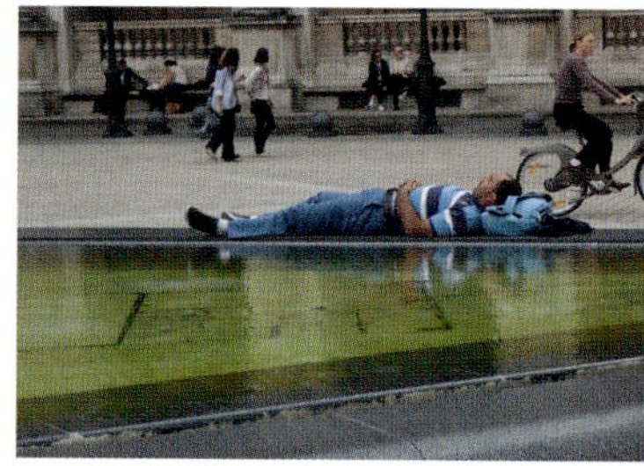

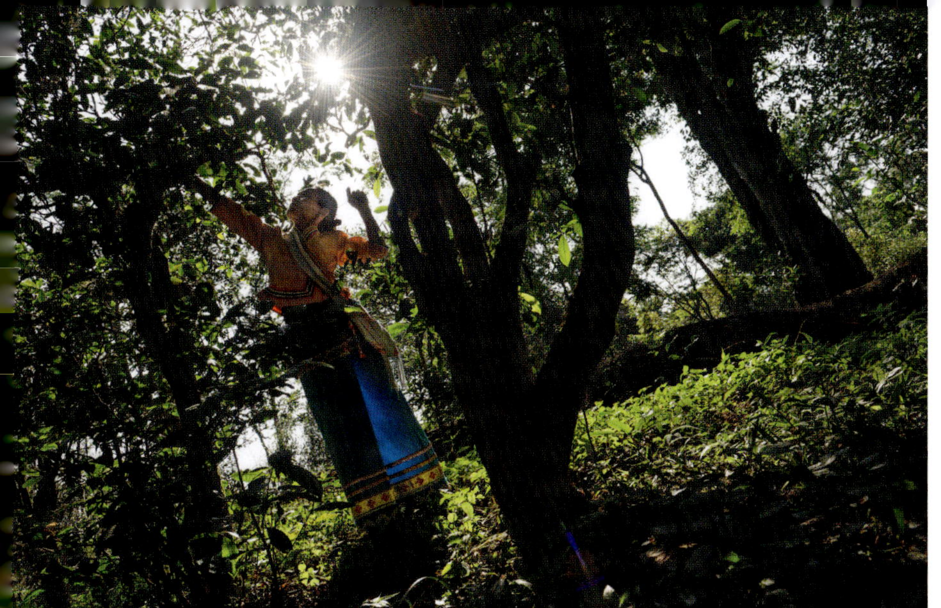

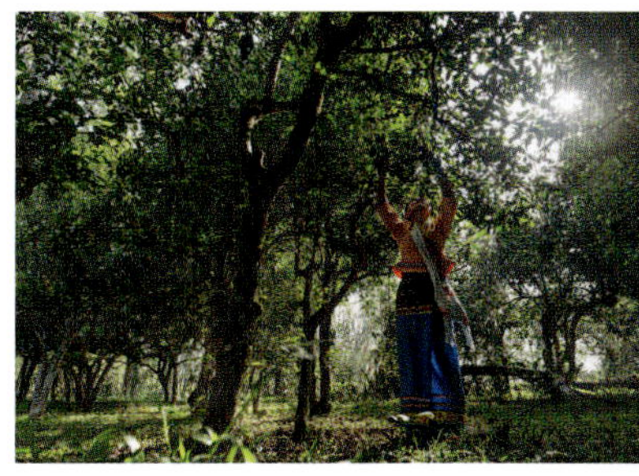

A woman from the Bulang ethnic minority in Yunnan, China picking leaves from an old tea tree. The backlighting, with the morning sun glinting through the branches and lighting up her blue sarong was atmospheric and attractive, but it was difficult to make the composition work in a visually interesting way in a normal, level view (above). Tilting turned the horizontal of the ground and the verticals of woman stretching and tree trunks into energetic diagonals.

In cinematography, the tilt attracts even more attention because action in the frame continues to unfold at an angle. Known as a Dutch angle (the name comes from 'German', relating to 'Deutsch' Expressionist cinema of the 1920s and 1930s), it has a history of being used to show scenes or characters that are off-kilter or crooked or wrong in some way. Carol Reed directed Orson Welles in *The Third Man* with so many Dutch angles that when the movie was finished, the crew (or perhaps the director William Wyler; there are two versions) presented him with a spirit level. There are many other examples, from *Jaws* to *Citizen Kane*, and there's typically a disorienting purpose behind the use.

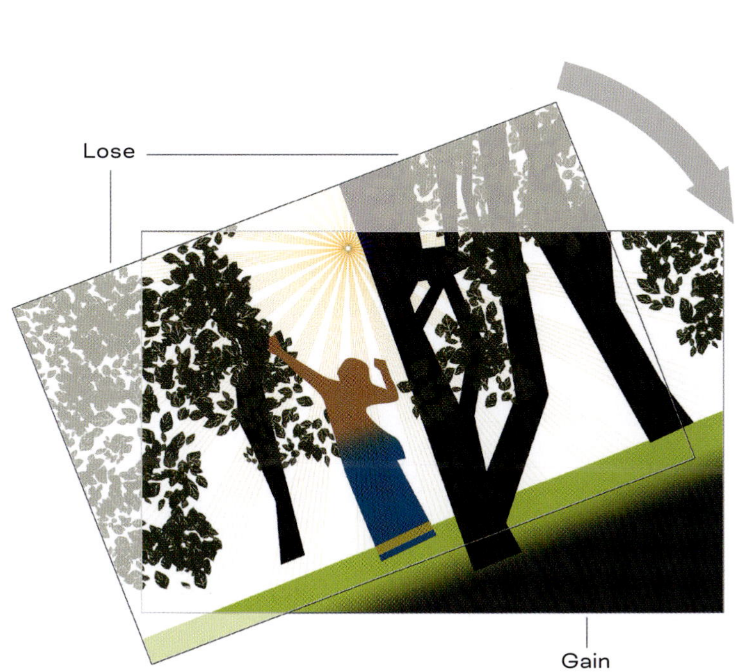

There can also be purely practical benefits from tilting. In a tilt, you always lose part of the scene and gain another part, and in this case the loss was a dark mass of upper tree (good) while the gain was more brightly backlit ground plants (also good).

REDUCTION

In an earlier book, at this point I'd have reached for the term 'minimalist'. Actually, I did, in *The Photographer's Eye*. By now, however, Minimalism has lost its currency through overuse and, frankly, misuse. I have no problem revisiting the art world's -isms, as in the previous constructivism, but we ought to stay true to the original ideas, and when most of us say Minimalist, we really mean just sweeping the image clean to leave as little as possible.

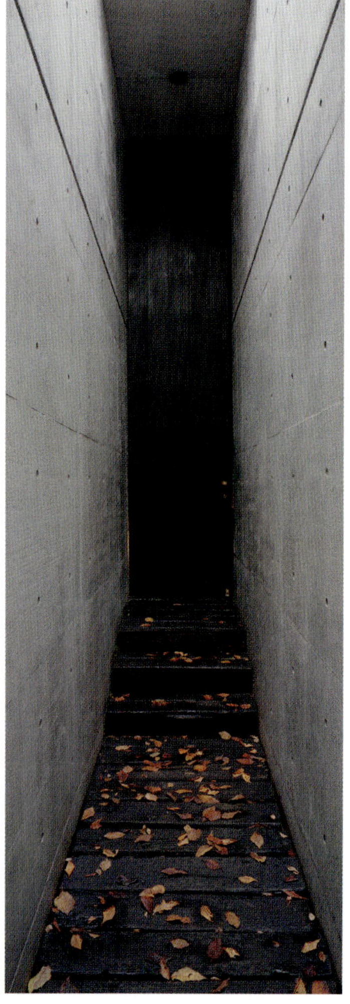

So, in photography, it doesn't mean aiming at an ideal as much as clearing stuff out and, as I think of it, reducing the image load. If there's any problem at all with it, it's that there's an almost knee-jerk approval to the power of simplicity. From the world of advertising, creative director John Hegarty wrote, 'Whatever you're creating, simplicity is the ultimate goal. The power of reduction, as we say in advertising, means taking a complex thought and reducing it down to a simple, powerful message.'[1] My favourite is from 17th-century French philosopher Blaise Pascal, who ended a letter with, 'My apologies for this letter being so long. Had I more time, it would have been shorter.'[2]

← Architectural details offer many opportunities to reduce clutter by closing in and searching out the appropriate viewpoint. This rigorously symmetrical and geometric image of the entrance to a contemporary Japanese house makes use of one of the staple methods in reductive shooting – liberal use of featureless texture. Bare concrete against a tall door and planking is only slightly relieved by a scattering of autumn leaves.

1 Hegarty, John, *Hegarty on Creativity: There Are No Rules*, London, Thames & Hudson Ltd, 2014.
2 Pascal, Blaise, *Les Provinciales Lettre XVI*, 1657.

A powerful reduction of a rock arch in Utah by combining three techniques – 1: eccentric framing to keep the arch at the bottom of the frame with no foreground to distract, 2: drastic underexposure with the sun just hidden behind the arch that abstracts the scene, and 3: a rich blue colour from the underexposed cloudless sky.

In photography it generally boils down to getting rid of stuff inside the frame, or at least, getting rid of clutter. The trick, if there is one, is knowing what to leave in and concentrate on – and having a reason for doing it. The techniques are generally to do with finding the right viewpoint that simplifies, framing that simplifies and a focal length that either excludes things or makes them appear too small to matter. One of the most convincing arguments for reducing in photography (apart from the fact that most viewers seem to like it) is that it's very much about exercising control – about putting your stamp on a scene. But as Pascal the letter-writer mentioned, reducing takes time and effort.

SEPARATE PLANES

The idea of clearly separated foreground, middle ground and background is an old one in photography, and it's a reliable way of ordering the depth of a scene. Typically, it enhances the sense of depth: you look past the foreground to the next plane beyond, and then beyond that.

This style here is different. It aims to put two planes together that don't have an expected logic. Instead of connecting, we're disconnecting, in the hope that two planes that appear together are so different from each other that the viewer wonders what's going on, at least for a short while. It's one of a group of disorienting strategies (as are the next two), and so its success is measured by how much puzzlement it creates. Clearly this is not for everyone nor for all occasions, but it's effective if used sparingly.

Because of its special requirements – two planes with a gap or 'window' in the nearer one – this is not a technique that you can easily turn to. It's opportunistic,

↓ A torn, fluttering banner offered a small window onto a group of Tibetans talking in the Sichuan town of Kangding, and worked as a device for focusing attention on them, while offering some ambiguity.

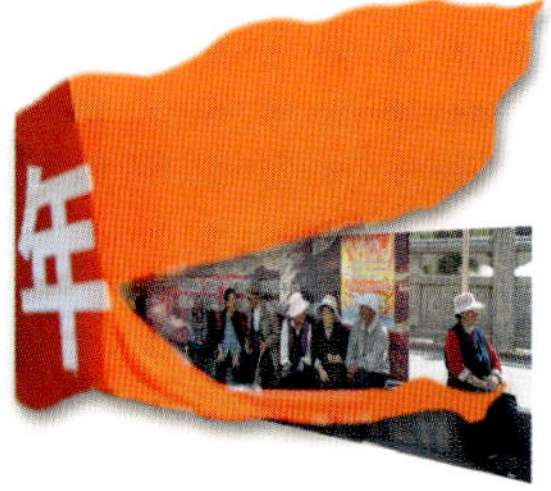

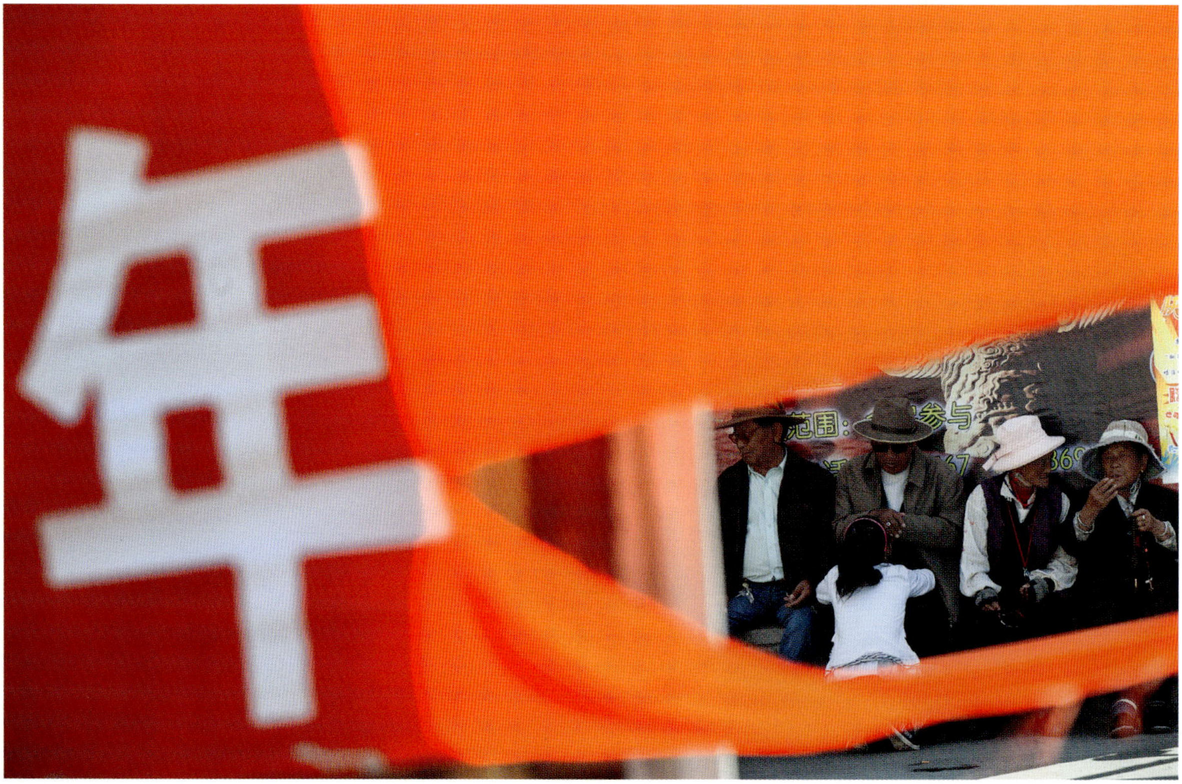

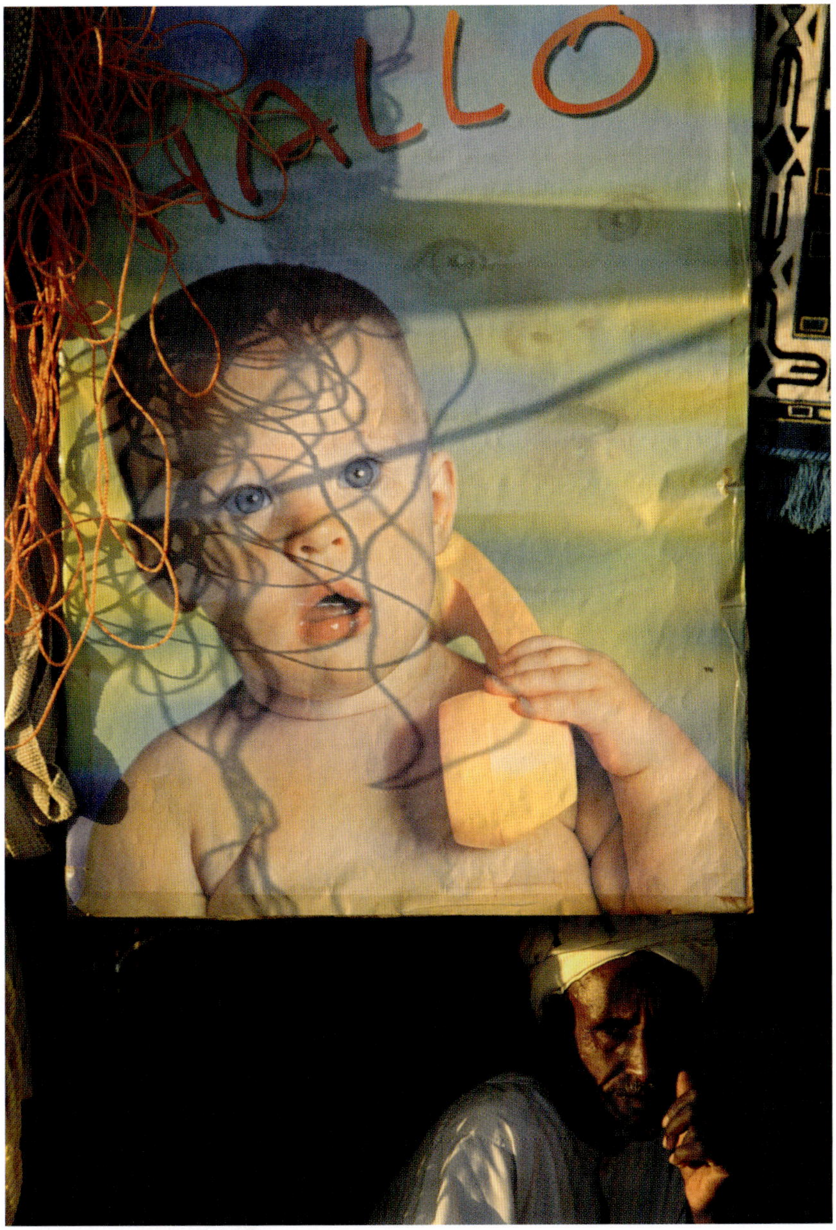

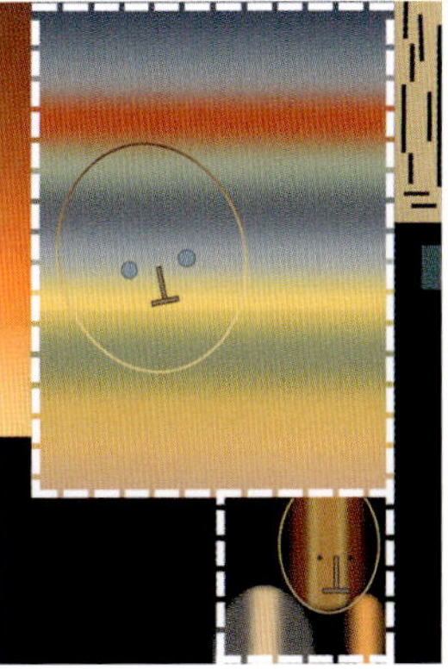

The tight framing of this stall selling mobile phones in Omdurman market, Sudan, removes the surroundings, leaving the slightly strange juxtaposition of a baby's face and the man's. The lack of context and squared-up viewpoint help to remove the sense of depth (see page 42), leaving few clues as to what is happening here.

and so one for staying attuned and on the lookout for possibilities, if it appeals. It usually works best if the depth of field is good enough to keep both planes sharply focused, which gives smartphone cameras with their short-focal-length lenses and small sensors an advantage. A slightly out-of-focus foreground plane can still work, provided enough detail is readable, as in the case of the image opposite.

LAYERING

Superficially it may seem that layering, like in these images, is close to the 'Separate Planes' technique we just saw, but they're put together differently and are also viewed differently. Layering means that something is superimposed, and reflections are by far the most common way that this happens.

There are other ways, such as artificially putting one scene on top of another, but since this is the province of Photoshop layers blended in a choice of modes, this kind of constructed layered shot has much less to do with photography and more with photo-illustration. In fact, the very ease of doing this in Photoshop has taken away most of its interest and the fascination it once had in the days of film-only. The techniques used then were double exposure, sandwiching and multiple printing with an enlarger in the darkroom. Two names from the past associated with this were the New York advertising and editorial photographer Art Kane and the American fine-art photographer Jerry Uelsmann. Kane mainly sandwiched slides together and rephotographed them as a way of juxtaposing ideas, while Uelsmann worked in the darkroom with a row of enlargers, each holding a different negative, to create his photomontages – all for a surrealistic effect.

Worn gilded lettering on the glass window of a pub overlays the reflection of houses opposite in a London street. The main concern was fitting the letters to the frontage and end of the buildings. The brightness of the gold called for an exposure that kept details inside the window dark and invisible.

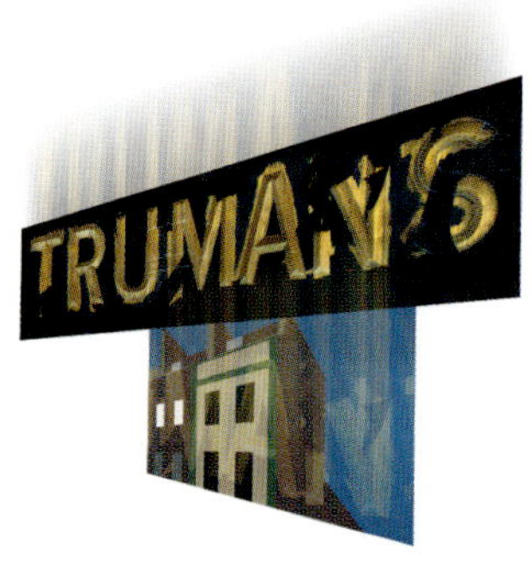

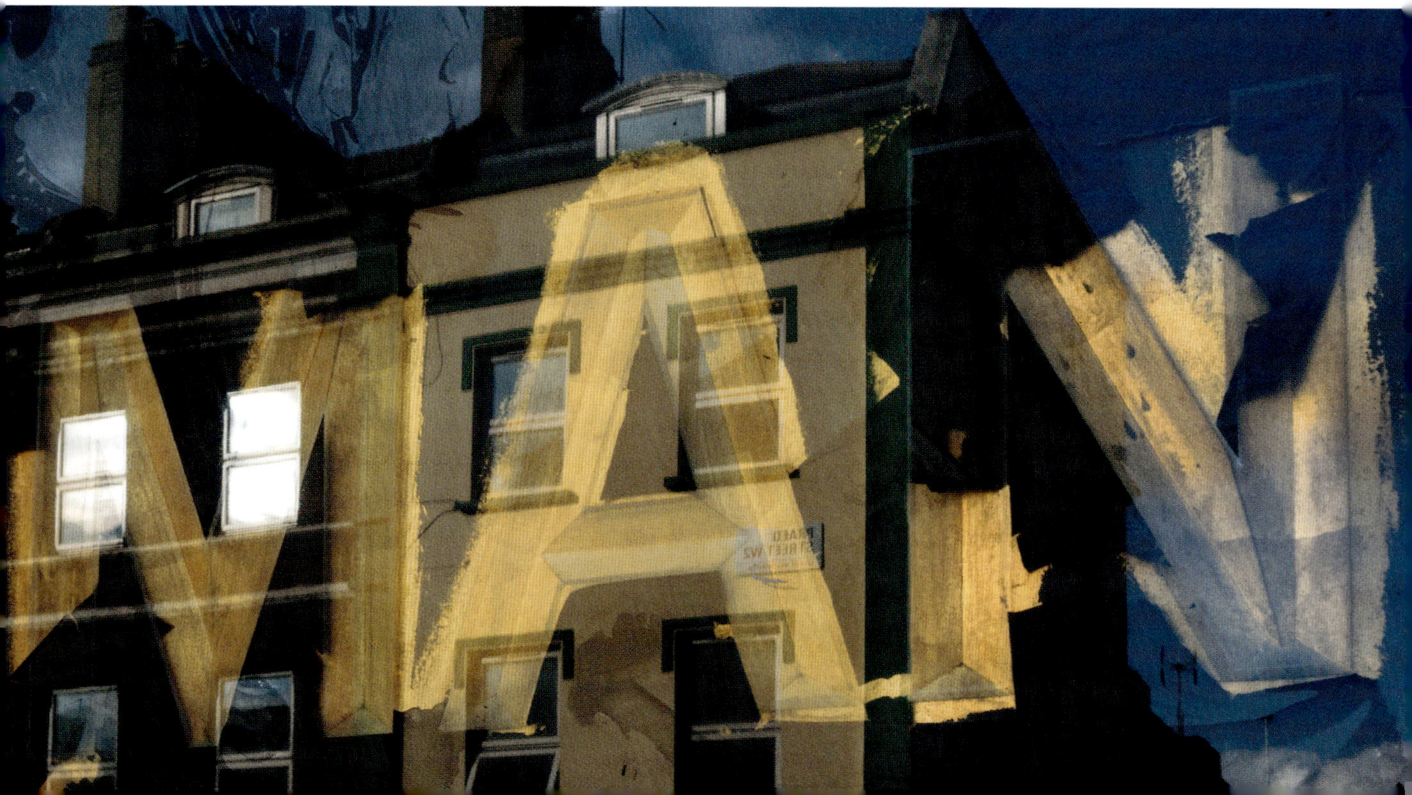

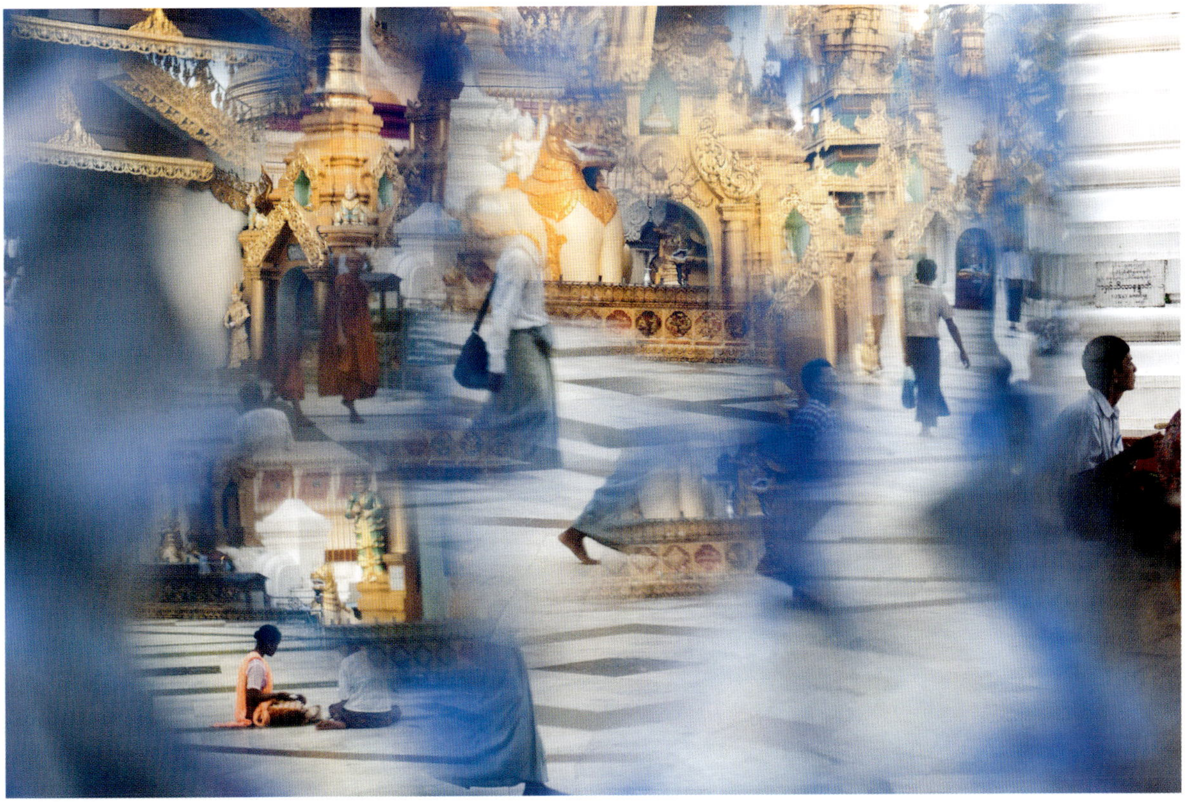

If we're keeping photography within the camera, superimposed layering operates mainly in reflections, and while it's possible to produce these in controlled shooting, much more interesting and less predictable are reflections found by chance. City streets are probably the most fertile hunting ground. This kind of shooting calls for two skills. One is fitting the two layers together so that they have some relationship, which could be purely graphic or might suggest something more meaningful – in any case, juxtaposition by shifting viewpoint or changing the lens. The other skill is balancing the brightness so that both layers are similar. Typically, this means waiting for the light to change or careful processing with local adjustments.

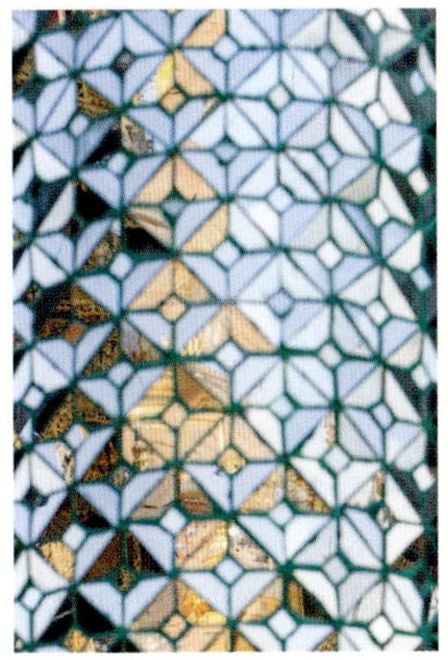

An ornate pillar clad in glass mosaic (above) gave a fragmented view of part of the Shwedagon pagoda in Yangon, Myanmar, which recalls a kaleidoscope (top). Shooting very close to the pillar, focused at infinity and with a wide aperture (*f*/2.8) reduced the pillar details and joins to an unrecognizable blur.

CONCEAL & OBSCURE

It's a short step from layering to obscuring, because the same techniques suit both. However, whereas the idea in layering is to balance the two superimposed scenes in such a way that we can see both, here the aim is the ambiguous one of hiding large parts of the subject.

There's still a balance needed, but the goal is different. The reasoning goes that because the default mode for photography is 'show and tell', to reveal and explain, and because many think that this is what photography does best, that's worth challenging. Many of us were trained, or trained ourselves, to follow this direct approach as an ideal. News photojournalism, for example, has to be clear and all-inclusive, getting as much information as possible into one image. Harold Evans, former editor of both *The Sunday Times* and *The Times* explained the virtues of a powerful news photograph as 'the sensation of being there and for an image the mind can hold.'[1]

However, there's possibly more dramatic potential in being less direct, more oblique, and to keep the audience guessing for a while. It works in other creative media. There's a creative risk involved (the viewer may lose interest after a second or two and move on), but if you carry it off successfully, your reward is drawing

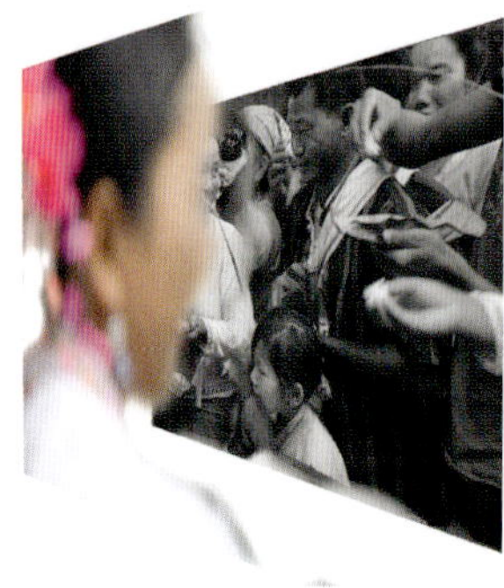

Throwing a close subject out of focus in favour of the background is an unusual technique that reverses expectations. At an annual celebration in an ethnic minority community in southwest China, it was used to turn a floral headdress into a colour wash – still readable to the viewer – while showing details of the event behind.

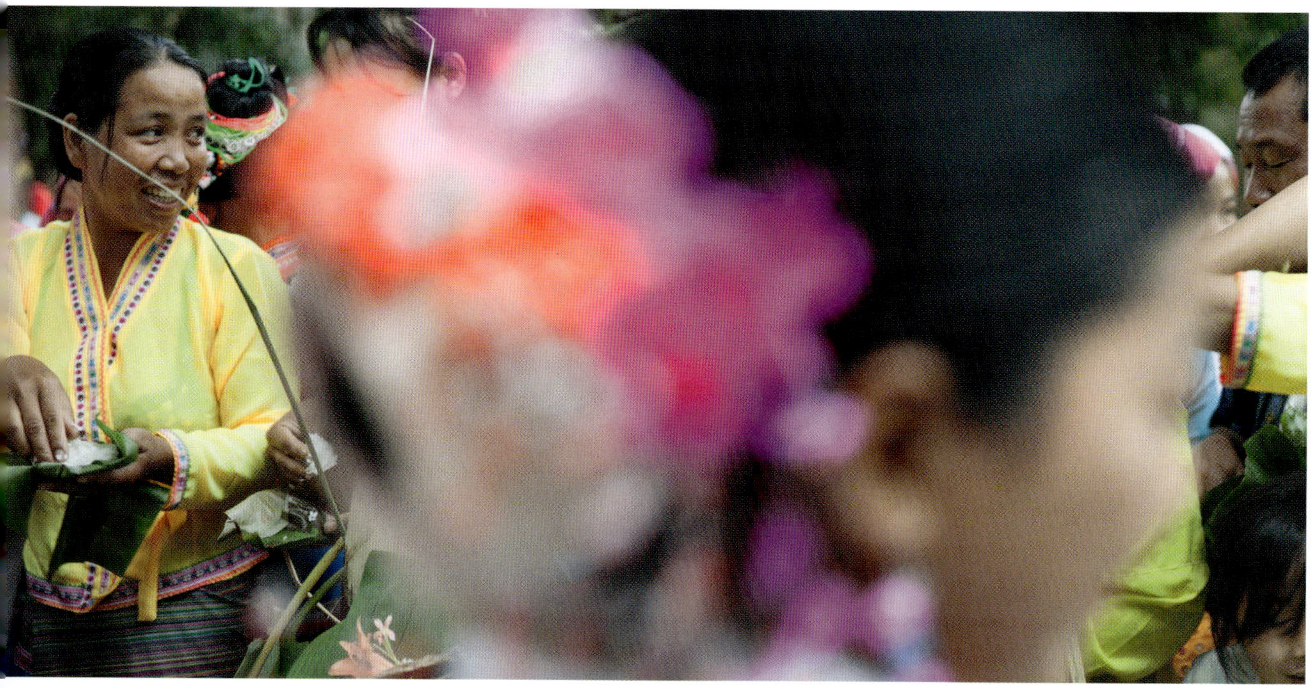

While this traditional Maldivian iron, heated by wood embers, is worthy of some attention in its own right, I was less interested in making a catalogue shot than playing with the billowing smoke that attends a domestic session of ironing clothes. Accordingly, the viewpoint was into the sun for the backlighting effect on the smoke, and the frame chosen was the one with most smoke.

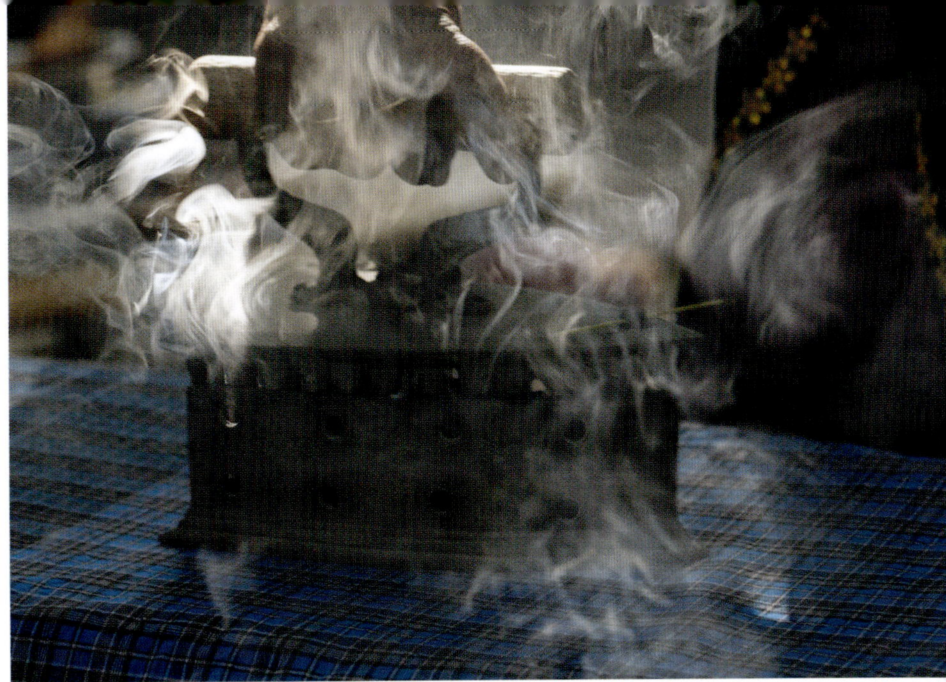

your audience more personally into your photographic world. In effect, you ask the viewer to get involved and do something. The traditional old iron, heated by smoking embers, is a case in point. There were moments when it was clearly visible but more times when the billowing smoke from the embers obscured it. Which is more effective? I'd suggest the smoke-filled picture, because first, that's what happens, and second, you have to look harder to see what's going on.

1 Evans, Harold, *Pictures on a Page*, London: Heinemann, 1978.

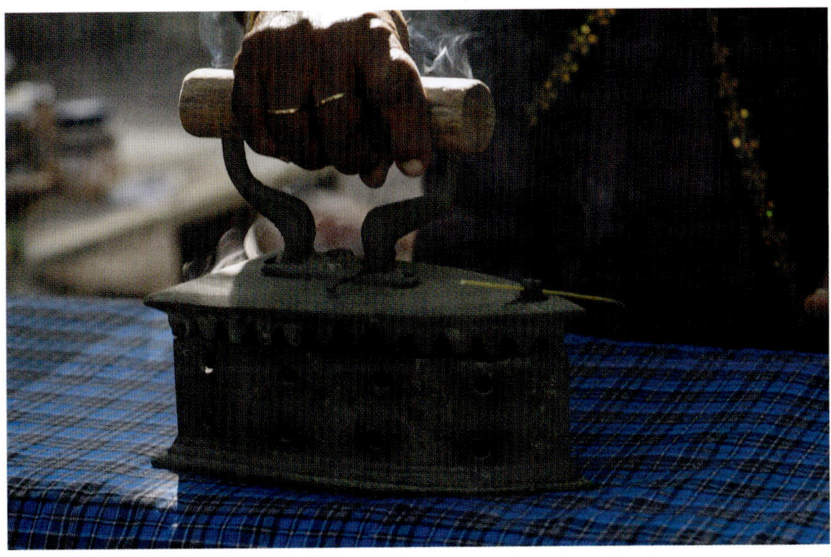

FREE FORMAT

More than painters, photographers have historically stayed committed to the shape of the frame that the camera and film gave them, with cropping usually viewed with suspicion. Digital changed this fundamentally.

We saw the variety of common aspect ratios – frame shapes – in Chapter 3, and the ways of fitting subject into frame and frame around subject. It is of course satisfying to work within the discipline of a fixed frame, but the ability to extend it by pan-and-stitch is a game changer, although not used as often as it might be. I could put that down to a basic conservatism, or perhaps also to a craftsmanship ideal that it's more proper to be able to work within the frame that the camera gives you.

In any case, this is an area for breaking out from the usual – though with caution. It runs some risk of being seen as a gimmick and not fully serious creatively. Against that, there's precedent. Jacques-Henri Lartigue, for example, experimented with tall narrow frames. In painting, J.M.W. Turner tried square, octagonal and circular at the end of his career. Chinese classical painting used extended formats in scroll painting, both horizontal and vertical, and the various shapes of fans.

Pan-and-stitch is the enabler, because at the actual time of shooting, you can use it, even on the spur of the moment, to simply go further (left, right, up, down) to see what happens. The most experimental of picture formats is surely the tall and narrow, as it has very rarely been used. One reason for this is practical – how do you display it effectively? On a gallery wall you can run a panorama very wide, because the viewer has only to walk along to see it all, but tall vertical is not so convenient. Pages and screens are similarly unreceptive, although larger smartphones are making it more familiar.

The issue with this format, and indeed any other odd shape, is to make full use of it in ways that you wouldn't normally think of with a normal aspect ratio. Elongated images are impossible for the eye to take in all at once; it has to travel along them. If you're leading the viewer through the frame, that calls for a composition that works in sequence – in a linear way. Or if you choose a shape that isn't even rectilinear, as the Polaroid shot on the right, that too calls for a composition, and possibly even a subject, that justifies it.

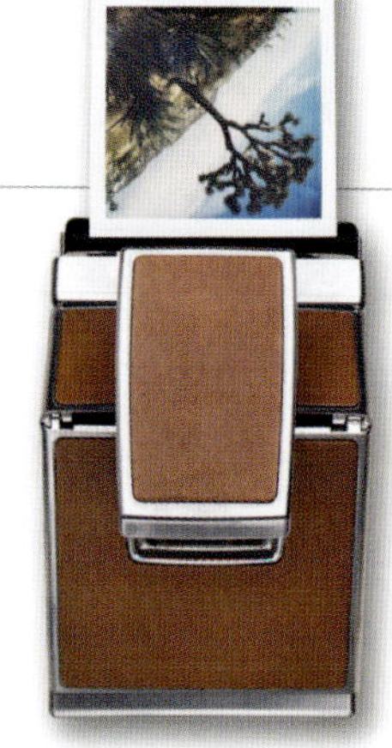

↓ The memorable Polaroid SX-70 produced a unique style of square photograph, but tilting it 45° creates a diamond frame – a perfect fit for a view of a Joshua tree in California, composed to use all four prominent corners. As for display, see what we've done with the text.

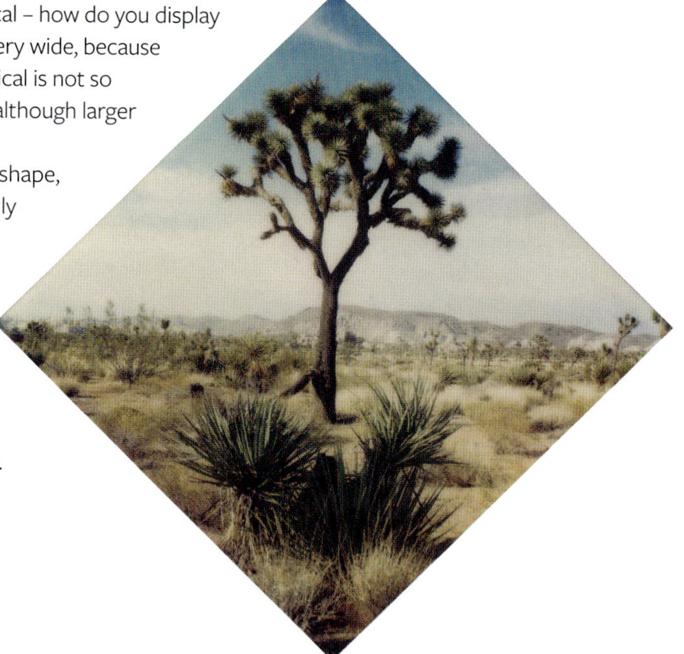

A black-and-white street scene in the old town of Lijiang, China, shot with a 500mm lens and looking down an incline, both of which make the tiered roofs seem stacked one on top of the other, directly over the woman walking. The unusually tall and narrow frame shape makes even more of this, and references the traditional Chinese vertical landscape scroll painting, with its technique of stacking elements on top of each other.

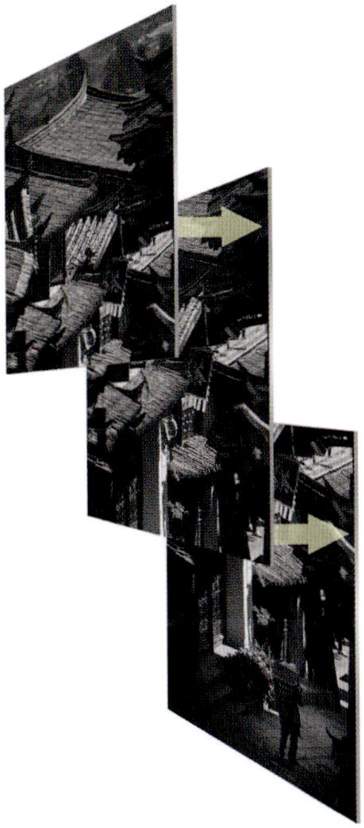

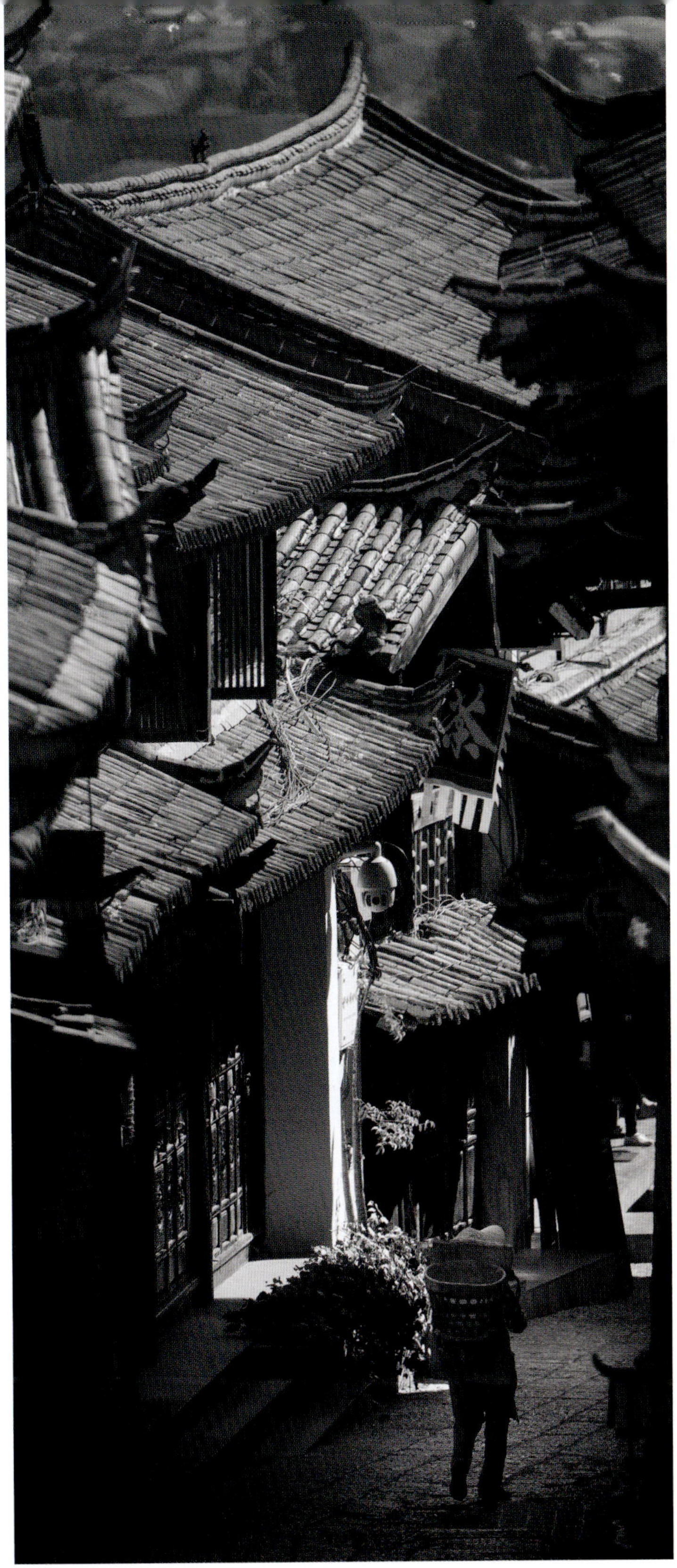

INDEX

INDEX

ACKNOWLEDGEMENTS

Special thanks to Dr. Jessica Wilson and the team at iMotions for the eye-tracking testing.

PICTURE CREDITS

All photographs by Michael Freeman.

Additional images: **74** Public domain, via Wikimedia Commons; **82** (top) Mariano Garcia/Alamy Stock Photo;
128 Rijksmuseum, Amsterdam; **149** (bottom) Artefact/Alamy Stock Photo.